Basic Economics

Basic Economics

Arnold Heertje, PhD,
Professor of Economics, University of Amsterdam

Brian R. G. Robinson, BA, MA,
Senior Lecturer in Economics,
Worcester College of Higher Education

1979
Holt, Rinehart and Winston
London · New York · Sydney · Toronto

Holt, Rinehart and Winston Ltd: 1 St Anne's Road,
Eastbourne, East Sussex, BN21 3UN

Set, printed and bound in Great Britain by
Fakenham Press Limited, Fakenham, Norfolk

ISBN 0–03–910196–7

Last digit is print No: 9 8 7 6 5 4 3 2 1

Preface

What can a completely new textbook in economics provide for the student and the teacher? Our book contains the major elements of microeconomic theory, but it also strongly emphasizes the macroeconomic basis of the modern economy and makes a special point of applying the theory to the real world of the British economy. We regard the modern textbook in economics as only one of several aids to learning for the student and his teacher. The textbook should therefore not be excessively long but provide the basis for the 'A' Level GCE courses in Britain. The companion *Teacher's Handbook* identifies for teachers the sources of a mass of wider resource material and provides work schemes for teaching the 'A' Level syllabus using this book and the resource material. In devising the text we have borne in mind the new Business Education Council courses in Further Education colleges; students on these courses can readily develop inter-disciplinary course links from some of our chapters. We also anticipate that students working for professional examinations which have an economics component will find the book of value and, as an introductory or revision text, so will some students in higher education.

We, the authors of this book, are a European combination of a university professor (responsible for the major theoretical element of the book) and a lecturer involved in the training of teachers of economics. A natural consequence of this combination is our emphasis on applying economic theory to the European Economic Community, in which Britain is now a major partner. In addition, the book extends the usual, very brief, textbook coverage of economic systems to include chapters specifically devoted to centrally planned economies, Marxist economic ideas, and comparative economic theory. This is to help the students working on the 'A' Level syllabuses which are now giving more weight to comparative economics.

It is our belief that what is taught in the British 'A' Level classroom should reflect relevant developments occurring internationally in the subject at university level. Thus we stress the crucial role of technical change in the modern economy, and the increasingly important environmental issues which are affected by economic decision-making. Moreover, we believe that the problems of the contemporary British economy, including its major institutions such as firms and trade unions, should be the starting and finishing points for the work on theory and concepts of the subject. This outlook will be conveyed by our serious attempt in the text matter of the book to relate theory to the real world.

Both of us were contributors to the First Working Conference on Secondary Economics Education in EEC countries in 1976 and we would like to thank Dr W. G. Jansen of the University of Amsterdam, now secretary of the Working Committee on Secondary Economics Education in the EEC countries, for his influence on the early development of the book. We are also highly appreciative of the close and continuous collaboration of the publishers Holt, Rinehart and Winston and are particularly grateful to the company's Editorial Director, Mr David Inglis, who has shown a most cooperative and practical sympathy with authors' problems, which in turn the authors hope they have shown towards the challenges of the publisher.

1979

Arnold Heertje
Brian R. G. Robinson

Contents

ECONOMICS is the study of the relationship between many wants and scarce resources which have alternative uses

Chapter One

Introduction: The Nature and Scope of Modern Economics

1.1 WHAT IS ECONOMICS?

To construct an answer to this question we would like you, the reader, to apply the definition given opposite to this chapter's reviews of:

1. the major economic problems of the present day;
2. the basic economic problem of the individual;
3. the basic economic problem of a nation; and
4. the wider economic issues concerning the environment.

By the end of this chapter it should be clear to you what the subject matter of economics is and how useful our definition is in capturing this.

1.2 CURRENT MAJOR ECONOMIC PROBLEMS

'We must get rid of inflation.' 'Youth unemployment will ruin the nation's future.' Such are the worried cries of politicians; indeed, major economic problems such as rising prices, unemployment, economic growth, environmental issues, and balance of export–import payments have become permanent concerns of national governments in the late twentieth century. During the whole post-1945 period persistent price increases have been an economic problem not only for governments but for firms, families and individuals. Indeed, most students and teachers will never have experienced periods of falling prices or even of stable prices. Recently the problem of rising prices has moved into a still more serious phase with the rapid world inflation which has followed the oil crisis of 1973–4. In fact rising prices relate to a basic feature of the subject matter of economics, the scarcity of economic *resources* in the world. *'Resources' here means physical supplies of land, labour, and capital* (e.g. machinery).

The mid 1970s saw the re-emergence on to the European scene of *mass unemployment*, that scourge of the 1920s and 1930s. This economic disorder spread throughout Britain and the rest of Western Europe to establish itself again as a major concern of government. The large-scale unemployment of the mid and late 1970s was paralleled in Britain and Western Europe by a very slow rate of growth of production of goods and services. In other words, economic growth was too slow to provide the goods and services which could, to some extent, satisfy people's *wants*. *Wants are the desires of the population for goods, services and intangible resources such as leisure time.*

The balance of *import–export payments* between Britain and other countries experienced heavy deficits in the early and mid 1970s, but this situation improved in the late 1970s. It ceased to be a month-to-month problem when the economic resource, oil, was developed from the North Sea, allowing Britain in the short term to be a net exporter of oil. Recent years have also seen environmental issues raise important economic problems: e.g., the proposed third London Airport would compete for land against the wants of local farmers for agricultural land and the wants of the local population for the low noise levels associated with agricultural use.

Running through all these economic problems is the central theme of people trying to satisfy their many wants from scarce resources. That some resources are scarce affects rising prices, the balance of import–export payments, and environmental issues. Slow economic growth worsens scarcity and makes it difficult to eradicate mass unemployment.

Scarcity The relationship between human wants and the scarcity of resources which have alternative uses is the very essence of economics. Scarcity is not the same as rareness; the latter merely means that something is found infrequently or in small amounts, while scarcity means that the store or availability of something which is wanted is inadequate. Thus, rotten eggs are normally a rare commodity; they constitute a scarcity only when they are in demand by some people to express their feelings at a bad speaker.

However, scarcity in itself is not a sufficient basis for the subject of economics: the scarce resources in question must also have alternative uses. This means that we are always faced with a choice of how to use these scarce resources, and this is the core issue in economic analysis. Thus, using an earlier example, an area of land can be used in different ways: it can be farmed, built on, or converted into a third London Airport.

1.3 THE PERSONAL ECONOMIC PROBLEM

Families and individuals also try to satisfy their many wants for food, clothing, housing and consumer goods from the limited means of the family or individual pay packet. Such an economic problem faces the student, as most readers of this book will need no reminding. From his limited grant a student must satisfy his wants of food, clothing, accommodation, transport, books, entertainment, etc. As you well know, the grant cannot satisfy all wants, and an individual must choose which wants will be satisfied. Effectively, this means drawing up a list of preferences of how to spend the money. In this way he is attempting to solve a basic economic problem of allocating his scarce funds among many competing wants. Clearly the funds have *alternative* uses. The allocation for entertainment could be spent on, say, a new LP record, on several paperback books or on the cinema, and a choice has to be made among them. Economics as a subject investigates how these choices are made and the subsequent effect of such choices.

1.4 THE NATIONAL ECONOMIC PROBLEM

Similarly, nations have to make choices to satisfy from scarce resources the many wants of all their people. In Britain, for example, there exist scarce resources in the form of coal, oil, gas and agricultural land (capable of producing foodstuffs for half the population) and the industrial skills of a large, trained labour force. From these limited resources the many wants of the British people have to be satisfied. But not only are coal, oil and gas required; nearly 75 per cent of Britain's raw material requirements has to be imported (e.g. copper and uranium). Moreover, as we have already implied, half her foodstuffs must also be imported. With the industrial skills of her labour force and imports of raw materials Britain could, if she wished, satisfy all her wants for consumer goods and industrial machinery from home production. However, before she can provide these consumer goods for her own people Britain must export large quantities of consumer and industrial goods to pay for essential imports. In this way the country attempts to reconcile the wants of the people to the nation's scarce resources.

Of course, people demand not only goods to satisfy their wants but also services such as transportation, catering, banking and police protection. Therefore, economics also examines how, from limited resources, a country provides services to meet the demands of its people. In Britain services are particularly important since nearly 60 per cent of the workforce is employed in supplying services both for home and overseas wants. British airlines and shipping, for example, transport passengers and goods worldwide, and British banking and insurance are heavily committed to business overseas. In all these cases the core economic issue is in evidence: choices are being made as to how scarce resources are used to provide goods and services which will meet people's wants.

Opportunity Cost A nation may decide to use its limited resources to build a motorway and not to develop the next best alternative in its list of priorities, a river barrage for a tidal power station. We call the river barrage the *opportunity cost* of the motorway, and every economic decision, whether made at the level of government, firm, family or individual, has its opportunity cost. The individual who decides to use his limited funds to buy an LP record must give up the purchase of several paperback books: the paperback books are the opportunity cost of the LP record. We can define opportunity cost as '*the forgoing of the next best alternative good or service in favour of the good or service actually used*'.

1.5 ECONOMIC PROBLEMS OF THE ENVIRONMENT

We generally exclude from economics resources which are in such plentiful supply, e.g. air and water, that all human wants for them can be satisfied. However, in certain cases, people's wants for clean water and a pollution-free atmosphere in which to live may be greater than the supply of these resources in a particular area. We are once more dealing with the core economic issue of reconciling people's wants with scarce resources that have alternative uses. People living near a river may desire clean water for the leisure activities of sailing and swimming but firms may wish to use the river to dispose of waste matter. Similarly, industrialists wishing to develop a new chemical factory in an urban area are competing for a scarce resource – a quiet and clean environment – with planners and tenants who desire a noise-free unpolluted housing estate.

Summary Economics is the study of the relationship between many wants and scarce resources which have alternative uses. Economics involves all wants and resources, including environmental wants, such as natural beauty and clean water.

1.6 PRODUCTION AND CONSUMPTION

Vital for the satisfaction of people's wants are *consumer goods* and *capital goods*, and it is important to distinguish between these. *Capital goods* (or, simply, *capital*) *are a stock of physical assets in being at a given point in time*. Capital plays a crucial role in the production of goods and includes items as diverse as machinery, buildings, office fittings and equipment. *In this book capital will usually have this meaning* unless it is qualified: for example, in everyday life capital often means money, but money will not be meant unless the term *money capital* is used. The term *human capital* is used by some economists to mean trained labour but we will not normally adopt this usage. However, there is one term, *working capital* (i.e. the processed raw materials in factories about to be consumed in production), which we will often use, since it refers to a subcategory of physical assets. Capital is one of the three *factors of production*. The other two are land, which includes all natural resources, and labour (see Figure 1.1). If we can increase these production factors we can reduce the severity of the basic economic

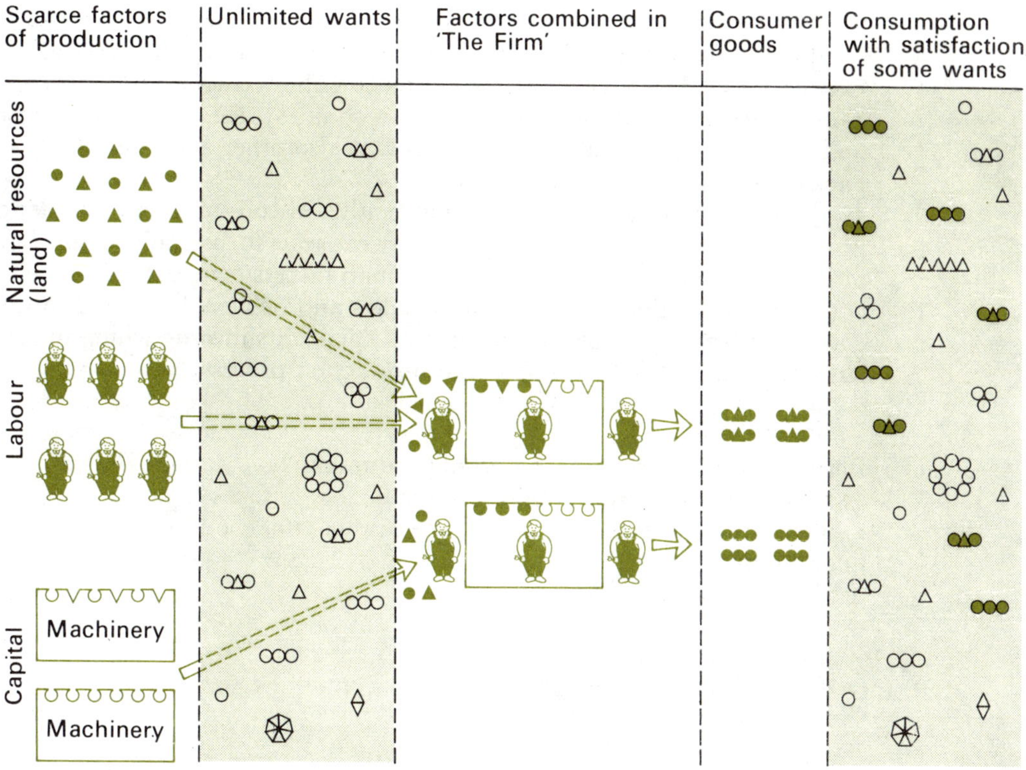

Figure 1.1 The factors of production, wants and consumption.

problem of reconciling many wants to scarce resources. Thus, more capital equipment per worker means a greater output of goods.

Land and labour are called primary factors of production, for they are always present. By contrast, capital is a secondary or derived factor of production, for it has to be created. Take the example of a primitive fisherman. To begin with he would catch fish with his hands. Then, by forgoing or cutting down on his food for some time he would make a net, i.e. a capital good. This would enable him to catch more fish than before, so that he could spend some time in doing other things.

Some economists regard entrepreneurial activity as a separate factor of production, the entrepreneur being a manager who combines land, labour and capital to produce goods. Although his activity introduces a new element – taking non-insurable risks – we shall include it under labour, since we consider that it is a type of specialized labour.

Production is the provision of goods and services through combining the factors of production, i.e. land, labour and capital, in a firm. For example, a steel firm combines elements of land (iron ore and coal), labour (its workforce, including managers) and capital (its blast furnaces, steelmaking equipment and rolling mills) to make steel. *Consumption is the purchase by an individual or family of the goods and services supplied by firms.* We use the term *household* to include both individuals and families.

The same good may be a capital good or a consumer good, depending upon the point production has reached. Thus, a loaf of bread is a *capital good* (a factor of production) when it lies in the bakery: it has to be combined with further factors of production to get it from the bakery to the kitchen table. It is a consumer good when it lies on your kitchen table. Thus production embraces not only the technical processes by which raw materials are converted into products but also other activities, such as packaging, storing and transportation.

The ultimate aim of production is always consumption. The long process of production of some goods may cause us to lose sight of this but ultimately the manufacturer making dough mixers owes his existence to consumption as does the baker who bakes and delivers his bread to the consumer. In consumption a household spends its income which in fact has been earned by working in the production process.

Summary There are three factors of production: land, labour and capital. Production is the combination of these factors in firms to produce goods and services while consumption is the purchase of goods and services by households.

1.7 SPECIALIZATION AND THE EXCHANGE ECONOMY

Societies developed specialization of labour when it was realized that more could be produced if each person concentrated on a small part of production. In a cotton factory some workers specialize in spinning, some in weaving, others in finishing the garment, and so on. Moreover, skill can be improved by gearing education and training to future specialization. This division of the labour task by specialization raises the quantity of goods produced per worker just as the provision of more capital equipment does.

The significance of the division of labour in factories was first appreciated by the great Scottish economist Adam Smith (1723–90), the founder of the classical school of economics, who, in his book *An Inquiry into the Nature and Causes of the Wealth of Nations*, published in 1776, discussed the case of specialization in a pin factory.

Extensive specialization is possible only in a highly developed economy, with money used both as a means of paying for work and for purchasing goods. It is essential that when an individual contributes to only a minute fraction of the production process, there must be some guarantee that he has access by exchange to all the consumer goods he may want. For example, a car-body worker at British Leyland can work assured that others will produce the food and clothes he needs: he will then buy those with the money he is paid for doing his job.

This exchange takes a primitive form in past and some present-day societies where specialization is much more limited than in ours. This form is called barter, in which goods are exchanged for goods. Historically, the trend has been for valuable objects (e.g. cattle, silver) to become the medium of exchange before finally being replaced by paper money as a means of payment and exchange. Thus the prehistoric bartering of hides for fish has been superseded by a token bartering, through money, of each individual's contribution to production. Therefore, in modern developed economies, people do their particular job, obtain money wages for their work, and use these wages to buy consumer goods.

Summary The production of goods by labour is increased when more capital equipment and greater specialization of labour (division of labour) are introduced. An important consequence of the division of labour is the development of an exchange economy, in which workers are paid in money and can use this money to buy goods to satisfy their wants.

1.8 WELFARE AND SCARCITY

Understanding welfare is important for grasping the nature of economics, since it refers not only to scarcity of material goods but also to scarcity of intangible resources such as natural beauty or leisure time. *Welfare is the level of satisfaction of the wants of an individual or a community in so far as it is based on the allocation of scarce resources which have alternative uses.* However, welfare is often crudely equated with tangible goods like motor cars, TV sets and dishwashers, and countries where such durable consumer goods are in abundance are said to have a high standard of living or a high level of welfare. Because these goods satisfy certain human wants, they assuredly contribute to welfare, but there is more to welfare than the satisfaction of material wants. Thus, depending on an individual's wants, his welfare can be enhanced not only by a higher income but also by more spare time. For some people, a day off work may bring greater satisfaction of wants than the money to be earned by the day's work, and this increase in welfare through the intangible resource, spare time, is at the expense of income which could be used on tangible goods. The economic significance of intangible resources is clear from the importance attached nowadays to holiday entitlement or early retirement in negotiations between employers and unions. An indication of the increase in welfare through intangible resources might be the worth of the next best alternative which frequently will be a tangible good.

The environment is another aspect of welfare. We desire clean air, clear water, quietness and natural beauty and these resources are becoming scarce. This is particularly true of densely populated areas, such as south-east England and Lancashire. Whether we can fulfil these wants depends on how we handle scarce resources in general. Preference for clean air and oil-free beaches may mean the suppression of certain cheaper techniques of production which pollute the atmosphere and the introduction of costly improvements to oil tankers. Again, a decision to preserve a potential quarrying area in the Malvern Hills of Worcestershire as a nature reserve where no industry is allowed will lead to conflict because both resources, the stone and natural beauty, are scarce. The decision to provide a nature reserve is made at the expense of industrial development. This illustrates that 'choice' in economics does not always concern cases where the pros and cons can be expressed in terms of money.

There is sometimes confusion between the meanings of welfare and happiness. The satisfaction of wants is of course not always connected with scarce resources, as is illustrated by man's wants for love and friendship. However, these wants do not have an economic aspect because they do not involve the use of *scarce* resources which have alternative uses. These aspects of man's state of mind come under the heading 'happiness', and should be distinguished from welfare.

Summary In economics, welfare is the level of satisfaction of the wants of an individual or a community in so far as it is based on the allocation of scarce resources which have alternative uses. It therefore brings within the bounds of economics the scarcity of non-tangible resources (e.g. clean air, natural beauty, leisure time) and we need to study the way their scarcity is related to man's many wants both for them and for tangible goods.

1.9 THE INVESTIGATIVE METHODS OF THE ECONOMIST: DEDUCTIVE AND INDUCTIVE

Deductive What methods does the economist use in his study of wants and resources? He tries to explain what happens in the real world by developing models of the way in which scarce resources are allocated to satisfy wants. *A model can be regarded as a simplified representation of reality, in which the simplification is achieved mainly by the introduction of certain assumptions.* An economic model of the price of coffee on the market can be developed in this way. Such a model would help us to see how effective price changes are in rationing people's demand for scarce goods. We therefore introduce assumptions in the model about supply and demand, follow a logical argument and draw conclusions from it about the price. This is called a deductive method of reasoning. A model is never completely valid when we apply it to the real world because we have made these assumptions to simplify matters, and this obliges us to be modest about such models. The economist's aim is to improve the predictions yielded by his models by improving the validity of the assumptions introduced into them. These remarks should serve to caution the reader about the limited validity of models and the dependence of the conclusion on the basis of assumptions made.

By using models and a deductive approach to teach economics, we shift the emphasis from descriptive aspects to more analytical work. We show how conclusions vary with the assumptions used and thereby how the student will learn about the limited nature of any conclusion reached by this deductive process of reasoning. It is hoped that this will promote a flexible and dynamic attitude rather than a rigid and static one. Working with models stimulates the critical faculty, imagination and creativity. When the basic assumptions concerning a model are being formulated and written up on the blackboard, they can be assessed by the student group, this being one of the most striking and immediate educational benefits of developing economic models. The model forms a framework that is subject to well-defined rules, so that the discussion cannot degenerate into an endless argument.

In such ways economists formulate models which can be used to predict economic behaviour. Models are also called theories and attempt to predict how, for example, income is distributed between workers and shareholders in firms, how firms determine their production and price decisions, and how government may attempt to take the national economy out of a situation of mass unemployment and low production.

In using the deductive approach economics shares with the natural sciences, such as physics or chemistry, a similar scientific method of inquiry. In the natural sciences, however, experiments play a much greater role than they do in economics. The scientists can study and test things in their laboratories, often under controlled conditions.

If economists want to know what will happen when the wages of manual workers are raised, for example, they cannot first limit the increase to a hundred workers in order to control and study their economic behaviour in isolation. They cannot stop the momentum of economic life. On the other hand, they can *treat* certain factors as constant when considering economic relationships. The factors which remain fixed are termed '*ceteris paribus*', and this is often used to gain an insight into complex economic situations. For instance, when considering the spending consequences of an increase in wages for manual workers we might choose to assume that the proportion of spending on imported goods remains constant.

Before applying the conclusions to the real world, however, we must carefully examine whether the *ceteris paribus* condition has been fulfilled, i.e. whether the proportion of spending does remain constant. An important way of finding out what happens in practice is by methodically collecting and analysing data from firms and households. We can then relate these data, derived from the real world, to our models.

Inductive In addition to the deductive model-building approach, there is the inductive method. The economist in this approach must firstly obtain the facts about the real world of producers and consumers. The inductive process involves gathering a large number of facts and then examining them to find connections among them. Statistical methods are used in both the collection and the testing of these data. For example, by studying the variation in the price of butter, bread, potatoes, etc., in the course of time and examining how much of the product is bought at each price, the economist can find a connection between the changing demand for essential foodstuffs and their price variations. A general relationship between changes in prices and variation in demand for essential foodstuffs can then be proposed.

Summary Models based on deductive reasoning are invaluable in developing an understanding of economics, and they encourage the practice of analytical thinking which is essential to the economist's methods of work. Although controlled experimentation is difficult in economic study the inductive approach relies on preliminary data collection similar to the observations and measurement of experiments in the natural sciences.

1.10 ECONOMIC SYSTEMS

How in reality do nations attempt to allocate scarce resources to satisfy wants? This allocation can be made by the state at national (or command) level or by firms and households at a decentralized (or market) level. The latter method encompasses the economic system explained in the main part of this book, since Britain and the other European Economic Community (EEC) countries take their economic decisions largely in this way. The former method is explained in detail later in the book, particularly in relation to the USSR. These two main economic systems are therefore the market economy and the command economy. However, in their pure forms they exist only in the economist's models and in practice each system contains some elements of the other. Western economies are basically market economies but with the government wielding a great deal of power, while Eastern Europe largely follows the basic pattern of a command economy but allows firms some limited decision-making. In fact most West European economies are so greatly influenced by government on levels of production and employment that they can be termed *mixed market* economies. In an economy with strict central control, the state decides on even the fine details of economic life, leaving little room for consumers' and producers' decisions. Thus there is no free market where supply of goods by producers and demand for goods by consumers may come to equate to each other. The function of government planners in command economies is not to make forecasts, as in Western economies, but to issue orders from the top which must be obeyed at most lower levels. In a recent development of this system, the lower levels are allowed to make some decisions about production, so that the decisions are to some extent decentralized. The USSR, the East European State Socialist countries, China, Cuba and some African countries such as Mozambique have command economies (see Table 1.1).

Market economies are based on the market mechanism whereby

consumer preferences for goods are expressed in the form of practical demand, i.e. a willingness to spend money. The producers respond to this demand and manufacture the goods required. The market, i.e. the total trading activity, relays to the producers the consumers' decisions about the types and quantities of goods wanted so that the allocation of resources

Table 1.1 Economic systems: examples of major countries.

Mixed-market		*Command*
United States	Japan	USSR
Canada	Iran	Poland
Britain	Australia	Czechoslovakia
France	Nigeria	Romania
German Federal Republic	South Africa	German Democratic Republic
Italy	Morocco	China
Netherlands	Argentina	Vietnam
Belgium	Brazil	Angola
Spain		Cuba
India		

to satisfy people's wants is determined by the decisions of households to buy and firms to sell. The pure form of the free-enterprise system is associated with perfect competition under which no supplier can corner the market, mainly because new firms are free to enter the industry and produce goods for this market.

Even in the strongest of the market economies complete freedom of consumption and production is curtailed by an often massive body of state regulations relating to health and safety at work, employment protection, and weights and measures.

As stated earlier, nowadays in the mixed market economies of most Western countries the government plays a very important role through the nationalized industries and the provision of a large welfare service. Moreover, government intervenes in the economy to attempt to prevent booms and slumps by introducing specific policies.

Summary There are various conflicting ideas about what kind of economic system should prevail in the world. The market system itself is being modified in EEC countries and in developing countries in Latin America, Africa and Asia, so that, for example, slumps in production are controlled by state intervention. The centralized command economies provide a very different system for allocating resources, but are now allowing firms to take decentralized decisions on some matters.

1.11 THE BRITISH ECONOMY AND THE EUROPEAN ECONOMIC COMMUNITY

Naturally we shall want to apply the economic theory we study to the British economy. However, the UK's home market for its goods and services now includes the 260 million people of the nine EEC countries and we must be prepared to extend our economic analysis to this supranational group, i.e. Britain, the German Federal Republic, France, Italy, the Netherlands, Belgium, Denmark, Ireland and Luxembourg. There is now complete free trade and free movement of labour between Britain and the other eight countries, and they share common agricultural, regional, social and industrial policies.

Britain and Ireland are members of a large customs union, with free trade throughout nine countries, and with a common tariff barrier towards the products of the rest of the world. All Britain's and Ireland's overseas trade agreements are now negotiated for them by the EEC, and all agricultural economic policies are part of the EEC's controversial common agricultural policy. In the fields of regional economic policy, social policy and structure of industry policy the EEC provides funds to develop British and Irish industries. The aim of the EEC treaties, signed by Britain and Ireland in 1972, is to create a complete economic union of the nine countries so that there might be a common currency, taxation system and banking system. If this should succeed, most government economic policy decisions concerning problems such as inflation and unemployment would be taken at EEC level and not at national government level. The EEC countries did, in fact, set 1980 as the date to achieve this economic union, but progress towards it has been very slow.

Nevertheless our belief in writing this book is that the application of economic theories must be primarily to the British economy and that this applied work should form an important part of the book. Theories are designed to help explain past and current economic events and predict future developments in the real world of economics: to have real life applications. Therefore, in Chapters 3 and 4 we not only study a theory of how production can be increased to create full employment but we also apply this theory to what has been done by government and firms to attempt to maintain full employment in Britain since 1945. To give another example, we not only examine the theory of how many goods are produced and how prices are fixed in vital industries in which only a few firms (oligopolists) operate, but we also apply these theories to the real-world situation in which these firms operate in the UK. *An oligopoly is an industry in which few firms compete,* e.g. motor car and tyre manufacturers.

In Britain, there is currently much discussion of whether the earnings of workers and shareholders should be limited by incomes policies. We shall examine the theories which attempt to explain how income is distributed in society, including in this analysis trade unions and employers' organizations which are responsible for negotiation of workers' wages. In short, we aim to relate all the most important theoretical work we discuss in this book to the real world of the British economy, so that the reader can understand what causes economic problems (e.g. unemployment, inflation) and assess how far economic theories can effectively explain the causes and justify the short-term solutions offered.

Summary The economic unit in which Britain participates extends to the European Economic Community of nine nations. Economic theory provides us with some explanations of how the economy of a nation and of a group of nations works, and we shall attempt to apply the theory to Britain and to the EEC.

1.12 THE LINKS BETWEEN ECONOMICS AND OTHER SUBJECTS

Economics is one of a number of social science subjects which analyse human behaviour and it is useful to examine the overlap that exists between it and the other social sciences.

The economist, the geographer, the lawyer, the sociologist and the psychologist are all concerned with analysing human behaviour according to their own particular frame of reference. An ailing pop record company, if studied by an investigator from each of these five disciplines, would provide from past and present corporate behaviour a rich source of data for interpretation. Nonetheless, if you were to read the five accounts, giving the view of each discipline on what was wrong with the company, you would have no great difficulty in distinguishing the viewpoints. There would of course be some common ground in the reports and the complete diagnosis would require consideration of all five analyses and perhaps some others. However, the common ground would not obscure the fact that the economist would concern himself only with the economic aspects (or effects or consequences) of the issues involved: e.g. the unattractive record sleeve design may lead to a lower sales level. He would concentrate on such matters as the fall in demand for this label, the company's subsequent upward price increase and the further fall in demand. Questions of consumer taste for the product or its packaging are *external data* or outside the scope of his subject as far as the economist is concerned. It is the role of other disciplines to analyse these aspects of behaviour. Amongst economists there is a consensus of what constitutes the subjects' boundaries but, as we shall see, certain traditional 'non-economic' factors are now showing themselves to be open to economic analysis. For example, consider the following four items: (1) consumer preference; (2) quality and quantity of the available factors of production; (3) the social and legal structure of society; and (4) technical change.

1. Consumers tend to show a scale of preference for goods such as clothes, shoes, food, and services such as the cinema. Economics is generally not interested in why some women prefer trouser suits to skirts and dresses, or how advertising influences the scale of preference. Nevertheless, advertising stems from the economic drive of firms to sell more goods and so increase sales income and profits. For this reason, economists are now probing more deeply into the question of how consumer demands arise and change. It is nonetheless from the findings of psychology that the major determinants of consumer preference can be derived.
2. The amount of national resources and the size of the total population are almost always taken as beyond the scope of economics. Capital, the third factor of production, is largely explainable by economic analysis. In the past the quality as well as the quantity of natural resources has been of as much interest to economists as to geologists and geographers. For example, the type and cost of capital equipment for mining coal will depend on the quality of the coal deposits. Another factor of production, labour, is now being assessed for quality by economic analysis. Thus the amount of money spent on education and training can have important implications for the quality of labour.
3. The social, political and legal structure of society is left largely for other subjects to explain. The general view of non-Marxist economists is that such questions as 'Why has the Soviet Union a command economy?' are not economic questions. In contrast, Marxist economists aim to explain changes in the social structure largely in terms of economic factors. However, amongst non-Marxist economists increasing attention is being paid to the 'economics of politics', which emphasizes the increasingly important role of government in Western European countries in producing goods and services and utilizing large parts of the national resources. Such analysis has confirmed the very close links between the political structure of societies and economic activity. The political scientist can provide much insight into politicians' decision-making in government economic policies designed to cure inflation or unemployment. Such analysis identified the possibility that the so-called 'pre-General Election boom' in the economy may be caused by a government's desire to win an election.

   Sociological explanations of worker attitudes towards work and strikes are relevant to understanding the background to negotiations of wages and general conditions in an industry. For example, car assembly-line workers, bored by a repetitive job, may be the more ready to strike in support of a pay claim.

   The legal structure has an important bearing upon whether firms can make price-fixing agreements among themselves, and whether the existence of a single dominant company in an industry is permissible. At a more mundane level the day-to-day functioning of firms is regulated by the Companies Acts and diverse legislation relating to safety, working conditions, employment protection, etc.

   A broader understanding of economics is thus gained if it is studied in the context of other social science subjects, particularly in relation to decision-making. This book attempts to link economics with these subjects whilst maintaining that economics can be studied legitimately as an academic subject in its own right. Most decisions have economic and non-economic aspects, and, as we will continue to emphasize, the former are concerned with the relationship between many wants and scarce resources with alternative uses.

4. Technical change perhaps best illustrates how a once-peripheral subject is now considered amenable to economic analysis. Until recently there was hardly any doubt that this was outside the scope of economics but now the view is gaining ground that the massive technical development in modern society depends on economic decisions which determine how much money is spent on education and training, and even the major directions of technical change. Space research is an example of how technical development is stimulated by government policy and government spending in a particular technological direction.

Summary The targets of economic analysis can be generally delineated but input from the other social sciences gives a broader understanding of economic topics.

1.13 OVERVIEW OF THE BOOK

This short section explains how we approach economics in this book. We start with the production factors and examine how society may increase some of these in attempts to cope with its economic problems (Chapter 2). The next section of the book (Chapters 3 to 7) studies how the production of goods and services is determined by the nation as a whole. This includes the use of money, as largely a paper representation of goods and services, and the influence of the British banking system and government in national production. Chapters 3 to 7 therefore overview the *macroeconomy, i.e. the study of the totals of economic activity in a nation* (e.g. national income, investment).

Microeconomics is the study of smaller decision-making units of the national economy (e.g. firms and consumers) and these we study in Chapters 8 to 11. There we will examine what, within the microeconomy, determines the decisions of consumers to buy goods and producers to make and sell them. In particular, we investigate how privately-owned firms make decisions on production, pricing and marketing goods to satisfy wants from scarce resources. This is related to the national situation of allocation of goods and services from scarce resources, discussed in Chapters 3 and 4, and we will also consider small businesses, firms, multinational companies and the concept of monopoly.

In Chapter 12 we move on to how income is distributed to workers and shareholders in the companies examined earlier, and in Chapter 13 we assess what causes a nation to increase its production of goods and services over a period of time. Technical change is a vital factor here in enabling people to satisfy their wants to an increasing extent. Finally, at the national level, Chapter 14 explains the economic role of government in an economy in which most production is from privately-owned firms. It examines how British governments have used economic policies involving control of money, the annual budget, prices and incomes to tackle national economic problems such as inflation, unemployment and balance of payments. The last part of the book analyses Britain's new economic role in the European Economic Community and the way in which economic decisions are made in communist countries. We examine why international trade takes place, and how at EEC level the wants of an economic community of 260 million people are satisfied from supra-national but still scarce resources. The Soviet Union, Eastern Europe and some developing countries have command economies in which economic decisions are made in a way substantially different from those in most Western countries, including Britain, and this subject is explained in detail.

Acting as both a summary and conclusion, the last chapter of the book reviews the different proposals made for the operation of national economies and the world's economy by the great economists of the last 200 years.

1.14 CONCLUDING REMARKS

After reading this overview of economic problems and issues it should be clear that the central issue of economics is to explain how mankind allocates scarce resources that have alternative uses in order to satisfy the many wants of people. Man attempts to satisfy these wants through the creation of goods and services by the production process, i.e. the combination of the factors of production: land, labour and capital. The wants are continuously changing, however, and are becoming more and more sophisticated as incomes rise and advertising becomes more persuasive.

In certain industrial locations the production of material goods has become so great that it precipitates a new scarcity of intangible resources such as clean air, clear water and natural beauty. If this occurs in a climate of public opinion which requires an increase in welfare there may be strong pressure to restrict, modify or stop a form of production that causes pollution.

The economic significance of choosing between growth of production and a pleasant environment still lies in the core issue of allocating scarce resources that have alternative uses, even though the advantages and disadvantages cannot readily be expressed in terms of money. Economics therefore is not restricted to choices where the alternatives can be given a financial value but covers all those decisions in which scarce resources are involved. However, economics alone cannot be used to make a decision because this may also depend on political, ethical, religious and other considerations which lie outside the scope of economics. We can, however, as economists, comment upon the ways in which resources are allocated, as far as their *economic* consequences are concerned.

QUESTIONS

1 What does scarcity mean in economics?

2 What do we mean by opportunity cost?

3 Name the factors of production. What is the combination of the factors of production called?

4 What is division of labour and how is it connected with an exchange economy?

5 What are the economic considerations involved in building a road across a nature reserve?

6 What do we understand by the term 'external data of economics'? Give some examples.

7 What is the difference between the inductive and the deductive method of investigation?

8 Give an example of nature as a consumer good.

9 What is a model?

10 What are the advantages of models in economics?

EXERCISES

1 Discuss the statement that butter is not scarce because we can buy it in any quantity.

2 Is a motor car a capital good or a consumer good?

3 Where is a washing machine a consumer good: (a) in the home, (b) in the shop-window or (c) in a laundrette?

4 Is it correct to say that the aim of economics is to show how a company can maximize its profits?

5 Is air scarce?

6 Which of the following observations is it the task of economists to explain?
(a) The price of butter has gone up by 4 pence.
(b) Consumers have switched from butter to margarine.
(c) The fat content of butter has been increased by a new technique.
(d) Foot-and-mouth disease has caused a drop in milk production.
(e) An indirect tax on butter has caused a drop in demand for this product.

7 Can it be said that someone's welfare is high if he earns a great deal?

8 What welfare effects are to be weighed against each other in the case where a new car manufacturing plant that could employ 500 men and give 10 000 more home-produced cars a year is to be built in a nature reserve with a large population of rare birds? Which of these welfare effects can be expressed in money?

9 Discuss the statement that land and labour as factors of production also directly satisfy wants.

10 Describe the basic differences between a command economy and a market economy.

11 Which major economic functions does the EEC perform which, prior to 1973, the British government performed?

Chapter Two

Production and the Factors of Production

How can a country become more prosperous and raise the living standards of its people? As far as material possessions are concerned the answer is that the country must increase its production of goods and services in order to make available a greater amount of consumer goods to satisfy people's wants. This is the essential economic problem which confronts developing countries of the so-called Third World (Africa, Asia and Latin America), where millions starve and millions of others suffer malnutrition. Even in developed countries, such as Britain, large numbers of the population are jobless, are living in poor-quality housing, and are even undernourished. They desire an increase in consumer goods to satisfy their material wants, and government normally attempts to increase national production to achieve this. Of course, in developed countries an increase in production may lead to a decline in intangible resources such as clean air and natural beauty.

In what ways can this increase in production over a period of time be achieved? To explain this we shall give a general description of the total process of production of goods by the economy. Thus, we shall not concentrate on production of one specific good but we shall examine total production and the totality of the agents or factors of production: total land, total labour and total capital.

2.1 CHANGES IN PRODUCTION

The obvious reason why the output of goods and services in Britain today is higher than a century ago is that our society has more capital, more labour and utilizes more land and raw materials. Less obvious, but as important, are the higher degree of specialization (division of labour) and the fact that capital equipment, due to technical change, is more advanced and can therefore produce more goods and different types of goods. These two factors of production, capital and labour, have increased not only in quantity but also in quality, embodying as they do both our technological progress and our progress in general education and vocational training.

The answer to the question 'What determines production over time?' is therefore first sought on the supply side: in the provision of more and better factors of production. However, the utilization of all these improved and more numerous factors of production calls for a sufficient level of *demand* in the economy. *Demand is the willingness and ability to pay for a particular good or service.*

If people do not buy enough consumer goods part of the productive capacity will stand idle and the level of production will be less than is possible. *The productive capacity of a country is the total amount of goods or services that the country is capable of producing if all the factors of production are used maximally.* It is determined by the three factors of production, specialization of labour and technical change available to a nation at a given point in time. So we must look at both the supply and demand side of the economy in order to understand what, in reality, determines production.

In the remainder of this chapter, after dealing with the supply side in general and giving a detailed characterization of the factors of production, we move on to case studies of the scarcity of production factors in relation to the demands of people for material goods and services. The case studies concern current basic economic problems related to (a) land and energy raw materials, (b) efficiency of labour and (c) capital in developing countries. We provide these so that the reader can examine, in a qualitative way, topical and crucial economic issues before proceeding to a more analytical approach through economic theory. Finally, we consider how Britain might increase its productive capacity, and we introduce the demand side of the economy.

2.2 SUPPLY FACTORS

The productive capacity of a country depends on the ready availability of the factors of production (labour, land and capital), and on the degree of specialization and the state of technology.

It is not only the quantity, but the quality that matters. More and better education of the workforce, including management, produces a more skilled labour force and technical change enables capital goods to be made more productive than similar capital 30 years ago. The production process is in a continuous state of change and new developments in this area are a major preoccupation of entrepreneurs. In fact, total productive capacity changes every day, with an overall tendency for more and better products to be made.

The skill of entrepreneurs or managers in a company is vital to increasing the supply and quality of the production factors labour and capital. It is management's decision whether to apply technical change to the company, that is, whether to install new capital such as machinery in a factory or to bring in new methods of work. Such decisions depend upon the expected rate of profit from sales of the products made with the new machinery and methods. For example, Imperial Chemical Industries Ltd is in the process of introducing both new machinery and new methods of making chemicals at its new coastal plants such as those in Teesside. The decision to do this required skilled managerial judgement, which can also be developed through greater specialization and training. I.C.I. managers are given specific management courses to complement their previous experience. Nowadays, therefore, the salaried executive manager is mainly a specialized decision-taker rather than an allrounder with knowledge of and experience in use of capital equipment, selling in the market and guidance of the labour force, as were owner-managers of companies in the early part of the century.

Technical change also has great economic importance and it has for too long been regarded by economists and other social scientists as something that is external to economics and is determined only by chance and the engineers. Indeed, the factors of production themselves can be used to produce new technical knowledge, so that we must include technical change in our discussion. For example, a car company can develop a new engine using existing plant and research engineers at a University.

Summary What can be produced depends in the first place on productive capacity, which is determined by the three factors of production, specialization of labour and technical change.

2.3 LAND

We stated earlier that land includes all natural resources such as soil, minerals and vegetation. It is a production factor the supply of which is fixed in the short run (i.e. one to two years) by rates of extraction or development and is limited in the long run by the total available. For example, the supply of physical land is difficult to increase even in the long run. There are rare examples of extending physical land such as the draining of the almost landlocked Zuider Zee (IJsselmeer) in the Netherlands in the mid twentieth century, but this success is the exception rather than the rule. However, the amount of land available for exploitation for agricultural purposes can be increased by, for example, irrigation of deserts. In Tunisia large areas of semi-desert are being reclaimed for raising sheep and even for the cultivation of arable crops. Thus the economic resources of Tunisia are being increased to satisfy more fully the wants of the Tunisian people.

Agricultural Land The area of agricultural land under production is not the only indicator of the effective use of land as a factor or production. India's agricultural land makes up 50 per cent of total land area, whilst in Western Europe it accounts for 44 per cent, but the latter produces much more than the former. Compared with India, Western Europe uses far more capital equipment, such as tractors and drainage equipment, in farming and also trains many more of its farmers in skilled agricultural techniques ranging from animal breeding to fertilizer application. It should now be clear that to increase the yield of agricultural land to a maximum requires the use of the other production factors – capital and labour. However, funds to do this cannot be reliably acquired by developing countries because the prices of most agricultural products on world markets fluctuate sharply: witness the large rises in wheat prices in 1972 and the large falls in potato prices in 1977.

Raw Materials The supply of raw materials such as coal, copper, lead, gas and oil is normally much easier to increase in the long run. The development of North Sea oil in the 1970s has been a classic example of increasing the long-run supply of raw material. In this way an economic resource has been substantially increased for use in production but this development, even more than with agricultural land, has required massive use of capital equipment and much training of skilled labour. As with agriculture, it used to be the case that accumulation of funds to develop raw material production was unreliable due to fluctuating world commodity prices. The fall in the world prices of raw materials in the 1950s was typical of this.

Increases in Raw Material Prices In contrast, the 1970s have witnessed some substantial rises in world prices of raw materials. Why did oil prices soar by a remarkable 40 per cent in 1974? This was initially due to a shortage of oil, created by a restriction of supply by some countries during the Middle East conflict of autumn 1973. This relatively small restriction of supply revealed that industrial countries were willing to pay considerably higher prices, and the major oil producers (already members of a 'club', the Organization of Petroleum Exporting Countries) saw the prospect of enforcing even higher prices. On 1 January 1974 they collectively quadrupled crude oil prices. Other cartels (i.e. price-fixing sellers' organizations) have developed in raw materials in the 1970s (e.g. in copper), and this has done much to maintain stable prices for producer countries. It was, of course, the huge rise in oil prices which led Britain to accelerate rapidly the development of North Sea oil, its most recently discovered major economic resource.

Summary Land is a factor of production whose supply is limited in both the short run and the long run. A more efficient and intensified use of labour and capital, the other factors of production, is required to increase its yield.

2.4 CASE STUDY: LAND AND ENERGY RESOURCES

Up to now we have merely hinted that there is a fixed limit to supplies of raw materials in the long run, but it is a vital point of debate in the late twentieth century whether the very last reserves of energy raw materials will be reached by the beginning of the new century.

Britain's Energy Resources In Britain the Advisory Council on Research and Development reported in 1976 that, in spite of North Sea oil and gas, imports of energy raw materials into Britain would need to be greater in 2000 A.D. than in 1976. Although North Sea oil production will rise to as much as 5 per cent of gross domestic product in 1985, by 1995 it will have been almost fully exploited.

What of the other energy raw materials? In 1976, of the home-produced materials, gas provided 17.7 per cent of energy requirements, coal 37.3 per cent and nuclear power 3.9 per cent; oil, largely imported, provided 41.1 per cent. Figure 2.1 demonstrates that in the following year, 1977, energy resources were used in similar proportions.

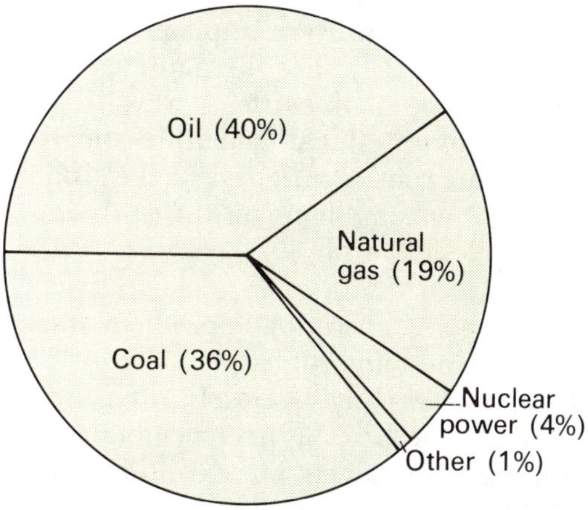

Figure 2.1 UK energy sources.

Gas The supply of natural gas from the North Sea has expanded meteorically since the 1960s but by the 1990s the proven reserves will be exhausted. Gas supplies will then become dependent upon oil and coal, since it is only as a by-product of processing these materials that gas will be available from United Kingdom sources.

Coal Coal has a much more promising future, with reserves proven for 300 years at the 1977 rate of production (121 million tons). The National Coal Board's 'Plan for Coal' (1976) proposes an increase in rate of production to reach 150 million tons per annum by 1985, through the development of Yorkshire, East Midlands and Staffordshire coalfields.

Nuclear Power Nuclear energy remains dependent upon supplies of imported uranium and existing thermal nuclear reactors in atomic power stations use that raw material inefficiently. If the fast breeder nuclear reactor were to be installed in power stations it would no longer be necessary to import uranium, since it produces more fuel than it consumes. If this new reactor is proven and deployed, Britain would be able, the Advisory Council report argues, to increase its economic resources of energy supplies to the level of self-sufficiency, even after the exhaustion of home-produced oil and gas. However, the fast reactor is criticized on grounds that it presents a permanent serious danger to the environment.

Scarcity of Energy Resources and Pricing The conflict therefore lies between the use of coal to supply all Britain's energy needs from the early part of the next century and the use of nuclear fuel to supply part of these requirements. Of course, the pricing of energy resources may be used to conserve different types of energy and save fuel. Some economists argue that coal could be conserved and would supply all Britain's energy requirements into the 21st century if a higher-price policy, which would reduce demand, were implemented.

These, then, are the main aspects of Britain's energy problem, but the same problem exists on a world scale. Although the energy problem encompasses ethical, scientific and social issues, it involves important economic considerations, and the economic theory of prices, in particular, will throw some light on the problem.

Summary The economic problem of energy is an illustration of the wider basic economic problem of increasing resources to combat scarcity. The theory of pricing is closely interwoven with planned solutions to this problem. In Britain the development of North Sea oil and gas has been a means of massively increasing material resources.

2.5 LABOUR

The production factor, labour, is not synonymous with total population since it refers only to the working population, i.e. those offering themselves for work. It therefore includes the unemployed but excludes students in full-time education, retired pensioners, and housekeepers within the family. Nevertheless a big increase in total population due to an increased birth rate will eventually lead to an increase in the working population. We must therefore examine the basic question of whether a large increase in total population (and consequently in working population) always constitutes an increase in economic resources, when viewed as a whole.

World Population Problem Malthus, the nineteenth-century English economist, argued that population increases in a geometrical progression, whereas production of foodstuffs increases in an arithmetical progression. In simpler terms, he was saying that population increases rather like this:

2,4,8,16,32,64,128 ...

whereas yields of agricultural foodstuffs rise much more slowly:

2,3,4,5,6,7 ... or 2,4,6,8,10 ...

If this is valid, a population increase could, in fact, lead to a rapid decrease in the basic foodstuffs available per person. There would be, it is true, an increase in labour, but with severe disadvantages.

Richard Bailey shows concern about the twentieth-century population explosion: 'perhaps the most important of the revolutions from the point of view of the world economy is the biological revolution, the sudden vast increase in the rate at which the human race is multiplying'. The evidence to support his contention is that world population has increased from 2 500 000 000 in 1940 to 4 000 000 000 in 1978, and a United Nations forecast estimates 6 500 000 000 by the year 2000 (see Table 2.1). The bulk of this increase is in Latin America, Africa and the non-industrialized countries of Asia, with annual rates of population growth exceeding 3 per cent. The doubling and re-doubling of world population in such a short space of time places enormous pressure on food production and can lead to a fall in the amount of foodstuffs available per person in the countries most seriously affected. In such cases a rise in total and working population, all else being equal, would only result in increasing scarcity.

Table 2.1 Increase in world population.

Year	*Population (millions)*
1800	1650
1900	1890
1950	2600
1970	3600
1978 (est.)	4000
2000 (est.)	6500

Source: Oxford Economic Atlas of the World.

Scarcity and Population It is true that in the nineteenth century the population of the industrial countries in Europe and North America rapidly doubled and re-doubled, but the application of capital equipment to home agriculture increased food supply. Moreover, industrialization led to development of manufacturing industries, which provided sufficient goods for export to pay for food imports as well as raising the standard of living within the country. A large increase in total population can therefore lead to an increase in the economic resource, labour, but this is usually of real value to society only if it is accompanied by the large-scale development of the other resources, capital and land. In very sparsely peopled countries such as Canada, however, a rise in population can lead to an increase in production without the need for further development of capital or land.

Summary The world population problem shows us that an increase in the labour resource will not necessarily lead to higher production and may increase the scarcity of foodstuffs.

2.6 CASE STUDY: THE EFFICIENCY OF LABOUR

One can increase the efficiency of labour in day-to-day work by improving the training of the working population and the general and vocational education of the future working population: the full-time school pupils and students. How is this achieved in practice?

Industrial Training The Industrial Training Boards set up in Britain in the 1960s have led to a substantial development of specific training by which young workers obtain specialist craft instruction, not only on the job, but also in training schools run by the larger firms. Such training can increase considerably the quality of the product: e.g. the well-trained skilled lathe operator in an engineering works should produce fewer substandard items in his work. The speed of production may also be increased by these methods, since a well-trained skilled welder in the shipbuilding industry should complete more work in a given time.

General Education The level of general education achieved is dependent on the educational facilities available in a country. It can be argued that a good general education will lead to improved quality and higher levels of industrial output. The study of such subjects as science, mathematics, English or economics requires a student to think analytically and express himself precisely, and this is a vital foundation for all production and service industries. Indeed, some educationists and economists go further and claim that a stronger vocational link between schools and industry is highly desirable and will motivate students to aspire to more skilled jobs.

Sickness In what other ways can the efficiency of the workforce be improved to increase production? A reduction in the number of working days lost due to ill health and industrial disputes would be a major improvement. In Britain more days are lost due to the former than to the latter and, where the absenteeism is genuinely a medical problem, improved preventive medicine and treatment would increase efficiency considerably.

Industrial Disputes Can there also be a preventive approach to industrial disputes? A major issue to be considered here is the conflict over income distribution between the production factors which earn income, i.e. wages accruing to labour, profits earned by capital for companies (giving rise to interest payments to shareholders), and in some cases rent earned by land for landlords.

In most Western industrial countries settlements between employees and employers concerning pay and general conditions are based upon a system of joint collective bargaining. In Britain this bargaining is usually done at two main levels: at the national level, to determine basic pay rates, and at plant level to determine additional earnings, e.g. bonuses, piece-rates. The system is further complicated in that, amongst employees, different-interest groups of workers are normally represented by different unions. For example, at Ford (UK) the workers are represented by more than 10 different unions. A few disputes occur between unions but the vast majority are between the employers and unions.

Income Distribution and Financial Incentives Solutions to these organizational problems have been suggested, such as bargaining at plant level only and one union per plant or per industry. These ideas, however, do not remove the basic issue of conflict over income distribution between labour and employers. Nevertheless, some economists argue that in Western industrial countries there has, in fact, been a shift in distribution of income towards labour in the last 40 years. On the other hand, it is argued that differences in income may act as incentives rather than disincentives to increasing efficiency and production. Managers, it is said, have special organizational skills and a company takes risks to develop economic resources of capital and raw materials: the manager and the company will expect high returns. Similarly, it is argued that some workers have special technical skills and require bonuses or individual piece-rate payments to encourage their full efficiency.

Summary The efficiency of labour can be increased by improved education and training, preventive medicine and a reduction in industrial disputes. These improvements are also valuable in themselves as they influence welfare in a positive way.

2.7 CAPITAL

A very powerful means of boosting production in the long run is to increase capital. An increase in capital equipment is called *Investment*. Investment can be defined more fully as *an increase in a stock of physical assets over a given period of time* (e.g. one year) (See Figure 2.2).

Investment, as we use the term, means new steelworks, new motorways, and new factory machinery; we are not thinking of investment as money or stocks and shares.

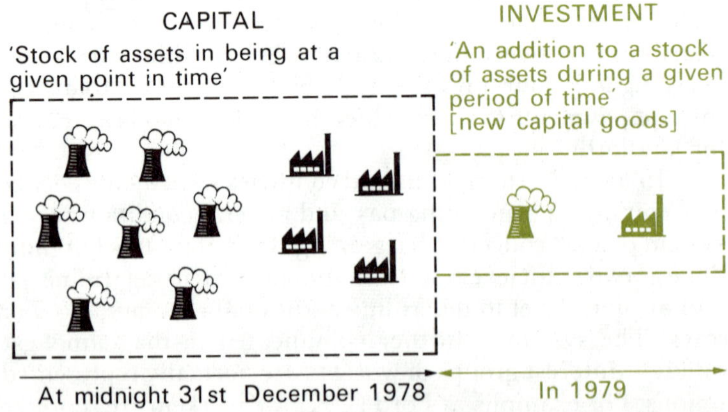

Figure 2.2 Capital and capital investment.

Investment is almost wholly produced by man and is usually swifter and more effective in increasing production than an increase in efficiency through training of the working population. For example, if a firm wishes to raise chemicals production, this can be achieved more rapidly by installing new semi-automatic plants than by training more chemical workers to man a second shift.

Investment and Technical Change A very important determinant of increased investment is technical change which we can take here as the discovery of techniques for producing new goods and the invention of improved techniques for producing existing goods. The invention of nylon as a new material in the 1940s is an example of the former, and the invention of the fast-breeder reactor for producing nuclear energy in the 1970s is an example of the latter. These technical developments require the building of new capital equipment to put them into effect, and they therefore increase the economic resource, capital. The potential for higher profit resulting from the sales consequent to the installation of this new equipment is also a vital factor in transforming inventions or discoveries into new capital goods. Private firms are unlikely to want to build new factories and machinery unless the profits earned by this capital equipment are greater than profits which could be earned by putting the funds into government stock or some other form of interest-bearing savings. Generally, in the private sector of the economy the rate of technical change and the potential for extra profit from new investment based on these advances will determine whether or not new investment takes place.

Summary New capital (i.e. investment) is generally a rapid means of increasing economic growth.

2.8 CASE STUDY: CAPITAL IN DEVELOPING COUNTRIES

An increase in new capital is a very speedy way of increasing production if one wishes to foster economic growth. The problem of expanding economic growth is particularly important in developing countries, which may possess much land, raw materials and labour, but lack major manufacturing plant for steel, engineering and chemical industries. Such countries generally have a lower material standard of living than industrialized countries and this is not only evident in the lack of home-produced durable consumer goods; thus the quantity and type of food produced at home is usually limited by the absence of industrial facilities for producing agricultural machinery and fertilizers which are needed to improve agricultural yields.

Investment in Developing Countries How can developing countries increase investment and accelerate the growth of their economies in the production of scarce goods? There are three possible major sources of funds for new investment: the savings of the wealthy, taxation of the population, and foreign funds in the form of investment, loans or grants. Even when combined, these three sources are usually insufficient to generate rapid economic growth.

The wealthy are usually a small percentage of the population and in a traditional society tend both to hold and to desire to hold wealth in the form of non-industrial goods such as jewellery and furniture. Taxation is difficult to impose since the population is generally poor and there are huge administrative problems involved in assessing and collecting taxes. Foreign investment flowed relatively freely into developing colonial countries in the nineteenth and early twentieth centuries, but it was not always into those industries, such as steel and engineering, upon which a country most effectively builds its industrial strength. Now, in the late twentieth century, such investment usually depends upon political stability in the recipient country and an agreement between its government and foreign firms on profit sharing, which gives a substantial income to both. Similar considerations also limit the availability of grants and loans from foreign governments.

Bangladesh Bangladesh is perhaps the most extreme example of a developing country, with all the difficulties described above and a rapidly increasing population (85 million in 1978, predicted to be 150 million by A.D. 2000). A World Bank research team has recommended that it should devote its industrialization to projects that will most improve agricultural yields (such as engineering and fertilizers) so that its increased population can simply survive at the present standard of living. Other countries are more fortunate and could, by industrialization, not only promote economic growth but also raise the individual's standard of living.

Investment Decisions in Developing Countries How are decisions about growth taken in a developing country? In a command economy, such as

China, central government allocates the resources, labour, land and capital, to produce new capital equipment in heavy industries and acquires funds largely from an efficient taxation system. In a mixed market economy, such as Nigeria, resources are allocated partly by central government in a similar way, together with foreign loans and grants, home savings and funds of foreign firms. In an advanced industrial mixed market economy, such as the United Kingdom, decisions about economic growth are made largely as in the Nigerian example, but with greater use of home savings as a source of funds. In all cases choices have to be made as to which goods and services should be developed first.

The analysis of how developing countries might grow through reorganized world trade is discussed in Chapter 15.

Summary Developing countries which have lower standards of living than have Europe, North America or Japan find difficulties in financing the costs of investment from their own means.

2.9 BRITAIN'S ECONOMIC RESOURCES

Britain's production from 1960 to 1969 grew by only 30 per cent, compared with 70 per cent in France and 80 per cent in West Germany. In comparative terms, Britain's real economic problem is that of increasing economic resources at the same rate as similar-sized neighbours in the EEC. If we apply our studies of economic resources in this chapter to this problem, we can see that by the 1980s home energy supplies will be plentiful, and that there will not be a rapid increase in population to put added demand on resources. Moreover, there could actually be an increase in the efficiency of labour through the development of more industrial training schemes, better industrial health, and a reduction in the number of industrial disputes.

Investment Decisions in Britain The production factor which most needs to be expanded, and can be expanded in the next decade, is investment which, in the 1960s, was much less in Britain than in France or West Germany. Despite some stunning successes in basic research and development there has been a deficiency of investment in Britain in the new technological industries of the late twentieth century, e.g. aerospace, telecommunications and computers. The nation may still be a leader in the research and development of new techniques but it has a poor performance in putting the techniques into practice in industry. Greater investment in manufacturing industry based on technical change would lead to increased production and increased exports. In turn, imports of scarce foodstuffs and non-energy raw materials could increase. All of this could raise the standard of living. The new investment could be carried out by private firms, by government or by both, but if it is to be done by private industry much would depend on the current level of savings and the level of profits predicted.

The problem of increasing Britain's economic growth will lead us into theories of how economic resources can best be allocated in a mixed market economy, i.e. how choices of what to produce are made.

Summary Britain has, in the medium term, sufficient energy supplies and a workforce sufficiently large and skilled to increase economic growth but it is relatively weak in the field of increasing investment, particularly that based on technical change.

2.10 DEMAND FACTORS

The excursion into Britain's economic resources should not distract us from the other factors which determine the course of production over time. Apart from the supply factors discussed, which determine what and how much can be produced, the demand factors are also important.

The demand placed on the productive capacity of a country comes from the demand factors: the consumers, producers, government and foreign countries. Demand may fall short of, be equal to, or exceed the productive capacity. In the first case, the actual level of production would indeed be determined by demand, for the economy could produce more and there would be some unemployed labour available: the only limiting factor would be demand. The recession in Britain in 1971–2 exemplifies this situation: effective demand was too low to create full employment. The production level had ceased to grow and we describe this situation as one of under-spending. In the second case (demand = productive capacity) the attainable output is in fact produced, and demand and supply keep abreast of each other. This situation has been short-lived in Britain in the post-war years, but can be identified as occurring in 1953, 1959–60, 1963, 1969 and 1973. Finally, the third case of demand (demand exceeds productive capacity) is characterized by overspending, as explained below.

Excess Demand Situation When the four demand factors – consumers, producers, government and foreign countries – together call for an output greater than the available productive capacity permits, the actual production level is determined by the productive capacity. Demand, however, is ahead of the productive capacity in this case, even though production is growing, and prices must necessarily rise as demand rises. In turn, the demand for labour, capital, land and raw materials is so high that their costs usually rise substantially. Economic life is then pervaded by a boom atmosphere: more labour is wanted than is available, and persistent demand creates a favourable climate for new capital equipment to be installed in factories.

The essential point, however, is that shortage of labour now holds back production. Because of this, entrepreneurs in investment goods industries sometimes find that they have over-reacted to the high demand and created an excess production capacity since the limited supply of labour has now restricted the demand of consumer-goods firms for these products. For example, a truck-manufacturing firm may have built more vehicles than are needed to transport to market the now restricted demand of the consumer-goods industries (e.g. cars, washing machines and television sets).

Summary Increases in production over time must be explained by a combination of supply and demand factors. The demand factors are vitally important in ensuring that increased productive capacity is used and full employment achieved.

2.11 CONCLUDING REMARKS

The expansion of production generally requires an increase in the supply of the production factors, land, labour and capital. An analysis of the means of increasing resources is central to any consideration of economic problems such as energy, efficiency of labour, and capital in developing countries. These current problems illustrate the need to make choices in attempting to satisfy demand by increasing the economic resources in some way. As we shall see later, economic theory can be used to make predictions about the effects of such choices.

The quality as well as the quantity of an economic resource is important. In advanced industrial countries the quality of the labour force and the sophistication of technology as related to production are vital features of any increase in economic resources. The quality of the environment is also related to economic choices, and if we rapidly increase production there may be a deterioration of non-tangible resources such as natural beauty and quietness. Economic theory also deals, therefore, with choices concerning the allocation of these scarce resources. Finally, the achievement of increased production also has to be explained in terms of the demand factors in the economy: consumers, producers, government and foreign countries.

QUESTIONS

1 What is the economist's definition of land?

2 Why did world oil prices rise so rapidly in 1973–4?

3 What are the main components of Britain's energy supplies?

4 What theory did Malthus produce in regard to population?

5 Is the rapid growth in world population a serious economic problem? Give reasons for and against this proposition.

6 In which ways could the general and specific quality of the British workforce be increased?

7 What economic arguments could managers make for increased profits, and workers for higher wages?

8 What is investment? Why is it a very important basis for economic growth?

9 How might economic decisions concerning increasing economic growth be implemented in a developing country?

10 What are the main difficulties in the way of increasing economic growth in Britain?

EXERCISES

1 Identify some economic problems in your local town. In what ways would an increase in economic resources overcome the problems?

2 Discuss the economic policy you would recommend to the British Government's Department of Energy as a means of helping to solve Britain's energy problem.

3 Examine (from U.N. Statistics) the growth in population of the following countries between (a) 1900 and 1950 and (b) 1950 and 1975:

The Netherlands, France, Sweden, India, Malaysia and Brazil.

Give reasons why rate of population increase has declined between 1950 and 1975 in the first three countries and not in the last three.

4 'Most economists agree that to secure a steadily expanding level of production in an industrial country, 10 to 15 per cent of the national production should be investment goods production.'
Comment on this statement and explain how increased investment goods can lead to growth in the productive capacity of a country.

5 What are the main goods produced in Nigeria? (See *Oxford Economic Atlas of the World.*) Which types of goods would you argue should be increased in production in order to raise living standards rapidly in this large developing country?

6 What are the main goods produced in Britain? (See reference as in Question 5 and/or *National Incomes and Expenditure* Blue Book.) Which types of goods should be increased in production to raise British living standards?

Chapter Three

National Income and Other Macroeconomic Concepts

Chapters 3 and 4 deal with macroeconomics which is concerned with the whole economy and involves such variables as aggregate (total) production, aggregate employment and aggregate consumption. The output of a firm, the level of employment in an industry and the consumption of an individual, which are only part of the whole economy (i.e. microeconomics), will not be studied in detail until Chapter 8.

This chapter is devoted to the general relationships between firms and households, this discussion paving the way for economic theory of the factors determining production levels and employment levels in the economy, which will be examined in Chapter 4. Here we will simply outline some of the relevant economic relationships, but give no theoretical explanations; nor do we give a complete set of these relationships, since no consideration is given to the government, the financial sector including banks, and foreign countries. Yet at the end of this chapter you will be able to give a full description of some basic macroeconomic concepts, such as aggregate output and national income, so providing the necessary foundations for economic analysis which follows. One of these basic economic concepts is the *national income* which is defined as *the value of the flow of goods and services becoming available to a nation during a given period of time* (e.g. a year). National income, investment, etc. are *actual* or measured values. Such actual values (totals) are sometimes in economics called *ex post* values, *ex post* meaning 'after the event'. The opposite of these are planned values (totals) or forecasts (e.g. planned investment). These planned values (totals) are sometimes in economics called *ex ante* values, *ex ante* meaning 'before the event'.

3.1 FIRMS AND HOUSEHOLDS

The concept of firms and households as economic units was introduced in Chapter 1. The following discussion will concentrate on these to the exclusion of the other economic units which are the government, the financial sector including banks, and foreign countries; that is, it will deal with a closed isolated economy.

Moreover, in macroeconomics, interest is focused not on a single, individual economic unit or subsection of the economy but on the totals of goods produced and consumed in the economy. These goods are produced by firms and consumed by households. Macroeconomics deals with the explanation of what determines the national income, and other so-called aggregate economic quantities, such as expenditure, saving and investment. *Saving* is essentially *that part of income which is not spent on consumption. Expenditure* comprises *purchase of goods and services by households for consumption and purchase of goods and services for investment.*

Summary For the sake of simplicity, only the relationships between production units (i.e. firms) and consumption units (i.e. households) are examined in this chapter.

3.2 THE CIRCULAR FLOW OF INCOME

The ultimate aim of all production is consumption – purchase of goods and services – so that the goods made and services supplied by firms must somehow come into the consumer's possession. We will assume that all the factors of production (labour, capital and land) belong to the households, and that the households place them at the disposal of the firms in return for wages, rent, interest and profit. There is therefore a stream of goods and services going from the producers to the consumers, and a stream of factors of production going from the consumers to the producers, thus setting up what economists call a circular flow between households and firms. The idea of the circular flow in the economic process was first proposed by the French economic philosopher Quesnay (1694–1774) who also served as doctor to Madame de Pompadour and King Louis XV.

Figure 3.1 shows two complete circles: one of consumer goods and factors of production (full lines), and one of money going in the opposite direction (broken lines). When the households (A) buy goods (D) from the firms (E), the goods (e.g. motor cars) go from E to A, while the money – the price of the goods – goes from A to E. It is not surprising, therefore, that money (C) circulates in the opposite direction to goods. The households provide the firms with the factors of production to do the work (i.e. labour, capital and land). These production factors (B) therefore flow from A to E. In return for these production factors the firms pay money to the households. They pay wages to labour, rent to landlords and interest and profit to shareholders in the firm. The money flows in the opposite direction to the stream of production factors. These four flows are generally called the *circular flow of income*.

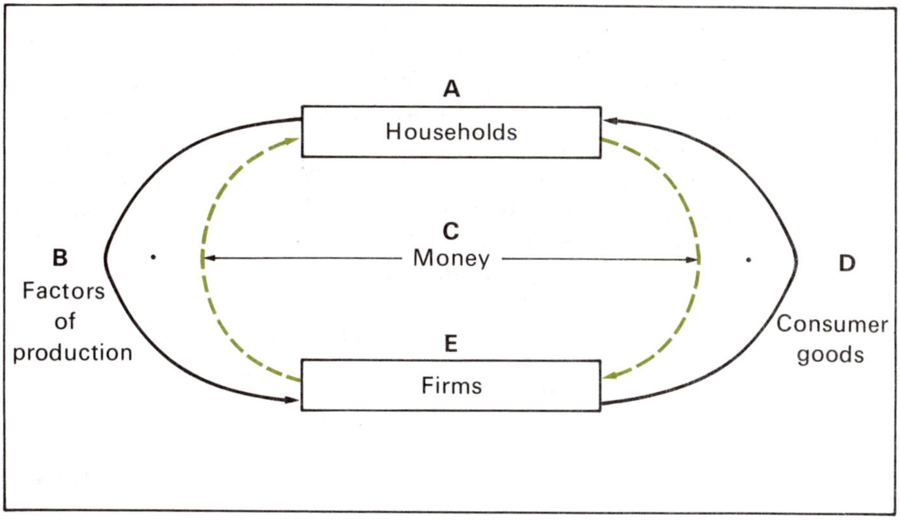

Figure 3.1 The circular flow of income.

To recap, the four flows are (a) the flow of goods and services produced by firms to the households, (b) the flow of money from households to firms as payment for these goods and services, (c) the flow of the production factors, labour, capital and land, from the households to the firms and (d) the flow of money payments from the firms to the households in the form of wages, rent, interest and profit.

Summary Even in the simple case where only firms and households are considered, there is a busy traffic between these economic units. Firms supply households with goods for money, while households provide the firms with labour, land and capital and receive in return payment as wages, rent, interest and profit.

3.3 CIRCULAR FLOW DIAGRAMS

The circular flow discussed above is very simple, and Figure 3.1 includes only firms and households, the government and foreign countries being left out at this stage. Yet however complicated the real world may be, this circular flow will be encountered time and time again as an underlying pattern.

For the sake of simplicity often only the money flow is shown, but to indicate the amounts involved the lines are replaced by arrows, the width of which is in each case proportional to the amount in question. The resulting figures are called flow diagrams. Figure 3.2 shows such a diagram in the case where only firms and households are taken into account. Comparison with Figure 3.1 shows that Figure 3.2 includes only the money flow, and the amounts involved in the transactions are indicated by the width (here equal) of the arrows in Figure 3.2. In the case shown in Figure 3.2 firms produce goods for the households, and in return the households pay the firms £32 000m for the goods. In order to produce the goods the households provide factors of production (labour, etc.) for the firms, and in return the firms pay the households £32 000m for the use of these factors of production.

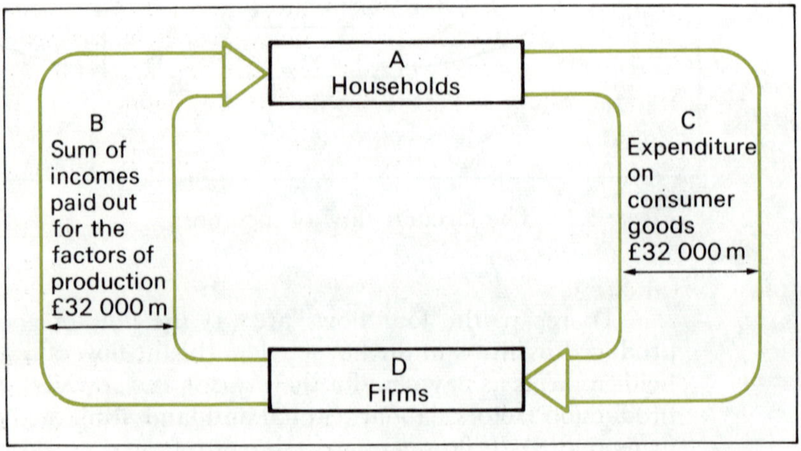

Figure 3.2 A circular flow diagram.

In Britain, the Central Statistical Office (CSO) periodically constructs flow diagrams for the national economy, which incorporate all the economic transactions of the previous year. These are derived from the national income accounts which are published annually by the CSO.

Summary Flow diagrams show the circular flow in quantitative terms, and specifically in terms of money. This is why in economics the circular flow concept is normally referred to as the *circular flow of income*.

3.4 CAPITAL AND ADDED VALUE

Capital goods which can be used repeatedly in production are called *fixed capital*. There is also *working capital* which is largely composed of raw materials in the factory about to be used up in the production process. These goods frequently reappear in some form or another in the end products (e.g. oil transformed into plastics). Fixed capital, such as tools, machines and buildings, can usually be used for many years. In contrast with working capital, only a small proportion of these goods is used up in annual production, this usage being termed *depreciation*. Depreciation is therefore *the wearing away of fixed capital during a period of time* (e.g. one year). An example is the guillotine blade in a paper mill, which has to be replaced because it can no longer be properly sharpened. Only fixed capital will be considered below; working capital will be discussed later in the chapter.

The purchase price of a good includes the manufacturing cost, which comprises wages, interest, rent and the cost of raw materials and components. The difference between the purchase price and the cost price is the *profit*.

If we multiply the purchase price of a single good (a *unit*) by the total number of units produced in a year, we obtain the *market value* of the goods. This is equal to the sum of wages, interest, rent, value of materials (i.e. raw material and components) and the profit. Consider motor cars: the combined annual totals of wages paid to workers, interest to shareholders, rent to any landlords, payment to other firms for materials, and *profit to the firm* are equal to the market value of the cars produced. In this example, the firm assembles motor cars from materials and components which already have value, a value expressed by what the firm paid for them. The act of assembly *adds value* to the *original* value and of course the *new* total value is the market value of the finished motor car. This *added* value, i.e. the difference between the market value of the motor car and the original value of the raw materials and components, is termed the *gross added value*. The firm adds this value by combining the factors of production.

Summary Fixed capital is composed of capital goods that can be used repeatedly in the production process, while working capital is composed of capital goods that are completely used up during production. The difference between the market value of goods made in a year and the value of materials used up in production is the gross added value.

3.5 NATIONAL INCOME: INCOME AND PRODUCT APPROACHES

Let us assume an economy composed of a number of households but only one firm, Great Britain Ltd, with all the factors of production being made available by the households to this firm. Let us continue to assume that this economy has no contact with government, the financial sector or foreign countries.

The firm makes goods and services by combining the factors of production, labour, capital and land. The gross added value of these goods and services is then the gross national income (i.e. the money value of the flow of goods and services becoming available to a nation during a given period of time). All the goods are supplied to the households which buy them with the money they have earned in production. There is no payment by one firm to another firm for raw materials and components in this example, because all raw materials and components are produced by our one firm, Great Britain Ltd.

Table 3.1.

Account for households (£m)

Outgoings		*Receipts*	
Supply of goods by the firm	£36 000	Wages	£23 000
		Interest	5 000
		Rent	1 000
		Profit	7 000
Total	£36 000	Total	£36 000

Account for the firm (£m)

Outgoings		*Receipts*	
Wages	£23 000	Supply of goods to households	£36 000
Interest	5 000		
Rent	1 000		
Profit	7 000		
Total	£36 000	Total	£36 000

The measurement of national income can be approached in three ways: the income approach, the product approach and the expenditure approach. We shall here deal with the first two. The national income by the *income approach* is the total of all incomes derived by households from working in the production of goods and services. It is composed of wages, interest, rent and profit, as presented in Table 3.1 above. The national income by the *product approach* is the total added value of all goods and services produced.

The firm has thus produced goods and services to a value of £36 000m, which is the national income by the product approach. This measurement is usually referred to as the national product. Wherever we use the term *national product* in this book we mean the national income by the product approach. All of these goods and services are supplied to the households. The sum of the incomes paid by the firm to the households (£36 000m) measures the national income by the income approach. Therefore the national income by the income approach is equal to the national income by the product approach. Of course, the above is a very simplified version of the real world and therefore we shall now make it progressively more complicated, and alter the figures accordingly.

Summary The national income by the income approach has the same value as by the product approach. The variables in the income approach are wages, interest, rent and profit, and the variables involved in the product approach are the added values of goods and services produced.

3.6 REPLACEMENT INVESTMENTS

Capital goods suffer wear and tear during their use, so that the stock of capital goods loses value in the course of production. To prevent this, one must install in each year new fixed capital goods of a value equal to the wear and tear incurred during production. In the last 20 years the British shipbuilding industry has failed to install enough new capital equipment to replace depreciating equipment, in contrast to the British chemical industry which has generally installed more new capital equipment than that which has depreciated. Wear and tear of capital equipment is taken account of under the depreciation heading in the accounts in Table 3.2. The production or acquisition of capital goods to make up for the wear and tear is termed *replacement investment*, the value of which must be equal to the depreciation as in Table 3.2.

To keep the stock of capital goods constant, therefore, the firm must produce – in addition to all the other goods – some capital goods to replace the worn out ones. This will necessarily absorb some part of the factors of production (i.e. land, labour and capital) so that fewer consumer goods will be produced (it is assumed that no extra factors of production exist, since all of them are already involved in production by the firm).

If the annual depreciation is £4000m, then at most only £36 000m – £4000m = £32 000m worth of goods can be supplied to the households, and the total payments of the firm to households (of wages, etc.) cannot exceed the difference between the gross added value and depreciation, this difference being termed the *net added value*. Similarly, the *gross national product* (GNP) is equal to the gross added value, and the *net national product* (NNP) is equal to the net added value. When replacement investment is taken into account, the situation is as shown in Table 3.2.

Table 3.2.

Account for households (£m)

Outgoings		*Receipts*	
Supply of goods by the firm	£32 000	Wages	£23 000
		Interest	3 000
		Rent	1 000
		Profit	5 000
Total	£32 000	Total	£32 000

Account for the firm (£m)

Outgoings		*Receipts*	
Wages	£23 000	Supply of goods to households	£32 000
Interest	3 000	Replacement investments	4 000
Rent	1 000		
Profit	5 000		
Net added value	32 000		
Depreciation	4 000		
Total	£36 000	Total	£36 000

The national income mentioned in Section 3.5 (Table 3.1) was £4000m higher, since replacement was not taken into account and the firm produced goods only for the households. An adjustment has now been made by reducing the interest and profit, each by £2000m, to allow for replacement investment.

It is only by reducing the payments to households (wages, interest, rent and profit) that the firm is able to keep its stock of capital goods constant by providing replacement investments. Note that the £4000m now spent on replacement investments is drawn from profit and interest payments. The value of the products available for consumption does not exceed £32 000m so that the households' income cannot be more than £32 000m.

Summary The net added value is equal to the gross added value minus depreciation. Therefore the net national product is equal to the gross national product minus depreciation. The net national product, the net added value and the national income, by the income approach, all have the same value.

3.7 EXPANSION INVESTMENTS

The firm may also decide to make more capital goods, so that its stock of capital goods increases, and this increase – termed *expansion investment* –

makes it possible to attain a higher national product in future. The National Coal Board in the 1970s developed new coal-face cutting equipment to boost coal production. This was an expansion investment.

Replacement investment and expansion investment together make up the gross or total investment. The expansion investment (or net investment) is thus equal to the gross investment minus the replacement investment, while the replacement investment is equal to the depreciation. In the late 1970s the National Coal Board's very substantial expansion investment in new collieries was greater than its replacement investment for older collieries, and the industry's productive capacity was therefore growing.

Since all the factors of production are assumed to have been introduced into the firm, the national income cannot exceed the figure given in Table 3.2. The entire *net* national product was supplied there to the households. However, some goods remain in the firms on account of the net investment, and if this is taken to be £7000m, then £7000m less of the national product will be supplied to the households.

Since the net national product is equal to the national income, the households will consume £7000m less of the national income than is shown in Table 3.3. This proportion of the income which is not used for consumption is called saving. The households' saving of £7000m is equal to the net investment. The net investment changes the situation as presented in Table 3.3.

Since a net investment of £7000m is made, the firm cannot supply £32 000m worth of goods to the households, but only £25 000m worth.

Table 3.3.

Account for households (£m)

Outgoings		*Receipts*	
Supply of goods by the firm	£25 000	Wages	£23 000
		Interest	3 000
Saving	7 000	Rent	1 000
		Profit	5 000
Total	£32 000	Total	£32 000

Account for the firm (£m)

Outgoings		*Receipts*	
Wages	£23 000	Supply of goods to households	£25 000
Interest	3 000	Expansion (net) investment	7 000
Rent	1 000	Replacement investment	4 000
Profit	5 000		
Net added value	32 000	Gross investment	11 000
Depreciation	4 000		
Total	£36 000	Total	£36 000

The change in the stock of capital goods is usually shown in the national income accounts by means of a calculation called the capital account, which in the present case is as shown in Table 3.4.

Table 3.4.

Capital account (£m)			
Outgoings		*Receipts*	
Replacement investment	£4 000	Depreciation	£4 000
Net investment	7 000	Saving	7 000
Total	£11 000	Total	£11 000

Summary Net investment is equal to the gross investment (i.e. replacement and expansion investment) minus depreciation, whilst saving is equal to net investment. Net investment is a vital factor in increasing a country's capacity to produce goods and to raise the material standard of living.

3.8 CHANGES IN STOCKS

It has been assumed so far that the households buy all the goods and services made by the firm for consumption – all £25 000m. We shall now assume that the households want to spend not £25 000m but only £20 000m of their £32 000m income on consumer goods, so that the saving will amount to £12 000m. The result is that the firm cannot sell all the goods made for consumption and is left with £5000m worth of goods and services in stock. Since by definition all goods in the possession of the firm are capital goods (i.e. the stock of physical assets at given point of time), the stocks of consumer goods are counted as capital goods. An increase in the stock of capital goods was termed net investment, and with the change in stock taken into account the net investment consists not only of expansion investment (fixed capital) but also of an increase in the stock of goods held.

This changes the accounts. In the case of households, the supply of goods by the firm is reduced by £5000m, while saving is increased by £5000m. In the case of the firm, the supply of goods to the households is reduced by £5000m while the stock is increased by this amount. Since this increase in the stock of goods held is regarded as a net investment, the latter is increased by £5000m. The gross investment must also increase by the same amount (see Table 3.5).

The capital account is changed accordingly in Table 3.6.

Table 3.5.

Account for households (£m)

Outgoings		*Receipts*	
Supply of goods by the firm	£20 000	Wages	£23 000
Saving	12 000	Interest	3 000
		Rent	1 000
		Profit	5 000
Total	£32 000	Total	£32 000

Account for the firm (£m)

Outgoings		*Receipts*	
Wages	£23 000	Supply of goods to households	£20 000
Interest	3 000	Expansion investment	7 000
Rent	1 000	Increase in stock	5 000
Profit	5 000		
		Net investment	£12 000
Net added value	£32 000		
		Replacement investment	4 000
Depreciation	4 000		
		Gross investment	16 000
Total	£36 000	Total	£36 000

Table 3.6.

Capital Account (£m)

Outgoings		*Receipts*	
Replacement investment	£4 000	Depreciation	£4 000
Net investment	12 000	Saving	12 000
Total	£16 000	Total	£16 000

Summary Net investment, which is equal to the gross investment minus depreciation, consists of expansion investment and changes in the stock of goods held. Saving is equal to net investment.

3.9 COMBINED ACCOUNT FOR A NUMBER OF FIRMS: NET NATIONAL PRODUCT

When an economy comprises more than one firm the national income accounts include all of the firms. These firms frequently supply goods to one another, the end product made by one firm often being the raw material for another. There are also some firms which render a service to

Table 3.7.

Account for firm A (£m)

Outgoings		*Receipts*	
Wages	£7 000	Supply of goods to firm B	£10 000
Interest	1 000	Expansion investment	
Rent	500	Increase in stocks	
Profit	1 500		
		Net investment	
Net added value	10 000	Replacement investment	1 000
Depreciation	1 000	Gross investment	1 000
Total	£11 000	Total	£11 000

Account for firm B (£m)

Outgoings		*Receipts*	
Wages	£16 000	Goods supplied to households	£25 000
Interest	2 000	Expansion investment	7 000
Rent	500	Increase in stocks	–
Profit	3 500		
		Net investment	7 000
Net added value	22 000	Replacement investment	3 000
Depreciation	3 000		
Goods supplied to firm	10 000	Gross investment	10 000
Total	£35 000	Total	£35 000

Table 3.8 Combined accounts for the firms A and B.

Outgoings (£m)	Firm A	Firm B	Total	*Receipts (£m)*	Firm A	Firm B	Total
Wages	7 000	16 000	23 000	Goods to households		25 000	25 000
Interest	1 000	2 000	3 000	Expansion investment		7 000	7 000
Rent	500	500	1 000	Increase in stocks		–	–
Profit	1 500	3 500	5 000	Net investment		7 000	7 000
Net added value	10 000	22 000	32 000	Replacement investment	1 000	3 000	4 000
Depreciation	1 000	3 000	4 000	Gross investment	1 000	10 000	11 000
Total	£11 000	£25 000	£36 000	Total			£36 000
Inter-firm sales			10 000	Inter-firm sales			10 000

others. Supply of goods and services by one firm to another is included in Table 3.7. These transactions between the firms have no effect on the gross and net national product. The GNP is always equal to the gross added value, which was defined in Section 3.4 as the market value of the products minus the cost of raw materials and components. The net and gross national product are obtained by calculating the net and gross added value for each firm in this way and then adding up the values for all the firms. The flow of goods from one firm to another is ignored in the combined account for all the firms. We shall now examine the case of two firms only, but the method can of course be extended to any number of firms. If we assume that firm A makes goods that are supplied only to firm B, the combined account for the firms is the same as that in Table 3.8 once the inter-firm supplies have been ignored.

Summary Only the combined account for the firms is considered when drawing up the national product accounts, and the inter-firm sales of goods are ignored. In the case of more than one firm, the net national product is calculated by adding up the net added values for all the firms, while the gross national product is calculated by adding up the gross added values for all the firms.

3.10 DEFINITIONS OF MACROECONOMIC TERMS

As we have seen (Section 3.5), the sum of the wages, rent, interest and profit gives the net added value, and this is equal to the national income, which will be denoted by Y. Part of the national income is used by the households to buy consumer goods, and this part is denoted by C. The other part of the income, not spent on consumption, has been termed saving, which will now be denoted by S. The letter O will stand for the net national product, which comprises the consumer goods supplied to households (C) and the net investment, denoted by I. An *identity* is an equality that holds by necessity. For example, since the students in a class are either male or female, the sum of the two groups must *equal* the total number of students in the class. We shall now introduce some identities of this kind that will be needed for our discussion later. Identities are really definitions of relationships.

Saving, S, is defined as the national income, Y, minus consumption, C. The national income computed by the income approach is equal to the sum of wages, rent, interest and profits. If Y = national income, C = consumption and S = saving, we have the identity

$$Y = C + S \quad (1)$$

This equation always holds, simply because this is how we have defined the relationship between the national income, consumption and saving.

According to a second identity, the value of the net national product, O, is equal to the consumer goods, C, produced and sold plus the value of the net investment, I, i.e.

$$O = C + I \qquad (2)$$

We have seen that the national income, Y, is equal to the net added value, which in turn is equal to the value of the net national product, O. The national income is therefore equal to the value of the net national product. Since these two quantities are by definition equal to the net added value, we have another identity, namely:

$$O = Y \qquad (3)$$

Since C has the same value both in Eq. (1) and in Eq. (2), S must also be equal to I. This equality between the savings and the net investment is purely a question of definition, i.e. it follows from the meaning we have given to the concepts of saving, investment, national income and national product. S denotes the amount by which the consumers refrain from buying consumer goods and the goods unsold in this period are taken as investment, i.e. treated as new capital. Even if the consumers burn the money saved, it is still true to say that they have refrained from buying consumer goods and have thus saved S. Eqs. (1) to (3) are called *macro-economic identities*.

Both the national income and national product accounts are found in the British national accounts (the annual *National Income and Expenditure* Blue Book). There is, however, in the British national accounts a *third* measure called the *national expenditure accounts* (i.e. national income, computed by the expenditure approach) which comprises spending on consumer goods and spending on investment goods. Therefore a further version of a macroeconomic identity may be derived: E (expenditure) = C + I. National expenditure will of course equal national income since Y (national product) = C + I (the consumer and investment goods themselves) and E = C + I. We have already proved that 0 = Y, so that E must also = Y, and hence Y = O = E (i.e. national income = net national product = net national expenditure). Thus, the national income can be computed by three approaches, the national income approach, net national product and net national expenditure, all of which are by definition equal to each other.

Summary I = S is a definitional equation that follows from the three macroeconomic identities: Y = C + S, O = C + I, and O = Y.

3.11 THE BRITISH NATIONAL INCOME ACCOUNTS

The Expenditure Approach The national income calculated by the expenditure approach, i.e. by computing expenditure on consumer goods and investment goods, is shown in Table 3.9. The spending by consumers and

Table 3.9. British national income: expenditure approach (£m).

Expenditure	1967	1968	1969	1970	1971	1972	1973	1974	1975	1976	1977
1. Consumers' expenditure	25 466	27 390	29 104	31 696	35 399	39 944	45 201	51 977	63 552	73 656	83 530
2. General government final consumption	7 194	7 640	7 973	8 964	10 212	11 630	13 198	16 503	22 746	26 562	29 121
3. Gross domestic fixed capital formation	7 523	8 200	8 590	9 453	10 515	11 604	14 127	16 947	20 656	23 427	25 429
4. Value of physical increase in stocks and work in progress	336	460	446	444	110	62	1 412	1 138	1 423	359	1 288
5. Total domestic expenditure at market prices	40 519	43 690	46 113	50 557	56 236	63 240	73 938	86 565	105 531	124 004	139 368
6. Exports of goods and services	7 365	8 949	10 045	11 451	12 881	13 547	17 130	22 876	26 801	34 837	43 446
7. less imports of goods and services	− 7 811	− 9 335	− 9 877	− 11 101	− 12 110	− 13 709	− 18 925	− 27 341	− 28 935	− 36 564	−42 354
8. less taxes on expenditure	− 5 997	− 6 809	− 7 782	− 8 415	− 8 787	− 9 264	− 10 122	− 11 435	− 14 146	− 16 660	−20 440
9. Subsidies	801	895	839	876	931	1 144	1 471	2 987	3 827	3 463	3 438
Gross domestic products at factor cost (gross national expenditure)	34 877	37 390	39 338	43 368	49 151	54 958	63 492	73 652	93 078	109 080	123 353

Source: Annual Abstract of Statistics, 1978, 1979, HMSO, reproduced with the kind permission of the Controller of HMSO.

Table 3.10. British national income: income approach (£m).

Factor incomes	1967	1968	1969	1970	1971	1972	1973	1974	1975	1976	1977
1. Income from employment	23 751	25 403	27 160	30 415	33 659	37 916	43 571	52 738	68 674	78 639	85 839
2. Income from self-employment	2 835	3 110	3 377	3 774	4 383	5 415	6 707	7 690	8 916	10 208	10 758
3. Gross trading profits of companies	4 625	5 254	5 668	5 930	6 695	7 469	9 233	9 962	9 677	12 445	10 767
4. Gross trading surplus of public corporations	1 132	1 363	1 451	1 447	1 520	1 681	2 063	2 556	3 057	4 460	4 666
5. Gross trading surplus of government enterprises	110	132	153	151	177	141	135	104	107	116	142
6. Rent	2 010	2 216	2 475	2 833	3 162	3 615	4 265	5 292	6 654		8 922
7. Imputed charge for consumption of non-trading capital	247	271	297	332	377	429	541	647	809	1 012	1 176
Total domestic income	34 710	37 754		44 882	49 979	56 665	56 515	79 017	97 940	114 655	122 270
less stock appreciation	− 190	− 600	− 745	− 1 157	− 1 090	− 1 401	− 3 183	− 6 147	− 5 358	− 6 577	
Residual error	357	236	− 498	− 357	268	− 306	160	782	496	982	1 083
Gross domestic product at factor cost (gross domestic national income)	34 877	37 390	39 338	43 368	49 151	54 958	63 492	73 652	93 078	109 080	123 353
8. Net property income from abroad	378	333	498	556	505	534	1 323	1 306	900	1 179	438
Gross national product (gross national income)	35 255	37 723	39 836	43 924	49 656	55 492	64 815	74 958	93 978	110 259	123 791
less capital consumption	− 3 272	− 3 577	− 3 899	− 4 437	− 5 082	− 5 813	− 6 900	− 8 384	− 10 919	− 13 533	−15 801
National income	31 983	34 146	35 937	39 487	44 574	49 679	57 915	66 574	83 060	96 670	107 990

Source: Annual Abstract of Statistics, 1978, 1979, HMSO, reproduced with the kind permission of the Controller of HMSO.

Table 3.11. British national income: product approach (£m).

	1967	1968	1969	1970	1971	1972	1973	1974	1975	1976	1977
1. Agriculture, forestry and fishing	1 106	1 101	1 174	1 242	1 359	1 518	1 881	2 136	2 575	3 116	3 447
2. Mining and quarrying	675	670	611	698	683	835	860	1 050	1 673	2 458	3 627
3. Manufacturing	11 194	12 003	13 051	14 300	15 562	16 884	19078	21 694	26 343	30 464	35 279
4. Construction	2 391	2 562	2 728	2 874	3 192	3 853	5 094	5 977	6 960	7 793	8 062
5. Gas, electricity and water	1 145	1 299	1 389	1 378	1 574	1 745	1 921	2 324	3 028	3 905	4 296
6. Transport	2 087	2 349	2 506	2 727	3 018	3 329	3 909	4 448	5 721	6 624	6 641
7. Communication	753	813	930	1 045	1 190	1 458	1 712	2 216	2 970	3 691	3 603
8. Distributive trades	3 911	4 053	4 240	4 522	5 246	6 046	6 618	7 230	8 838	10 379	12 657
9. Insurance, banking, finance and business services	2 137	2 416	2 535	2 974	3 582	4 356	5 471	5 628	6 430	7 717	9 171
10. Ownership of dwellings	1 693	1 861	2 073	2 372	2 636	3 011	3 552	4 485	5 732	6 723	7 787
11. Public administration and defence	2 246	2 403	2 614	2 930	3 463	3 908	4 414	5 436	7 288	8 458	9 159
12. Public Health and educational services	1 779	1 929	2 086	2 359	2 757	3 314	3 721	4 812	7 163	8 055	8 786
13. Other services	4 391	4 799	5 081	5 642	6 139	6 899	7 680	8 718	11 522	13 417	14 546
Total	35 508	38 258	41 018	45 063	50 401	57 156	65 911	76 154	96 243	112 750	127 061
Adjustment for financial services	− 988	− 1 104	− 1 182	− 1 338	− 1 518	− 1 892	− 2 579	− 3 284	− 3 661	− 4 702	−4 791
Residual error	357	236	− 498	− 357	268	− 306	160	782	496	982	1 083
Gross domestic product at factor cost	34 877	37 390	39 338	43 368	49 151	54 958	63 492	73 652	93 078	109 080	123 353

Source: Annual Abstract of Statistics, 1978, 1979, HMSO, reproduced with the kind permission of the Controller of HMSO.

by the government is indicated in the first two items. Gross domestic fixed capital formation is replacement investment and expansion investment within the country added together, with no allowance for depreciation. Stocks are indicated in the fourth item. Imports, exports and taxes are in these accounts but we shall explain these in Chapters 14 and 15 more fully. However, exports are added and imports subtracted from this account. Then, finally, taxes are deducted, and subsidies (grants) added. The total, called *gross domestic product at factor cost*, is in fact the gross domestic national expenditure on consumer and investment goods (£123 353m in 1977). Note that there is a slight fall in the proportion of investment over the 11-year period 1967–77, and a substantial rise in stocks during 1973–5.

The Income Approach The national income calculated by the income approach, i.e. by computing all incomes, is shown in Table 3.10. Wages are included in items one and two. Profits to companies and interest payments to shareholders are in the third item, and profits of state-owned firms in the fourth and fifth items. After these we have rent income. In the income approach the value of stocks is deducted to avoid double counting. The total is called again *gross domestic product at factor cost* which is in fact the gross domestic national income (£123 353m in 1977). The gross national income includes income from overseas property. A notable feature of the period 1967–77 is the decline in gross trading profits of companies relative to other sources of income.

The Product Approach The national income by the product approach in the British national income accounts is computed by adding up all production of goods and services, as shown in Table 3.11. We again obtain gross domestic product at factor cost of £123 353m in 1977. This total is gross domestic national product and equals the totals for gross domestic national income and gross domestic national expenditure given in the income and product approaches, and simply enables them to balance with the expenditure approach in statistical terms. By definition, all three approaches must of course be equal.

A very interesting feature of Table 3.11 is the very substantial decline shown in manufacturing industries during 1967–77, and the increased output of services such as insurance and health care.

Summary The British national income accounts give an overview of the economy by revealing types of expenditure on goods and services, types of incomes from producing goods and services and the production of particular goods and services themselves. The accounts can be used as the basis for a description of changes in the economy and for pinpointing particular changes which affect the whole economy (e.g. increase in the production of services, fall in the proportion of profits and fall in the proportion of investment).

3.12 CONCLUDING REMARKS

We have described here a simple circular flow of income comprising only firms and households, with the aid of a flow diagram and accounts. The items featuring in the model accounts are the same as those included by the CSO in the corresponding national accounts. The government and foreign countries, however, have not so far been included in our explanation of what determines the national income.

We derived three identities from definitions borrowed from the national accounts. These identities do not *explain* anything but rather they express succinctly the relations between the macroeconomic quantities introduced. The identity (or equation) $O = C + I$ shows the composition of the net national product, while $Y = C + S$ shows how the national income is spent. Finally, $Y = E = O$ shows how the national income, product and expenditure are related.

QUESTIONS

1 What is understood by the circular flow of income?

2 What are the two ways of expressing this circular flow?

3 Who compiles the national accounts?

4 What is added value? What is the difference between the net and gross added value?

5 Why do we choose to speak of added value at all?

6 What do you understand by gross national product, net national product, gross investment, net investment and net national income?

7 Does the net investment consist only of manufactured fixed capital goods?

8 What is the difference between fixed and working capital?

9 What is understood by saving? Can it be said according to this definition that someone who burns his money is saving?

10 Does profit increase the added value?

11 Show that the macroeconomic identities are valid.

12 Fixed capital goods are produced by the firms during the year. How can the effective increase in the stock of capital goods be calculated from this? If £6000m of new fixed capital goods are added, can the net investment take a negative value?

13 How is the contribution of a firm to the national income calculated?

EXERCISES

1 Complete the calculations below, given that the national income is £27 000m.

Account for households (£m)				*Account for firms (£m)*			
Outgoings		*Receipts*		*Outgoings*		*Receipts*	
Supply of goods by firms	.....	Wages	14 000			Supply of goods to households	......
Saving	.....	Interest	....	Wages	......	Net investment	......
		Rent	....	Interest	3000	Replacement investment	......
		Profit	....	Rent	3000	Gross investment	10 000
	—		——	Profit	......		
Total	.....	Total	....				
Gross investment			10 000	Depreciation	3000		
	—				—		
				Total	......	Total	......
Total	.....			*Capital account*			
				Depreciation	......		
				Saving	......		
					—		
				Total	......		

2 The firms produce £30 000m worth of consumer goods and £14 000m worth of capital goods in a given year. The households receive £20 000m as wages, £10 000m as interest and £5000m as rent. The net added value is £40 000m. (a) Draw up the accounts. (b) How large is the net national product?

3 The value of the fixed capital goods produced is £5000m while the depreciation is £3000m. The national consumption amounts to £30 000m. The firms pay out £23 000m as wages, £5000 as interest, £3000m as rent and £8000m as profit. (a) Draw up the accounts. (b) How large is the national income? (c) How large is the net investment and how is it made up?

4 If newly created firms in a country have the sole purpose of providing the established firms with raw materials and components, will this raise the total production? Does this affect the added value? Give reasons for your answers.

5 The following table gives the value of the goods produced, the material inputs (raw materials, components and services from third parties) and the depreciation for a number of industries. Calculate the contribution to the national income coming from two of these industries.

Industry	*Value of goods (£m)*	*Material inputs (£m)*	*Depreciation (£m)*
Textiles	3091	2174	86
Clothing	2650	1268	38
Timber	1099	620	34
Paper	1349	882	49
Chemicals	6359	4192	266
Pottery and glassware	991	450	47

Chapter Four

The Determinants of National Income

In view of the economic difficulties currently experienced by many countries, the level of national income is of particular importance, for it is closely related to the level of employment: the greater the economic activity, the higher the national income and the level of employment.

In recent years, mass unemployment has once more reappeared in the Western nations recalling the Great Depression of the 1930s. However, there are two important differences: unemployment is not as high now and social security guarantees an income to the unemployed. On the other hand, unemployment still means a great deal of personal distress to the individual, and can have significant social and psychological effects on the family.

There are many causes of unemployment. For example, the fall in demand for a certain good can lead to a contraction of production and thus to redundancies. If this drop in demand is general, cyclical unemployment has occurred, so called because it is caused by recurring slumps (periods of low production) in the trade cycle. The high unemployment rates of the mid 1970s were caused by a period of low production (slump), which followed the period of high production (boom) in 1973–4. A major contribution to understanding this situation was made by Keynes and his theory will be discussed below.

Unemployment can also be caused by the introduction of labour-saving machines or reorganization of labour. There is no drop in demand in this case; the cause is found in the supply side of the economic process. For example, new capital equipment introduced into the British Steel Industry in the 1970s caused redundancies. Again, if two competing firms merge, the now-combined capital assets may lead to loss of jobs. In both of these cases we speak of *structural unemployment*.

The causes of structural unemployment were discussed by Marx (1818–83), whose work *Das Kapital* has attracted much attention since its first appearance in 1867. He said that capitalist production is characterized by a class struggle between the employees (proletariat) and the employers (capitalists). He argued that although as the capitalists introduce labour-saving methods more and more goods are placed on the market, the number of impoverished unemployed grows larger and larger.

His prediction was that this contradiction in the system would cause the downfall of capitalism and he believed that this feature of capitalism is reinforced by the concentration of the ownership of firms in the hands of a few, with the larger firms growing by taking over the smaller ones. He also foresaw the emergence of large multinational companies. Whatever we may think of Marx's views, it is a fact that technical development and the concentration process do play a part in unemployment. This chapter, however, will deal mainly with the demand side of the economy, cyclical unemployment, and Keynes' theory, while Chapter 13 will deal with the supply side and thus with the causes of structural unemployment recognized by Marx.

4.1 DETERMINATION OF SIZE OF THE NATIONAL INCOME

The government, the financial sector and foreign countries were ignored in our simplified description of macroeconomic concepts in Chapter 3 and our attention was confined to a description of households and firms. This was a closed model.

The question of what determines the value of the national income and the national product in a closed economy now arises. This is important for society because the national income greatly affects the employment situation. Lower production means fewer jobs; in addition, the lower the production, the lower the utilization of the other factors of production, such as machines and buildings. To discuss the factors that affect the national income, we shall first assume for the sake of simplicity that there is no change in the overall productive capacity of the firms. In other words, the available labour force, stock of capital goods, land, degree of division of labour and the state of technical change remain constant during the period under consideration. In this case, the degree of use of the productive capacity depends on the demands of households and firms. The central theme of this chapter is how the size of the national income is determined by these demand factors and our approach is largely based on the theory of Keynes.

Of course, in the long run the productive capacity changes with increases in population and capital goods, the discovery of new natural resources, further specialization (division of labour) and advancing technical change. Consequently, when changes in the national income are viewed over the course of time, the supply factors must also be taken into account. This approach, in which the productive capacity is considered to vary, will be discussed in Chapter 13. For the time being, we shall examine only the demand side of the economic process, starting with the total demand of the households.

Summary In assessing what causes the level of national income in a given year, the productive capacity of firms can be taken as fixed, in which case demand for goods and services is the only determinant. When changes in national income are examined over a longer period, however, both demand and supply factors must be taken into account.

4.2 THE MACROECONOMIC CONSUMPTION FUNCTION

We saw in Section 3.11 that consumers spend a certain part of their total income, Y, on consumer goods. It is reasonable to assume that the amount households spend on consumer goods is related to their income and, more specifically, that the higher the national income, the more they generally tend to spend on consumer goods. However, in reality it has been found that beyond a certain level of national income, consumption rises less steeply than the national income. The relationship between consumption and the national income can therefore be quite complex. Nonetheless, we shall here assume for our model that consumption C is proportional to income Y in a fixed manner, as in the case shown by the figures in Table 4.1.

Table 4.1 Consumption function (£m).

C	*Y*	*C/Y*
10	15	2/3
20	30	2/3
30	45	2/3
40	60	2/3
50	75	2/3

Clearly $C = \frac{2}{3}Y$, which is an example of a *macroeconomic consumption function*. This simply is the relationship between total consumption and total income. The ratio of C to Y is called the *average propensity to consume* or, in simpler language, the *average tendency* to consume. As stated in this example the value of the ratio C/Y is the same here ($\frac{2}{3}$) for all levels of national income.

Saving is of course related to both national income and consumption and is simply Y − C, i.e.,

$$S = Y - C,$$

or the average propensity to save $\frac{S}{Y} = 1 - \frac{C}{Y}$

and on substituting values $= 1 - \frac{2}{3}$

$$= \frac{1}{3}$$

Another important relationship is the ratio between the *extra* consumption and the *extra* income that makes the *extra* consumption possible, this ratio being called the *marginal propensity to consume* (c) or, in simpler language, the tendency to consume from extra income (see Table 4.2). In the present case, we have

Table 4.2 Marginal propensity to consume.

C	*Extra C*	*Y*	*Extra Y*	*Extra C (Δ C)* / *Extra Y (Δ Y)*
10	–	15	–	–
20	10	30	15	2/3
30	10	45	15	2/3
40	10	60	15	2/3
50	10	75	15	2/3

$$\frac{\text{extra consumption}}{\text{extra income}} = \frac{2}{3} \text{ or } \frac{\Delta C}{\Delta Y} = \frac{2}{3}$$

where delta (Δ) is the symbol for change.

The marginal propensity to consume is usually less than 1, since the increase in consumption can at most only equal the increase in national income. In the example given above in which $C = \frac{2}{3}Y$, the marginal propensity to consume has the same value as the average propensity to consume, both being equal to $\frac{2}{3}$. The counterpart of the marginal propensity to consume (c) is the *marginal propensity to save* (s), i.e. the tendency to save from extra income. It follows from our consideration of the average propensity to save that $s = 1 - c$.

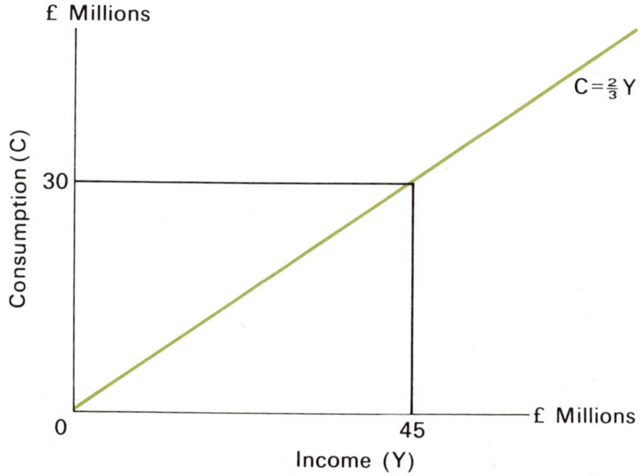

Figure 4.1 The consumption function.

Figure 4.1 is a graphical presentation of the consumption function with the national income Y plotted along the horizontal axis and the consumption C along the vertical axis. The consumption function $C = \frac{2}{3}Y$ is a straight line that passes through the origin 0. The graph can be constructed by taking two values: when $Y = 0$, C is also 0, so that the origin 0 is a point on the graph, and when $Y = 45$, $C = 30$, which gives a second point to form the line. We can now simply read off the graph the value of C corresponding to any value of Y. If, for example, we want to find the consumption associated with a national income of 45, we first draw a vertical line from the horizontal axis of $Y = 45$ to the graph, and then a horizontal line from there to the vertical axis. The intercept, i.e. the point where this line intersects the vertical axis, gives the value of C corresponding to $Y = 45$ (here $C = 30$). The consumption function $C = \frac{2}{3}Y$ therefore defines the value of consumption (C) for each value of income (Y).

The equation $C = \frac{2}{3}Y$ is a behavioural relation and as such is very different from the identities mentioned in Chapter 3. For example, the identity $Y = C + S$ tells us nothing about the value of Y, but merely that, whatever its value, national income will be equal to the sum of consumption and saving. By contrast, the consumption function quantifies the behaviour of all the households, i.e. that, in the present case, they plan to spend two-thirds of the national income on consumer goods. Behavioural equations are the proper building blocks of a theory, because they are based on assumptions about the real world actions of people.

Human behaviour is generally too erratic to give a straight-line relationship such as that in Figure 4.1 but, however complicated a pattern it may show, the fact remains that there is a relationship between the total amount spent on consumption and the level of the national income. As long as we remember that this relationship is more complicated in reality, there is no objection to representing the macroeconomic consumption function in our model as a straight line going through the origin.

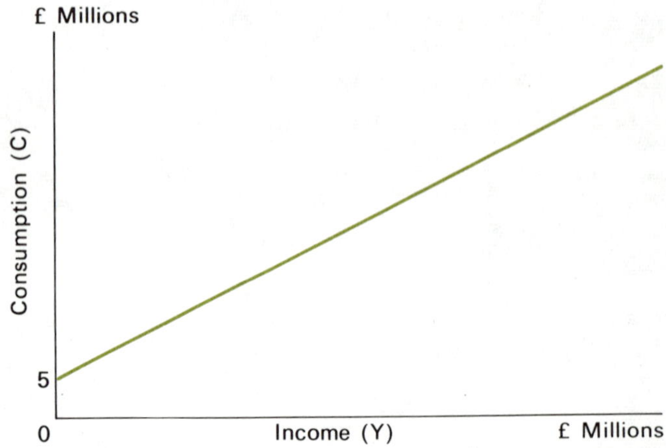

Figure 4.2 The consumption function, including autonomous C.

A somewhat more general consumption function is obtained if we include the type of consumption that does not vary with the national income, called *autonomous consumption*. Figure 4.2 shows the consumption function $C = \frac{2}{3}Y + 5$ where 5 is the magnitude of the autonomous consumption. In this case households plan to spend on consumer goods $\frac{2}{3}$ of national income, plus a further £5m whatever the actual value of national income might be.

Summary The macroeconomic consumption function is a behavioural equation. It embodies the assumption that has been made about the levels of spending on goods and services in the economy by households.

4.3 NET INVESTMENT

Just as the households want consumer goods, firms want capital goods and hold a certain stock of them. An increase in the stock of consumer goods in the households is consumption (C) and an increase in the stock of capital goods in the firms is investment (I). We shall assume that the firms have decided to install investment goods to the value of £20m irrespective of the size of the national income (*autonomous investment*), i.e. they intend to make a net investment to the value of £20 million, for example in building steelworks, chemical plants, etc. However, we do not know yet whether this plan will be realized, i.e. whether the actual or ex post investment will really be to the value of £20m. The latter is only the planned figure (ex ante 'investment') and must be clearly distinguished from the actual investment made in the given period.

In the opposite case when the investment does depend on the

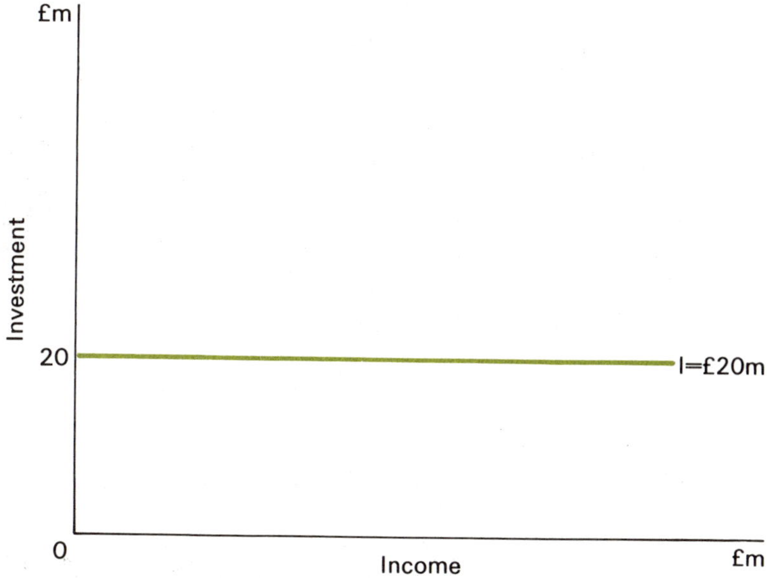

Figure 4.3 Investment function.

national income, we speak of *induced investment*, for it is then induced by a change in the national income. However, only autonomous investment will be considered here. I = £20m is also a behavioural equation, for it describes the behaviour of the firms. It says they spend £20 million on investment goods. The investment function is simply the relationship between total investment and national income. As can be seen from Figure 4.3, the graph for this investment function is a straight line running parallel to the horizontal axis since I is constant at £20 million for all values of Y.

Summary The investment function is a behavioural equation that describes the investment plan of the firms. It is assumed here that the investment does not depend on variations in national income and is therefore called autonomous.

4.4 AGGREGATE (TOTAL) EFFECTIVE DEMAND (ED)

This is obtained by adding the households' planned demand for consumer goods (E) to the firms' planned demand for investment goods (I). Thus ED = C + I.

The aggregate effective demand is satisfied by using the productive capacity of the country to make goods and services available. The value of ED can be calculated for various values of income (Y). For example, if Y = £12m, C = £8m ($= \frac{2}{3}$Y) and I planned = £20m (independent of Y), then the effective demand is given by ED = £8m + £20m = £28m. The effective demand exceeds here the national income, i.e. the households and firms demand more than is produced. Thus not all the demand will be satisfied, for although the households consume as much as they want to (i.e. $\frac{2}{3}$Y, which is £8m), the firms cannot spend more than £4m on investment goods, i.e. £16m less than they intended to. However, in our model we will assume that the firms will not let this discrepancy of £16m come about between their planned (or *ex ante*) investment (£20m) and their actual (or *ex post*) investment (£4m). They will strive for a production figure that permits their investment plan to be realized. This implies that a national income of £12m is not an *equilibrium* value, and the economy is not at a stable state in this case.

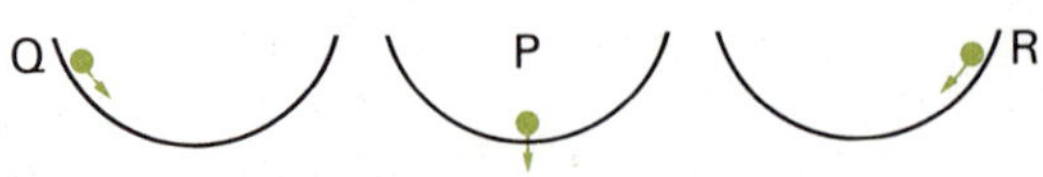

Figure 4.4 The concept of equilibrium.

The concept of equilibrium is borrowed from natural sciences and can be illustrated by a marble rolling inside a dish (Figure 4.4). At point P it is at rest and is said to be at equilibrium: no forces are acting on it to make it assume a different position. Points Q or R on the other hand do not represent an equilibrium position, for the forces acting on the marble make it roll down. Of course, the forces in the economic model we are developing in this chapter are the economic behaviours of the households and firms.

In economics, we often want to find the equilibrium position values of certain economic variables. As an example we will now show how to find the equilibrium value of the national income Y by calculating the effective demand for various values of Y (Table 4.3).

Table 4.3 Calculation of effective demand (£m).

Y	$c = \frac{2}{3}Y$	$I = £20m$ (*planned*)	*ED*	*I (actual)*
12	8	20	28	4
24	16	20	36	8
36	24	20	44	12
48	32	20	52	16
60	40	20	60	20
72	48	20	68	24

Just as in the case of Y = £12m, with Y = £24m, £36m and £48m the national income is exceeded by effective demand so that equilibrium cannot be achieved. Since the *actual* amount spent on investment goods would then be £8m, £12m and £16m, the firms would be spending respectively £12m, £8m and £4m less than they wanted to. So, again, there is no equilibrium, for the firms cannot realize their plans.

When the national income reaches £60m, however, production is at equilibrium with the wants of households and firms, and both can achieve exactly what they set out to: the households can consume two-thirds of the national income (C = £40m) and the firms can actually invest the *planned* sum (I = £20m). The effective demand in this case is exactly equal to national income, ED = Y = £60m. We also have then that I *planned* = I *actual* and since I = S, we can write I *planned* = S. This means that the sum the firms want to spend on investment goods now agrees with the sum the households want to save. Therefore, when the national income is £60m they can both realize their plans.

Let us now see what happens if national income is increased to Y = £72m. The effective demand would then be £68m, which is not enough to absorb all that has been produced, and the firms are forced to stockpile their goods; as a consequence, the *actual* investment (£24m) exceeds the *planned* figure (£20m). Just as when the national income was too low, there is again no equilibrium in this economic situation, for the firm's intentions are still frustrated.

We have thus seen that the level of national income is determined by the effective demand both for consumer goods and for investment goods, and the model has revealed that these demands are satisfied only when Y = ED = C + I = £60m. The equilibrium point lies where the total effective demand is equal to the national income. Figure 4.5 shows how the equilibrium national income comes about, this graph being obtained by plotting Y along the horizontal axis against C + I along the vertical axis (the units are the same on both axes).

We first plot Y = C + I, which is the condition for equilibrium, i.e. that spending should be equal to the national income (the figures are taken from Table 4.3). This condition does not fix the actual value of Y, but merely stipulates that for equilibrium to prevail the point should lie on the Y = C + I line. The actual point has still to be determined. The graph for the consumption function $C = \frac{2}{3}Y$ is also a straight line, passing through the origin, as stated before. The total effective demand is found by adding I *planned* to each C value, i.e. ED = C + I *planned* or $ED = \frac{2}{3}Y + 20$. When Y is plotted along the horizontal axis against ED along the vertical axis, the resulting straight line will meet the vertical axis at £20m. This is so because the *planned* investment is fixed at £20m. To construct the line, it is enough to take two values, e.g. Y = 0 and Y = 30, for which the C + I *planned* will be £20m and £40m respectively.

We already know that at equilibrium the effective demand for goods and services is equal to the national income level which can be attained in the country (ED = Y). This is the case in Figure 4.5 at the point of intersection S, where Y = £60m and C + I planned (i.e. ED) = £60m. The graph shows that the equilibrium value of Y is composed on a consumption of £40m and an investment of £20m. Since Y is equal to £60m, the *actual* investment is exactly the same as the *planned* investment, i.e. £20m. The hatched area in Figure 4.5 shows the difference that can arise between the *planned* and the *actual* investment at different values of Y. At equilibrium, this difference is reduced to zero.

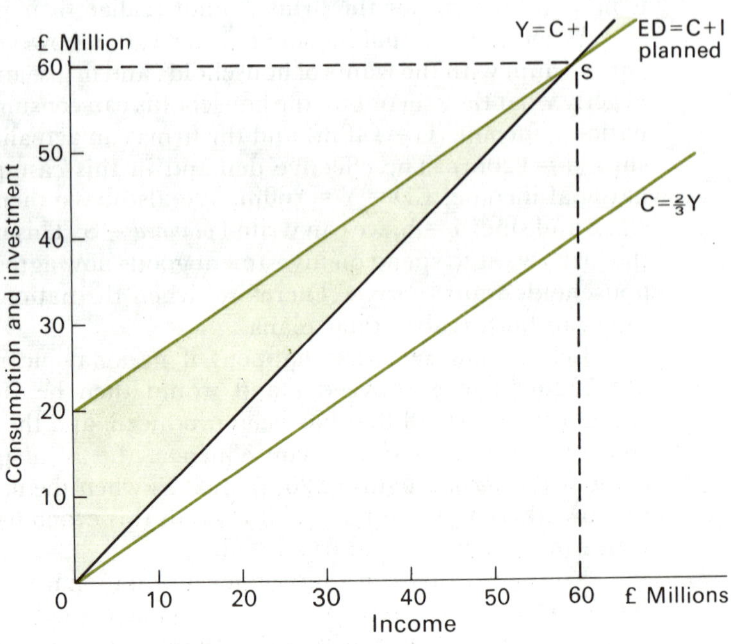

Figure 4.5 Equilibrium national income.

To calculate saving at the equilibrium income remember that saving is national income minus consumption. Therefore, in this case, when the income is £60m and consumption £40m, saving must be £20m. The actual saving (£20m) is thus equal to the actual investment (£20m).

The situation in which the national income is such that the households and firms can exactly satisfy their wants is called *income equilibrium*.

Summary The level of national income is determined by the effective demand for consumer and investment goods. At income equilibrium, the effective demand for goods and services equals the national income, the actual investment is equal to the planned investment, and actual consumption is equal to planned consumption.

4.5 CHANGES IN THE PROPENSITY TO CONSUME AND THE PROPENSITY TO INVEST

The gist of Section 4.4 can be presented in three equations:

$$Y = C + I \qquad (1)$$

$$C = \frac{2}{3}Y \qquad (2)$$

$$I = 20 \qquad (3)$$

Eq. (1) gives the condition for income equilibrium, i.e. national income equals the sum of the demands for consumer and investment goods, Eq. (2) describes consumer behaviour, i.e. consumers plan to spend two-thirds of national income, and Eq. (3) describes the behaviour of the firms, i.e. they plan to spend £20m on investment goods. These equations give a simplified picture of economic events and together represent a model of economic reality.

Since this model consists of three equations with three unknowns (C, I and Y), i.e. consumption, investment and income, it will have a solution, giving the equilibrium value of Y with the values of C and I that belong to it. The solution is obtained by inserting into Eq. (1) the values for C and I from Eqs. (2) and (3):

$$Y = \frac{2}{3}Y + 20 \qquad (4)$$

When we work out this equation it leads to the result:

$$\frac{1}{3}Y = 20$$

$$\therefore Y \text{ or } \bar{Y} = 60.$$

The symbol $\bar{Y}$ denotes the equilibrium value of national income. This method therefore gives the same result as the graphical approach, namely that the equilibrium national income is £60m. We thus have the identity of the equilibrium quantities $\bar{Y} = \bar{C} + \bar{I}$ in the form of $60 = 40 + 20$.

We shall now test to see if the introduction of a small change into the model leads to a different equilibrium position. To do this, we will assume that the value of the marginal propensity to consume has changed and is no longer two-thirds but half of any increment in national income (i.e. $\Delta C = \frac{1}{2}\Delta Y$). In other words, the marginal propensity to consume – which in this case is equal to the average propensity to consume – is assumed to have dropped from $\frac{2}{3}$ to $\frac{1}{2}$. The propensity to consume is thus lower, and conversely households' propensity to save is higher. Put more simply, the households' tendency to save is higher and their tendency to spend is lower. In fact, we have $S + C = Y$. It will also be assumed that the autonomous investment is £15m, i.e. the producers decide to invest £5m less than before. Both changes mean the same thing, namely that the effective demand is less than before because both groups spend less. The model using the same three equations as before now has the following form:

$$Y = C + I \tag{1}$$

$$C = \frac{1}{2}Y \tag{2}$$

$$I = 15 \tag{3}$$

Substitution from Eqs. (2) and (3) into Eq. (1) now leads to:

$$Y = \frac{1}{2}Y + 15 \tag{4}$$

When we solve this equation it leads to the result $\frac{1}{2}Y = 15$. Therefore $\bar{Y} = 30$.

The equilibrium value of Y is now £30m: the national income has thus dropped to half its previous value because of the drop in effective demand. If consumer demand by households and investment demand by firms drop, the equilibrium level of national income drops.

Figure 4.6 shows the new equilibrium in which Y = £30m, and C + I *planned* = £30m. Now, a change in the consumption function from a marginal propensity to consume of $\frac{1}{2}$ back to the original marginal propensity to consume of $\frac{2}{3}$ would mean an increase in consumer demand with $C = \frac{2}{3}Y$ again. An increase in investment demand from £15m back to £20m will result in an overall increase in effective demand by households and firms, which returns us to the previous equilibrium position in which Y = £60m, C ($\frac{2}{3}$Y) = £40m, and I = £20m. Figure 4.6 shows the return to this position. The equilibrium value of the national income can also be found by using the equality between planned investment and planned saving as a condition for equilibrium. If the consumption function is $C = \frac{2}{3}Y$, the saving function can be formulated as $S = \frac{1}{3}Y$ on the basis of the equations $S = Y - C$ and $C = \frac{2}{3}Y$. It has also been assumed here that the *planned* autonomous investment is £20m. Income equilibrium is achieved when the planned saving of the households is exactly equal to the planned investment of the firms. Our macroeconomic model then consists of the following equations:

$$S = \frac{1}{3}Y \quad (1)$$

$$I = 20 \quad (2)$$

$$S = I \quad (3)$$

Since S = I, and I = 20, then S = 20 also. S is $\frac{1}{3}$Y and therefore $\bar{Y} = 60$.

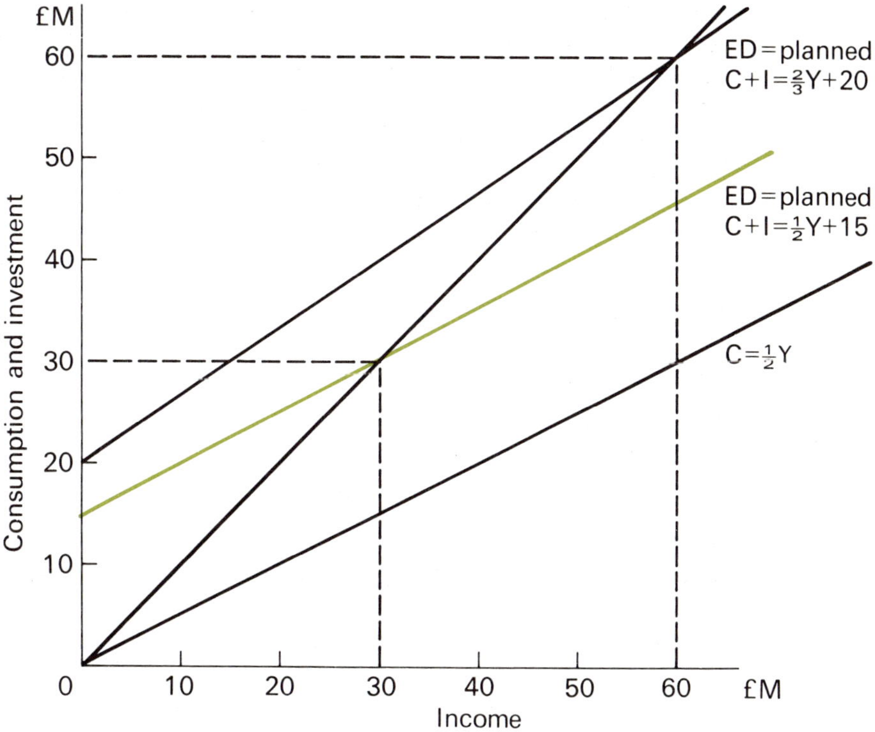

Figure 4.6 Changes in national income.

Summary If the effective demand of the households and firms decreases, the equilibrium value of national income falls; if it increases, the equilibrium value of national income rises.

4.6 THE MULTIPLIER

An increase in autonomous investment leads to a greater increase in the equilibrium value of the national income. Let us illustrate this by writing the model in the following general form:

$$Y = C + I \qquad (1)$$
$$C = cY + C_0 \qquad (2)$$
$$I = I_0 \qquad (3)$$

Eq. (1) states that the sum of consumption and investment at equilibrium is equal to the national income. This is the condition for equilibrium in this model.

Eq. (2) defines consumer behaviour, it being assumed that planned consumption is a function of national income. In this general form of the model, the marginal propensity to consume is denoted not by a figure but by a symbol (c). The consumption function also includes a term (C_0) for the autonomous consumption. So we have consumption that is autonomous (C_0) and consumption related to variations in national income.

Eq. (3) shows that investment is taken to be autonomous (I_0), i.e. the firms are assumed to invest the same sum, (I_0), irrespective of the level of the national income.

In this model, c, C_0 and I_0 are given for example as $\frac{2}{3}$, 0 and 15 respectively, but Y, C and I are to be found. The first three are called exogenous variables – they are determined by factors external to the model – and the second three are called endogenous variables – they are to be determined within the model. The equations will now be solved for Y, i.e. the equilibrium value Y of the national income will be determined. Since we have $Y = C + I$ we can substitute $(CY + C_0)$ for C, and I_0 for I. Therefore,

$$Y = cY + C_0 + I_0 \qquad (4)$$
$$Y(1 - c) = C_0 + I_0$$

the value of $\bar{Y}$ is given by

$$\bar{Y} = \frac{C_0 + I_0}{1 - c} \qquad (5)$$

$$\bar{Y} = \frac{C_0 + I_0)}{1 - c}$$

Substitution of $C_0 = 0$, $I_0 = 15$ and $c = \frac{2}{3}$ gives a result of $\bar{Y} = 45$. Substitution of the previous values, namely $C_0 = 0$, $I_0 = 20$ and $c = \frac{2}{3}$ gives a new equilibrium value of $\bar{Y} = 60$.

The increase in the equilibrium value of national income from £45m to £60m, following the change in autonomous investment from £15m to £20m, is an example of the *multiplier effect* in action. Since the increase in I_0

of £5m gave rise to an increase in Y of £15m the magnitude of the multiplier effect, or simply the *multiplier*, is $\frac{15}{5} = 3$.

Eq. (5), $\bar{Y} = \frac{C_0 + I_0}{1 - c}$, actually shows us that the equilibrium value of national income is directly related to the sum of autonomous consumption (C_0) and autonomous investment (I), i.e.

$$\bar{Y} = \frac{1}{1 - c}(C_0 + I_0).$$

If the letter k is the *multiplier*, the formula for this is

$$k = \frac{1}{1 - c}$$

The multiplier, k, is the factor by which autonomous demand (consumption plus investment) is to be multiplied to obtain the equilibrium national income.

It should be clear from $k = \frac{1}{1 - c}$ that since c is always less than one, k is always greater than one as the following examples demonstrate

$$c = \tfrac{2}{3}, k = \frac{1}{1 - \frac{2}{3}} = 3$$

$$c = \tfrac{1}{3}, k = \frac{1}{1 - \frac{1}{3}} = \tfrac{3}{2}$$

$$c = \tfrac{1}{4}, k = \frac{1}{1 - \frac{1}{4}} = \tfrac{4}{3}.$$

In addition, we know that the marginal propensity to consume (c) is related to the marginal propensity to save (s), $s = 1 - c$, thus on substituting $c = 1 - s$ into $k = \frac{1}{1 - c}$ we have:

$$k = \frac{1}{1 - 1 + s} = \frac{1}{s}$$

or, in words, the multiplier is the reciprocal of the marginal propensity to save.

Let us now look at a worked example of the multiplier effect in action. Assume a civil engineering company invests in a new motorway programme and £30m is earned from this as wages, profit, interest and rent. If the marginal propensity to consume is $\frac{2}{3}$, £20m of this income will be spent on consumer goods and this in turn will give rise to £20m income earned from the production of these consumer goods. As before, $\frac{2}{3}$ of this £20m, £13.3m, will be spent on consumer goods and in turn will give rise to an income of £13.3m which will itself create £8.86m of extra income.

The total multiplier effect is the sum of the series:

$$30 + \tfrac{2}{3} \times 30 + \tfrac{2}{3} \times \tfrac{2}{3} \times 30 + \tfrac{2}{3} \times \tfrac{2}{3} \times \tfrac{2}{3} \times 30 + \tfrac{2}{3} \times \tfrac{2}{3} \times \tfrac{2}{3} \times \tfrac{2}{3} \times 30 \ldots \text{ or}$$
$$30 + \tfrac{2}{3} \times 30 + (\tfrac{2}{3})^2 \times 30 + (\tfrac{2}{3})^3 \times 30 + (\tfrac{2}{3})^4 \times 30 \ldots$$

If we present this as a *table* the total effect of the multiplier and the diminishing nature of the effect are clearly seen:

	£m
$(\frac{2}{3}) \times 30$	20.0
$(\frac{2}{3})^2 \times 30$	13.333
$(\frac{2}{3})^3 \times 30$	8.888
$(\frac{2}{3})^4 \times 30$	5.926
$(\frac{2}{3})^5 \times 30$	3.950
$(\frac{2}{3})^6 \times 30$	2.634
$(\frac{2}{3})^7 \times 30$	1.756
$(\frac{2}{3})^8 \times 30$	1.171
$(\frac{2}{3})^9 \times 30$	0.780
$(\frac{2}{3})^{10} \times 30$	0.520
$(\frac{2}{3})^{11} \times 30$	0.347
$(\frac{2}{3})^{12} \times 30$	0.231
$(\frac{2}{3})^{13} \times 30$	0.154
$(\frac{2}{3})^{14} \times 30$	0.103
$(\frac{2}{3})^{15} \times 30$	0.069
	89.862 = Total at the 15th round

The series, if calculated far enough, would reach 90, or as near as makes no difference in this context. Such series can be expressed in a general equation which shows that an increase in total extra income (ΔY) equals the initial investment (ΔI) divided by one minus the marginal propensity to consume (c):

$$\Delta Y = \frac{\Delta I}{1 - c}$$

If we substitute from our numerical example $\Delta I = £30m$ and $c = \frac{2}{3}$, then the increase in total extra income is given by:

$$\Delta Y = \frac{30}{1 - \frac{2}{3}} = 90.$$

Since the initial investment of £30m gave rise to a total increase in income of £90m, the multiplier has a value of 3.

Summary The increase in the equilibrium value of the national income is a multiple of the increase in the autonomous investment and autonomous consumption.

4.7 LEVEL OF EMPLOYMENT AND CAUSES OF CYCLICAL UNEMPLOYMENT

Level of Employment As we have seen, the level of national income at a given productive capacity of the economy depends on the amount spent on consumption and investment goods. In a closed model, without government, a financial sector or overseas trade, the sole determinant is the effective demand of the consumers and producers for goods and services. When the government, the financial sector and overseas trade are also included in the model, the effective demand also includes government expenditure and exports. This will be discussed in later chapters (Sections 14.5 and 15.11).

We shall now examine from a macroeconomic viewpoint the labour market as a function of the effective demand alone, i.e. without taking into account the other factors that influence the number and nature of jobs available. We shall not consider here unemployment caused by the introduction of labour-saving machines or techniques, since this does not stem from demand falling short of the available productive capacity.

Since only the demand side of the economy is taken into account here, saving is viewed only as a decrease in effective demand and not as a prerequisite for capital formation and thus for raising the productive capacity. If the households at progressively higher income levels decide to save more (i.e. if their propensity to save increases), then the consumption (C) and hence the effective demand (ED) will decrease, so that production drops, since it is determined by the effective demand. This is one major cause of economic depression. Thus in the mid 1970s the British economy suffered from a depression, which can be explained partly in terms of a lack of effective demand.

Expenditure Equilibrium and Income Equilibrium When for one reason or another the effective demand picks up again, production rises but only as long as there is some surplus labour. National product can be regarded as the volume of goods produced multiplied by the price level of these goods. *Volume* here means the total number of all goods produced, and *price level* means the average price of the goods. Before full employment is reached, extra demand can easily be met by employing more labour and increasing the output of goods. There is no reason for prices to increase, and the growth in national product is real, i.e. attributable to increased production. Once labour is fully employed and productive capacity is being utilized to its limit, further demand will remain unsatisfied. In this situation, although output cannot be increased, prices can be raised and this indeed is then the only way the monetary value of the national product can grow.

The situation in which the effective demand is such that there is full employment is called *expenditure equilibrium*. If the effective demand is higher, we speak of *overspending*: if lower, so that there is some unemployment, of *underspending*. An essential point of Keynesian economics is the distinction between income equilibrium, where the households and firms can exactly satisfy their wants, and expenditure equilibrium, where the productive capacity is fully employed. Let us assume a labour force of three million and an annual per capita productivity of labour of £30 000m.

To establish expenditure equilibrium, the national income must be £90 000m. If $C = \frac{2}{3}Y$ and $I = £20\,000$m and the condition for national income equilibrium is $C + I = Y$, the equilibrium value of Y is £60 000m.

The national income is then £30 000m, too low in the case of full employment, and one million people lose their jobs due to *cyclical unemployment*. To achieve expenditure equilibrium the autonomous expenditure must be raised by £10 000m, since the multiplier in this model is 3. Thus we can raise the £10 000m either by an autonomous consumption or autonomous investment or by a combination of the two.

Cyclical Unemployment This is one of several possible types of unemployment. Here we will confine our attention to the causes of cyclical unemployment and to a description of the other, almost inevitable, types of unemployment: seasonal and frictional.

Cyclical unemployment, as we have seen, occurs when there is not sufficient demand for goods in the national and international economy for full employment to be achieved. It is termed *cyclical* rather than the more explicit *demand-deficient* unemployment, because the fluctuations in world and national trade from boom to slump tend to follow a pattern (or cycle) of four to five years from boom to boom with an intervening slump. Cyclical unemployment can be overcome by use of the measures recommended by Keynes, some of which are based on the multiplier concept.

Frictional and Seasonal Unemployment However, some types of unemployment are almost inevitable and of these the major ones are frictional and seasonal. *Frictional unemployment* is short-term unemployment of workers who leave one job and seek another. It is essentially unemployment of weeks rather than months. A lorry-driver, for example, might be made redundant because a small road haulage firm for which he worked in his home town of Mansfield has gone bankrupt. He signs on as unemployed at the local Department of Employment Office and goes to their Job Centre to look for job vacancies for drivers. After some unsuccessful applications after five weeks he is employed as a lorry driver by the National Coal Board in the same area. Yet another example is of an Oldham woman made redundant in a declining industry, cotton textiles, and employed locally, after being unemployed for six weeks, as a machine operator in an expanding light engineering factory. Of course, her basic machine-minding skills have to be developed by training at her new firm. This case illustrates the point that some frictional unemployment is inevitable as people become redundant in declining industries, and are re-employed in expanding ones after training.

Seasonal unemployment is an inevitable consequence of there being seasonal industries, such as the hotel trade, professional cricket and tourism in general. Winter can find hotel waiters, salmon fishers and even some cricketers unemployed.

Any interpretation of full employment must allow for some workers unemployed for seasonal and frictional reasons. In Britain this means about 500 000 people, i.e. nearly 2 per cent of the working population, and in the Irish Republic about 30 000 people, again nearly 2 per cent of the working population.

Summary The net national product is equal to the volume of output multiplied by the average price level. The productive capacity determines the maximum that can be produced, while the effective demand determines the extent to which the capacity is utilized. Until full employment is reached, an increase in the effective demand causes a rise in real national income; when full employment has been reached, an increase in the effective demand leads to a rise in the national income only through price increases. Cyclical unemployment occurs if effective demand is insufficient to employ the available workforce.

4.8 THE AVERAGE PRICE LEVEL

The measurement of the price level is a simple numerical procedure. A change in the price level is expressed by an index number. This is a ratio of the weighted average price in the current period (year or month) and that of the base period (year or month), the latter being taken as 100.

Let us assume for the sake of simplicity that only one consumer good (a loaf) and only one capital good (a railway locomotive) are produced, and that their prices in the base year are £0.20 and £100 000 respectively. Let us further assume that in the year under consideration these prices have risen to £0.25 and £150 000. What is then the average price rise?

To answer this question, we first calculate the partial price index for each good separately:

	£ price	*PPI*	*£ price*	*PPI*
Base year	0.20	100	100 000	100
Year X	0.25	125	150 000	150

You might now be tempted to say that the average price index would be the average of the two partial price indexes, i.e.

$\frac{125 + 150}{2} = 137.5$, but this is wrong. Consider the case when only one loaf and one locomotive are produced in both years:

	Combined £ price	*Price index*
Base year	100 000.20	100
Year X	150 000.25	149.99 (not 137.5)

Clearly the loaf has a negligible effect on the overall price index here because its price is so small in comparison with that of the locomotive. We can achieve the same result by '*weighting*' the partial price indexes by the price and the number sold in the base year:

$$\frac{1\ (\text{loaf}) \times 0.20 \times 125 + 1\ (\text{loco.}) \times 100\,000 \times 150}{1 \times 0.20 \qquad + \qquad 1 \times 100\,000}$$

$$= \frac{25 + 15\,000\,000}{100\,000.20} = 149.999$$

Effectively, we are weighting by *turnover* of the goods, i.e. quantity sold and price. Thus if three million loaves were sold in the base year the average index will change:

$$\frac{3\,000\,000 \times 0.20 \times 125 + 1 \times 100\,000 \times 150}{3\,000\,000 \times 0.20 \quad + \quad 1 \times 100\,000}$$

$$= \frac{75\,000\,000 + 15\,000\,000}{600\,000 + 100\,000} = \frac{90\,000\,000}{700\,000} = 128.57$$

In this case the lower partial price index of 125 for the loaf, associated with the larger turnover in bread as compared with locomotives, reduces our general price level to 28.57 per cent over the base year.

The calculation of such a price index is one of the most important tasks of the Central Statistical Office, which publishes the retail price index every month. This is a weighted mean of the partial price of consumer goods bought by an average householder. If, for example, the partial price index for clothes rises by 200 points, the overall significance of this for the aggregate price index depends on the consumer preferences of the people involved in the group under consideration. If they prefer jeans and T-shirts it will scarcely matter to them, but if they spend a large proportion of their income on a wide range of clothing, it will mean a great deal to them.

Summary The average price level is a weighted mean of the prices of all goods, and is expressed by index numbers. The weighting factor is of great importance in this connection. The central Statistical Office publishes the retail price index every month.

4.9 KEYNES

The theory of employment outlined earlier was proposed by the great British economist, John Maynard Keynes (1883–1946), in the 1930s, precisely at a time of great unemployment. In *The General Theory of Employment, Interest and Money*, published in 1936, Keynes argued that the Great Depression was due to insufficient effective demand. In his view, the consumption function is fairly stable, since consumer habits change slowly and it is therefore difficult to influence consumer demand in this way. In a depression, the producers have no motive to invest in new factories and new machinery. This is because investment is made in order to enable producers to supply more consumer goods in future, and in the absence of a great demand for consumer goods investment may turn out to be unprofitable, with the producers being left with a stock of unsold goods. This is, of course, contrary to their desire to make a reasonable profit and to remain active in the market. In a period of stagnating sales, the entrepreneurs cannot be expected to raise their production capacity by investing; instead, both components of the effective demand – consumption and investment – will drop together.

According to Keynes, an economy can be put on its feet again only by the government stimulating the effective demand, e.g. by embarking on a programme of public works, such as building roads, bridges and schools. The multiplier effect discussed in Section 4.6 is of great importance here, for a public expenditure of, for example, £100m will raise the national income by some multiple of £100m.

Indeed, one of the first attempts to reduce mass unemployment through the multiplier effect of stimulating consumer and investment goods was the building of highways and major waterpower projects in the 1930s New Deal policy in the USA. Keynes and American economists were thinking on similar lines. Closer in time, the unemployment of the mid 1970s did not stem entirely from insufficient demand, but this was one of its causes. So in recent years several Western governments have attempted to combat cyclical unemployment by stepping up public spending.

Keynes' theory can also account for the opposite situation in which the effective demand outstrips the production capacity, and over-full employment results, but it does not explain unemployment that is connected with changes on the supply side.

Summary The Great Depression in the 1930s prompted Keynes, one of the greatest economists of the century, to re-examine the factors that determine the national income, national product and the level of employment. In the short term, the level of effective demand is decisive for the course of events in economic life.

4.10 GOVERNMENT POLICY TO MAINTAIN FULL EMPLOYMENT AT NATIONAL LEVEL

During the period 1945–74 unemployment in Britain rose to more than 2 per cent of the working population in 1951–2, 1957–9, 1962–3, 1966–9 and 1971–2. Each time, government intervened in the economy, and through macroeconomic policies overcame the problem. These policies were laid down in the Government White Paper on Employment Policy of 1944, in which government said it was '... prepared to accept future responsibility for taking action at the earliest possible stage to arrest a threatened slump'. The major method recommended was that government should ensure a sufficiently high level of consumer and investment demand to prevent the deficiencies of demand which had created the pre-war mass unemployment. In other words, government should put into practice the recommendations developed from the Keynesian theory of cyclical unemployment discussed in this chapter. For example, this method was adopted in 1951–2 when a fall in effective demand and rise in unemployment were countered by cuts in the rate of interest to make private investment more profitable and by cuts in hire-purchase rates to encourage more consumer demand. The result of these measures was a fall in unemployment to well below 2 per cent. Similar measures were used in 1959, but with the addition of taxation cuts to encourage a more rapid increase in consumer demand, and some increase in public spending to create more investment demand. This anti-unemployment package of 1959 was largely repeated in 1963 and 1968–9.

The main example we shall use to illustrate this approach fell in 1971–2 when unemployment soared to nearly one million and to over 4 per cent of the working population (January 1972, 927 000; 4.1 per cent). To deal with this massive problem government in 1971–2 reduced both the rates of interest to encourage private investment (bank rate down to 5 per cent) and hire purchase rates to motivate consumer demand, and substantially increased the money supply to supplement the means by which firms could expand. In the budgets of 1971 and 1972 there were also large personal taxation cuts (£950 million and £1200 million, respectively) to encourage consumer demand. Moreover, a range of public investment programmes was instituted to raise employment directly and to bring about by the multiplier effect an increase in the consumer demand of those re-employed (e.g., £2900 million Motorway programme 1972–81, £118 million on health services buildings 1971–5, British Steel Corporation's £225 million investment programme 1971–2). The direct effects of these measures can be seen in the fall in unemployment during 1972 and 1973 from 4.1 per cent (January 1971) to 2.2 per cent

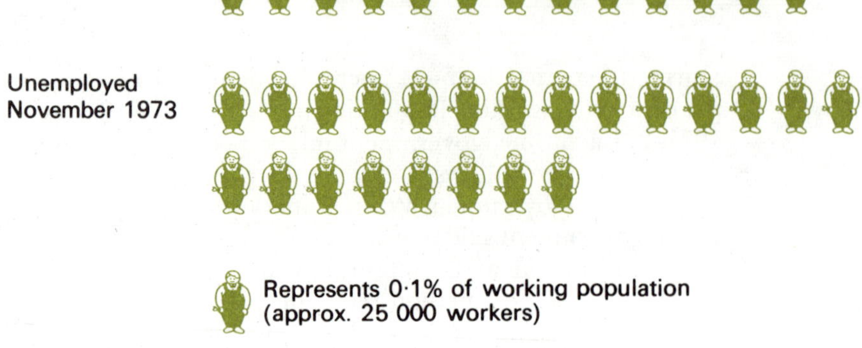

Figure 4.7 Unemployment falls as government expands production in UK.

(November 1973). These measures had therefore been successful in controlling demand-deficient or cyclical unemployment by massively increasing effective demand (Figure 4.7).

In the still more severe recession of 1974 onwards, government did not use these policies to cure our mass unemployment, which rose to 6.8 per cent in July 1977 (1.6 million). The prime aim of government at this stage was to contain an accelerating rate of high inflation, and it was argued that increased public spending, tax cuts and low interest rates would have forced up demand and worsened the inflation problem. Unemployment fell to less than 6 per cent in 1978–9. (Inflation will be dealt with more fully in Chapter 6.)

Summary In the British economy in the post-1945 period the government has normally applied the recommendations of Keynesian economic theory in order to prevent the development of large-scale cyclical unemployment. Keynesian economic theory therefore provided government with a basic strategy for maintaining full employment until the appearance of complicating factors, such as rapid inflation, in the 1970s.

The economic theory, which attempts to explain the general working of the economy, has been dealt with in this chapter. In order to simplify this topic for the student, we have so far specifically excluded the roles of international trade and government economic activity in the general economy. These aspects are explained in Chapter 14 (Section 5, Macroeconomic Theory and Government Economic Activity), and Chapter 15 (Section 14, Macroeconomic Theory and International Trade), but they can, of course, be studied immediately after this chapter.

4.11 CONCLUDING REMARKS

We have seen that the level of national income at a given productive capacity is determined by the effective demand, which is made up of the households' demand for consumer goods and the producers' demand for investment goods.

The national income, O, is at equilibrium only when the firms invest as much as they have planned to. From the corresponding income equilibrium, the households save an amount, S, which is exactly equal to the firms' net investment, I. When full employment is reached, any further increase in the effective demand leads to a rise in the price level, P.

When there is a shift in the consumption function and/or the investment function, another income equilibrium presents itself. Since a certain level of employment is appropriate to each level of production, a drop in production leads to redundancies. This prompted Keynes to analyse the factors that govern production, income and employment.

Keynes's theory as discussed here covers only the demand side; changes connected with the supply side, which lead to a change in the productive capacity, will be discussed in Chapter 13. This implies that

Keynes's theory should not be used to explain all unemployment, since structural unemployment, which is due to changes in the structure of production and to technical development, has been mentioned only briefly so far.

QUESTIONS

1 What is the macroeconomic consumption function?

2 What are the marginal and the average propensity to consume?

3 What is effective demand?

4 What is planned (*ex ante*) investment?

5 What are unemployment and economic depression?

6 What is over-full employment?

7 How is the price index of household consumption calculated?

8 What were Keynes's main economic ideas?

9 What is expenditure equilibrium?

10 Illustrate the equilibrium discussed in Section 4.5 by a graph for the saving function.

EXERCISES

1
(a) Calculate the equilibrium income when the consumption function is $C = \frac{3}{4}Y$ and the autonomous investment is £50m. It is assumed that income equilibrium prevails if the sum of consumption and investment is equal to the national income.
(b) How much of the equilibrium income is saved?
(c) Give a graphical derivation of the equilibrium.
(d) Calculate the multiplier involved in this model.

2 Assume that the consumption function is $C = \frac{3}{4}Y + 20$ and that the autonomous investment is £10m.
(a) Tabulate the planned (*ex ante*) consumption and the planned (*ex ante*) investment figures for Y = £15m, £30m, £45m, £60m, £90m, and £120m.
(b) At which value are the consumers' and the producers' plans realized?
(c) How much does saving amount to in this case?
(d) Give a graphical derivation of the equilibrium.
(e) Calculate the equilibrium value of Y algebraically.

(f) Derive the saving function from the consumption function.
(g) Determine graphically the equilibrium value of Y with the aid of the saving function and investment.
(h) Calculate the multiplier involved in this model.

3 Take a closed economy without government intervention and take the national income Y, consumption C, investment I, consumption function $C = \frac{3}{4}Y + 100$, and an autonomous investment of £300m.
(a) Calculate the equilibrium value of the national income by assuming that it is determined by the total effective demand.
(b) If the productivity of labour is constant at £20m, will there be full employment for a labour force of 100 000?
(c) By how much should the expenditure be increased to reach expenditure equilibrium?

4 The firms pay out bonuses from time to time. Can this phenomenon be explained by the concept of effective demand?

5 Try to form a picture of the national employment or your local situation on the basis of newspaper data or information from a job centre, not forgetting to mention seasonal and frictional unemployment in your report.

6 The following figures give the British *ex post* consumption and national income in 1965–75 in billions of pounds (at 1970 constant prices). Though we are not dealing here with a *planned* consumption function, it is worth examining the connection between C *planned* and Y *actual*.

	C	*Y*
1965	28	45
1966	29	47
1967	30	48
1968	31	50
1969	318	50
1970	32	52
1971	33	53
1972	34	54
1973	36	58
1974	37	58
1975	35	57

Source: Annual Abstract of Statistics, 1976, HMSO. Reproduced with the kind permission of the Controller of HMSO.

(a) Plot the C values against the Y values to obtain a graph showing the connection between them. This will give you a cluster of plots.
(b) Construct a line through these in such a way that approximately the same number of plots lie above it as under it.
(c) Estimate the consumption for 1976 if the national income was a billion pounds.

Chapter Five

The Nature and Types of Money

What is the nature of and need for money? We have seen that the most important aspect of the satisfaction of wants is the provision of goods and services. It is these, and not money, which reduce scarcity. However, in an advanced industrial society such as Britain, there must be an intermediary between the goods and services we produce as workers and the goods and services we need as consumers. Money is the intermediary. It is required as a token, to be received for producing goods and services at our places of work and later to be used, in part, for purchasing goods and services. Money is also required by firms to use as a token in the same way. Firms carry out investment goods production, but finance this activity partly from the savings of households. Members of households have been paid in money for their production of goods and services and they part with some of this, for an interest payment, and the firms which receive this money have use of it to help finance their investment goods production. In this chapter the nature of money is examined in relation to its functions in the economy, and the various types of money in use are explained.

5.1 THE FUNCTIONS OF MONEY

Money is an acceptable medium of exchange, a measure of value, a store of purchasing power and a standard for deferred payments.

Exchange Money is a *medium of exchange* which has been invented independently in many different places at different times, probably when the exchange of goods by barter became unwieldy. Imagine being paid today in shoes, light bulbs or books: no barter system could cope with the many wants of modern society. In the 1970s, however, barter is making a comeback in a limited way, e.g. a hotel might give a printer a free conference weekend in return for his printing the hotel stationery.

Measurement of Value Goods and services can be *valued* using money. Thus, in the example of barter given above, the hotel will have valued the printing of its stationery in terms of money and estimated that the cost to them of a weekend conference was a fair exchange. The facility of valuing allowed the development of our sophisticated accounting and taxation systems.

Storage of Purchasing Power Goods can be stored as a reserve of purchasing power (i.e. wealth) but money is much more convenient for this purpose. Money is compact, easy and cheap to store, and does not physically deteriorate. Goods are generally bulky, costly to store and insure, and sometimes have limited lives (e.g. soft fruits). Both goods and money are subject to falls in value but the money value of goods is more precarious than the exchange value of money. Finally, the distribution of goods is slow, and even difficult, during exchange but the use of money makes for a speedy transaction, i.e. it has liquidity. *Liquidity is the property of being acquired and disposed of quickly and easily without loss in nominal value.*

Deferment of Payment The importance of various types of deferred payment really stems from the flexibility, convenience and relatively stable value of money as an exchange medium. Credit and loans are types of deferred payment and modern economic activity, from capital investment down to consumer hire purchase, is utterly dependent on this use of money.

Summary *Money* is an exchange medium and a measure of value. Money can be stored as wealth, and with its introduction the techniques of accounting, taxation and deferred payment quickly develop.

5.2 THE HISTORY OF MONEY

The commercial history of man reveals that the development of the functions of money determined its nature at particular times. Table 5.1 presents the prerequisites for a money system and compares the use of silver metal and sheep as examples of primitive money.

Table 5.1 Prerequisites for a money system.

Prerequisite	*Comparison*	
	Silver metal	*Sheep*
1. Acceptability	Yes, it has intrinsic worth as a precious metal	Yes, it has intrinsic worth as a raw material supply
2. Portability	Yes, it has high ratio of value to bulk	Much less convenient to trade with
3. Divisibility	Yes, susceptible to very fine division by weight	Much less convenient even when dead
4. Durability	Yes, does not deteriorate	Limited life and subject to disease, drought and accident
5. Limited supply	Yes, relatively difficult to find and exploit	Yes, animal husbandry demands skill and land

Of all the commodities used as money the precious metals gold and silver had overwhelming advantages and the only significant development in their use was the creation of coins. Coinage increased the portability of the money and introduced standard divisibility.

Gold and silver coins began to circulate quite early in the history of civilized man and the state guaranteed the quantity and fineness of these precious metals by minting the coins in a special shape and size. People could still offer these metals for minting, and ask for coins to be melted down, but both operations were controlled by the state so that the money was really 'state money'. A practice arose which was later to acquire great significance: in 17th-century England people gave gold and gold coins to goldsmiths for safe-keeping. The receipts of deposit given by these goldsmiths to the owners started to circulate as money, because they were fully *covered* by gold. In short, the receipts were accepted as having the value of the deposited gold metal or gold coins. The receipts were fully backed up by the deposits and if all of the receipts were presented all of the gold would return to the owners. Transactions between the owners using the receipts simply meant that the gold moved from one deposit account to another. These receipts or notes, which were the forerunners of banknotes, gradually became less tied to gold as the goldsmiths realized that over a period of time only a small proportion of the receipts were taken back to them to be converted into gold. They *issued more notes than they had gold deposits*. Thus the goldsmiths created money in order to loan it and so bankers and banknotes came into existence. The original circulation of receipts, and then banknotes, as money was based on people's confidence that these could always be exchanged for gold. Of course some banks failed by bringing too many banknotes into circulation with too little cover of gold: there were crises of confidence, with panic rushes to convert notes to gold.

Most countries now have only one bank authorized to issue banknotes. In Britain, this is the Bank of England, which will be discussed later, and in Ireland it is the Central Bank of Ireland. The money issued by this authorized bank is called notes. However, there is another kind of money – bank money – which evolved alongside the development of notes and is now of paramount importance. The basis of bank money was the account the goldsmiths opened in their accounting records (or books) for a gold depositor. Payments between depositors could be made by transferring an amount from one account to another by means of a bill of exchange (or later, a cheque) and so these deposit accounts gradually acquired the character of money. This is another reason why the goldsmiths can be regarded as forerunners of the multi-purpose commercial banks, such as Lloyds and Barclays. The modern commercial banks, like the goldsmiths, accept deposits from the public and industry, make short-term loans to government and industry, and create bank money (i.e. chequebook money).

Summary As commercial transactions developed, gold coins, used as money and left with goldsmiths for safe-keeping, gave rise to notes and bank money.

5.3 FROM GOLD TO MODERN PAPER MONEY

Gold coins were in circulation until 1914, and these were called *coins of the realm*. With this form of currency the face value of the coins was the same as the actual value of gold as a commodity. Of course, bank notes were also in circulation and could be exchanged for their value in gold coins. After 1914, this situation again existed in Britain, in a very modified form, between 1925 and 1931.

Britain finally abolished the internal use of gold as legal tender and changed completely to using paper money in 1931. Paper money here means banknotes and coins which have no intrinsic value. Gold and scarce foreign currencies (e.g. US dollars) are used only to pay off deficits on the balance of trade.

The following types of money are currently in use in Britain and Ireland:

1. Coins struck by the Government Mint.
2. Notes issued by the central bank (e.g. Bank of England).
3. Bank money, brought into circulation by the commercial banks.

Types 1 and 2 represent state money, and type 3 represents bank money. State money is note or coin money while bank money is essentially credit (see Figure 5.1) and amounts to over 90 per cent of the total.

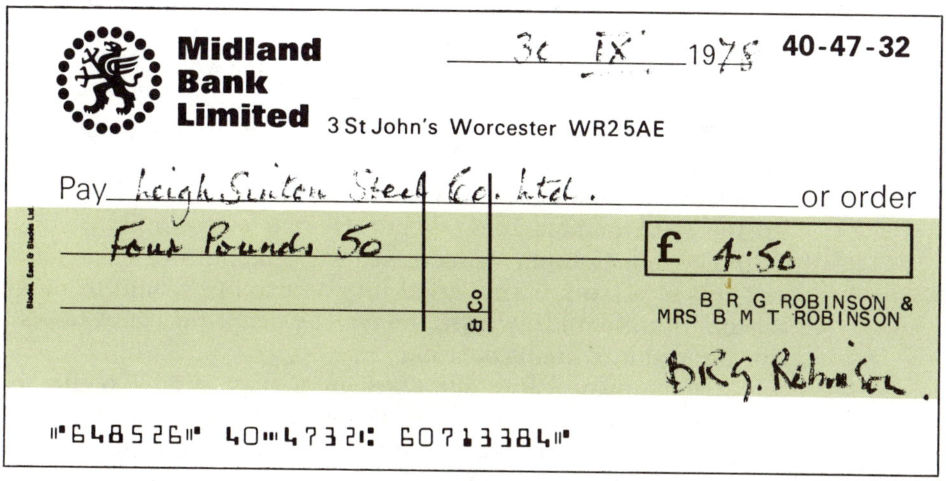

Figure 5.1 A cheque: a major method of transfer of bank money.

Summary The history of the money system in Britain shows the gradual divorce of money from gold. Notes and coins are at present issued by the state through its central bank. Bank money is a speciality of the commercial banks but constitutes the largest proportion of total money.

5.4 THE CREATION OF MONEY

The creation of money means simply increasing the amount of either coin, notes or bank money, and its opposite is demonetization or the destruction of money. Cash is created by printing banknotes, striking coins and bringing them into circulation. Bank money is created by commercial

Table 5.2 Bank balance sheet items.

Liabilities	*Assets*
Capital	Cash (notes and coin)
Current and deposit and other accounts	Cheques in course of collection
	Money at call
Other liabilities	Treasury bills
	Other bills (commercial bills, bills of exchange)
	Special deposits
	Certificates of deposit
	Investments
	Advances

banks, by their granting credit in various ways. The balance sheet items of a commercial bank are given in Table 5.2. Liabilities are the deposits made with banks by individuals and firms. Assets are the bank money and cash of the commercial bank, which are used by that bank in the economic system. Liabilities and assets are dealt with in detail in Chapter 7.

We shall now examine some of the ways in which the money supply is changed. In general, the money supply increases when the current or deposit accounts are increased through the granting of credit by the bank. An exception is when people put cash into a current account, because this leaves the total money supply unchanged: it 'destroys' as much cash as it creates bank money, i.e. it substitutes one for the other.

The money supply is increased when money in a customer's deposit account at a bank is converted into a current account from which the customer can withdraw cash freely. The deposit account funds here are not the result of credit creation.

Other examples of increases in money supply relate to foreign exchange and treasury bills. When a bank releases funds from its accounts under UK foreign exchange control to purchase foreign currencies, it increases the money supply. A treasury bill is a receipt for lending a specified sum to the government for a period of up to three months. The central bank increases the supply of money when it purchases treasury bills from the client of a bank. The central bank does this by paying the client through his bank account.

Money Creation through Loans By far the most important way of increasing the amount of money supply is the granting of loans to householders and firms by commercial banks in the form of *advances*, i.e. loans to people and institutions with current accounts at the bank. This increases the quantity, not of cash, but of bank money, or credit, as it is also called. Consider the example of Mr Grimethorpe, the owner of a small cutlery works in Sheffield, who goes to his local bank for a loan (an advance) of £20 000 to buy a new cutlery-making machine from Smith and Platt Ltd, the manufacturers. The bank agrees to the loan, and writes into its assets columns an advance of £20 000, but it also writes into its liabilities columns a deposit of £20 000 in Mr Grimethorpe's own account. Mr Grimethorpe can now pay from his account a cheque for £20 000 for the machine to Smith and Platt Ltd. Grimethorpe's bank honours this cheque, and the £20 000 is now credited to the account of Smith and Platt (see Figure 5.2). The £20 000 is in fact new 'bank money' (or credit) which has been created by the bank in addition to all of its other loans and deposits. This sum is

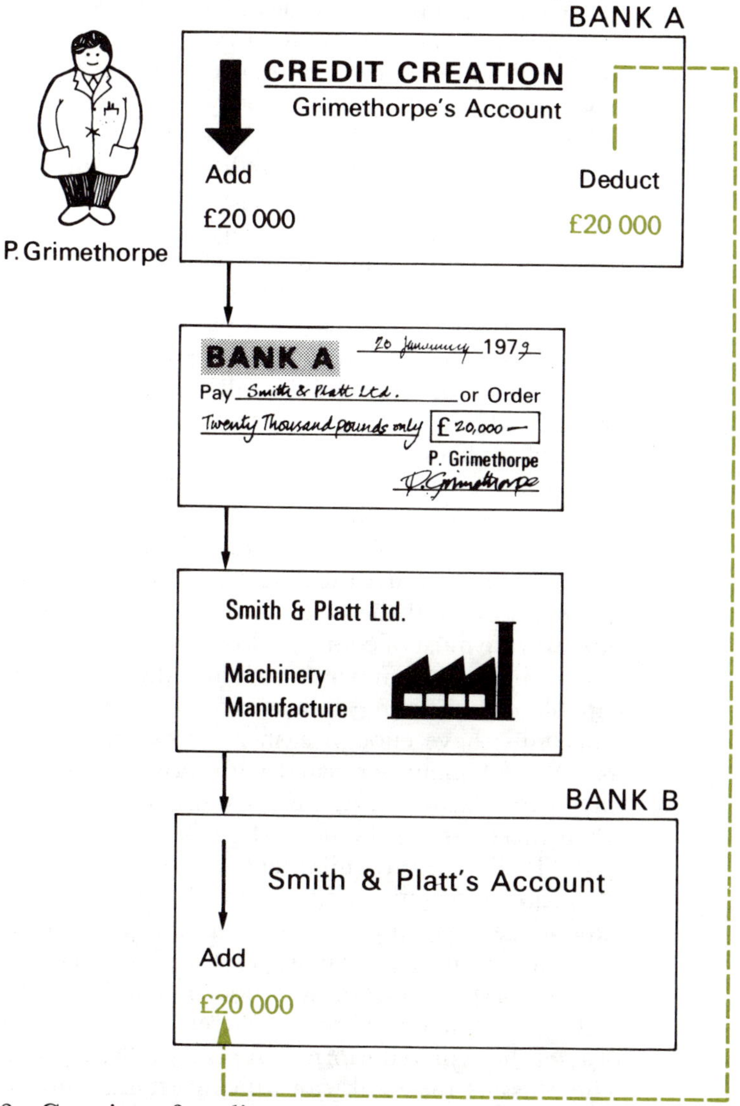

Figure 5.2 Creation of credit.

therefore an addition to the money supply. The loan (asset) of £20 000 has been balanced by the deposit of £20 000. As a consequence the balance sheet of the bank shows assets and liabilities equal to each other.

Money Creation through Purchase of Government Stock Another method whereby banks increase the money supply is the purchase of government stock (i.e. loans to the government over a ten-year period). The bank pays for the stock by a cheque written out for a particular sum to the government, and the government is credited with the same sum in the bank's deposit account. The sum of the loan is put into the bank's assets column as 'Investment', and into the bank's liabilities column as a deposit. This sum is new 'bank money', created in the same way as the 'bank money' created for Mr Grimethorpe.

Creation of money in these ways is based on the experience of banks that over a period of time depositors withdraw only a small proportion, usually about 4 per cent, of their money. As a result, the banks can give more credit than the actual money they have received. The banks know that they need keep only about 6 per cent, or less, of assets as cash reserves, for not all the beneficiaries of credits will ask simultaneously for the credits they have been granted in the form of cash. A large part of such money is never even used as cash, but merely for transfers by cheque from one person's current account to another.

This type of money creation is different from that practised by, for example, savings and merchant banks, which simply make available the money they have received from depositors. The commercial banks are institutions which provide a full range of banking services, including credit creation, whereas other banks specialize in particular services or a range of services.

Limitations on Banks' Money-creation Powers The key issue in banking is how much credit can be granted. The policy of a commercial bank is normally to maximize the difference between the rate of interest it pays to its depositors and the rate of interest it charges to its debtors (the first interest rate must of course be lower than the second). However, while so attempting to maximize its profits, the bank must remain liquid (i.e. capable of honouring cash withdrawals immediately). To be liquid, a bank must have enough cash reserves (in Britain, about 6 per cent of assets), to honour the usual withdrawals in normal times, and it must have extra cash or near cash resources to cover withdrawals in periods when these exceed the normal level.

The liquidity requirement is a guarantee that banks do not exceed their money creating activity. As we have seen British banks know from experience that they must keep 4 to 6 per cent of their assets in cash. Government no longer enforces a cash-to-assets ratio, but does require banks to keep a substantial proportion of their assets in the form of 'near cash'. This is achieved by the current legal requirement that $12\frac{1}{2}$ per cent of assets be kept in the form of treasury bills, other bills, and money at call. These assets the bank can quickly transfer into cash whenever this is required. If government wishes banks to create more bank money it can simply increase the supply of banknotes to them from the central bank. However, any such decision by government is taken in the context of its macroeconomic policies, i.e. involves consideration of the effect on the earning and spending of the national income by firms and households. We must therefore examine whether or not the introduction of money influences the interplay between the effective demand for goods and services and the net national product.

Summary Through their ability to create money, banks can alter the country's money supply. This activity is not open to abuse for although the banks try to maximize their profit, they are careful to remain solvent and liquid. We shall see later that the commercial banks' money-creating activity is subject to limitations because of its impact on effective demand for goods and services. It is through the central bank, on which the commercial banks rely, that any restriction on the money-creating power is exercised.

5.5 THE MONEY-CREATION MULTIPLIER

Let us assume a situation in which there is a central bank that does not grant any credits to the private sector and there are three commercial banks, A, B and C. We further assume that there is no cash in circulation so that the clients pay one another in bank money and cannot withdraw any cash. Furthermore, we suppose that the banks must keep 10 per cent of the immediately withdrawable deposits as cash reserves, either because this is a statutory requirement or because it is supported by reasons of good business economics.

Bank A now receives a claim against the central bank – and therefore a cash reserve – amounting to £1000, e.g. by the state paying this amount from its account with the central bank to the account of one of the clients of bank A. Since the latter needs to keep only 10 per cent or £100 as cash reserve, it can lend the rest, £900, to Mr X. The latter owes Mrs Y £900 and instructs bank A to transfer this sum to her account with bank B. This bank therefore acquires £900 from bank A, or the credit balance of this bank's account with the central bank is increased by a transfer from bank A's account with the central bank. At the same time, Mrs Y's deposit account is credited with the same sum. This sum is now in the hands of bank B, which again needs to keep only 10 per cent (i.e. £90) of it as cash reserve, and can lend the other £810 to Mr Z who has it transferred to the account of someone who has an account with bank C, and so on, and so on, with this process. In other words, starting with a £1000 claim received by bank A against the central bank, the commercial banks together eventually create £9000 of bank money. In our simple case, the cash reserve ratio is 1/10 (i.e. 10 per cent), and the money-creation multiplier is the reciprocal of it.

By changing the stipulated cash reserve ratio, the central bank can influence the funds available for lending and the money-creation multiplier, thereby affecting also the credit potential of the commercial banks.

Summary The commercial banks together can create an amount of money that is a multiple of the original amount which they have available for lending. The public itself will decide in what form it wants to have this newly created money.

5.6 CONCLUDING REMARKS

We have examined the nature, and type, of money without discussing how it operates in the economy. The two primary functions of money are as a medium of exchange and as a measure of value, while its derived functions are those of a store of value and standard for deferred payments. The larger part of the money supply in Britain and Ireland is in the form of bank money, which can be withdrawn from banks without any notice. All British money since 1914 has been paper money, except for some use of gold during the period 1925–31.

The commercial banks' ability to create money raises the question of what limits should be set on the increase in the amount of circulating money. Commercial banks like the Midland Bank and the National Westminster are able to increase the total money supply by creating money. In the banking sector of the economy this ability is restricted by the banks' need to remain solvent and liquid, but we have yet to examine whether there should be any limits to the banks' credit expansion as far as effective demand for goods and services is concerned. This will be discussed in the next chapter, together with the creation of money by the central government.

QUESTIONS

1 What uses has money?

2 Why is it that a banknote is accepted by everyone as a medium of exchange, but is not exchangeable for gold and is not even fully covered by it?

3 How can a commercial bank increase the money supply of society?

4 What are the limits set on the creation of money by commercial banks?

5 What is the basis for the principle of the money-creation multiplier?

6 What does the credit potential of the commercial banks depend on?

7 How can the banks influence the cash-to-total-money ratio, and how does this affect their credit potential?

EXERCISES

1 Someone converts £1000 from his current account into his deposit. What accounting operations are carried out by the bank, and what does this change mean for the money supply of the country?

2 Someone sells 100 French francs to his bank and has it put in his current account there. What accounting operations are carried out by the bank, and how does it affect the money supply of the country?

3 Someone sells some goods in France for 100 000 francs and wishes to convert this back into pounds. How does this affect the British money supply?

4 Show that on the basis of central bank money, the maximum money created in Exercise 3 is the same as in the case discussed in the text.

5 Does it make a difference if a bank, A, receives an initial additional sum of money in the form of (a) a payment by the state to a client of this bank, or (b) payment by the central bank for treasury bills bought from bank A?

Chapter Six

The Theory of Money

We have examined the nature and types of money, and in this chapter we shall assess its effect on the economy. This is a particularly topical problem, since the value of money in most Western countries has been falling. This fall in the purchasing power of money can be looked at in another way: prices have been rising rapidly, i.e., there has been inflation. But as we shall see, inflation can also occur without price rises. Nevertheless, in practice, it is generally true to say that the more money there is in circulation, the higher prices are, so that inflation can almost always be identified with rising prices. The theory of money will give us a thorough and realistic insight into this problem.

6.1 ACTIVE AND INACTIVE MONEY

To assess the importance of money in an economy we must first find out whether it affects production or merely flows through a system, as a necessary but inert medium, or accumulates somewhere during its flow, thereby changing things.

Reasons for Holding Money Firms and households use a large amount of the money they receive to meet their daily purchases of goods and services. Keynes called this wish to hold money so that it could be ready to purchase goods and services: the *transactions motive*. He called the money involved *transactions money*, but we shall call it *active money*. If one has active money, one can exert an effective demand for goods and services, whenever one wishes.

The opposite is *inactive money*, kept either for emergencies (e.g. ill health) or for buying securities such as shares in firms and government stocks. These two reasons for holding money were called by Keynes respectively the *precautionary* and the *speculative* motives. Both the active and the inactive money are examples of people's preference for liquidity (i.e. for holding funds in money or other liquid items such as three-month treasury bills). According to Keynes, the demand for active money depends mainly on the level of national income (i.e. on production of goods and services), while that for inactive money depends on the rate of interest. If production is high, demand for active money to buy goods is high. Keynes's liquidity-preference theory of interest is discussed in Chapter 12.

Hoarding and Dishoarding Any transfer from active to inactive funds, made either by consumers or by producers, is called *hoarding*. The opposite transfer, from inactive to active funds, is *dishoarding*, or the release of money. Dishoarding is exemplified by a consumer who buys a durable consumer good (e.g. a car) for the money that he has put aside in case of emergencies. He releases his money and exerts an effective demand for motor cars. In the case of hoarding, on the other hand, the effective demand is reduced, and more is put into inactive-money funds. The individual may decide to postpone purchase of a deep-freezer and hoard funds in order to purchase shares when the price of them is optimum.

Since only firms and households are taken into account here, the country's total money supply, M, is divided into money demanded by firms (L_f) and money demanded by households (L_h), so that $L_f + L_h = L$. We denote active and inactive money in both cases by the letters 'a' and 'i', so that we have $L_h^a + L_h^i = L_h$ and $L_f^a + L_f^i = L_f$. The total active money is given by $L^a = L_h^a + L_f^a$, and the total inactive money by $L^i = L_h^i + L_f^i$. The complete situation is presented in Table 6.1.

Table 6.1 Active and Inactive Money.

	Active money	*Inactive money*	*Total*
Firms	L_f^a	L_f^i	L_f
Households	L_h^a	L_h^i	L_h
Total	L^a	L^i	L

When firms transfer money from inactive to active funds, so that L_f^i is reduced, and L_f^a is increased, they are said to dishoard or release money. When households transfer money from active to inactive funds, they are said to hoard money. There is a continual hoarding and dishoarding of money by firms and households but it is the net effect of hoarding and dishoarding which is important for the economy as a whole.

When money hoarding predominates in an economy, money remains idle for a longer time on average – or, to put it differently, it circulates more slowly, taking a longer time to change hands – than when dishoarding takes place. If the money supply, M, is multiplied by the velocity of circulation of money, V (i.e. the speed with which money changes hands), the 'money stream' MV is obtained. The money supply M is a *stock* variable, i.e. like all stocks it refers to a measurement made at a certain *point* in time, while the money stream MV is a *flow* variable, i.e. like all flows it refers to a measurement made over a given period of time. If V increases, the flow of money at a given value of M becomes faster, and MV increases, and vice versa. Conversely, if M is increased at a given value of V, the money stream MV similarly becomes larger, and vice versa.

Money, Liquid Assets and Goods We have so far assumed for the sake of simplicity that money is either hoarded or used to buy goods. Reality is more complex, however, and there is a spectrum of types of money, assets, goods and services which are progressively less liquid in nature, such as those in the following list. We begin with cash, the most liquid asset.

Cash
Bank money (current account)
Bank money (deposit account)
Bills of exchange and treasury bills
Government stock
A rare stamp
A piece of land
A television set
A suit of clothes
A meal in a restaurant

Cash is fully acceptable everywhere as a medium of exchange, and normally so is bank money. Short-term assets such as bills of exchange and treasury bills can usually be converted quickly into cash, through sale in the market. By contrast, long-term assets such as government stock are less easy to sell rapidly and convert into cash. It is not much more difficult to sell certain goods such as a rare stamp, and convert it into cash. However, it becomes progressively more difficult to exchange a piece of land, a TV set, a suit of clothes and a meal in a restaurant for liquid assets, including cash.

Summary The money supply is demanded by firms and households; it can be divided into active and inactive categories, on the basis of which we define hoarding and dishoarding. There is a spectrum of money, assets, goods and services which are progressively less liquid in nature.

6.2 INCREASE IN EFFECTIVE DEMAND, THE RELEASE OF MONEY, AND INFLATION

Increase in Effective Demand We have seen in Chapter 3, where a fixed productive capacity was assumed, that the net national product, O (equal to the level of prices, P, multiplied by the output of goods produced), increases when the effective demand, ED, rises, and that an increase in the effective demand raises the output only until full employment is reached. The question we now have to pose is whether such an increase in the output raises the money supply, M, i.e. whether doubling the output of, e.g., ten loaves of bread, each sold at 20 pence, without changing the price doubles the value of M. The answer is that this need not be the case, because it can also happen that the households release some money from their inactive into their active funds, and the money changes hands faster, so that twice as much bread can be exchanged with the aid of the same amount of money. The money thus released is used here to raise the effective demand for a consumer good (bread), and an increase in the ED is already known to lead to a higher national product and national income. In this situation the effective demand can grow only if money is dishoarded, which can of course be done only until the inactive funds are exhausted. At a given money supply in the economy, the effective demand can therefore rise only as long as some inactive money is still available or, in other words, if the velocity of circulation increases.

We have seen that the money stream is equal to MV, which must in turn be equal to the money value of all transactions, PT (average level of prices, P, multiplied by number of transactions, T). The identity $MV = PT$ is Fisher's quantity equation of exchange, which is an important element of his quantity theory of money. If PT increases, MV must also increase, and – assuming that the money supply M is constant – this is possible only if the velocity of circulation of money, V, increases.

Release of Money Whether the effective demand stays at the higher level depends on what firms do with the extra money received. If they keep it as active money, the effective demand stays at the higher level, but if they transfer it to inactive funds, the effective demand falls to the old level; as also does the national income, because the households' dishoarding of money is accompanied by the firms' hoarding of it.

The households' withdrawal of money from inactive funds held for speculative purposes need not increase the demand for consumer goods, since the money involved may be used for buying securities or acquiring other subjects of investment, which means that the money is now held in a less liquid form (e.g. as deposit accounts in banks or as government stock). The money involved may, of course, find its way to the firms, who will use it for financing their investments. In this case, the effective demand increases even though the households did not dishoard any money, that is to say, they did not transfer it from their inactive to their active funds. The reason for this increase in the effective demand is that the money in question has gone from the inactive funds of the households to the active funds of the firms. The important point is that an increase in the total effective demand always stems from a net dishoarding of money since, overall, inactive money is converted into active money. This need not hold for one particular household, because it may use the money withdrawn from the inactive funds to buy securities like bonds.

(We have ignored here the fact that the effective demand can also be stimulated by an increase in the money supply, M, through the creation of money by the central banks, the commercial banks and the state.)

Inflation When this money is released, through dishoarding, and effective demand consequently rises, we can say inflation is taking place in the monetary sector. The dishoarding and the rise in effective demand may or may not lead to price rises. This depends on how near the economy is to full employment level. However, inflation is nevertheless present, since inflation is a situation of net dishoarding and consequent increase in effective demand for goods and services.

The question now, in real production terms, is whether or not this expansion of output as a response to the rise in effective demand continues until there are no more people to employ, i.e. until there is full employment. The answer is that this need not be the case, for it all depends on whether or not the effective demand continues to increase: it may stop increasing before full employment is reached. This may happen either because people do not want to increase their expenditure, although their inactive funds have not been exhausted, or because, although they want to spend more, their inactive funds are empty: all of their available liquidities have been used up.

Inflationary Gap However, if people's propensity to spend persists and they have enough liquid assets to allow the release of money to continue, full employment is eventually reached, and the output then cannot be increased any further. A further increase in the total effective demand then leads only to a rise in the level of prices. *An inflationary gap* then exists, in which the money-backed demand for goods and services in the economy exceeds the capacity of the economy to produce the goods and services required. From a monetary point of view, expansion is stimulated by the dishoarding of money in this case too, and the resulting inflation is then price inflation. However, as we have seen, inflation need not always lead to price rises.

It is true that inflation mostly leads to price rises because the productive capacity is usually already fully utilized when the volume of money stream increases from one period to the next. Since the early 1970s, prices have been rising rapidly, this inflation reaching an annual average of 15 per cent in Britain and Ireland in the mid 1970s.

Changes in the monetary sphere (i.e. money supply) in this model follow changes in the commodity sphere (i.e. production of goods). The national income and thus the number of jobs increase because the propensity to spend and hence the effective demand increase. Money is released because of the growth in effective demand. Events in the commodity sphere are regarded here as the primary phenomena, while those occurring in the monetary sphere are a necessary condition for them. There is an alternative viewpoint in which a more important role is attributed to money, the presence of liquid assets in the inactive funds being itself a factor that influences spending, i.e. money is released and *therefore* the effective demand goes up, and so constitutes a cause of an increase in the effective demand. Those who adhere to this view are called *monetarists* and they hold that inflation is due mainly to an excessive expansion of the money supply.

Summary As long as the money supply is assumed to be constant, an increase in the effective demand means the release of money, inactive money being converted into active money. Money then circulates faster. This leads to a rise in output before full employment is reached, to a rise in prices, after full employment has been reached, and a resulting inflationary gap.

6.3 DECREASE IN EFFECTIVE DEMAND AND THE HOARDING OF MONEY, DEFLATION AND STAGFLATION

Decrease in Effective Demand If at a time of full employment the effective demand decreases, there will be a decrease not only in consumption, C, and investment, I (and hence in the national income, Y), but also in the amount of active money, L^a, since less money will then be needed for the daily purchases. Money shifts from active to inactive funds, i.e. it is hoarded. In short, a decrease in effective demand is accompanied by hoarding in the monetary sphere. This contraction of the money flow is called deflation. It is again open to discussion which way causality operates, i.e. whether hoarding is a result of the drop in effective demand or the cause of the lower propensity to spend; if the latter is the case, the public are assumed to want to hold in the inactive form more money than before.

Deflation and Deflationary Gap Under-employment is then explained by insufficient demand and is coupled in the monetary sphere with a strong tendency on the part of the public to hold its money in the inactive form. In the ensuing depression, we paradoxically have a surfeit of money on the one hand, and poverty, caused by unemployment, on the other. People hold their money now in inactive non-liquid funds rather than as active money.

A deflationary gap then exists in which the money-backed demand for goods and services in the economy is less than the capacity of the economy to produce goods and services. Unemployment will result from a lack of demand.

We followed a Keynesian approach in the last two sections by ascribing changes in the employment situation only to changes in spending, and concluding that, at a given productive capacity, unemployment is due to a drop in effective demand. In view of the late-1970s situation, however, we must stress that this explains only the trade-cycle side of unemployment, called cyclical unemployment (as discussed in Chapter 4).

Stagflation Keynes concentrated on demand inflation, arising through the demand-pull mechanism, in which prices are 'pulled upward' by a high level of expenditure relative to the productive capacity. Cyclical unemployment results from the opposite situation, i.e. when the level of expenditure is lower than is needed to exercise the whole labour force. According to Keynes, we have either cyclical unemployment or inflation with price rises, but not both at the same time.

Keynes therefore did not explain the situation where there are both price rises and high unemployment, a picture characteristic of the 1970s. To understand the combination of industrial production stagnation and inflation which has been called 'stagflation', we must abandon the Keynesian model and concentrate on the supply side of the economy. First of all, a steep rise in costs (e.g. wage rises) raises prices just as the increase in demand does, this being known as the 'cost-push' mechanism of inflation. In such a case, manufacturers simply 'pass on' to the consumers the increases in the cost of their raw materials, energy or wages (an increase in monopoly profit can also mean increased costs for those who buy goods from monopolist firms). When firms experience difficulties because of their rising costs, production begins to stagnate. In a special but important response, firms may introduce machines to replace labour which has become more expensive. This situation illustrates the connection between cost inflation and structural unemployment. Structural unemployment is related to the supply side of the economy and it is not only more expensive labour that exerts a cost-push, and not only the introduction of labour-saving machines that causes it. Recent unemployment has both cyclical and structural components and the price rises are due both to a strong propensity to spend and to a steep rise in costs, the first occurring on the demand side and the second on the supply side of the economy.

Summary In monetary terms, a decrease in the effective demand means hoarding and deflation, active money being converted into inactive. Money then circulates more slowly. This deflation reduces production to below the level associated with full employment, and ultimately lowers the price level. There is an excess of hoarded money, accompanied by ever-worsening unemployment – a paradox that was explained by Keynes in 1936. The 1970s' economic problems of concurrent stagnation in industrial production and inflation cannot be explained by the Keynesian model.

6.4 MONETARY EQUILIBRIUM AND EXPENDITURE EQUILIBRIUM

If in a certain period (at a given money supply in the economy) the amount of money hoarded is equal to that dishoarded, we speak of monetary equilibrium, in which the inflationary trend and the deflationary trend cancel out each other.

On the other hand, expenditure equilibrium exists when, at a given productive capacity, the effective demand is neither higher nor lower than the value that corresponds to full employment. When the effective demand is insufficient, cyclical unemployment results.

Most people think that both underspending and overspending should be avoided, the first because it means cyclical unemployment and an incomplete use of the available capacity, and the second because it leads only to nominal increases but not to a real increase in the net national product. In the second case, overspending forces up the general level of prices and therefore net national product increases in money value but not in terms of actual goods and services. The principal aim is therefore to maintain expenditure equilibrium, with its avoidance of cyclical unemployment. The various cases are shown in Figure 6.1.

Monetary equilibrium is also of great importance. The fact is that the dishoarding can change an expenditure equilibrium into a situation of

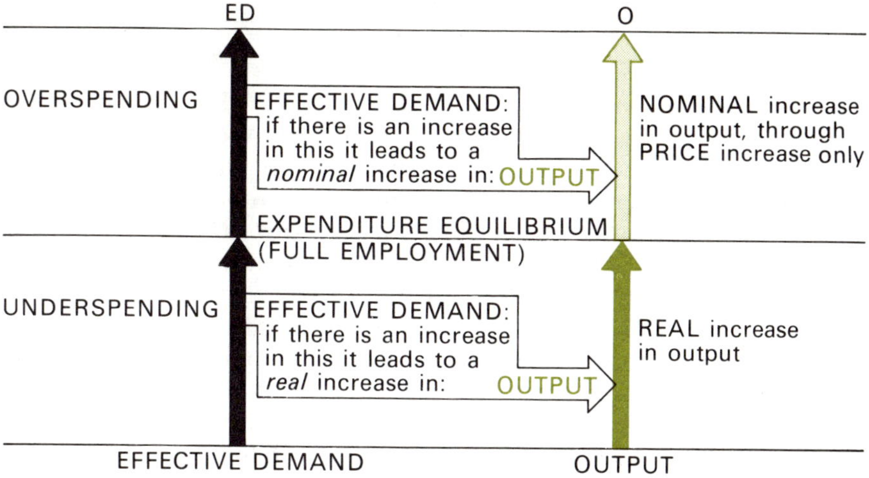

Figure 6.1 Expenditure equilibrium and monetary equilibrium.

overspending. This destruction of monetary equilibrium creates excess demand and therefore an inflationary situation with price rises results. This fall in purchasing power has a particularly serious effect on people who have a fixed income, such as pensioners. This has recently given rise to the suggestion that various payments and allowances should be pegged either to the price index of household consumption in order to keep them at a fixed value, or to the wage index, which will tend to compensate for price increases. Either way should keep people at a relatively constant level of welfare. Steep price rises have made it attractive to have debts (which are repaid in depreciated money in future), and people who have saved money see the value of their savings fall. In the 1970s, there have been substantial moves by people towards saving through the purchase of property rather than by buying shares or government stock. Property values have matched, and are sometimes ahead of, inflation. Also, when our home inflation is higher than that abroad, we run the risk of pricing our goods out of the international market.

The government is expected to ensure both monetary and expenditure equilibrium, since firms and households cannot easily ascertain whether their transactions lead to these equilibria.

Summary Monetary equilibrium (at a given money supply and over a certain period) occurs when dishoarding and hoarding are equated and expenditure equilibrium exists when the value of effective demand is sufficient to create full employment. Most people expect the government to aim at establishing expenditure equilibrium and monetary equilibrium at the same time.

6.5 CHANGES IN THE MONEY SUPPLY AND MACROECONOMIC POLICY

Government Action to Change Money Supply The money supply, which has so far been assumed to be constant, can be changed by the government. Thus, the government can increase it by (a) advising the central bank and the other banks to make payments to the public, through purchases of treasury bills (see Chapter 7), (b) government's repaying loans, and (c) making more money and introducing it into circulation. Conversely, the government can decrease it by (a) asking the public to make payments to the government, by sales of treasury bills, (b) raising government loans, and (c) withdrawing banknotes and coins from circulation. Finally, the commercial banks can change the stock of money by creating or destroying bank money (i.e. credit). Although the money supply is not a constant, the Bank of England in the United Kingdom, and the Central Bank of Ireland in Ireland can impose restrictions on the commercial banks' liberty to create credit (see Chapter 7, Section 4).

Precariousness of Monetary Equilibrium The effect of the extra money depends on the use it is put to. If it is used as active money, then it obviously means the financing of increased effective demand, and there will be an increase in spending, the national money income, and the number of jobs. The extra money here has the same effect as the release of money, i.e. an inflationary destruction of the monetary equilibrium. If, however, the extra money created goes into inactive funds (i.e. is hoarded), it balances out its creation, and the monetary equilibrium is maintained.

The possibility of creating and destroying money calls for a modification of our previous definition of monetary equilibrium. Taking only hoarding and dishoarding into account, we defined monetary equilibrium as an overall balance between these two opposite phenomena over a certain period. We must now say that monetary equilibrium prevails when the sum of money created and dishoarded is equal to the sum of money destroyed and hoarded.

Although hoarding all the newly-created money maintains the monetary equilibrium, the increase in the amount of inactive money involved here means, for the firms and households, an increased liquidity which can be mobilized and spent at short notice. Consequently, a latent inflationary potential is inherent in this situation.

Government and Monetary Equilibrium Furthermore, the source of the increase in the money supply is significant, since the state, the central bank and the commercial banks each have a different reason for increasing money. Thus, the commercial banks do it when firms and households ask for more money. When their inactive money proves insufficient, firms or households can increase their spending by borrowing from their banks money as advances at a rate of interest. This is how the banks can create the possibility of overspending, i.e. by the inflationary financing of firms and households. This is the macroeconomic effect of the banks' ability to create money: it may happen that banks embark on the inflationary financing of the firms and households at a time when stimulating the effective demand is undesirable. In such a case, the result is price inflation and the over-expansion of the economy. A similar state of affairs is produced when the central bank creates more money by printing more banknotes and purchasing treasury bills, and when government creates more money by repaying loans.

Monetarist Ideas Some economists argue that control of the money supply by government, central bank and commercial banks is the major means of solving the problems of inflation and stagflation. The American Milton Friedman, in putting maximum emphasis on the monetary factors, in theories developed in the 1960s, has contended that the authorities must equate the growth of the money supply with the growth in real national income. If this is done during a period of inflation the reduction in the money supply will create high unemployment, since effective demand will have been reduced. However, the inflation will be removed as soon as the growth of the money supply is just sufficient to finance the increase of real national income. Critics of the monetary approach would argue that monetary control alone is insufficient to reduce the rate of price inflation. A further important criticism is that it takes too little account of the real factors that influence inflation, such as power of pressure groups, e.g. trades unions.

Summary **Banks, through credit creation, and firms and households, through dishoarding, act in such a way that effective demand for goods and services rises so high that monetary inflation may result. Government through the central bank attempts to enforce limits to the expansion of the money supply and use of money in order to curb inflationary tendencies.**

6.6 CONCLUDING REMARKS

We have discussed in this chapter some concepts which, though difficult at first to comprehend, are necessary for an understanding of the real world of economics. To examine the effect of money on the economy, we distinguish between active and inactive money or funds. Active money, held to make payments in the production of goods and services sphere of the economy, is therefore also called *transactions money*. Inactive money is partly a precautionary reserve, but is mainly held to buy objects of speculation such as stocks, shares and bonds, and may therefore be also called *speculation money*. A rise in the national income is due to an increase in the effective demand, which presupposes that more money is available for daily transactions. This means that, at a constant money supply, active money, L^a, increases and inactive money, L^i, decreases. The transfer of money from inactive to active funds is called dishoarding or release of money, and an increase in the effective demand at a constant money supply is necessarily accompanied by release of money. This dishoarding is inflationary and signifies the destruction of monetary equilibrium and its replacement by inflation.

If the economy also includes banks that create money, then the condition for monetary equilibrium is that the sum of money created and dishoarded should be equal to the sum of money destroyed and hoarded in the same period.

Expenditure equilibrium implies that the effective demand is neither less nor more than is needed to put to employment the whole working population so that there is full employment. We try to avoid both overspending, which is accompanied by price rises, and underspending, which is accompanied by unemployment.

An attempt has also been made in recent years to combat stagflation, where prices are rising although there is unemployment. In this situation, increasing spending, as prescribed by Keynes, may be self-defeating, since unemployment here is partly a result of cost inflation (see Chapter 14).

Banks can change the money supply, and thus exert a macroeconomic influence, so that their activities must be supervised – a task discharged in the United Kingdom by the Bank of England and in Ireland by the Central Bank of Ireland.

QUESTIONS

1 What is monetary equilibrium?

2 What is expenditure equilibrium?

3 Does the creation of money by the banks invariably lead to price rises?

4 In which ways can money be withdrawn from active funds?

5 A private individual converts £10 000 of cash into stocks from one period to the next. Does this raise the effective demand he exerts? Is there in general an increase in the effective demand?

EXERCISES

1 Can the effective demand increase while monetary equilibrium prevails?

2 Is the presence of a great deal of money in the inactive funds sufficient in itself for the economy to move out of a depression?

3 Does money make a difference to the statement that, at a given productive capacity, the national product is determined by the effective demand? What is the connection between a rise in the price level, P, the money supply in the economy and the velocity of circulation of money, V?

4 Starting with expenditure equilibrium, describe what happens when monetary equilibrium is destroyed and replaced by deflation.

5 Assume a constant money supply in a country over a certain period. How can a general rise in share prices be explained if the profit of enterprises does not show an upward trend?

Chapter Seven

The British Banking System

The system of British banking is a combination of largely privately-owned banking institutions supervised by a state-owned central bank, the Bank of England. The banks comprise both the commercial banks, including the seven London clearing banks, which deal with general business, and the specialist banks, such as merchant banks and overseas banks. In addition, several important ancillary institutions in the London Money Market (e.g. discount houses and accepting houses) support the functioning of the banking system. Through the banks the Bank of England controls credit creation, and by its own actions determines the supply of cash, and plays a vital role in the day-to-day overseas economic relations of Britain. Nevertheless, the Bank of England is a nationalized firm, subordinate to the national Treasury and to the government, and it is therefore through the Bank of England that government in its turn influences the policies of the banks and money-market institutions.

7.1 THE COMMERCIAL BANKS

The functions of the commercial banks are to accept deposits from the public and industry, to make short-term and medium-term loans to government and industry and long-term loans to government, and to create credit through lending. The London clearing banks are the major institutions in this business of general banking, and comprise seven companies: Barclays, Lloyds, Midland, National Westminster, Co-operative Bank, Williams & Glyn's, and Coutts & Co. The first four are by far the largest in turnover and also have branches throughout all counties of England and Wales: in fact, Williams & Glyn's are owned by Lloyds, and Coutts by National Westminster. Through their other subsidiary companies the 'Big Four' also enable their branch banking service to operate throughout Scotland and Northern Ireland.

The detailed functions of the commercial banks are perhaps best analysed through the combined balance sheet of all of them, shown in Table 7.1.

Table 7.1 Balance sheet of London clearing banks (19 July 1978) (£m).

Liabilities		*Assets*		
Eligible liabilities	25 991	Cash: notes and coins	869	
Total liabilities	43 583	balances with Bank of England	599	
		Total	1 468	
		Money at call	1 545	
		Treasury bills	345	
		Other bills and government stock of less than 1 year	858	
		Total reserve assets	3 347	
		(Reserve assets ratio		12.9%)
		Special deposits	506	
		Certificates of deposit and other market loans	3 659	
		Investments	2 080	
		Advances	20 065	
		Other assets	12 057	
		Total assets	43 583	

Liabilities These are mainly the current and deposit accounts made with banks by individuals and firms. Much of the deposits are created credit which has derived from the loans made by the banks to customers. In this way loans have helped to create deposits (see Chapter 5, Section 4). There could be competition in the rates offered to customers for deposits, but in spite of government encouragement in 1971 to do this, there has been little change in banks' policy.

Assets These are analysed in detail as follows:
Cash: This is kept both on the banks' premises and at the Bank of England. The former is to ensure that the banks have the minimum cash necessary to satisfy customers' needs, and the latter represents a potent means of last-resort control by the central bank (as well as control of any new entrants to the London clearing banks' 'club').

Cheques in course of collection: This item refers to inter-bank payments at a point in time, and therefore it is not included in the combined balance sheet of all commercial banks given in Table 7.1.

Money at call: This element is very short-term lending to the discount houses in the London money market, and it can be 'called in' by the banks at as little as a day's notice or up to 14 days' notice. This asset is easy to collect, but is lent at a low rate (11 per cent on 23 April 1979).

Treasury bills: The treasury bill is a short-term borrowing (up to three months) by the government, and therefore to buy them is a good security for part of the banks' assets since they can be exchanged for cash in a relatively short period. The rate is, of course, lower than for most forms of lending (11 per cent on 23 April 1979).

Other bills: On a similar basis the banks lend money to local authorities (local authority bills) and to some firms (bills of exchange) for a short period. All three types of short-term bills, money at call, and other short-term loans to government (up to one year) are *reserve assets*. Banks must, in general terms, possess 12½ per cent of their assets in the form of these reserve assets. In full, the rule is that total eligible bank liabilities (all deposits except foreign currency deposits) must be matched by 12½ per cent of the bank's assets, these being the reserve assets.

Special deposits: The Bank of England requests commercial banks to transfer to it a percentage of their assets at times of government anti-inflationary policies, and 4 per cent is the maximum which can be demanded. The calling in by the central bank of special deposits increases in reality the banks' reserve assets ratio, and therefore reduces their power to lend in the medium and long term to industry.

Certificates of deposit: These are medium- to long-term securities provided by a bank to a customer who guarantees a deposit with the bank for at least three months and at most five years.

Investments: These are medium- and long-term investments in government securities for periods varying from two to ten years. The rate of interest upon these is higher than for treasury bills.

Advances: This part of the banks' business is their most lucrative in terms of rate of interest upon money lent. It takes the form of short-term lending to individuals and short- and medium-term lending to nationalized firms (12½ per cent on 24 April 1979) and private firms (13 per cent on 24 April 1979). Medium-term advances are a development of the 1970s and these are used to finance, for example, factory building by companies. Previously, banks lent to industry only short term, usually on an early repayment basis. Loans to a farmer to purchase sheep would be one example. When he had raised and sold them, he would repay the bank out of his profits.

Rates of interest in the money market are shown in Table 7.2.

Table 7.2 Major rates of interest in London (6 September 1978).

Money at call	8½%	Government long-term bonds	$12\frac{1}{10}$
Treasury bill rate	$9\frac{1}{20}$%	Advances to nationalized industries	11%
Minimum lending rate	10%	Advances to large private companies	12–13%

A banker's main practical problem is reconciling profitability with liquidity. Advances are his most potent source of funds, and yet he must abide by both the government's imposed reserve assets ratio of 12½ per cent and his own prudence to ensure that he has enough cash or liquidity (i.e. 'near cash' – call money, treasury and other short-term bills) to deal with any demands by depositors. The banks' head offices work out an overall strategy for coping with this problem, and usually restrict advances to less than 60 per cent of assets whilst normally maintaining a reserve assets ratio of more than 12½ per cent. Holding cash in a rigid ratio to assets is not the most important safeguard for banks' security of operations: the essential safeguard is to hold sufficient 'near money', i.e. liquid reserve assets, which can bring in interest and be speedily transferred into cash.

Summary The commercial banks must possess 12½ per cent of their assets in the form of liquid reserve assets. The most profitable source of business for banks is the short- and medium-term loans to industry and individuals.

7.2 THE SPECIALIST BANKING INSTITUTIONS

There is a wide variety of specialist banking forms which operate in London. The merchant banks have two major functions: that of sponsoring on behalf of clients new issues of shares on the London capital market; and that of underwriting new issues of shares. These institutions therefore provide a clear link between commercial banks, as holders of almost all private bank accounts, and the process of raising funds for new industrial and property developments. They have also developed in recent years a new function, a limited service of general banking, and continue to provide specialist advisory services.

The foreign banks in London are the most rapidly expanding of all the banking institutions in the United Kingdom. Their specialist role has been to provide an international service to their home customers and advice to British firms which might wish to operate overseas and to use the banks' home-country facilities (e.g. Banco Commerciale Italiana). However, like the merchant banks, the foreign banks have begun to develop a limited general banking service to British customers, and some of them have opened provincial offices to enhance this trade further.

Foreign banks, like British banks, find it difficult to provide sufficient funds for the borrowing requirements of multinational companies, and have therefore formed international banks to carry out this highly specialized and costly operation (e.g. Europartners, comprising Banco di Roma, Banco Hispano Americano, Commerzbank and Credit Lyonnais). Overseas banks are, paradoxically, British-owned banks with head offices in London, but are engaged in providing banking services in a particular region of the world (e.g. Standard Chartered Bank Limited, in the Middle East). In addition, these banks have developed a limited general banking service for British customers. Therefore, in 1971 the British government imposed reserve asset ratios not only on commercial banks but also on the other specialist banks.

Summary The specialist banking institutions provide a variety of specific services to customers, but most are also gradually developing a general banking role.

7.3 THE BANK OF ENGLAND: PRODUCER OF BASIS OF MONEY SUPPLY

The central bank has four major functions: (1) to provide the cash basis of the money supply, (2) to control credit creation, (3) to act as banker for the government, (4) to manage day-to-day overseas monetary relations. Since its foundation in 1694, the Bank of England has exercised all these functions, and since 1844 it has concentrated upon them almost to the complete exclusion of general banking business. As producer of the cash basis of money supply, the central bank provides the English note issue and controls the availability of Scottish and Northern Irish banknotes, by requiring cover for most of these by Bank of England notes. The Royal Mint makes the coin issue at the direction of the Bank of England. It is this cash and the reserve assets basis which enables the commercial banks to create credit. Whenever this basis expands, more credit can be created by the banks (see Chapter 5, Section 4).

Summary The Bank of England not only controls the supply of cash but, through this control of variations in cash, also determines broadly the quantity of credit which the commercial banks can create.

7.4 THE BANK OF ENGLAND: SPECIFIC METHODS OF CREDIT CONTROL THROUGH THE COMMERCIAL BANKS AND LONDON MONEY MARKET

An analysis of the further wide range of specific methods of controlling credit by the central bank will enable us to examine the functions of some major institutions in the money market which are important links in this chain of control. The Bank of England's additional methods of control are, essentially, through adjusting interest rates and liquidity ratios, together with some more directly interventionist weapons such as the directive and special deposits.

Minimum Lending Rate (12 per cent in April 1979) The key rate of interest is the *minimum lending rate* (MLR), which can be set by the Bank of England, acting on government instructions. However, if government does not intervene, MLR is determined in the market as a rate $\frac{1}{2}$ per cent above treasury bill rate, and rounded up to the nearest $\frac{1}{4}$ per cent. During a period of rapid inflation the Bank of England may raise MLR and also force up other interest rates by ensuring that the discount houses (dealers in treasury, local authority and commercial bills) have to borrow money from the central bank at the high MLR. Government has increasingly intervened in this market and since May 1978 it has officially taken on the task of directing MLR changes through the Bank of England.

How are the interest rates forced up by the central bank? The discount houses borrow money at call from the commercial banks in order to buy treasury bills, but if the central bank announces a tightening of credit restrictions by raising MLR the commercial banks will be less willing to lend out call money to the discount houses. The latter will then be forced to borrow money from the Bank of England itself at high MLR (instead of low call-money rate), with the central bank acting as 'lender of last resort' to the houses. When the discount houses in their turn sell these treasury bills to the commercial banks, they consequently charge them higher rates, therefore raising treasury bill rates and rates of interest more generally.

Open Market Operations Although the Bank of England has never yet raised the reserve assets ratio to increase the liquidity of banks, reduce their advances and therefore cut credit lent to industry, it does very indirectly increase liquidity and curb advances at a time of credit restriction. One measure for achieving this is *open market operations*. In Figure 7.1

Figure 7.1 Open market operations.

the central bank obtains £1000 from the assets of a commercial bank by selling a treasury bill to Mr A., one of the bank's customers. If the selling of treasury bills happens on a large scale the commercial banks have less money to lend in advances: since they have paid large sums to the central bank, they cannot reduce their holdings of reserve assets such as treasury bills, and therefore they must lend less in advances and/or in long- and medium-term investments. In this way credit is reduced, and in effect the reserve assets ratio has been raised by the banks' holding greater stocks of treasury bills and fewer medium-/long-term assets.

Special Deposits As defined earlier in this chapter (Section 7.1) this measure enables the central bank to acquire from the commercial banks, on a temporary basis, funds worth up to 4 per cent of assets and therefore, in reality, increases the reserve assets ratio. As long as the central bank also refuses to sell medium- and long-term investments, the banks must reduce their advances to pay the special deposits, and can therefore lend less to industry and individuals.

Funding At a time of credit restriction the Bank of England wants to convert short-term government bills (treasury bills) into long-term holdings of government stock. This operation, which is known as funding, is achieved when the central bank tempts holders of treasury bills to re-invest funds in new long-term government stock at higher rates of interest. This measure reduces banks' treasury bills holdings and, in order to maintain the reserve assets ratio, the banks must reduce advances, therefore lending less to industry.

Directives The Bank of England has the legal power to issue directives to commercial banks on banking policy, including credit restraint. It has never resorted to this, since the banks in a gentlemanly code accept its 'requests' to limit credit for particular purposes, e.g. to property purchasers. Such acts of moral persuasion by the Bank of England are received very seriously by the banks. Since 1971, the central bank has requested only such qualitative reductions in bank lending, as given in the example in Section 7.5 below, and it has not requested any quantitative ones.

In 1971–2 the government introduced a new banking and monetary policy called *Competition and Credit Control*, which was designed to introduce more competition into banking services and to move towards much more indirect control of credit. It is true that the directive has not been used to reduce bank lending quantitatively, but government has often changed minimum lending rate (MLR), rather than leave its determination to market forces. The other three controls are also used in ways broadly similar to those in use before 1971, so that it is not so much that the mechanism of credit control has been drastically altered, but that the approach to operating the control has been more flexible.

Summary The central bank has at its disposal a wide range of detailed methods of credit control, all of which can result in reductions in bank lending to industry and individuals.

7.5 THE BANK OF ENGLAND: USE OF CREDIT CONTROLS; 'THE CREDIT SQUEEZE'

The operation of credit control by the central bank tends to be concentrated into major efforts to combat inflation by imposing most of the controls, or an intensification of most of them, in one package, or *credit squeeze*, as it is popularly known. One of the most dramatic, perhaps the most dramatic, was the credit squeeze instituted in October 1976, which vigorously intensified existing controls. This was a response to a combination of rapid inflation, rapid increase in the money supply and consequent liquidity, and the falling external exchange rate of the pound. MLR was raised from 9 per cent to a record 15 per cent, and other interest rates soared with it. The Bank of England attacked the excess liquidity by open-market operations and funding, whilst maintaining a high level of special deposits and making a qualitative request to banks to restrict non-industrial lending. The result by the end of 1976 was a mopping-up of liquidity, a rise in the external exchange value of the pound, a further reduction in investment, and a small reduction in the rate of inflation.

Since the new competition and credit control policy of 1971–2, credit squeezes have been imposed not only on the commercial banks, but also on the specialist banks. However, firms can still acquire funds from such non-banking sources as investment trusts and pension funds. The Radcliffe Committee on the monetary system stated as long ago as 1959: 'There was general agreement among witnesses that firms denied bank credit they wanted resorted to finance companies, accepting houses and even discount houses.' These institutions have been subject since 1971–2 to a 10 per cent reserve assets ratio, but the other sources still largely exist.

A clear attempt was made in 1971–2 to introduce market forces more fully into the banking system. However, the financial crisis of 1973–4, and the need for credit squeezes during rapid inflation led to a swift return to central bank control through MLR. The use of special deposits and the directive was not abandoned even in 1971–2. Nevertheless, greater competition for deposits from the specialist banks has developed, and, in an attempt to control this more fully and to plug the gaps in credit squeeze restrictions, in 1976 the government prepared, as a policy document, a White Paper called 'The Licensing and Supervision of Deposit Taking Institutions.'

Summary The credit squeeze is a major weapon of overall government economic policy, and its use in the 1970s has necessitated continued government control of MLR and the use of specific interventionist monetary weapons, although quantitative restrictions on bank lending are no longer used.

7.6 THE BANK OF ENGLAND: THE GOVERNMENT'S BANKER

The government deposits with the Bank of England its main Exchequer account, and the accounts of government departments of state. As we have already seen the central bank, on behalf of government, issues treasury bills and medium- and long-term stock, and manages the National Debt. In addition, if the government runs into short-term deficit on its accounts, the central bank accords it overdraft facilities, as a commercial bank would do for a credit-worthy customer. This large role of the central bank means that not only is the Bank of England's relationship with the Treasury and other government departments legally a close one, it is also in day-to-day relationships a very intimate one. In this way the Bank of England has become a 'financial conscience' of the government, and gives very firm and independent judgements to it. This function of the central bank as banker to the state has developed more rapidly in the post-war period, since increased government expenditure has resulted in more of the national income passing through its own accounts.

Summary **The central bank has a close working relationship with government, partly because it handles all the state's major accounts.**

7.7 THE BANK OF ENGLAND: EXTERNAL FUNCTIONS

The central bank, like most of its counterparts in Western countries, is responsible for much of the day-to-day management of Britain's monetary relations. These external functions are basically threefold: management of the exchange equalization account; exchange control; and relationships with other international financial institutions.

Management of the Exchange Equalization Account Since 1946, the Bank of England has held and managed this account, which is designed to prevent undesirable fluctuations in currency, even during a period of floating exchange rates. Part of the account's holdings are some of the gold and foreign currency reserves of the UK, all of which are kept by the central bank. At a time of fixed exchange rates the Bank of England had to use the exchange equalization account (EEA) very regularly to keep the pound within the very narrow limits allowed. Since 1972 the pound has floated against foreign currencies, but whenever there has been excessive pressure for or against the pound, the central bank has moved in, either to buy pounds with EEA funds (to prevent a rapid fall in the pound; e.g. in September/October 1976), or to sell pounds with EEA funds (to prevent a rapid rise in the pound; e.g. in the summer of 1977). This policy of limited intervention to prevent rapid changes in currency values is known in the 1970s as *managed flexibility*. It is central bank intervention which prevents the forces of supply and demand from determining currency values. Sometimes the very basis of EEA is threatened, i.e. when there is an outflow of gold and foreign currencies from London, and in this situation the central bank raises MLR to draw back these currencies by the lure of higher interest payments (as in October 1976).

Exchange Control Free movement of currency, securities, gold and property is controlled by the central bank under the Exchange Control Act 1947. The commercial agents of the central bank, who undertake the detailed administration of these wide-ranging regulations, are approved travel agents and, once again, the commercial and specialist private banks. There has been some increase in the amounts of these valuable commodities which individuals are permitted to take out of or bring into the country in the 1960s and 1970s, with the liberalization of trade between Western countries.

Relations with Other International Financial Institutions The Bank of England is not only a national central bank but also has a role as an international financial institution, and thereby has close relations with other central banks and international financial bodies. On behalf of the small number of countries now in the sterling area (e.g. some colonies and associated states) the Bank of England holds, buys, and sells their sterling assets, and holds, buys and sells their gold and foreign currency reserves. Some foreign countries permit the Bank of England to hold and manage their sterling assets for them.

Since Britain joined the EEC in 1973, the bank has developed much closer day-to-day relations with its European counterparts. It does not participate in any EEC fixed currency arrangements, but cooperates in a practical way in maintaining currency and general monetary stability in the EEC.

In the mid 1970s the Bank of England has developed still closer relations with its counterparts in the other six major industrial countries in the non-communist world, particularly to ensure monetary cooperation and stability in major recession.

At a broader international level the bank participates in the Bank for International Settlements (BIS), and the International Monetary Fund (IMF), the Governor of the Bank of England being the British Governor (i.e. senior British official) of the IMF. The bank both advises government on IMF policy decisions (e.g. those concerning loans to countries in acute balance-of-payments deficit, or new funds for IMF), and also does the practical work, with IMF, of organizing loan facilities from that body when Britain is in serious balance-of-payments trouble. The massive IMF loan arranged for this purpose in December 1976 was negotiated by the British government, but the 'nuts-and-bolts' job of administering the loan facility practically was the bank's role. In a similar way, the bank represents the UK at an official level in the International Bank for Reconstruction and Development (IBRD), advising government on decisions about the IBRD's role as a provider of funds for projects in the developing countries.

The Bank of England's developing administrative partnership with foreign central banks and its role in foreign exchange markets require it to learn and retain information, and this principle can conflict with that of public accountability to Parliament as Britain's central bank, and as a nationalized firm. A select committee of the House of Commons examined this matter in the late 1960s, and tried to establish which activities of the central bank required confidentiality. The committee clearly established that foreign exchange was one such activity, and that helping important financial institutions in difficulties was another. As a result of the committee's and of internal reviews by the central bank itself, much more information about its work is made available to Parliament and the general public. The *Bank of England Quarterly Bulletin*, in its external relations sections, is no longer a generalized summary of events, but provides a valuable and detailed picture of the important aspects of day-to-day management of external monetary relations. The 'Old Lady of Threadneedle Street' has become up-to-date, but by no means trendy.

Summary The central bank manages the day-to-day monetary external relations of the UK and it intervenes, using the exchange equalization account, in international currency markets to prevent large changes in the value of the pound. Its cooperation with other central banks concerning monetary stability, particularly in the EEC and with the USA, Canada and Japan, has developed considerably.

7.9 CONCLUDING REMARKS

The British banking system in the early 1970s has undergone some apparently important changes, such as the Competition and Credit Control policy and the floating of the pound, but the effects of these changes have been much less than were envisaged. The central bank still uses, basically, the same array of monetary restrictions to control credit issued by the private banks. It is true, however, that nowadays all banks, not only the commercial banks, are in the central bank's net. The central bank still intervenes in foreign exchange markets to prevent large fluctuations in the value of the pound, although it does so less regularly than in the years of fixed exchange rates. The private banking institutions still do not offer full price competition to acquire deposits, but they do compete in quality of service and there is a persistent expansion of specialist banks into this general banking business. It is the latter development which might accelerate into the most fundamental change in the British banking system in the 1970s.

QUESTIONS

1 What was 'Competition and Credit Control' policy?

2 What is the purpose of open-market operations?

3 What is the function of specialist banks?

4 Explain the value to commercial banks and government of treasury bills.

5 What controls on credit supply does the Bank of England use?

6 What are advances?

7 What is the exchange equalization account?

8 List the main external functions of the Bank of England.

EXERCISES

1 Discuss the main reasons for the introduction of 'Competition and Credit Control' policy.

2 Has the 'Competition and Credit Control' policy been more a change of form than of substance?

3 What are the credit control techniques actually operated by the Bank of England, and which would you argue is the most powerful?

4 What examples are there of qualitative credit controls?

5 Which financial institutions really possess credit creation powers?

6 What is the influence of cheque cards (e.g. Barclaycard) on the banks and on monetary expansion?

7 Should specialist banks be as rigidly controlled by the Bank of England as are commercial banks?

8 What is the effect upon the economy's production, employment and price levels of a 'credit squeeze'?

Chapter Eight

Consumer Behaviour Theory

We shall now focus attention on microeconomics, first on the economic behaviour of individual consumers and then on individual producers in the market. The forces of demand and supply meet in the market for goods and services, and prices are formed there by the interaction of the demand and supply factors. Therefore we shall go on to discuss prices and production under perfect competition, where there are so many consumers and producers in the market that no one can influence prices. Later, we shall examine prices and production under other market conditions, in which the competitive element is considerably reduced or non-existent (e.g. monopoly and oligopoly).

As we shall see, the behaviour of consumers and suppliers can be expressed by demand and supply functions respectively, and we shall first look at how the demand function can be derived from consumer behaviour. Consumer behaviour is based on consumer preferences which are usually accepted as data external to economics. This approach has recently been criticized, and not without reason, partly because advertising – which is, of course, motivated by economic considerations – can mould consumer preference, and partly because, when new products are being developed, it is the firms which take the initiative and the households which are at the receiving end. We shall emphasize in Chapter 10 the role of advertising and companies which have oligopoly and monopoly power. The fact remains, however, that even according to traditional economic theory, a knowledge of consumer behaviour is important in understanding how the prices of goods are formed. We shall see how much this behaviour is based on personal preference. It should also be stressed that the overall purchasing pattern reflects not only the consumers' preferences but also that part of their demands which is backed up by their purchasing power, and that therefore the level of individual income and of income distribution play an important part in this respect.

This supply and demand behaviour determines prices on the market. Suppliers like ICI and British Leyland and consumers in the households use prices as general guidelines for their decisions about the production and purchase of goods. Thus, the high price of an article created by a high demand for it will encourage firms to produce this good, or make more of it, from resources that could be used for other purposes. There is much discussion at present about the operation of the price mechanism, the role of the government in this connection, and the need to correct the results of the price mechanism. If we want to follow this discussion and participate in it, we need to gain an insight into the way prices are determined in our economy.

8.1 THE CONSUMERS' PREFERENCE PATTERN

Consumers consciously or subconsciously compare various possible purchases and finally express a preference for one article by buying it. The theory of consumer behaviour is based on the finding that consumers can, in fact, express their preference. This preference may be for a combination of goods, e.g. ten apples and two pears rather than nine apples and four pears. The reason why more *utility* (i.e. consumer satisfaction) is apparent in the first combination is not discussed in economics; the way consumers arrive at their preference patterns is something on which economists simply accept the data obtained in other branches of social science, such as psychology.

It used to be thought possible to tell how much greater the utility of one good or set of goods was than that of another, for utility was thought to be measurable. However, the Italian economist Pareto (1848–1923) did not agree with this view and said that the consumer could only put the goods in order of preference or priority, i.e. could only say whether he values a certain combination of articles more or less than another combination, without putting numerical figures on his valuations. If consumers can express preferences, they are also able to express indifference.

Expression of Consumers' Indifference between Combinations of Goods To understand consumer behaviour we start first by establishing which combinations of products give the same satisfaction. Once this approach is grasped the remainder of consumer behaviour theory is much more readily understood. For example, we can show apple–pear combinations that are equally acceptable to the consumer, by plotting the amount of pears along the horizontal axis and the amount of apples along the vertical axis, obtaining curves of the type shown in Figure 8.1. Here a combination of 18 kg of apples and 2 kg of pears, represented by point P, has exactly the same utility for a given consumer as the combination of 10 kg of apples and 4 kg of pears, represented by point Q. Such graphical presentations are called indifference curves, because the consumer is indifferent as to which combination lying along a particular curve he chooses, i.e. he is indifferent as to whether he consumes 18 kg apples + 2 kg pears or 10 kg apples + 4 kg pears. A combination of 18 kg of apples and 4 kg of pears, represented by point T, gives the consumer more utility than the combination represented by point P. Point T therefore lies on a higher indifference curve, together with all the other combinations of the same higher utility, for the consumer. It is possible to construct an infinite series of indifference curves, each being further from the origin and representing a higher utility, in the way that indifference curve 3 in Figure 8.1 represents a higher utility than indifference curve 2. Of course, to simplify the

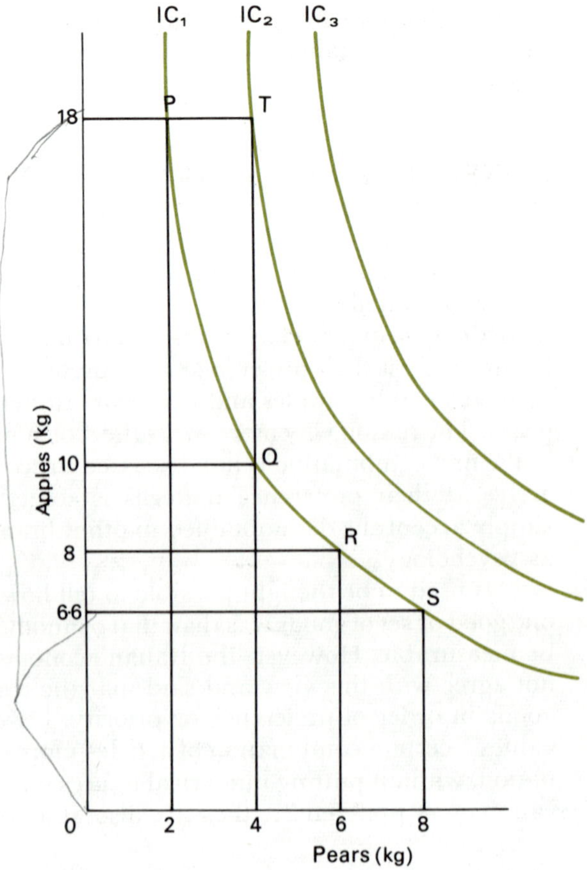

Figure 8.1 Consumer indifference pattern.

situation only three such curves, representing only three different levels of satisfaction, are drawn in here.

Marginal Utility We must now explain why these curves are convex to the origin. If we move from point P to points Q, R and S, the amount of pears always increases by 2 kg, while the amount of apples decreases first by 8, then by 2 and finally by 1.4 kg. This means that, in the first instance, the consumer is prepared to forgo more apples (8 kg) for an extra 2 kg of pears (i.e. when moving from point P to point Q) than in the second instance (2 kg, when moving from point Q to point R). In other words, he finds it more difficult to forgo an apple in the second case. In general, the fewer units of a certain good he consumes, the more extra utility – *marginal utility* – he attributes to an extra unit of the good in question. Conversely, he finds less utility in extra quantities of pears as his stock of pears increases. In general, the marginal utility of a good decreases as the stock of this good held by the user increases. Thus the more Coca Cola he consumes the lower is his satisfaction from each extra unit of Coca Cola. The situation in Figure 8.1 provides an extension of this explanation in terms of two goods. It shows how the consumer is less willing to give up apples for one pear as his consumption of pears in relation to apples increases. The number of apples being given up for one pear reflects the rate of substitution between apples and pears. As we follow the indifference curve from left to right, we see that the rate of substitution (the slope) is diminishing. This also refers to small changes, i.e. marginal changes, and therefore we can also say that the marginal rate of substitution is diminishing. This *law of diminishing marginal rate of substitution* therefore explains why indifference curves are convex to the origin, as in Figure 8.1. The law of diminishing marginal rate of substitution states that a consumer is less willing to give up one good for another as his consumption of the latter increases in relation to the former.

When there are more than two goods, the preference pattern cannot be illustrated by two-dimensional graphs, but it can still be discussed, and the discussion then covers the consumers' expression of their preference or indifference for a large number of goods.

Summary The consumers' scale of preference, which is the starting point of the theory of consumer behaviour, can be illustrated very clearly by indifference curves. All the combinations of two given goods which represent the same utility or satisfaction for the consumer lie on the same indifference curve. The further the curves lie from the origin, the greater the utility. The indifference curves are convex to the origin.

8.2 MAXIMUM SATISFACTION OF WANTS AND CONSUMERS' EQUILIBRIUM

Consumers want to maximize the satisfaction of their wants, i.e. utility, and will therefore choose combinations of goods that lie on the highest indifference curves compatible with their income. The question is therefore which combinations of goods maximize the consumer's utility, or, to

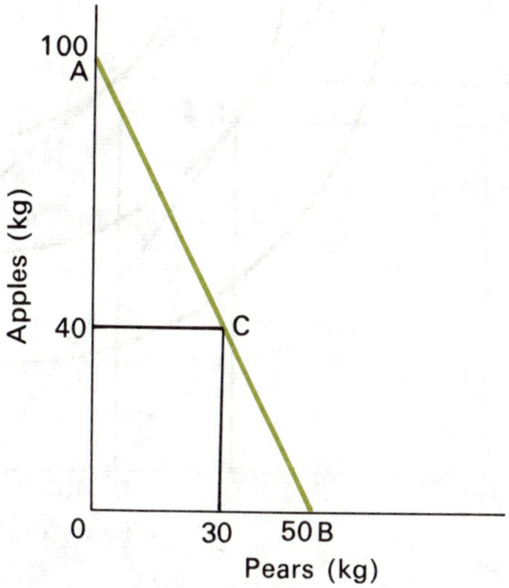

Figure 8.2 Budget line.

use the alternative term, his satisfaction at a given income and given price of goods.

Budget Line Let us assume a consumer with an income of £100 who spends it all on apples and pears costing £1 and £2 per kg, respectively, and suppose that these prices remain the same irrespective of the amounts purchased, so that the consumer does not get a discount. In this situation, the consumer can adjust only the quantities of his purchases. Our consumer can buy either 100 kg of apples or 50 kg of pears if he spends his whole income either on apples or on pears. These extreme cases are represented by points A and B in Figure 8.2. He could also buy any combination of apples and pears that lies on the line between points A and B, which is called the budget line. At point C he can therefore buy 40 kg of apples and 30 kg of pears, thus spending his total income of £100. This line is the boundary between combinations the consumer can afford and those he cannot afford. He can afford those combinations to the left of the budget line but cannot afford those to the right of the budget line. This line is a straight line because we have assumed the prices of apples and pears do not change if the consumer demands more apples and pears. The slope of the budget line is determined by the price ratio of apples and pears: the lower the price of apples relative to the price of pears, the steeper the slope of the budget line.

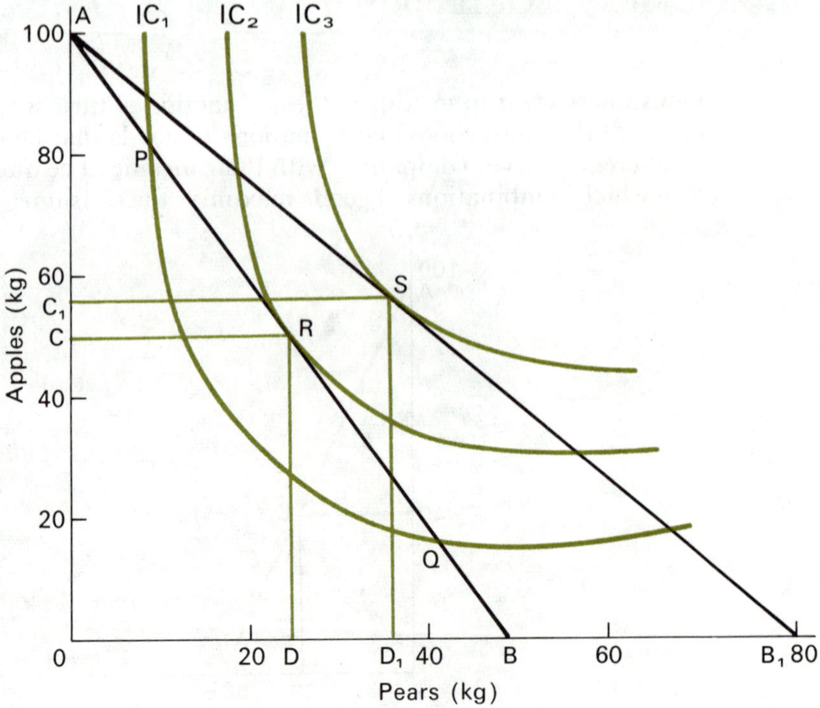

Figure 8.3 Consumer maximization of satisfaction.

Consumer Maximization of Satisfaction of Wants To discover which combination of goods lying on the budget line offers the consumer the highest utility (satisfaction), we construct a number of indifference curves, as shown in Figure 8.3. The first curve represents combinations of goods having the same utility (i.e. satisfaction), including points P and Q on that curve.

The budget line meets the second indifference curve at point R, which represents a greater utility (i.e. satisfaction) than any point on the first indifference curve, since the second curve is placed further from the origin. R therefore also represents the maximum utility available to him, given his income and the current prices. The consumer will therefore choose the combination of goods represented by point R, since this is where the budget line meets at a tangent the highest indifference curve compatible with his present income and prices. This point, which corresponds to a combination of 50 kg of apples at C and 25 kg of pears at D, represents an equilibrium state for the consumer: any other combination lying on the budget line would offer him less utility, so that he will not want to change the situation represented by point R. If, for example, he substituted £1 of apples for £1 of pears, or vice versa, and moved therefore a small way up or down the budget line, he would in both cases arrive at a point on the same lower indifference curve. Thus at point R we can say that the marginal utility (or extra satisfaction) from consuming £1 worth of apples or of pears is the same.

Now R lies on both an indifference curve and a budget line, the slopes of which will be identical at R. The marginal rate of substitution of apples for pears is measured by the slope of this indifference curve. At this equilibrium point the ratio of the price of apples to pears, i.e. the slope of the budget line, equals the marginal rate of substitution of apples for pears which is the slope of the indifference curve at R. Since the ratio of the marginal utilities of apples and pears equals the marginal rate of substitution of apples for pears, it must also equal the price ratio of apples to pears at point R.

Therefore $\frac{P_a}{P_p} = \frac{M_{ua}}{M_{up}}$.

So for maximum satisfaction the marginal utility of apples divided by its price equals the marginal utility of pears divided by its price, i.e.

$$\frac{M_{ua}}{P_a} = \frac{M_{up}}{P_p}.$$

Summary The point where the budget line meets the highest possible indifference curve compatible with the consumer's income and prices represents the state of equilibrium for the consumer, where a change to any other combination of goods would only lower the total utility he can obtain. It is assumed here that the consumer can only select quantities of goods and cannot influence prices.

8.3 CHANGES IN PRICES AND INCOMES

We have seen so far how many apples and pears are demanded by the consumer when the prices of apples and pears and his income are known and fixed. Let us now examine how these quantities of apples and pears demanded will change when firstly prices and secondly income alter.

Change in Price If, for some reason such as a glut of pears, the price of pears drops from £2 kg to £1.25 kg, the consumer could buy as many as 80 kg of pears if he spent all his income on them. This situation, too, can be seen in Figure 8.3. The point of intersection of the budget line AB with the horizontal axis shifts from B to B_1, since the consumer can now purchase a maximum quantity of pears of OB_1 instead of OB. The point of intersection of the budget line with the vertical axis remains the same, because the maximum quantity of apples the consumer can purchase is still 100 kg. The budget line is still a straight line because we maintain the assumption that both prices are constant, and this line now runs from A on the vertical axis to B_1 on the horizontal axis.

The indifference curves remain the same, and using the new budget line, AB_1, we see that the consumer has a new equilibrium point, S, on indifference curve 3 in Figure 8.3. This point S represents a combination of 56 kg (OC_1) of apples, and 35 kg (OD_1) of pears. We note that the drop in the price of pears has led to an increase in the demand for them of 10 kg, and also to an increase in the demand for apples of 6 kg. Therefore, the change in the price of pears has not only altered the consumers' demand for them; it has also changed his demand for apples. This is a very important element in the theory of consumer behaviour: the demand for a good depends not simply on its own price but also on the prices charged for all other goods. Therefore, any price change will also alter the real income of the consumer. This real income is represented by the basket of goods that can be purchased with his money income. If his money income were to be unchanged, and prices then went up, his real income would decline, because he could not buy as large a basket of goods at the new higher prices.

When money income remains unchanged and the price of pears falls, as in our example, the consumer's real income increases. He can therefore buy a larger basket of goods at the new lower price, and he demands both more pears and more apples. Figure 8.4 depicts these changes.

Change in Income Let us now examine the effects on consumer demand of a change in monetary income when the prices of apples and pears remain constant. If the consumer's monetary income per week rises from £100 to £150, a new budget line (A_1B_1) parallel to the old budget line (AB) is attained. There has been no change in the price ratio of the apples and pears, so the slope of the budget line remains the same, and it is therefore parallel to the old budget line. If the consumer were to spend all his new higher money income on apples, he would buy 150 kg of them, and if he were to spend it all on pears, he would buy 75 kg of those. The new point of intersection of the budget line with the horizontal axis is at B_1, and with the vertical axis at A_1. The consumer in this new situation is able to reach a higher indifference curve (IC_4), and the optimal combination of apples and pears, where he maximizes utility, is point T on Figure 8.4. At this point he consumes 75 kg of apples and 40 kg of pears. We can see that the rise in income has led to an increase in demand for apples of 25 kg, and an increase in demand for pears of 15 kg. The demand for both goods is therefore changed by a rise in income.

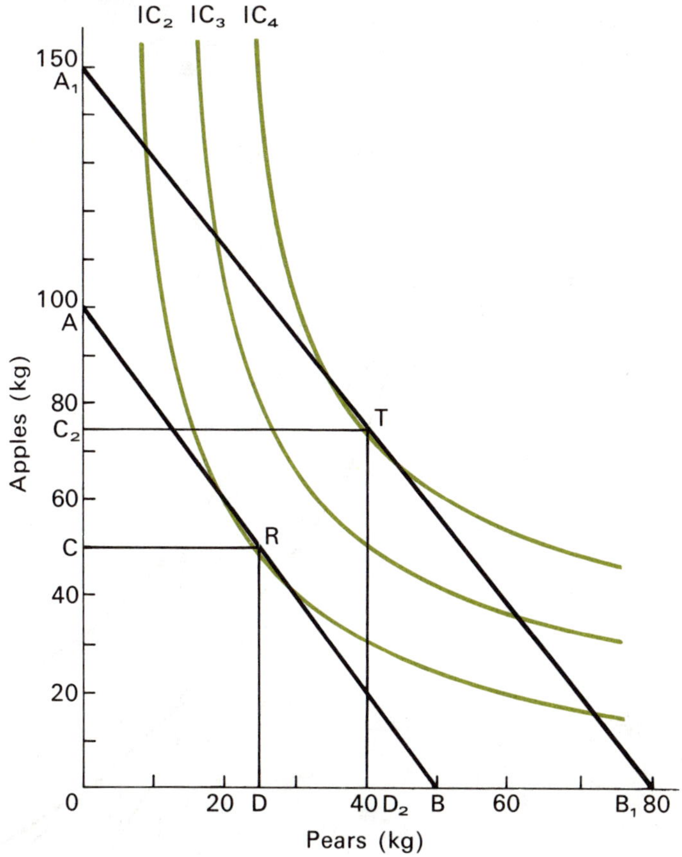

Figure 8.4 Income changes.

Summary The optimum combination of goods demanded by the consumer depends on the prices of all goods and income.

8.4 THE INCOME EFFECT AND THE SUBSTITUTION EFFECT

It is now possible to analyse the effect of a fall in the price of a good on the optimal combination of goods demanded by the consumer.

A fall in the price of a good has both a substitution effect and an income effect. The substitution effect is that, at a constant price of the other goods, the good in question becomes cheaper in relative terms, and the consumer demands more of it to substitute it for the other goods which have become more expensive in relative terms. The substitution effect will always raise the amount demanded of this good. The income effect is that at a constant monetary income the real income increases due to the fall in price of any good. The income effect can raise or lower the amount of a good demanded.

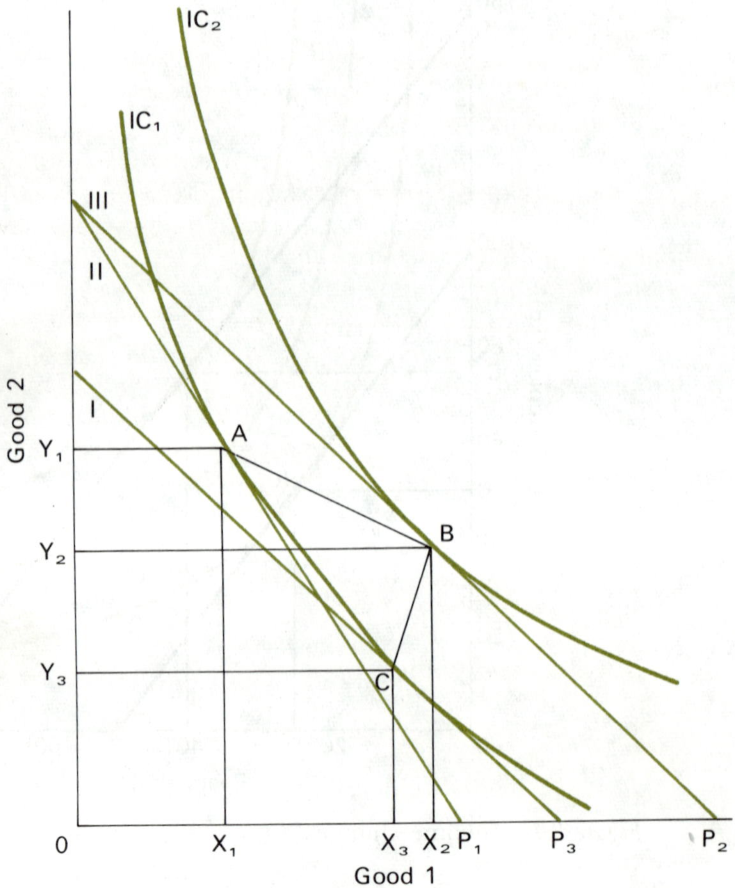

Figure 8.5 Income and substitution effects.

These effects are illustrated in Figure 8.5 in the case of two goods, 1 and 2. Before the price fall the maximum satisfaction is represented by point A on the indifference curve IC_1. After the price fall represented by budget line III, the maximum satisfaction derives from point B on the indifference curve IC_2. Now any budget line which we draw parallel to budget line III, so giving it the same slope as III, will also express the new price relationship between good 1 and good 2. If we draw such a line (I) just touching IC_1 at C, C represents the point at which the *same* satisfaction is obtained as at A, taking into account the new price of good 1 but *without* spending the total income available. Thus the price change allows the same satisfaction of A and C through the *substitution* of good 1 (X_1X_3) for good 2, the consumption of which drops by Y_1Y_3. This is the substitution effect, i.e. the extent to which the change in price alters the proportions of good 1 and good 2 which need to be purchased to give the same satisfaction as before. However, a satisfaction *higher* than A or C can be obtained by moving to III and spending all the money available. This occurs at point B where the indifference curve IC_2 meets the new budget line III. In moving from C to B we see the *income* effect in action with an increase X_3X_2 in good 1 and Y_3Y_2 in good 2. For the cheaper good 1, the price change has meant a total increased consumption of X_1X_2 comprising a substitution effect X_1X_3 and an income effect X_3X_2. For good 2 the negative effect of substitution Y_1Y_2 is counteracted by the income effect Y_2Y_3 so that the total decreased consumption is Y_1Y_2. The overall result here is that the demand for good 1 increases and that for good 2 decreases. This is the normal case, since good 1 is now relatively cheaper and good 2 is relatively more expensive.

However, there are two important exceptions to this normal case: *inferior* goods and *status* goods. With inferior goods the income effect works in the opposite direction to the substitution effect and is greater than it. A case in point would be with a rise in the price of bread. The substitution effect would work in favour of more purchases of another good but nevertheless the greater income effect on the consumer would result in a net increase in the purchase of bread rather than the other good. Goods which are treated in this way are often called Giffen goods after Sir Robert Giffen who analysed purchasing patterns of poorer members of the community in the nineteenth century. He argued that bread was the staple diet of the poor and an increase in its price meant less income available to purchase more expensive substitutes and therefore more bread was actually purchased.

With status goods the income effect and the substitution effect work in the same direction although the income effect is more powerful than the substitution effect. This combination results in the consumer purchasing less of the lower status good, e.g. linoleum, and more of the higher status good, e.g. carpet.

Both inferior goods and status goods are unusual in the context of consumer patterns in the late twentieth century; our normal case is much more typical.

Summary **The magnitude of the substitution effect and the income effect determines the ways in which a consumer may react to a change in the price of a good.**

8.5 THE DEMAND CURVE FOR THE INDIVIDUAL AND THE MARKET DEMAND CURVE

Individual's Demand Curve The matters we have discussed so far in this chapter lead us to an important conclusion: the individual's demand for each good depends on all prices of all goods and on the individual's income – as long as we assume that the individual's preferences are given and fixed. We shall refer to this relationship as the *individual demand function*. We denote the individual's demand for quantity of goods as Q, the prices of goods as P_1 (for article 1), P_2 (for article 2), P_3 (for article 3), etc., and income as i. Therefore the individual's demand function is

$$Q = f(P_1, P_2, P_3 \ldots P_n, i)$$

This demand function follows immediately from the theory of consumer behaviour which we have discussed in the earlier sections of this chapter.

It is common practice to study the relationship between the individual's demand for a good and the price of the good, assuming that all other prices, consumer income and consumer preferences remain given and fixed. In this situation, we are making use of the *ceteris paribus* principle, i.e. that all other things remain given and fixed, whilst we study the behaviour of two variables, in this case the individual's demand for pears and the price of pears. In Figure 8.6 a demand curve, DD, is drawn which depicts the individual demand function. If the price of pears is

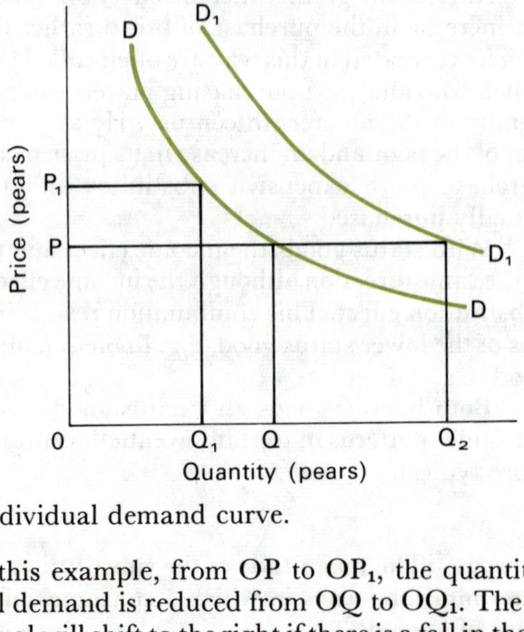

Figure 8.6 Individual demand curve.

increased, in this example, from OP to OP_1, the quantity of pears the individual will demand is reduced from OQ to OQ_1. The demand curve for the individual will shift to the right if there is a fall in the prices of other goods (and income and preferences are constant and fixed). In this case we obtain a new demand curve, D_1D_1, and at the same price of pears, OP, the demand for pears increases to OQ_2. We should distinguish between a shift in the demand curve as in the latter case, and a movement along the demand curve as in the former case.

Engel Curve We can also study the relationship between the quantity of pears demanded and income, leaving all prices and preferences given and fixed. In this case a curve, as in Figure 8.7, can be drawn: this is called an Engel curve after the nineteenth-century German statistician of that name. Engel argued that the consumer initially increases his demand for the good more than in direct proportion to the increase in income, but that after a certain level of income is achieved his consumption of the good increases less than in proportion to further increases in income (see Figure 8.6).

Figure 8.7 Engel curve.

Market Demand Curve As well as constructing the individual demand function, we can also construct a market demand function. The market demand function accounts for the demand for a good in terms of the prices of all goods and the income of all consumers – as long as we assume that the preferences of consumers are given and fixed. In order to obtain the market demand function some kind of aggregation procedure is required, and in a simplified form this can mean aggregating the individual demand functions. We can construct this simplified market demand function by adding up the demand functions for all individuals, and in Figure 8.8 we do this for two individual demand functions.

It is not only the prices of goods and incomes which influence the market demand function, however; changes in size of population and income distribution also have their effects. If population rises there are more consumers and therefore the demand for goods will rise, as long as these form a basic part of people's wants, as do fruits in most countries. When there is a redistribution of income which favours lower-income groups, who tend to spend more of their incomes than do those with higher incomes, more fruit will be bought – as long as it forms part of people's basic wants.

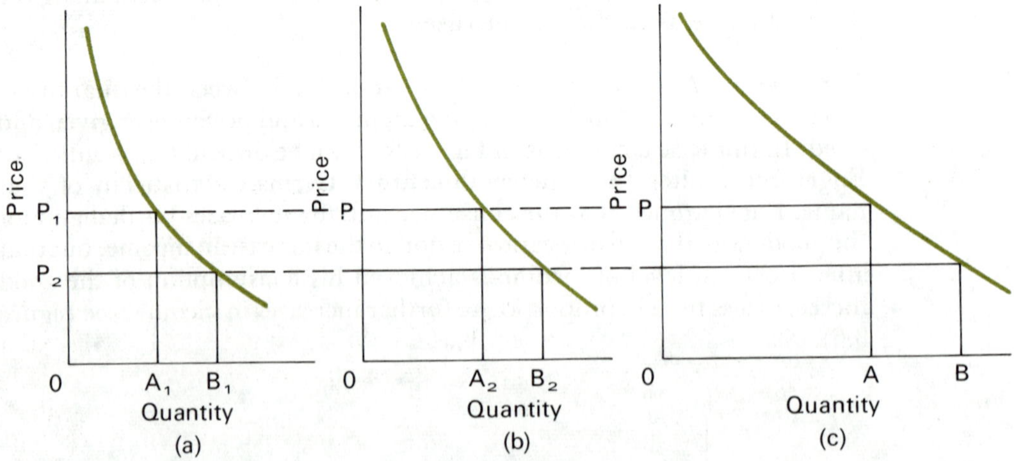

Figure 8.8 Market demand curve.

Market Demand Curve and Macroeconomic Consumption Function The market demand functions are necessary complements of the macroeconomic consumption function, which we discussed in Section 4.2, because they tell us the composition of total spending and indicate the factors that influence it. The macroeconomic consumption curve shows how much is spent at various levels of the national income, but it does not give us details of how much is spent on particular goods. Analysis of consumer behaviour has now shown that the detailed pattern of consumption depends in particular on prices. At given consumer preferences, changes in relative prices lead to a change in the combination of goods consumed and thus in the structure of consumption. When the price of a product falls for some reason such as technical development, the consumers use this as a signal urging them to change their market position. A certain 'communication' thus arises between different parts of the economy. The market demand curve derived for a certain good from the theory of consumer behaviour does not tell us the price that will actually emerge on the market, only how much the consumers would buy at various prices. However, only one of these prices will actually prevail, and it will be shown later (Chapter 10) how this price is determined.

Summary The individual demand curve shows how the amount of a given good demanded by one consumer varies with its prices when all other conditions such as the prices of other goods, consumer's income and preferences are given and fixed. The Engel curve shows the relationship between quantity demanded and individual consumer income when prices and consumer preferences are given and fixed. The market demand function explains how demand for a product depends on its price when the prices of all other goods, consumers' incomes and consumer preferences are assumed to be given and fixed.

8.6 PSYCHOLOGICAL AND SOCIAL ASPECTS OF CONSUMER BEHAVIOUR

The consumer behaviour theory discussed here is based on the adoption of a consumer preference pattern, including consumers' tastes, which has been given to us by non-economic forces. Once the preferences are given, the total demand for goods is determined by the incomes, income distribution, prices and the number of consumers, and we now have a fairly large body of information on how these factors affect the market situations. For example, market research uses various statistical techniques for predicting the effects of changes in prices and incomes. However, more and more economists want to know why a consumer makes a certain purchase – a question which, involving as it does the preference pattern, lies outside economics. To analyse the purchasing motives, we must turn to psychology. This reveals the involvement of a great variety of partly subconscious motives which can, in addition, vary in the course of time. However, motivation research, based on various psychological techniques, yields useful information for guiding more effective marketing of companies. For example, once consumers' motives for buying motor cars are known, an advertising campaign, geared to these motives, can be devised for making a new model attractive to consumers.

Consumers' perception and ability to learn are also important factors in consumer behaviour. The first determines how they will view the virtually infinite variety of goods and distinguish between them. Will they, in fact, accept the claimed difference between detergent A and detergent B in terms of cleansing power? Or will they simply buy detergent A because it is in a red packet? The consumers' ability to learn will determine the extent, quality and frequency of information which, through advertising, needs to be presented. Although the investigation of these two characteristics is still in its infancy, it is here that we can expect a further refinement in the analysis of purchasing behaviour. Moreover, the consumer is also a member of several distinct social groups (e.g. family, business or profession, and sports club), and his purchasing behaviour is further influenced by the interaction with the other members of these groups. The commercial value of detailed classification is illustrated by the case of 'consumer first-purchasers', those who are the first to buy a new product. They share particular character traits and also exhibit a clearly definable group behaviour.

Summary Consumer behaviour theory gains still more practical importance if consumer preferences are subjected to detailed psychological and sociological analysis.

8.7 CONCLUDING REMARKS

This chapter has dealt with the consumer behaviour theory, first developed by Pareto. As Pareto pointed out, utility cannot be measured, merely ranked. Gossen's first law of diminishing marginal rate of satisfaction defines the shape of the indifference curves. Gossen, who lived in the middle of the nineteenth century, was a forerunner of the *marginal utility school*, which was founded around 1870 and included Menger, Jevons and Walras, and concentrated on the role of the consumer in economic life. This was a reaction to the earlier classical school of Smith, Ricardo and Malthus, which focused attention on the production side of the economy, particularly on free enterprise production at national and international levels.

The marginal utility school, or 'marginalism', had three branches, the Austrian, the Cambridge and the Lausanne schools. The first one counted Menger, Wieser and Böhm-Bawerk among its members, and Schumpeter was a later advocate of its views. The Cambridge school was founded by Marshall, who researched developments, on production in the macroeconomy, shown by the advocates of the classical school, and also strongly developed consumer and producer marginal theory. Finally, the Lausanne school was founded by Walras and included Pareto among its members. Walras and his followers also made extensive use of mathematical methods.

The equilibrium condition of the consumer can be defined with the aid of a budget line and indifference curves. By changing the income and the prices, one can gain an insight into the valid construction of the individual demand curve. Finally, the market demand function can be derived by aggregating the individual demand curves. The theory outlined in this chapter has recently come under serious criticism, partly because it ignores the effect of personal wealth on consumer spending, and partly because it adopts consumer preference as fixed and not susceptible to change. The increasing importance of advertising in creating wants and the realization that the goods available are also largely determined by the state of technology all cast doubts on the traditional view of consumer preference. These factors are much more fully considered in Chapter 11. In conclusion, this criticism undermines our confidence in the validity of our model of the price mechanism, on the grounds that consumers can receive signals from the producers but consumers have only a limited ability to send out signals themselves.

QUESTIONS

1. What is the indifference curve?
2. What is the difference between consumer behaviour theory before Pareto and that after him?

3 Why is the budget line straight?

4 What is marginal utility?

5 What is the law of diminishing marginal rate of substitution?

6 Why must the marginal utility of one good divided by the price equal the marginal utility of another good divided by its price?

7 What is an individual demand curve?

8 What is a market demand curve?

9 What can shift the market demand curve?

10 Why will the consumer choose the combination of goods that corresponds to the point of contact between the budget line and one of the indifference curves?

11 What are the income effect and the substitution effect?

12 When investigating the question why a consumer buys something, one has to leave the subject of economics at a certain point. Why is this so?

EXERCISES

1 Can two indifference curves intersect?

2 What does it indicate when the indifference curves are straight lines?

3 A youth has £9 of pocket money, which he spends on chicken-portions and petrol for his motor bike. The price of the former varies, while that of the latter is constant at £0.75 per gallon. When the portion of chicken costs £0.30, his best combination of goods will be 12.5 chicken portions and 6 gallons of petrol. When chicken portions cost £0.75, the best combination is 6 portions and 6 gallons; when chicken costs £1.20, it is 4 portions and 5.5 gallons; and when chicken costs £1.50, it is 3.5 portions and 5 gallons.

(a) Draw this youth's demand curve for chicken portions.

(b) How does this demand curve change when his pocket money is increased?

4 Use the figures in exercise 3 above to construct the budget line and draw suitable indifference curves against it.

5 What combination will this boy buy if chicken portions cost £0.15?

6 The following connection exists between the price of a product and the amount of it purchased:

Price (pence)	*Amount purchased (in units)*
74	20
62	30
55	40
48	50
43	60
33	80
25	100
19	120
14	140

Draw the demand curve on the basis of these figures.

7 The following figures have been obtained on the relationship between incomes and the money spent on tea and coffee:

Income (× 1000) pence	*Money spent on tea and coffee*
5	92
6	108
7	110
8	117
9	127
10	135
11	134
12	152
13	149

Plotting the income along the horizontal axis and the consumption along the vertical axis gives an Engel curve. Calculate the percentage increase in consumption that results from a percentage increase in income in some income groups.

8 Discuss how much effect advertising has on consumer preference. Does advertising interfere with the operation of the price mechanism?

Chapter Nine

Producer Behaviour Theory

When producers or firms are mentioned one may think of very large or multinational companies which exert a great influence on economic life and often feature in the news, because of large profits or redundancies. However, business life is not synonymous with these large companies – we also have numerous small firms, tradesmen and shopkeepers. While large companies provide employment for very many people (and contribute a great deal to state funds in the form of taxes), nearly 40 per cent of the working population earn their living in another unit of business life, the small firm.

Many controversial issues relate to the role and nature of firms in our society: What is the aim of the firm? Is profit necessary? How should it be used? Do firms have too much power? Should investment be determined only by the firms or also by the nation via the government? These are just a few of the topical questions under discussion in economics, and the answers will involve both positive statements or descriptions ('what there is') and value judgements or prescriptions ('what there ought to be'). In other words, the problem involves both an analysis of reality and proposals as to how production should be organized. The prescriptive answers are beyond the scope of this textbook, so it must suffice to raise these important social questions in order to stimulate discussion.

However, we must have some idea of the factors that condition the behaviour of the firm, namely costs of production, revenues from production, the market situation and objectives. We shall accept, without giving approval or otherwise, that profit maximization is a major determinant of the behaviour of the firm. In neither approving nor condemning this, our aim is to analyse reality. Influencing or changing the nature of the economic situation is a political matter and as such will not be considered here.

We have seen in the last chapter how the market demand function, derived from consumer behaviour theory, shows how society's demand for a given good varies with its price and we shall now examine how the total supply of a given good varies with its price, that is to say, we shall derive the market supply function. However, this is possible only if perfect competition is assumed, because only then do the firms have to accept the market price as a given factor, so that they can decide only the quantities that are the best for them to produce.

As with the market demand function, the market supply function is obtained by aggregating – i.e. adding up – the individual supply functions. We must therefore firstly obtain these individual functions, each of which shows how much a given firm will supply of a certain good at various prices. The firm must first of all derive the cost function, which shows how the costs vary with the output.

The greater the output, the higher the total cost, but not necessarily in the same proportions. If we assume a constant state of technology and a constant amount of capital within the firm, the more labour is combined with this capital, the higher is the resulting output. However, the output does not rise in strict proportion to the extra amounts of labour employed. This will be examined in the following section.

9.1 THE LAW OF INCREASING AND DIMINISHING RETURNS

To repeat what has been said before, experience has shown that when a constant amount of a factor of production (say, land) is combined successively with increasing units of a variable factor of production (say, labour), the total output (e.g. grain) first increases more than in proportion to the increase in the variable factor, labour, then less than in proportion to it, and later still it actually decreases. This applies not only to agriculture but also to industry. This empirical rule is illustrated by the figures given in Table 9.1.

Imagine a farmer with a certain plot of land which he initially works with one man, and from which he harvests five tons of grain. Now suppose that he hires more and more workers to cultivate his land. At first, every time he hires an extra man, his output goes up more than in proportion. Thus, by working with five men (i.e. five times as many as initially) his output is 55 units (i.e. 11 times as much as the initial five units). But then, starting with the sixth man, the output increases less than that resulting from the employment of the last man. For example, 12 men produce 126 units, while six produced 70 units, so that a doubling of the manpower has not doubled the output (it is not 140). The fifteenth worker adds nothing to the output of the first 14 workers (see column 3 of the table) and with the employment of further workers the total output in fact drops and the extra output is negative. Does the fifteenth man stop the fourteenth working, or what?

Average Product and Marginal Product The output per worker, shown in the last column, is of course obtained by dividing the total output by the number of workers in each case. The figures are seen to increase up to the eighth worker, after which they steadily decrease. The highest addition to output (or, as we would call it in economics, the highest *marginal product*) is obtained with employment of the fifth worker and the highest output per worker with eight workers. This means that the average product per

Table 9.1 Increasing and diminishing returns.

Workers	*Physical product*	*Marginal physical product*	*Average physical product*
1	5	5	5.0
2	13	8	6.5
3	25	12	8.3
4	39	14	9.7
5	55	16	11.0
6	70	15	11.6
7	84	14	12.0
8	96	12	12.0
9	106	10	11.8
10	114	8	11.4
11	121	7	11.0
12	126	5	10.3
13	130	4	10.0
14	132	2	9.4
15	132	0	8.8
16	130	−2	8.1

person (or *average product*) carries on increasing after the marginal product has reached the maximum and started to fall. This is not surprising, since the seventh worker still adds 14 units to the total output and the average product for the first six workers is only 11.6 units, so that the average product for seven workers will be higher than with six workers. For a given number of workers, as long as the extra (i.e. marginal) output from an additional worker is greater than the current average product, the latter will rise with his employment; when it is smaller than the average product, the latter will decrease.

Graphical Presentation of this Law These relationships are illustrated by Figure 9.1 where diagram a is obtained by plotting the number of workers along the horizontal axis and the total product along the vertical axis, while diagram b is obtained by plotting the number of workers along the horizontal axis and the marginal product and the average along the vertical axis. Since the scale is the same for both horizontal axes, it is easy to read off that with four workers, for example, the total output is 39 units, the marginal product is 14 units and the average product is 9.7 units.

The proportionately greater increase in the total product (OB) as the number of workers increases corresponds to a steady increase in the marginal product (O_1B_1) and a less sharp rise in the average output (O_1C_1). Over the next section, BD, the total product increases less than in proportion to the increase in workers and the marginal product declines to zero (B_1D_1). Finally, after reaching its maximum, the total product begins to fall at point D and the marginal product is then negative beyond D_1. It should be clear from graph b that as long as the marginal product curve is above the average product curve each additional worker will increase the per capita output. C_1 represents the point at which average product equals marginal product and thereafter the decline of marginal product

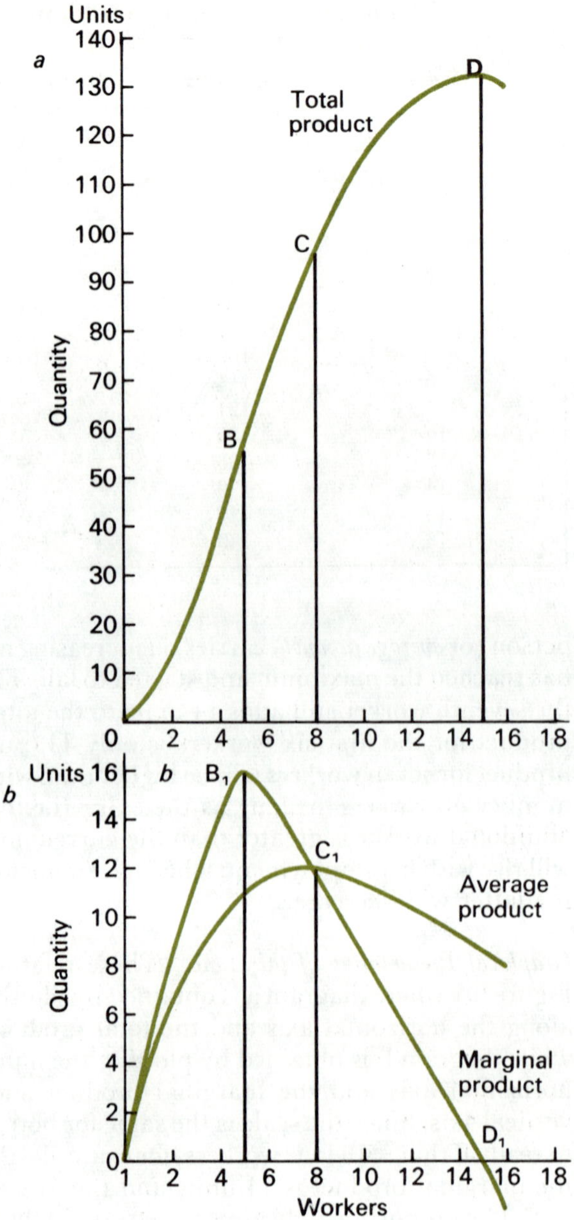

Figure 9.1 Increasing and diminishing returns.

from C_1 to D_1 means that with every additional worker the average output declines.

Summary The law of increasing and diminishing returns has been derived from practical life and states that when more and more units of a factor of production are added to another factor of production that is being held constant, the total product rises at first more than in proportion to the increase in the variable factor, then less than in proportion to it, and finally decreases, while the marginal product correspondingly increases, then decreases, and even becomes negative.

9.2 THE TOTAL COST FUNCTION

Figure 9.1 can be converted into a cost curve in two stages. We first change the axes, plotting the total output along the horizontal axis (while ignoring the declining section beyond point D), and the number of workers along the vertical axis. This gives Figure 9.2, which shows the amount of labour needed to produce a certain output. We then multiply the amount of labour by its price (i.e. wages), which gives the labour cost curve shown in Figure 9.3.

At first, the production of a unit of output needs less labour, the variable factor, than it does later. This formulation of the law of diminishing returns takes us half way to the cost function, showing as it does how much labour is used up for a unit of production. Assuming that this is all human labour, the labour cost or wage bill is obtained by multiplying the number of workers by the wage. If the wage for each worker on the farm is taken as constant at £100 per week, irrespective of the number of workers employed, the producer operates as a quantity adjuster on the labour market in so far as he, as a buyer of labour, is faced with a constant price (wage) of labour and adjusts the amount he wants to buy of it.

If, for example, the production of 55 units of grain requires five workers (see Figure 9.2) and if this process takes 20 weeks, the wage bill will be $5 \times 20 \times £100 = £10\,000$. Since the number of workers is always multiplied here by $20 \times £100 = £2000$, the shape of the curve in Figure 9.2

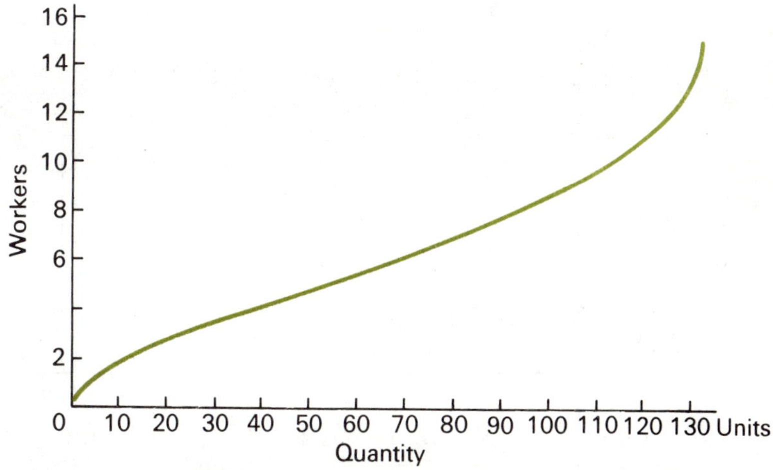

Figure 9.2 Output per worker function.

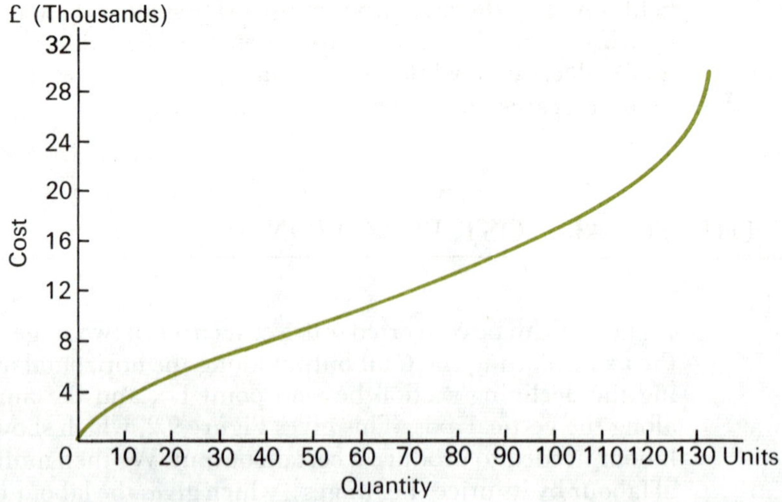

Figure 9.3 Labour cost curve.

will remain the same after this multiplication, as can be seen in Figure 9.3, where the vertical axis now tells us how much money must be spent on wages to produce a given amount of product. This, then, is the curve for the total variable costs – variable because they vary with the output. By contrast, fixed costs do not change when the output is varied. In the case of agricultural production, for example, the fixed cost is the rent for the land and it remains the same whether we produce on it a lot, a little or nothing at all. If we take the fixed cost to be £4000, for example, and combine it with the variable cost, we obtain the total cost curve shown in Figure 9.4. This also retains the shape of the curve in Figure 9.2. It can be seen that to

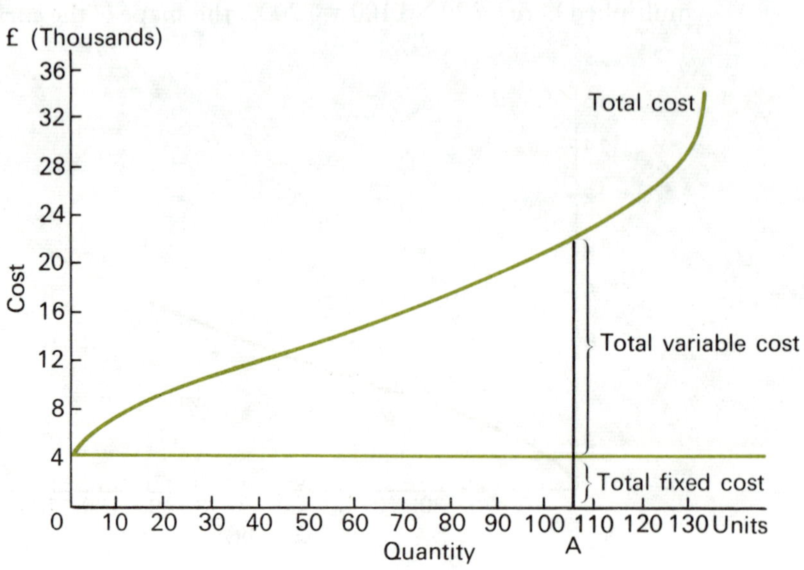

Figure 9.4 Fixed variable and total costs.

obtain an output (OA) the total fixed cost is £4000 and the total variable cost is £18 000.

Summary The total cost function can be derived from the law of diminishing returns by changing the axes of the curve. It is assumed here that the producer 'buying' the factor of production – labour – is a quantity adjuster.

9.3 AVERAGE AND MARGINAL COSTS

Assuming that in the situation shown in Table 9.1 each worker on the farm works for 20 weeks for a weekly wage of £100, we obtain the figures shown in Table 9.2 for the total variable cost.

Table 9.2 Average and marginal costs.

Units produced	*Total variable cost (£)*	*Units produced*	*Total variable cost (£)*
5	2 000	106	18 000
13	4 000	114	20 000
25	6 000	121	22 000
39	8 000	126	24 000
55	10 000	130	26 000
70	12 000	132	28 000
84	14 000	132	30 000

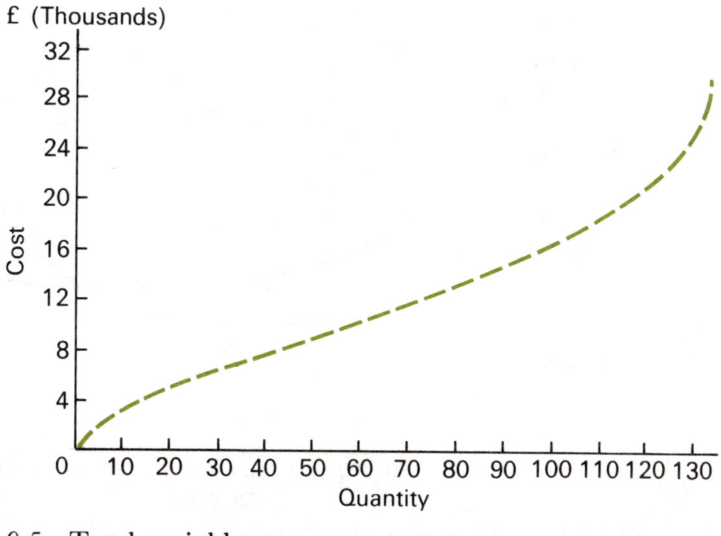

Figure 9.5 Total variable cost.

The corresponding graph is shown in Figure 9.5. By joining the points we obtain a continuous curve for the total variable cost (like those in Figures 9.3 and 9.4) which also tells us the labour cost for any output including outputs which would mean that some workers are employed on a part-time basis. A tabulation of the total variable cost up to an output of 25 units is shown in Table 9.3. The average variable cost (AVC) is

Table 9.3 Total variable cost.

Production	*Total variable cost (£)*	*Production*	*Total variable cost (£)*
1	500	14	4200
2	900	15	4400
3	1300	16	4600
4	1700	17	4800
5	2000	18	4950
6	2300	19	5100
7	2600	20	5250
8	2900	21	5400
9	3150	22	5550
10	3400	23	5700
11	3600	24	5850
12	3800	25	6000
13	4000		

obtained in each case by dividing the total variable cost (TVC) by the output, and for an output of 10, it is found to be 3400/10 = 340, while for an output of 25, it is 6000/25 = 240. The corresponding figures for the output range 0 to 132 units give the curve marked AVC in Figure 9.6.

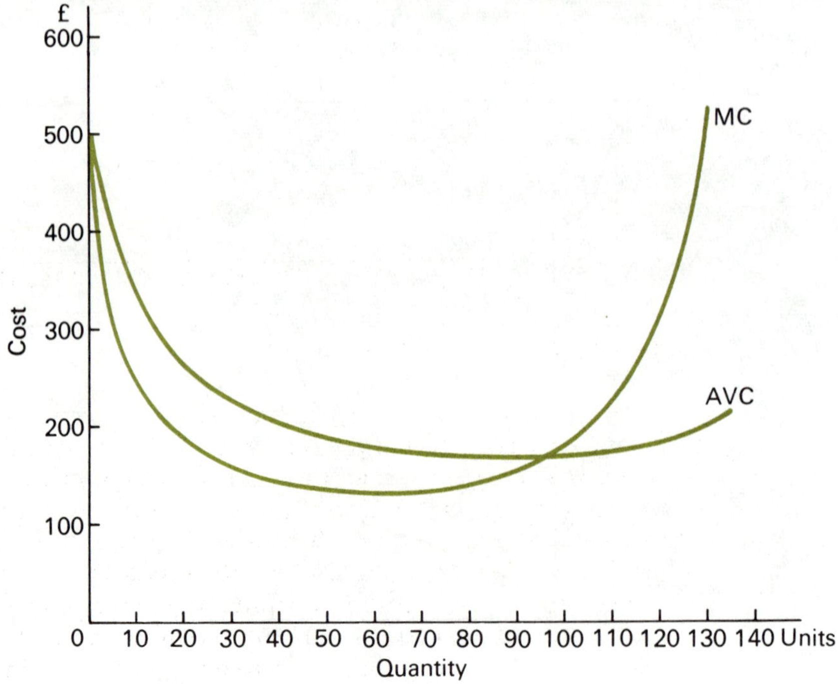

Figure 9.6 Average variable cost and marginal cost curve.

The curve for the marginal cost (MC), also shown here, is obtained from the data in Table 9.3, the marginal cost being the cost incurred in the production of the extra unit of grain in each case. Thus, if the total variable cost of the production of one unit of wheat is £500 and that of two units of wheat is £900, the marginal cost of the second unit is £400; for the eighth unit, for example, it is £300.

The two curves intersect at the lowest point of the curve for the average variable cost. As long as the marginal cost is below the average cost, the average cost is seen to fall; when the marginal cost is higher than the average cost, the average cost is seen to rise. At the point where the average cost neither increases nor decreases, i.e. at the minimum of the average cost graph, the marginal cost is equal to the average variable cost.

Let us again assume, as in Section 9.2, a fixed cost of £4000 for the whole output range. The average fixed cost (AFC) is obtained by dividing this figure of £4000 by the output and it can fall rapidly with increasing output, being in the present case £400 for 10 units of output and £40 for 100 (see Figure 9.7).

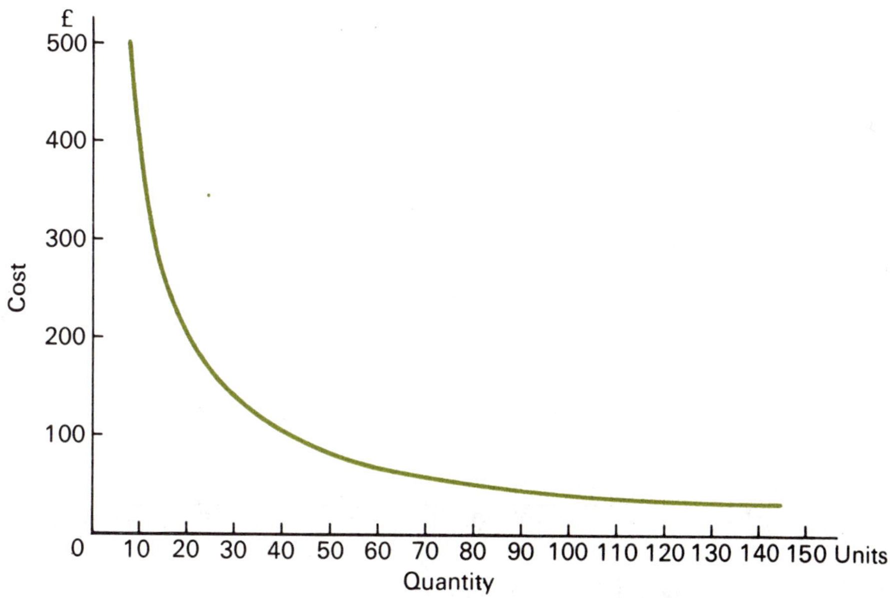

Figure 9.7 Average fixed cost.

The average total cost (ATC) is the sum of the average fixed cost and the average variable cost and is shown by ATC curve in Figure 9.8. The same figure also gives the marginal cost curve (MC) which intersects the curves for the average total cost (ATC) and the average variable cost (AVC) at their lowest points. The distance between these last two curves diminishes with increasing output, because as the fixed cost is spread over more units the variable cost of the units becomes a progressively greater proportion of the total costs, i.e. the curves will tend to merge together.

The cost functions will shift when there are changes in the amount of the factors of production that is assumed to be constant (i.e. in the size of the farm), in the state of technology (e.g. the machinery used) or in the price of the machinery used. Thus a farm's cost functions will change if the farm is enlarged, if mechanization is increased or if the prices of land or machinery go up. Shifts in cost functions mean simply a re-positioning on the graph; their shapes remain the same. Cost analysis explains one aspect of the firm's behaviour, but we must now examine the sales situation of firms, since we generally assume that firms want to maximize their profit. The profit is the difference between the total sales revenue and the total cost.

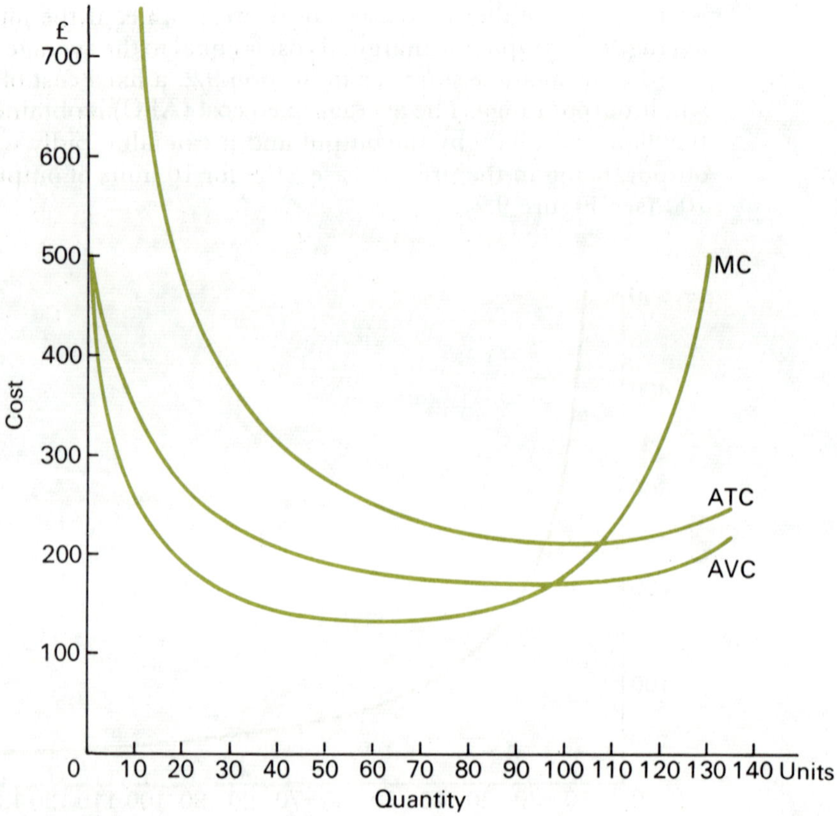

Figure 9.8 Cost functions.

Summary The average total costs of a firm are the sum of its average fixed and average variable costs. The marginal costs of the firm are the extra units of cost it incurs for each unit increase in output. The marginal cost curve must intersect the average cost curve at the latter's lowest point. This is because whenever average cost is falling marginal cost is less than average cost and whenever average cost is rising marginal cost is higher than average cost. The cost situation is important in determining the output at which the firm's profit can be maximized.

9.4 THE INDIVIDUAL SALES FUNCTION

We must stress that in a perfectly competitive situation the producer is assumed to be a quantity adjuster when buying labour, and that he does not influence the price of labour, i.e. the wages, but pays the same wage, irrespective of the size of his labour force. It is further assumed now that he is a quantity adjuster also with respect to selling his product and does not vary his price with the amount he sells. This applies, for example, to a farmer who, owing to his limited contribution to the total supply, always gets the same price for his grain, irrespective of the amount he sells of it. It also applies to a small glove-manufacturer, whose contribution to total supply is so minute that he obtains the same price for his output, whatever it is.

Since the amount a firm can sell depends on the demand for the product it makes, the individual sales function, which shows how much a firm sells at various prices, depends on the market demand function. In the case of quantity adjustment the price is constant, whatever the amount of product sold, so that when the sales are plotted along the horizontal axis against the price along the vertical axis, a set of horizontal straight lines is obtained (see Figure 9.9).

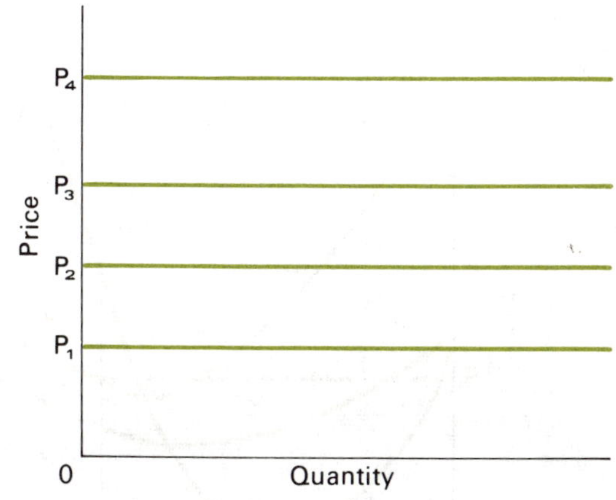

Figure 9.9 Individual sales function.

The individual sales function gives a straight line parallel to the horizontal. There may be small, medium or large quantities sold at any given price, and the price is not affected by a change in the sales volume.

The total revenue is equal to the quantity sold times the price, so that the average or unit sales revenue is always equal to the price. The marginal revenue is the extra revenue obtained from the sale of the one additional unit. If the firm is a quantity adjuster, the marginal revenue is equal to the average or unit revenue (the price), since each extra unit sold raises the total revenue by the price of one unit of the product. If 10 units are sold at £5 apiece, the total revenue is £50 and the average revenue is £5; if 11 units are sold, the total revenue is £55, while the marginal revenue and the price remain £5.

Profit Maximization by the Producer This implies that the firm will continue to expand its output as long as the marginal revenue is higher than the marginal cost, i.e. if a unit still has a higher marginal revenue than marginal cost, the firm will want to make it. The maximum profit is obtained when the marginal revenue is equal to the marginal cost, for beyond that point the marginal costs of further units exceed their marginal revenue, so that there is no incentive to produce them. If a firm continues production until the marginal revenue is equal to the marginal cost it does not mean that the profit is nil on the grounds that the 'costs' are equal to the 'receipts'. On the contrary, it means that the profit is maximized, since up to that point each and every unit of output that has been produced and sold has made a profit, albeit a progressively declining one.

Optimum Production Level The question which now arises is 'How much will the firm produce at a given price of its product?' We have assumed that marginal revenue equals the average revenue and so the plots of marginal revenue (MR) and average revenue (AR) will coincide. They are represented in Figure 9.10 by the straight line MR/AR. The curves for

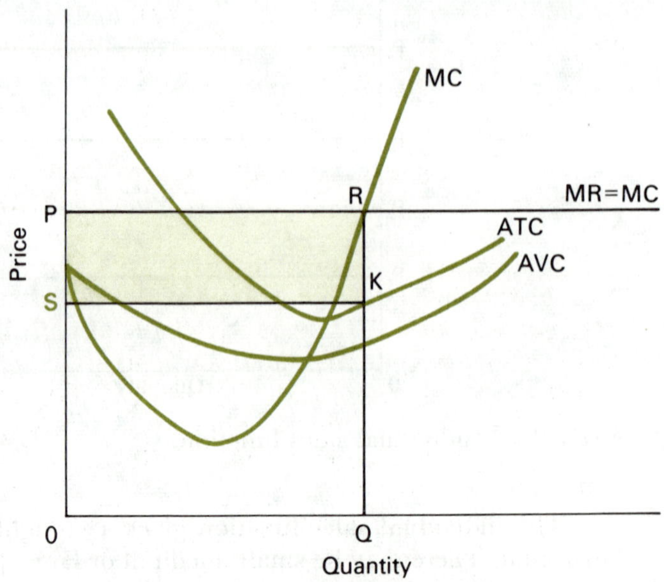

Figure 9.10 Production at profit maximizing level.

marginal cost (MC), average total cost (ATC) and average variable cost (AVC) are also plotted and, at the intersection R, the marginal revenue and marginal cost are equal. This means that for all units sold from O to Q the marginal revenue has exceeded the marginal cost, i.e. MR always lies above MC until the intersection R. At quantity OQ the average total cost is given by QK so that the cost QK times the quantity sold OQ equals the total cost of producing OQ units. The total revenue from OQ units is obviously this quantity OQ times the price OP and profit is the difference between total revenue and total costs. Since the points P, S, O, Q, K and R delimit rectangular areas the profit is actually represented by the shaded area in the graph, i.e. we have been multiplying the sides of rectangles, and total revenue and total costs can be represented by the areas OPRQ and OSKQ, and their difference, total profit, by the shaded area SPRK.

Summary For firms which are quantity adjusters, the sales function is a straight line running parallel to the axis along which the amount sold is plotted. The average revenue is equal to the marginal revenue. On the assumption of profit maximization, the output at which the profit is at a maximum can be determined for any given price (OP). This amount is the supply offered for sale at a price OP and is not to be confused with the sales volume.

9.5 THE SUPPLY CURVE

Firm's Supply Curve The supply curve reveals the amounts a firm will offer for sale at various prices on the assumption that it will want to maximize its profit at the given price. From Figure 9.10 we saw that for price OP this occurred at the intersection of the curves for marginal revenue (MR) and marginal cost (MC) and this holds true for all of the prices OP, OP_1 and OP_2 plotted in Figure 9.11. The supply curve coincides with the marginal cost curve (MC) as shown by the green line in the diagram. Thus at price OP the intersection is point S and the quantity sold to maximize profit is OQ; similarly, at price OP_1, the intersection is R and the quantity sold is OQ_1. Now both OP and OP_1 lie above the average total cost curve (ATC) and clearly when the price falls below the minimum point of ATC, say to OP_2 (T), the total cost of producing OQ_2 exceeds the total revenue and a loss is made. Nonetheless, the revenue obtained still exceeds the average variable cost (the revenue line lies above AVC) and contributes towards the fixed costs of buildings and machinery which have already been incurred. However, if the price falls further, to OP_3, and the revenue line intersects MC at the minimum point of AVC then here the revenue covers only the variable cost exactly, with no contribution to fixed costs remaining. Obviously, with a price below OP_3, the total revenue will not even cover the total variable cost, and production must stop otherwise the loss will simply increase.

The individual supply curve is shifted by the same factors as those which shift the marginal cost curve, namely changes in technology and changes in the prices of the factors of production. In addition, it can also be shifted by changes in the size of the firm. Once again, such shifts do not alter the shape of the supply curve, simply its position on the graph.

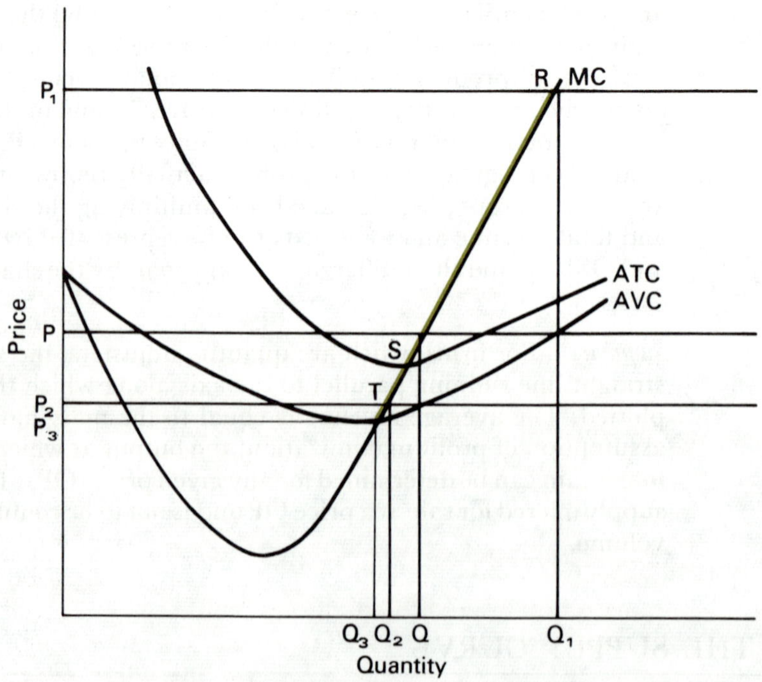

Figure 9.11 Individual supply curve.

Market Supply Curve For identical competing goods this can be obtained by aggregating the quantities corresponding to all points on the individual supply curves, as is shown in Figure 9.12 in the case of two suppliers. Thus for OP_1 the market supply curve will have a quantity value of $OB_1 + OB_2 = OB$ and, for OP_2, $OA_1 + OA_2 = OA$.

The market supply curve shows what quantities the suppliers will together offer for sale at various prices. Again, it does not tell us what price will be formed on the market, merely the amounts the firms will offer for sale. The supply curve rises, indicating that the higher the price, the more

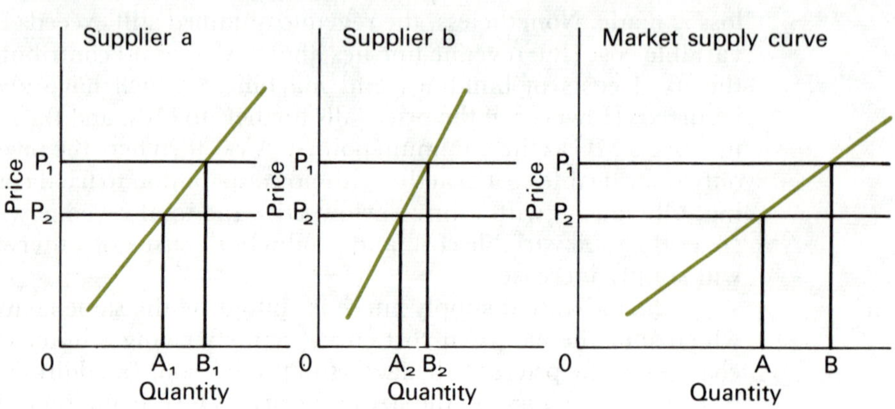

Figure 9.12 Market supply curve.

the firms will supply. In Britain, manufacturers of such essential products as springs and nuts and bolts have their market supply curves determined for them in an approximation to this way. The manufacture of cotton textiles which is subject to intense competition, national and international, shows similar market supply curves.

Summary The assumption of quantity adjustment, which leads to the market demand function in the case of consumer behaviour, similarly gives the market supply curve in the case of the producer behaviour. As will be shown later, the equilibrium price can be determined by combining the market demand curve and the market supply curve.

9.6 CONCLUDING REMARKS

In discussing the behaviour of producers in this chapter, we have obtained various cost functions from the law of increasing and diminishing returns. The cost functions are shifted by changes in technology, in the prices of the means of production and in the factor of production that is assumed to be constant.

To maximize their profit, firms raise their output until the marginal cost is equal to the marginal revenue. If we assume that firms are quantity adjusters it is easy to find the best output value at each price. We have thus obtained the supply function which shows how much the firms would offer for sale at various prices, if these existed, but in reality, as will be seen later, there is only one price.

We have assumed that firms want to maximize their profit, without saying whether this is a good or a bad thing; we have made no value judgement about it. Nonetheless, firms can also have other objectives, as will be seen in Chapter 11.

The production side of the economy was mainly analysed by the classical school, important members of which were Adam Smith (1723–90), Ricardo (1772–1823), John Stuart Mill (1806–73) and Say (1767–1832). Apart from Say, classical economists held that prices were determined mainly by the production cost. They therefore concentrated on the supply side and mostly ignored the demand side of economics, though this, as we have seen in Chapter 8, is just as important.

QUESTIONS

1 What is the law of increasing and diminishing returns?

2 What are variable costs?

3 What is marginal cost?

4 What is the connection between the supply function and the law of increasing and diminishing returns?

5 What is the connection between the curves for the average product and the marginal product on the one hand and those for the average and marginal costs on the other?

6 When is the individual firm's sales curve a horizontal line?

7 What is the difference between the individual firm's sales curve and the individual firm's supply curve?

8 What is the connection between the marginal revenue and the marginal cost if profit maximization is assumed?

9 Why is it that the supply curve coincides with that part of the marginal cost curve that lies above the point of intersection with the average *variable* cost curve and not with the part that lies above the point of intersection with the average *total* cost curve?

10 What factors can shift the market supply curve?

EXERCISES

1 A farmer produces the following amounts of grain on his land with the help of an increasing number of workers. Calculate the average product and the marginal product in each case and plot them on a graph.

Number of workers	*Output (tons)*
1	4
2	9
3	15
4	22
5	29
6	35
7	40
8	43
9	44
10	44

2 A furniture manufacturer produces the following quantities of chairs at the total labour costs specified; the total fixed cost for the chair manufacture is £300 per chair. Calculate the total and the marginal cost for each level of output and plot them on a graph.

Number of chairs	*Total labour cost (£)*
1	15.0
2	25.0
3	32.5
4	38.5
5	43.5
6	50.0
7	59.0
8	72.5
9	87.5
10	107.5

3 An engineering firm making machines has a total fixed cost of £140 per machine and its total variable cost increases with its output as shown below. The firm is a quantity adjuster on the supply side. Calculate (a) how many machines the firm will sell if the sales price is £150 per machine and the firm aims to maximize its profit, and (b) how much its profit or loss in this case is (use a graph, but also try to express the profit or loss in figures).

Number of machines	*Total variable cost (£)*
1	100
2	160
3	195
4	260
5	360
6	510
7	714

4 A sewing machine manufacturer operating with a total fixed cost of £300 per sewing machine finds from his books that he has the following total costs:

Number of sewing machines	*Total cost*
1	500
2	620
3	690
4	800
5	980
6	1260
7	1660

(a) Calculate the average total cost, the average variable cost and the marginal cost and show these on a graph.
(b) Calculate the total profit or loss when the manufacturer can sell his sewing machines at a price of £180 apiece. Show the profit or loss by shading the appropriate area on the graph.

5 Give three formulations of the law of increasing and diminishing returns.

6 Show on a graph what happens to the market supply curve when the number of suppliers increases.

7 Show on a graph how an increase in the price of oils and fats – the main ingredients of soap – affects the market supply curve for soap.

Chapter Ten

Perfect Competition in Theory and Practice

We have now discussed the demand behaviour of consumers and the supply behaviour of producers separately and in this chapter we shall examine the interaction of these demand and supply forces in the market situation. First, we shall assume that the market is characterized by perfect competition in which no firm has an economic advantage. It should be pointed out, however, that this is an extreme case which nowadays exists in practice only to a very limited extent in Britain. In actual fact, firms in most industries have the power to fix their prices and other conditions of sale to a significant extent, as has recently been illustrated by the oil companies. Nevertheless, it will be useful to start with perfect competition before examining the other types of competition encountered in reality. This approach will enable us (a) to compare these types of competition with perfect competition which was commoner earlier this century; and (b) to describe the form of price determination under perfect competition which some economists still consider to be very desirable. In perfect competition theory we assume that there are so many consumers and suppliers that no individual consumer or supplier has the power to fix price levels. We have already examined the combined demand of consumers (studied in Chapter 8) and the combined supply of producers (studied in Chapter 9), and we shall now analyse how the interaction of these combined forces determines price. Later in the chapter we shall apply this theory to the real-world behaviour of firms and consumers.

10.1 THE MARKET

The market is the interaction of the demand for and supply of a given good. The market need not have a physical location such as the local open retail food market in Walsall town square or the cattle market in Worcester. Indeed, the purchasing of grain from the USA by a transatlantic telephone call made by a UK customer is a transaction in the world grain market.

In the market for a good the equilibrium price of the good will be determined by the forces of supply and demand. In the case of perfect competition certain conditions will apply which affect these forces. These are:

1. The good in question must be 'homogeneous', i.e. no matter who offers it for sale the good is identical.
2. The market for the good must be 'transparent', i.e. all of the suppliers and consumers have full information on the prices asked and offered.
3. There must be large numbers of suppliers and consumers with each individual making only a small contribution to supply and demand.
4. There must be freedom of entry to new sellers or buyers.
5. There must be no segmentation of the market so that suppliers sell and consumers buy in any part of the market without, for example, suffering the cost of transport.

Of course, homogeneous goods are rare and even when they do occur packaging and advertising can serve to make them heterogeneous from the consumer's point of view. However, if goods are homogeneous the market transparency ensures that no supplier can raise his prices without consumers knowing they can obtain the identical good more cheaply elsewhere. Again, the absence of any 'friction' in moving from one part of the market to another allows the consumer to do just that in pursuit of the lowest price. Since individual suppliers and consumers have such a small impact on supply and demand, no-one can affect price by varying his contribution; price is fixed by the total supply and demand. Thus a supplier will adjust his output to maximize profits and a consumer will adjust his demand to maximize satisfaction of wants.

Summary The market is the interaction of the demand for and supply of a good. It is the series of transactions which constitutes the market and these may or may not occur at a fixed location. Perfect competition is the market form in which suppliers and consumers cannot influence the equilibrium price of a good.

10.2 EQUILIBRIUM OF SUPPLY AND DEMAND

When there is perfect competition in a market it is possible to derive a market demand curve and a market supply curve, such as those shown in Figure 10.1. The supply curve rises from left to right (i.e. the higher the price, the more is offered for sale), while the demand curve falls from left to right (i.e. the lower the price, the more is demanded). Both curves are hypothetical to some extent, in so far as they show how much *would be* supplied and demanded at various prices, whereas in reality there is only one going price (OP), where the amount demanded is equal to the amount supplied. This one price is determined by the total demand of consumers for the good and the total supply of the good by producers. All producers know this price, and maintain it. At this point the market is at equilibrium, and OP represents the equilibrium price, while OQ is the quantity that changes hands at this price.

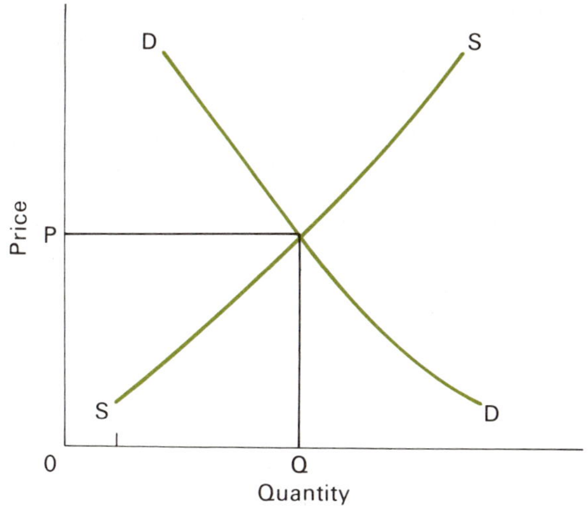

Figure 10.1 Equilibrium of supply and demand.

Now that the equilibrium price is known, every consumer and supplier can decide how much he wants to buy and sell, respectively. It can therefore be seen again that the equilibrium price is determined in the market, and that all we can say prior to this moment is how much they *would* buy and sell at various hypothetical prices. The actual individual supply and demand of quantities of the product bought and sold are determined only after the equilibrium price has come into existence.

Shifts in the Demand Curve When deriving the market demand function (in Chapter 8, Section 5), we found a connection between price and total demand on the assumption that the following items remained constant: the consumers' income, the number of consumers buying the goods in question, and the price of all other goods. A change in any of these can raise or lower the demand at the same price, so that the demand curve is shifted to the right or left, respectively, as can be seen in Figure 10.2.

Here we have a demand curve (D_1) in situation 1, and a demand curve (D_2) in situation 2, i.e. the demand curve has shifted to the right, indicating a rise in demand. This may be due to an increase in consumers' income or to an increase in the total number of consumers, or to a change in the price of the other goods, or simply to the fact that the consumers now want more of the product in question. In any case, the amount (OA) they purchased at price OP_4 in the first situation has now increased to OF (at the same price), and the quantities purchased at all the other prices have similarly increased, i.e. the demand has increased.

The opposite change in the four factors mentioned above will lead to a decrease in demand, when the consumers want to buy less at a given price than before, and the demand curve then shifts to the left.

Shifts in the Supply Curve The market supply curve can be similarly shifted to the right by technical change, a change in the price of the means of production, or an increase in the number of suppliers. A change in the number of suppliers of course implies free entry to the market (and exit from it), which as we have seen is a mandatory condition for perfect competition. If would-be suppliers are not allowed to enter the market, the existing supplier might easily become powerful enough to influence the market terms. New suppliers will be attracted to a market, under perfect competition, until all producers can achieve no more than normal profit levels, i.e. profit which is sufficient only to maintain the financial viability of a firm.

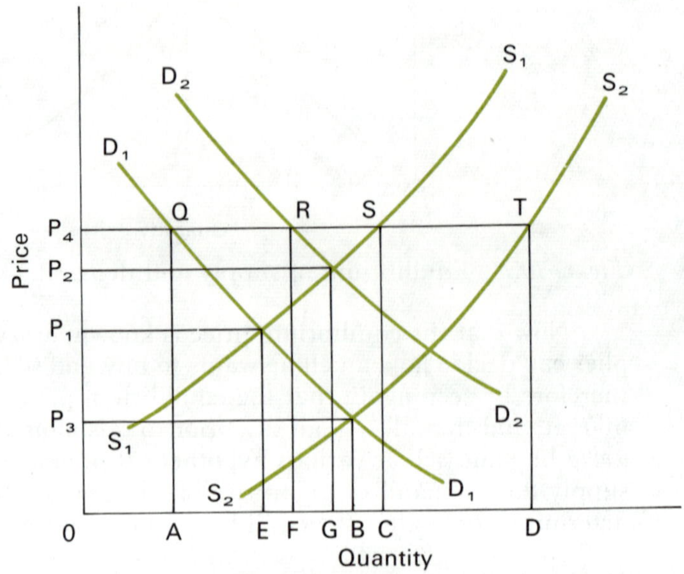

Figure 10.2 Changes in supply and demand equilibrium.

Let us imagine that, owing to a change in one or more of the three factors mentioned above, supply curve 1, which holds for situation 1, is replaced by supply curve 2, which holds for situation 2, i.e. the original supply curve shifts to the right, indicating an increase in supply. Here, the amount OC supplied at price OP_4 before (see supply curve S_1) has now increased to OD, again at the same price (see supply curve S_2). Conversely, if the supply decreases, the supply curve shifts to the left.

Price Determination under Perfect Competition Now we can go on to examine how supply and demand forces act to determine the price of a product under this situation of perfect competition.

In situation 1, with supply curve S_1 and demand curve D_1, the equilibrium price for the product is OP_1 and the equilibrium quantity bought and sold is OE. If the demand for the product rises, the demand curve D_1 now shifts to position D_2 while the supply curve remains at S_1, and a new equilibrium price OP_2 emerges, i.e. the price of the product rises from OP_1 to OP_2. If, on the other hand, the demand remains unchanged while the supply of the product increases, the supply curve will shift from position S_1 to position S_2, and the new equilibrium price is at point OP_3 (where curve D_1 and S_2 intersect), which means that the increased supply has reduced the price from OP_1 to OP_3. A shift in these curves is very different from moving along them, even though this too will lead to new quantities supplied or demanded. A shift is produced by a change in the forces of supply and demand mentioned, while a move along the curves reflects a change in the quantities supplied or demanded, caused by price changes under otherwise the same conditions. Changes due to price alterations and the related moves along the curves have been explained in Chapter 8, Section 5.

Summary Under perfect competition, the equilibrium price in the market is determined by the point at which the amount demanded for the product is equal to the amount of the product supplied. A shift in the demand or supply forces is shown by a shift in the demand and supply curves, and a change in equilibrium price results.

10.3 ELASTICITY OF DEMAND AND SUPPLY

Price Elasticity of Demand How does the supply and demand for products react to small changes in price? Demand for some products is highly responsive to changes in price, but for other products demand alters little when prices change. In economics we call the responsiveness of demand to price change the *price elasticity* of demand.

A small price change for some goods leads to a very large change in demand for them. These are normally less essential products, such as new motor cars, perfume, plastic gnomes, etc. A small rise in the price of

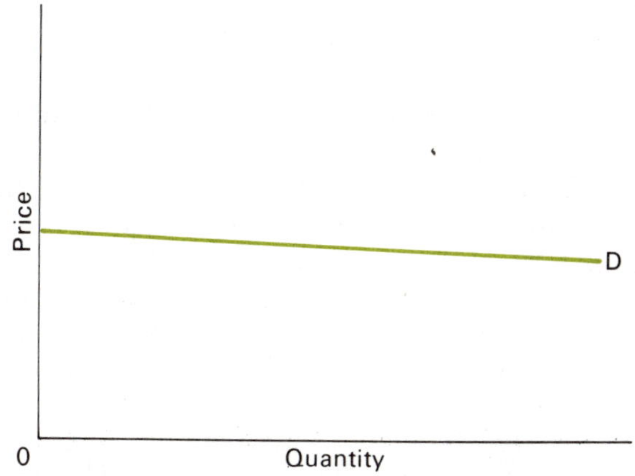

Figure 10.3 Demand curve for elastic product.

plastic garden gnomes will normally lead to a substantial fall in demand for them, since not only are they non-essential goods but also other products, such as garden figures made of wood or clay, are easily substituted for them. A product whose responsiveness of demand to small price changes is as strong as this is called an *elastic* product. The demand curve for such a product is shown in Figure 10.3, and is almost a horizontal straight line. In this case the proportionate change in demand is much greater than the proportionate change in price, and here we say the elasticity of demand is greater than 1 (i.e. it is greater than unity).

A small change in price for other goods leads to a barely measurable change in demand for them. These are normally essential everyday products such as bread, milk, sugar, etc. A small rise in the price of bread will usually result in an almost insignificant fall in the demand for the product. A good whose responsiveness of demand to small price changes is as weak as bread is called an *inelastic* product. The demand curve for such a product is shown in Figure 10.4, and is almost a vertical straight line. In this case the proportionate change in demand is much less than the proportionate change in price, and here we say the elasticity of demand is less than 1 (i.e. it is less than unity).

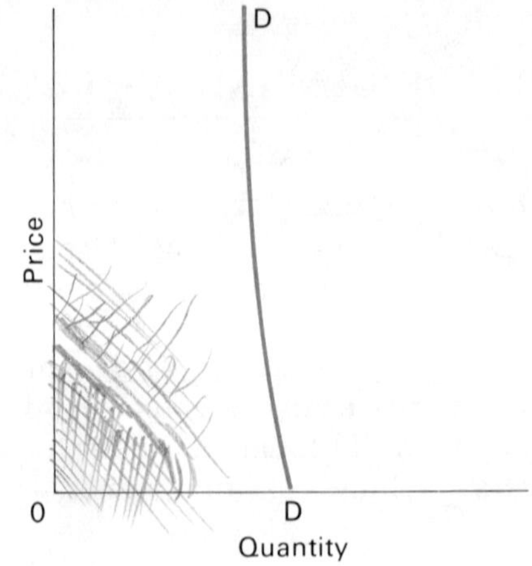

Figure 10.4 Demand curve for inelastic product.

When the proportionate change in demand for a product is equal to the proportionate change in price, we say that the elasticity of demand is 1 (i.e. it is equal to unity). It is important for firms and consumers to know what will happen to the demand for products if price changes are made. If British Rail increases fares it needs to know what effect this will have on the travelling public in order to judge whether the measure will be of financial advantage or not. It is important, therefore, to measure elasticity of demand for products. The way to measure elasticity of demand is in terms of proportionate change in demand related to proportionate change in price. Therefore the proportionate change in demand should be divided by the proportionate change in price. The first is found by dividing the change in quantity demanded by the former quantity demanded. The second is found by dividing the change in price of the product by the former price of the product, i.e.

$$\frac{\text{change in quantity demanded}}{\text{former quantity demanded}} \div \frac{\text{change in price}}{\text{former price}}.$$

We can now substitute in this word-equation the following symbols:

Ep : price elasticity of demand
Q : quantity demanded; ΔQ : change in quantity demanded
P : price ; ΔP : change in price

$$\text{Thus, } E_p = \frac{\frac{\Delta Q}{Q}}{\frac{\Delta P}{P}} = \frac{P}{Q} \times \frac{\Delta Q}{\Delta P}.$$

Applying this formula to Figure 10.5 we can see that the price change (ΔP) from OP to OP_1 of minus one penny is accompanied by a change in the quantity demanded (ΔQ), an increase from OQ_1 to OQ of 0.5 kg.

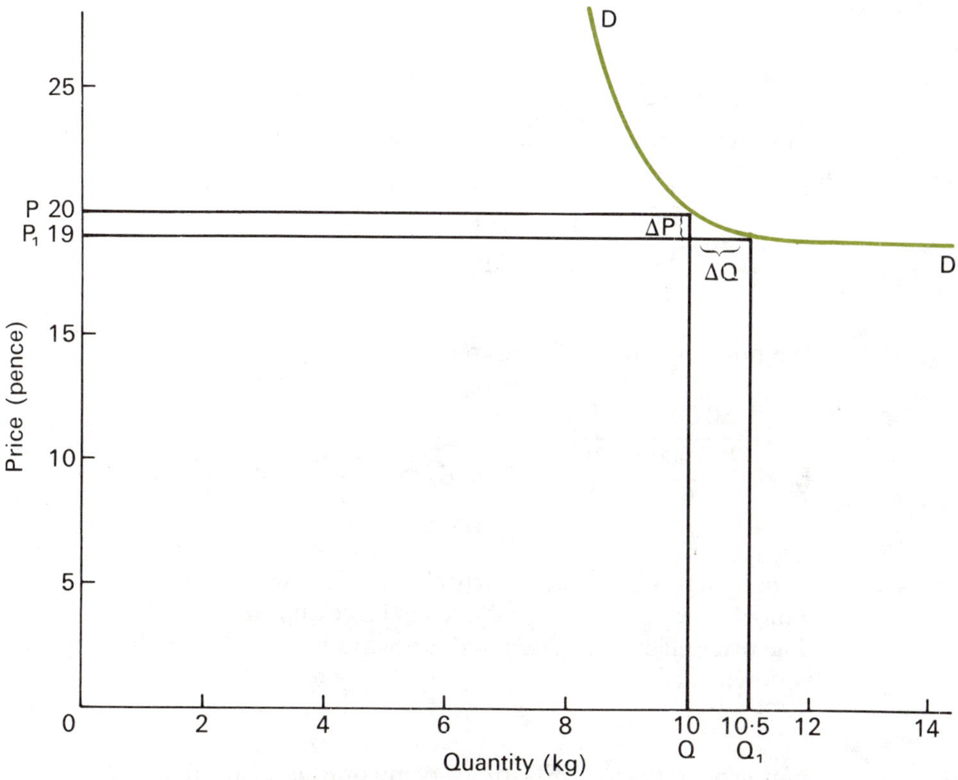

Figure 10.5 Price elasticity of demand.

$$\therefore E_p = \frac{\frac{\Delta Q}{Q}}{\frac{\Delta P}{P}} = \frac{\frac{0.5}{10.0}}{\frac{-1}{20}} = -1.00 \quad \text{or } E_p = \frac{20}{10} \times \frac{0.5}{-1} = -1$$

The price elasticity of demand is always negative since the demand curve is downward sloping.

Price Elasticity of Supply We also have price elasticity of supply, which is the relation between a proportionate change in quantity supplied and a small proportionate change in price. Price elasticity of supply can be *inelastic*, when a product is fixed in terms of quantity supplied regardless of price offered for it. The famous 'Mona Lisa' painting would be an example of a good which is completely inelastic in supply. The perfectly inelastic supply curve is vertical.

Normally, however, the higher the price offered, the more of a good will be supplied. In Figure 10.6 the price of bicycles at OP is £50 and the quantity supplied at OQ is 100 000. A rise in the price of bicycles from OP to OP_1 (from £50 to £60) will lead to an increase by bicycle manufacturers in the supply of bicycles from OQ to OQ_1 (from 100 000 to 130 000).

We establish the elasticity of supply by a similar formula to that given for the elasticity of demand:

$$\frac{\text{change in quantity supplied}}{\text{former quantity supplied}} : \frac{\text{change in price}}{\text{former price}}$$

$$\text{i.e. } E_p = \frac{\frac{\Delta Q}{Q}}{\frac{\Delta P}{P}} = \frac{P}{Q} \times \frac{\Delta Q}{\Delta P}$$

We now substitute the figures

$$E_p = \frac{\frac{30\,000}{100\,000}}{\frac{10}{50}} = \frac{\frac{3}{10}}{\frac{1}{5}} = 1.5 \text{ or } E_p = \frac{50}{100\,000} \times \frac{30\,000}{10} = 1.5.$$

Supply in this example is fairly elastic, since we are dealing with an article, a bicycle, which can be produced in large quantities by simple technology. The price elasticity of demand is always negative since the demand curve is downward sloping.

Elasticity of Income Elasticity of income is also an important concept. Here we are examining the relation between a proportionate change in

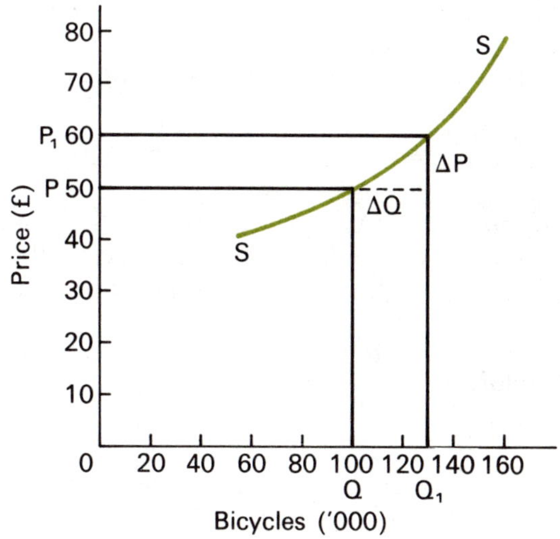

Figure 10.6 Price elasticity of supply.

income and a proportionate change in quantity demanded. This can be formulated with reference to the Engel curve, showing the connection between the quantity (Q) and income (i). The income elasticity of demand (E_i) is expressed by a similar formula to that of the price elasticity of demand just examined (i = income):

$$E_i = \frac{\frac{\Delta Q}{Q}}{\frac{\Delta i}{i}} = \frac{i}{Q} \times \frac{\Delta Q}{(\Delta i)}.$$

This is the ratio between a small proportionate change in the amount demanded and a small proportionate change in income. Thus if E equals

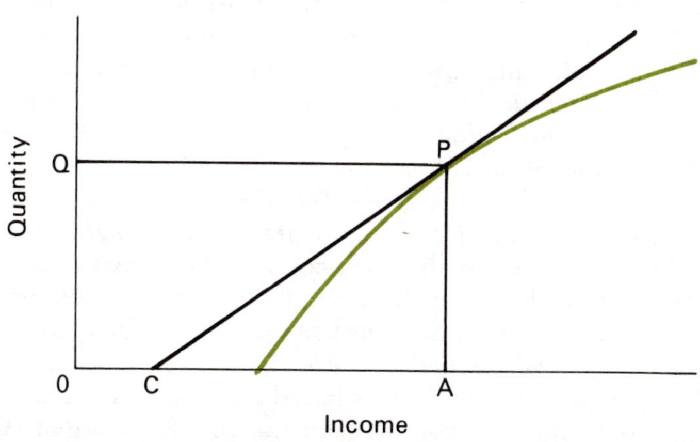

Figure 10.7 Income elasticity of demand.

3.2 it means that a 1 per cent rise in income causes a 3.2 per cent rise in quantity demanded.

In Figure 10.7, E_i is found graphically as follows:

$$E_i = \frac{\Delta Q/Q}{\Delta i/i} \text{ which can be rewritten as } E_i = \frac{i}{Q} \times \frac{\Delta Q}{\Delta i}.$$

Now when $i = OA$, $Q = OQ$ and $\frac{\Delta Q}{\Delta i}$, the slope of the Engel curve at P is found by drawing a tangent to the curve at P. This tangential line cuts the x-axis at C and clearly the slope of the line and therefore $\frac{\Delta Q}{\Delta i}$ is given by $\frac{AP}{CA}$.

$$\text{Therefore } E_i = \frac{OA}{OQ} \times \frac{AP}{CA}$$

$$= \frac{OA}{CA} \qquad \text{since } OQ = AP.$$

Should the tangential line intersect the x-axis at the origin O, $OA = CA$ and $E_i = 1$.

Summary The price elasticity of demand is the ratio between a proportionate change in the quantity demanded and a small – possibly infinitesimal – proportionate change in price. The price elasticity of demand and the income elasticity of demand can also be determined graphically.

10.4 PERFECT COMPETITION IN BRITISH INDUSTRY

Food Retailing During the past 30 years there has been a massive increase in the size of firms and a growth in the number of British industries which do not approximate to the perfect competition situation. However, some important industries still price their products and conduct their economic behaviour in a way which roughly corresponds to the perfect competition analysis in Section 10.2 above. The retail food industry in city centres is an example of this. Worcester, a town of 75 000 inhabitants, has eight large supermarkets and a score of smaller retail outlets in the city centre dealing with grocery products, e.g. vegetables and general food products. Surveys have shown that strong price competition exists among the many sellers, and that this competition leads to an equilibrium price for each product within narrow limits. The price is not absolutely fixed by the market, as in the perfect competition model, because there are low price strategies carried on by some firms based on massive bulk buying by national food companies. The volume of demand by thousands of consumers in a county capital, and the number of competing retail outlets prevent the establishment of prices much above the perfect competition equilibrium of supply and demand.

Housing Market The market for semi-detached private housing approximates to perfect competition analysis. The size of this market depends not only upon new additions to supply, but also upon demolition of and the stock of existing houses. We can, however, try to relate the market for private housing for sale in Britain to the four main conditions relating to perfect competition. Firstly, the good is almost homogeneous. There may be differences in design, but the size of and area occupied by most semi-detached private houses for sale vary to only a very limited extent. Secondly there are many sellers and buyers. On the supply side large firms have only a moderate share of new housing output. There are as many as 88 017 private firms involved in house building, of which only 71 employ more than 1200 or more workers. On the demand side the buyers in a given year in Britain are measured in millions rather than thousands. Thirdly, the flow of information amongst buyers and sellers is considerable, since most houses are produced on a speculative sale basis rather than for a particular consumer. In every major town, therefore, information on numbers of houses for sale at particular prices is well known to both firms and buyers (through estate agents and newspaper advertisements). Finally, entry to the industry is not difficult for a firm. Many sub-contractors are employed in the industry, and thereby develop funds and skills which they can then utilize as independent building firms.

Demand for Private Housing We can apply the theory of perfect competition to the factors which determine supply and demand in the market for private houses for sale. On the demand side family income increases are an important factor in raising the demand for housing, and the rise in real income per head in Britain in the 1950s and 1960s helps to explain the increased demand for home ownership in that period.

A simple increase in the number of buyers will increase demand, of course, and such a phenomenon occurred in the massive housing boom of 1973. A change in the price of other goods and services related to the housing market has led to increases in demand for new houses. For example, the escalating cost of repairs to older houses has been a factor in motivating home owners to purchase new houses. When consumers want more of a given product an increase in demand results, and in this respect private housing is no exception. Thus in the 1960s and 1970s there has been a trend towards the purchase of second homes. Finally, price will also affect demand, of course, particularly the price of borrowing money for house purchase. The fall in the rate of interest in 1977 and 1978 led to an expansion in the demand for private housing, whereas the sharp rise in mortgage interest rates in 1976–77 resulted in a slump in house building.

Supply of Private Housing Changes in technology can increase house production, and such developments as replacement of labour by capital in site clearance, and prefabrication, are examples of this. An increase in the number of producers of private housing occurred in the 1950s, and this factor had an important influence not only on the production capacity of the industry but also on restraining price increases at a time of increasing demand. Increases in costs of production will also affect supply at given prices. A rise in price of labour or building may lead to a fall in house production.

In manufacturing industry there are still a few industries with conditions approximating to perfect competition. The furniture industry has many firms, and of course many purchasers. In engineering, the spring industry and the nut and bolt industry approximate to perfect competition, and in agriculture so do beef farming, dairy farming and horticulture.

Summary Some sectors of agriculture and manufacturing industry in Britain approximate to perfect competition but these sectors constitute a small proportion of total production and total employment.

10.5 GOVERNMENT INTERVENTION

The price system that results from the interplay between supply and demand under perfect competition is termed a *free pricing system*. However, this mechanism may bring about prices that are socially undesirable. Thus, the uncurbed operation of market forces can lead to a disproportionately high price of milk in the event of a sudden serious milk shortage, and this in turn can cause serious social problems, since poorer families will not be able to buy milk. The government then intervenes and fixes a maximum price which is lower than the price at which the market forces would produce milk (see Figure 10.8). This was done during the rapid rise in milk and other basic commodity prices in 1974–5 in Britain.

Here, the free-market price (OP_1) is considered socially undesirable, and the government fixes a maximum price (OP). However, at this price supply is not at equilibrium with demand but is below it. This is a typical situation that quite often arises with government intervention, however justified it may be. Supplementary measures may be needed in the form of rationing in order to make sure supplies are available to all and to rectify the imbalance between supply and demand. However, poorer people will now have the products which they could not otherwise buy.

By fixing a maximum price, the government protects the consumer: by fixing a minimum price, it protects the firms. It may do this when, owing to a temporary slackening of demand, an industry is forced to stop production because the equilibrium price is falling too low. The government then fixes a minimum price that is higher than the price would otherwise be, so that production can continue. The European Commission does this for prices of farm products, on behalf of the nine member states of the EEC (see Chapter 15).

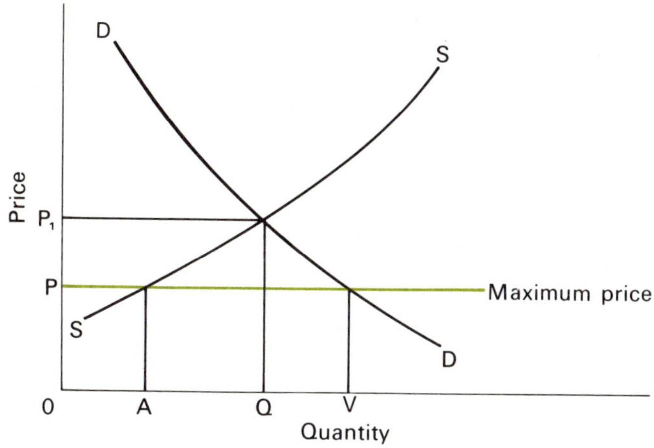

Figure 10.8 Government maximum price action.

Summary The price mechanism in a free market does not always lead to prices that are socially acceptable, and government intervention, in the form of fixing maximum and minimum prices, is then considered necessary to protect the consumer or the producer. Such intervention usually requires additional measures as well.

10.6 CONCLUDING REMARKS

We have derived here the equilibrium price in a market where the firms and households are quantity adjusters and have no influence on prices. The discussion focused on the case of perfect competition, which assumes the existence of very many buyers and sellers in a perfect market.

While the previous macroeconomic chapters dealt with total consumption, here we have talked about the price of goods in particular markets. While the consumption function is concerned with the total amount spent on consumption, in this chapter our microeconomic investigations have also given an insight into the structure of total consumption.

Both the demand side and the supply side are important in the formation of the equilibrium price, so both the classical school, which dealt only with supply, and the marginal utility school, which put the emphasis on demand, were one-sided.

The model of perfect competition is often encountered in the work of Marshall (1842–1924) who also dealt with elasticity.

Economists concentrated on perfect competition for a long time, neglecting the increasing progressive deviations from it in the form of monopolies and oligopolies. They put their trust in the price mechanism and held that competition would always bring about the lowest prices.

However, one important prerequisite for perfect competition – namely, freedom of entry to the market – is not often fulfilled, so that the sale of a product can be concentrated in the hands of a few large companies. Nevertheless, housing, many sectors of agriculture, retail food industry and some manufacturing industries do experience conditions approximating to perfect competition.

The classical economists always assumed perfect competition when they argued that the price mechanism ensured satisfactory results in the allocation of the factors of production, and in the use of scarce resources. Adam Smith wrote about the invisible hand which ensures that, though each consumer and producer pursued his own individual ends, this at the same time benefited society as a whole, free competition leading to the best results. Under perfect competition, the price just covers the average cost, including normal profit, in the long run. So long as it is possible to make abnormal profit in the industry in question, the established manufacturers expand their output or new competitors are attracted to the field. This profit depends on the level of demand; an increase in demand leads to a higher equilibrium price as a result of a shift in the demand curve to the right which in turn urges the producers to supply more. Firms will enter the industry up to the point that profit reaches normal levels.

One may wrongly suppose here that, by expressing their preferences, the consumers dictate both the nature and the level of production. However, we should not forget that only those consumer preferences that are backed up by purchasing power appear in the market. Besides, the constant shifts in the demand and supply curves can create a great deal of instability in the market under perfect competition. Finally, not even perfect competition guarantees that the external disadvantages of production, such as atmospheric pollution, are not added automatically to the production cost and thus to prices. Therefore, if there is reason to study and question the price mechanism under perfect competition, there is even more reason to do so under imperfect competition, in which firms have much more individual power. This will be done in the next chapter.

QUESTIONS

1. What is (a) a market, (b) a perfect market, and (c) perfect competition?

2. What factors can shift the supply curve?

3. What factors can shift the demand curve?

4. What is price elasticity of demand?

5. Draw an inelastic demand curve.

6. What is income elasticity of demand (E_i), and what does it mean if $E_i = 1$?

EXERCISES

1 (a) Is the motor car market homogeneous?
(b) Is it transparent?
(c) Are there so many suppliers that the price is a fixed entity for each of them?

2 Show how the entry of new suppliers to the market affects the profit of the existing suppliers.

3 Can there be cost differences between the manufacturers under perfect competition?

4 The equilibrium price in a market with perfect competition is £1.50. The government wants to set a minimum price at which the consumption is halved. What will this price be if the price elasticity of demand is constant at −2.5 per cent?

5 What is meant by elasticity as applied to demand and supply? Discuss the main factors which determine elasticity in each case.

6 What does the concept 'elasticity of supply' mean with respect to price? Discuss examples of this concept.

7 'The demand for rice is inelastic.' Explain what this means in a South Asian country, and whether it is a valid statement for such a country.

8 Discuss the environmental costs in your region that are manifested neither fully nor at all in the prices.

9 Discuss the production of agricultural products in Britain in terms of whether the producers are in perfect competition with each other.

10 Draw an Engel curve in the case of which the income elasticity at low incomes is greater than 1, and as the income increases it assumes values smaller than 1 but greater than 0, and finally becomes negative.

Chapter Eleven

Monopolistic Competition, Oligopoly and Monopoly in Theory and Practice

This chapter will bring us closer to economic reality since it will no longer be assumed that firms are powerless to do anything about prices. Large companies like Ford, I.C.I., British Oxygen Company and Esso can set their own sales prices and influence the market through advertising. The intensity of competition with their rivals will depend on how much oligopoly power they have.

The multinational companies occupy a special place. They operate in numerous countries through a large network of subsidiary companies, often too complex for outsiders to disentangle, and they usually have more economic power than other companies. It is possible for them simply to transfer their activities away from a country where local conditions or legislation creates a climate unfavourable to them. Multinational companies often lead in the development, diffusion and application of new techniques, and provide employment for a large number of people. Despite such advantages, however, some people consider that these companies wield too much economic, financial and even political power. Of course this is a debatable point which often involves political and ideological value judgements.

Value judgements will also play a part in the justification of profit. Does profit come from the exploitation of workers and consumers? Is it essential for the survival of the company? Is it just a reward to the shareholder for taking a risk and placing their assets at the disposal of the company? In any discussion of profit, we must not forget that in Britain nearly half of the gross profit is paid to the government as corporation tax and serves to finance public spending, while a considerable part of the rest is used within the company to create new machinery and factories, and to replace depreciated machinery and buildings.

Whatever your personal opinion is, it is undeniable that companies nowadays often have a great deal of economic power and are capable of affecting the welfare of individuals, groups and even society itself. It is also undeniable, however, that many people earn their living by working for oligopoly and monopoly companies.

Another area of debate is the decision-making process in companies and the relative contributions management, shareholders and workers should make to the development of a company. In this country the government appointed a Committee of Inquiry to investigate the feasibility of bringing about joint management of firms by shareholder and worker directors. The Committee's majority report (the Bullock Report) in 1976 has led to intense public debate, but as yet no legislation. This issue will not be discussed in depth here because inevitably political value judgements are involved. Nevertheless, after reading this chapter some of the challenges and complexities of developing greater industrial democracy should become clear.

11.1 PRICE DETERMINATION IN MONOPOLISTIC COMPETITION, OLIGOPOLY AND MONOPOLY

In our modern society, the supply side of the market, in particular, often deviates from the conditions of perfect competition discussed in Chapter 10. None the less certain markets, such as the grain market and the Stock Exchange, do operate under perfect competition, and other markets can be described more easily as deviant forms.

In reality, goods are rarely homogeneous; coffee, for example, is not a single homogeneous good but comprises a number of different products – brands – competing for the consumers' favour. In addition, differences in quality, the associated service provided, etc., all serve to make the market heterogeneous, so that the consumer is influenced not only by his preference for the price, but also by other considerations. Thus, he may be prepared to pay a little more if he finds the service better. However, if there are still very many suppliers, one is faced not with monopoly, but with an intermediate form called monopolistic competition, in which each supplier is a monopolist with respect to his own brand but is still competing against the makers of other brands. For example, a restaurant is in one sense a monopolist in that it differentiates its range of food and services from others but has to compete with all other eating houses which will sell a wide range of food. This, therefore, is an example of monopolistic competition.

When an industry has only one producer (a monopolist) or only a few producers (oligopolists) a manufacturer does not have to accept the price of its goods as beyond control. Price can be fixed by the company and at a level that is as favourable to profit or sales as required. In brief, the company can pursue its own price policy. One cannot now consider a supply curve that shows how much the manufacturer would offer for sale at various prices, since the price is fixed by the manufacturer.

In addition, an oligopolist can also adjust the quality of its products, and can advertise. It can offer goods of different qualities and each oligopolist tries to convince the consumers that its product is best. In our earlier description of quantity adjustment under perfect competition there is of course no advertising. While these other aspects will be discussed later the main emphasis here is on the price policy.

We shall examine three systems of price fixing, namely monopolistic competition, monopoly and oligopoly. A monopolist itself can charge the price it wishes without having to take into account other manufacturers, whereas an oligopolist such as Chrysler has to take into account its few competitors, just as does a producer working under monopolistic competition. In oligopoly there are only a few sellers on the market, and this is precisely the situation that frequently occurs in real life.

Summary Homogeneous goods are rare in practice, and the normally heterogeneous nature of a good such as coffee therefore segments the coffee market. Manufacturers can fix their prices, and the individual and market supply curves no longer exist.

11.2 MONOPOLISTIC COMPETITION

Market Segmentation and the Demand Curve In this form of competition there are still many sellers in the industry, as in perfect competition but, as described in the previous section, they differentiate their product. Products are presented by the seller in a way designed to encourage consumer 'loyalty' to the seller's brand. For example, an Indian restaurant attempts to create a special market for its own services by differentiating them from the nearby Chinese restaurant, thereby hoping to capture consumer loyalty. Similarly, Heineken attempt to create special, almost heroically mythical, qualities for their lager beer, and to develop consumer attachment to it.

In this situation a producer can increase the price of a product and because of its brand image still retain most of its market. Under perfect competition he would lose sales to competitors.

Figure 11.1 shows how a price increase from OP_1 to OP_2 will lead to a reduction in quantity bought from OQ_1 to OQ_2. Similarly, if the producer lowers his price he will increase sales at the expense of his competitors, but will not gain all their sales, as under perfect competition, since his rivals have also differentiated their product and gained 'loyal' consumers. If he lowers the price from P_1 to P_3 he will obtain the extra sales at OQ_3. The demand curve is therefore downward sloping and to the right.

Transparency and Entry Barriers Another feature of monopolistic competition is that the many sellers and purchasers do not have full information on all the prices and products of their competitors. Departmental stores in large cities (e.g. Liverpool and Birmingham) which sell clothes and many other products are an example. The ranges of clothes of various types in these large stores and their prices are such that it is difficult either for the other sellers or for the consumer to be up-to-date with this information. Prices can therefore be raised by sellers without losing much of their market to their ill-informed rivals. In monopolistic competition there is not usually free entry to the market. In this case, the costs of building new departmental stores, for example, are a real barrier to entry for new firms.

As we saw in Figure 9.10, in perfect competition a firm produces at a level where the price equals marginal cost, but in this situation of short-run excess demand a price above marginal cost can be charged and

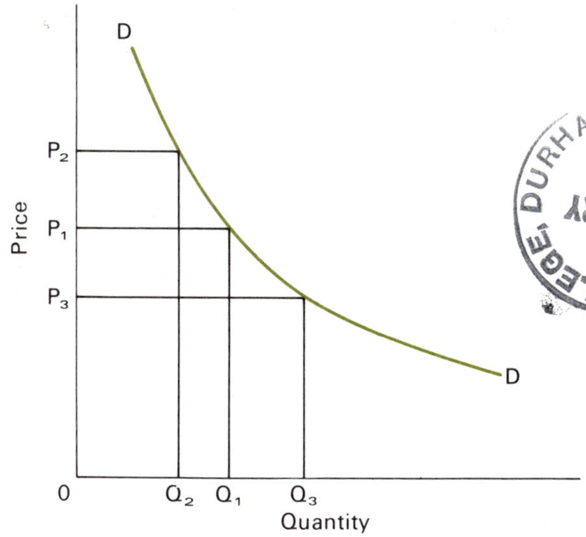

Figure 11.1 The demand curve under monopolistic competition.

abnormal profits made. Figure 11.2 shows the behaviour of the firm in the short run under monopolistic competition. Note that unlike the perfectly competitive situation the marginal revenue (MR) and average revenue (AR) curves are not identical because here the monopolistic characteristics ensure a falling sales curve rather than a horizontal one. The quantity (OQ) manufactured when marginal cost equals marginal revenue has total costs, including normal profits, represented by the area OKLQ. But the price charged allows the abnormal profit represented by area KPCL to be made over and above OKLQ. The firm in the short run under monopolistic competition is little different from the monopolist discussed in the next section.

It is useful at this point to investigate why the marginal revenue and average revenue curves are not identical. Since quantity sold varies with price, the marginal revenue is now equal to the revenue from the last unit of output *minus* the loss of revenue that is due to the fall in prices and must be applied to the other units sold. Thus, if 10 units (1 to 10) are sold at £2 apiece and 11 units (1 to 11) at £1.90 apiece, the marginal revenue is £1.90 (i.e. the revenue from the eleventh unit) minus 10 times £0.10p (the amount by which the price of 10 units (1 to 10) is less than that of the old price of the first 10 units (1 to 10)) to give MR = £0.90. The same result is obtained by comparing the total revenues from units 1 to 10 (10 × £2 = £20) and units 1 to 11 (11 × £1.90 = £20.90): £20.90 − £20 = £0.90). The following table illustrates the total and marginal revenue.

Units	*Total revenue*	*Price*	*Marginal revenue*
0	–	–	–
1	2.90	2.90	2.90
2	5.60	2.80	2.70
3	8.10	2.70	2.50
4	10.40	2.60	2.30
5	12.50	2.50	2.10
6	14.40	2.40	1.90
7	16.10	2.30	1.70
8	17.60	2.20	1.50
9	18.90	2.10	1.30
10	20.00	2.00	1.10
11	20.90	1.90	0.90

After the first unit, the marginal revenue is seen to be smaller than the price, so that the marginal revenue curve (AT) lies to the left of the sales curve (AB) (see Figure 11.2).

Short Run and Long Run What is the position of the monopolistic competition firm over the two time periods of short run and long run? In the short run no new production factors (e.g. labour and capital) can be used by the firm, and almost certainly no new firms can enter the market. An increase in demand for the product in the short run cannot be matched by an equivalent increase in supply.

The long-run situation is quite different, because new factors of

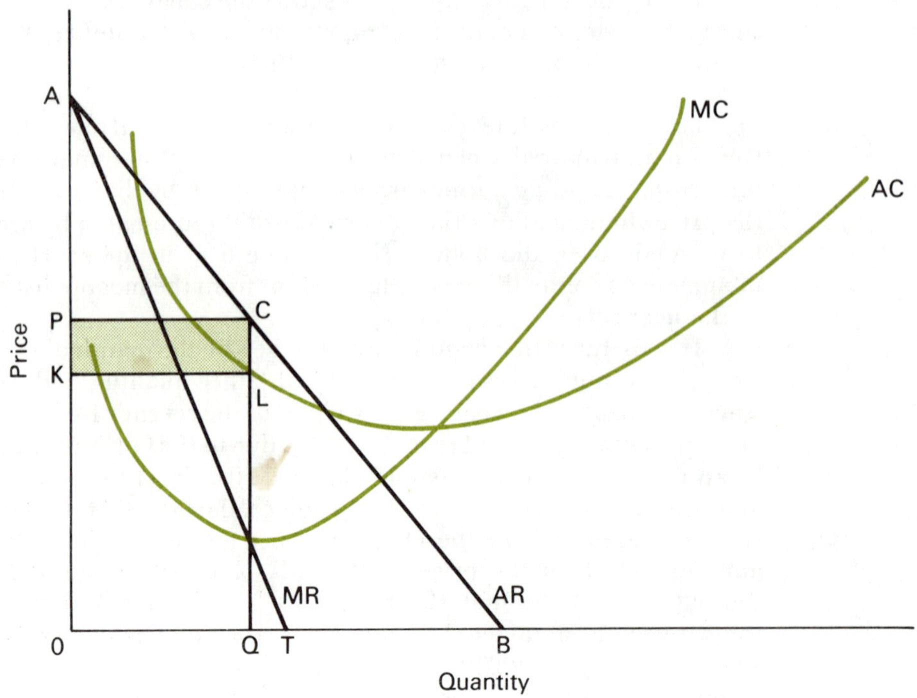

Figure 11.2 Monopolistic competition (short run).

production, and in some cases new firms, enter the industry to boost output. None the less, the supply side does not always fully equate with the demand because the good in question is differentiated into products and these encourage brand loyalty. Unlike perfect competition in which supply and demand would equate, and profits be reduced to normal, the firm under monopolistic competition may continue to make small amounts of abnormal profit. It does this because it can price its product slightly higher than under perfect competition, since it makes a differentiated product. However, many new firms can enter the market even for differentiated products and there can arise a situation of substantial excess capacity in the industry which will reduce firms' profits to the level of normal profits. The sales function has shifted such that it will be tangential to the average cost curve (see Figure 11.3) and here total costs including normal profits are represented by OP_1C_1Q.

Summary Monopolistic competition assumes the existence of many sellers in the market, making differentiated products, and without full knowledge of all prices and products. Firms therefore can change prices without losing or gaining substantial numbers of customers.

11.3 MONOPOLY

The monopolist's sales situation is depicted by the average revenue sales curve, which is based on the market demand curve and similarly falls from

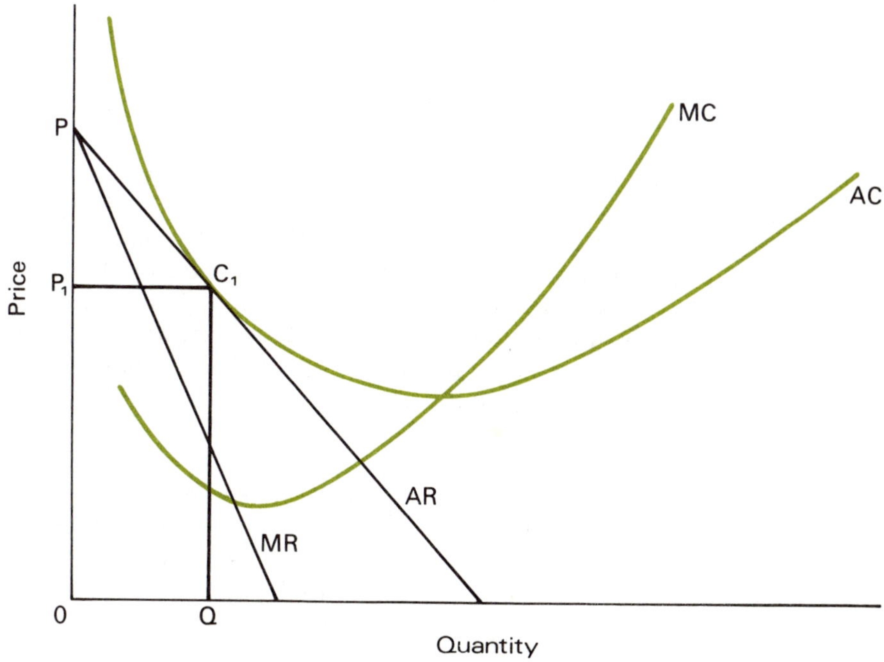

Figure 11.3 Monopolistic competition (long run).

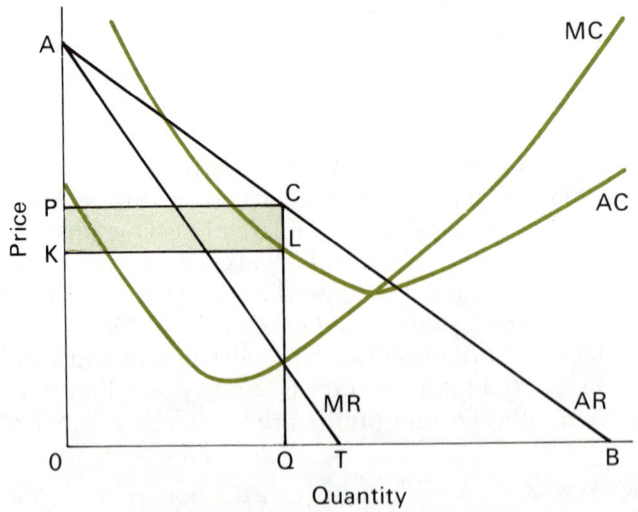

Figure 11.4 Monopoly.

left to right, i.e. the monopolist can also sell more at a lower price (see Figure 11.4). He maximizes his profit by the appropriate choice of the price and the quantity which, as always, corresponds to the output where the marginal cost is equal to the marginal revenue. While the curves for the marginal and average cost are the same as under perfect competition, the curve for the marginal revenue again differs here from the average revenue curve, in contrast to the situation under perfect competition shown in Figure 9.10.

The marginal cost corresponding to a sales volume OQ is equal to the marginal revenue, and so the profit is maximized here. The corresponding price is OP. Since the average total cost (AC) at volume OQ is QL (which is the same as OK), the profit per unit is PK. The total profit is given by this unit profit (PK) multiplied by the number of units sold (OQ), i.e. by the area of the shaded rectangle PCLK. The equilibrium point C on the sales curve is called the Cournot point after Cournot who formulated this monopolist's equilibrium in 1838. He was far ahead of his time, since he did pioneering work on monopoly while his contemporaries concentrated mainly on perfect competition.

Summary Given the sales curve, the monopolist fixes his price himself. However, he cannot set his prices at too high a level or he would lose all his customers. The Cournot point on the sales curve gives the price and output at which profit is maximized.

11.4 OLIGOPOLY

Oligopoly often occurs in practice but has not yet been fully explained in theoretical terms. As soon as we have a few competing manufacturers in a market, various things can happen. They can wage an economic war against one another which will hurt all of them and eliminate the weakest or they can cooperate with one another to varying degrees.

Price Policy Profit-maximizing firms find that any move on their part elicits a reaction from their competitors, but it is difficult to say what this reaction will be: competitors may make an identical change in prices, or may make an entirely different change, or may make no apparent change at all. The equilibrium situation varies with the reaction, but the latter cannot be predicted. However, as a general rule one can say that the prices of all firms in the industry tend to be similar, presumably because of reluctance to use price as a weapon in competition. There is instead a preference for competition in terms of product type and quality, allied services and advertising.

Pricing of products in reality shows a greater variation than is predicted by the hypothesis of profit maximization. Thus, there may be reasons to set the price at a level lower than that required for profit maximization, for example to ensure a rapid growth in the market. A firm attempting this is known as a *sales maximizer*.

What is the pricing policy of an oligopoly firm? It is generally found that where there are between two and four firms in an industry, any firm which reduces its price will be followed by the others. However, if it raises prices it may not be followed, because the others may believe their market will increase at the expense of the first firm.

In Figure 11.5 OP is the current price level, and the demand curve is BAD. If the price is cut to below OP then the part of the demand curve which is relevant to the firm is AD, which is the more inelastic part of it, reflecting the firm's belief that its price cut will be followed by the other firms.

On the other hand if the price is raised above OP, then the part of the demand curve which is relevant to the firm is BA, which is the more elastic part of it, reflecting the firm's belief that its price rise will not be followed by the other firms.

We often obtain in oligopoly the kinked demand curve BAD. This kink in the demand curve is related to a discontinuity in the marginal revenue curve BFEM. This discontinuity in the MR curve shows that in oligopoly markets one can observe the same price and output being compatible with different costs. If the marginal revenue curve shifts between E and F, there will be no change in the price charged by the oligopolist as long as he tries to measure his profits. This explains some of the price rigidity which exists under oligopoly conditions.

An alternative view of pricing under oligopoly is one which argues that when one oligopolist raises his price the others follow. Substantial evidence for this 'price-leadership' idea has been provided by investigations in the post-war period into such British industries as cables, tyres, and tea supply. In cables, tyres and tobacco British Insulated Callender Cables, Dunlop, and Imperial Tobacco, respectively, have been cited as companies which act as leaders in raising prices, which the other firms follow. It is argued that in an expanding economy (as in Britain between 1945 and 1975) brand loyalties are very strong and therefore all firms in the industry benefit from price rises, there being no need to fear a loss of market share by any company. A case study of pricing in the tea supply industry can be found in Section 11.7. At present, this alternative view is the one most widely accepted as representing the firm's behaviour under oligopoly conditions. Indeed, it is true to say that few oligopolists cut prices during the present inflationary conditions; in fact, rapid inflation in the 1970s has reinforced the need for a form of upward price leadership in oligopoly industries. For example, the British car industry doubled the prices of basic saloon cars over the period 1972–7 as the four firms concerned followed upward price leads.

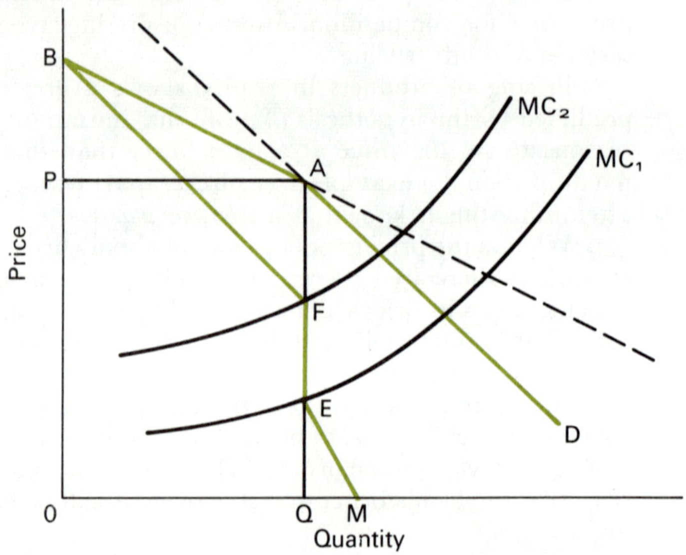

Figure 11.5 Oligopoly.

Non-price Forms of Competition As indicated earlier, these are important areas of competition between oligopolists and the three sections below deal with them.

Product policy concerns the number and type of products to be supplied, the characteristics that are to be attributed to them, the degree of product differentiation, and the development of entirely new products. In the British detergent industry there are two oligopolist firms, Unilever and Procter and Gamble. Both firms market a wide range of soap powders, each product being differentiated and subject to much advertising. They are able to maximize profits and control much of the market by ensuring the popularity and therefore the sales of at least one of each firm's products all the time.

Distribution policy deals with two main questions: one concerns distribution to wholesalers as opposed to retailers, and the other the actual routes and modes of distribution and the way to stimulate the sales effort along the chain. The costs of production of a new product for oligopoly companies are so great that they need to control routes and modes of distribution to the consumer very carefully. Motor car companies therefore have agents as retailers in all major towns, and make agency agreements with them to optimize sales outlets and after-sales service publicity. Many oligopoly firms sell direct to retailers and cut out wholesaling operations altogether. In this way they cut the costs of employing a 'middleman' and hope to increase profit as well as sales.

Advertising policy concerns the various forms of product promotion that are known to all of us from television, radio, newspapers and direct mail. More specifically, it deals with the advertising theme, the amount to be spent in comparison with research development or distribution and how the advertising budget should be spent. Advertising is vital to ensure that the huge production costs of an oligopolist can be met by adequate sales at a price established (usually) by price leadership. The Ford Fiesta car produced in 1977 was supported by a massive advertising campaign to help promote a sales level which should pay the costs and lead to profits.

Competition is directed not only against other established firms but also against would-be entrants to the market, attracted to it by a considerable profit margin. It is possible, therefore, that the established firms take the possibility of entry into account when fixing their prices. Apart from this, competition occurs only occasionally in the oligopolistic market. However, the oligopolistic firms can easily form a power block, i.e. adopt a common policy against would-be entrants and agree not to compete with one another through prices. If independent companies in a certain sector come to such an agreement to restrict competition, we speak of a cartel and – in the case of a price agreement – a *price cartel*. The danger for society is that cartels sustain inefficient forms of production and keep prices high. The British government, among others, therefore prevents by law the development of cartels.

The government is also watchful of *mergers* (the fusion of two or more independent companies), *takeovers* (one company absorbs another) and entry barriers. Mergers and takeovers are on the increase in Britain and because of this the situation for medium and small companies is becoming increasingly precarious. On the other hand, this form of industrial concentration could promote economic growth and technical development.

Summary In practice, oligopoly often means a certain rigidity of prices which is 'asymmetric', since it applies only in one direction, namely upwards: prices may be raised but rarely lowered. Such behaviour is often based on price leadership in an industry in which all firms by custom fix their prices at a level similar to that of a key company.

11.5 THE OPEC CARTEL

OPEC is the recently formed organization of Oil Producing and Exporting Countries. It is a cartel, concentrating on the maintenance of a common price for oil, and such a cartel is one of the possible forms of oligopoly. By agreeing in principle to coordinate their price policy, the oil producing and exporting countries forestall a self-destructive price competition among themselves which would push the price of oil down. Their aim is clearly to maximize their joint profit, so that the profit made by each country is proportional to the oil it produces and sells. The power of the cartel depends on (1) how united the consumers are in their response, and (2) how compatible the interests of the parties to the cartel are. Both a concerted consumer response and differences in interests within the cartel could lead to the dissolution of the cartel. First of all, the West can cut down on its consumption of oil. The demand is more sensitive to the price than was once thought. Saudi Arabia, for example, appreciated that a much higher price means a considerably lower sales volume in the short run and even more so in the long run. Therefore neither Saudi Arabia nor the Union of Arab Emirates subscribed to the OPEC price agreement of 1977.

Collective profit maximization may thus be undermined through the desire to ensure individual profit. In addition, the oil consuming countries will develop or encourage the development of new sources of oil from deposits and harness alternative forms of energy. All this works against the oligopoly power of the oil producing and exporting countries.

The conflict of interest between the members of the cartel, based on differences in their investment programmes, should also be considered. Some members have an ambitious, mainly internal, investment programme, based on the expectation that oil prices can continue to be increased greatly for a long time. Others, with less optimistic expectations, have embarked on more modest investment programmes located mainly in the West. Members of the first group, such as Libya and Algeria, are compelled to ask a very high price for oil and ignore the effect of this on the world economy, while those of the second group, including Saudi Arabia, pursue a less extremist policy and have a direct interest in the recovery of the world economy. This conflict may increase and eventually destroy the cartel. However, the cartel unanimously agreed to increase oil prices in January 1979, largely in order to combat the decline in value of the American dollar (the currency in which oil prices are expressed) and price rises are aided by production cutbacks.

Much depends also on how the West will respond to large OPEC price rises. These will raise all prices in the short term and accentuate the difficulties of numerous companies, while aggravating inflation and recession in general. On the other hand, some economists would claim that a small increase would not sustain interest in and research on alternative energy sources and, from this point of view, a smaller rise in oil prices would be even more damaging to the West in the long run.

Summary The OPEC cartel has great economic power, but not absolute power. Like all oligopolies it has to pay attention to long-run profits in the market supplied, for it would be counter-productive to aim purely at maximizing short-run abnormal profit.

11.6 STRUCTURE OF PRIVATE INDUSTRY IN BRITAIN

Private industry in Britain is characterized by a mixture of the market forms we have examined (i.e. perfect competition, monopolistic competition, oligopoly and monopoly), and it is owned in a variety of ways including sole trading, partnership, and private and public companies. Nationalized firms account for about 11 per cent of production in Britain and these companies are studied in Chapter 14, Section 7. During the past two decades there has been a strong trend towards concentration of ownership of private industry into fewer hands, due to mergers, and a substantial increase in the size and importance to the national economy of the largest companies. In 1958, the 50 largest firms in the United Kingdom were responsible for 24.7 per cent of the net output, and by 1968 their share had risen to 32.4 per cent. Similarly, their share of labour employed had also increased from 21.2 per cent of the working population in 1958 to 29.4 per cent in 1968. These changes are due to a growth of the largest form of ownership, the public company, and the market form called oligopoly, in which as we have seen only a few firms exist in an industry.

The Sole Trader The sole trader is the simplest form of industrial ownership and tends to be associated with perfect and monopolistic competition conditions of trade. The street-corner retailer, who sells a wide range of general products, including groceries, is one of the most typical examples of the sole trader. He usually owns one retail outlet, and has full freedom to manage the business and employ staff as he wishes. Similarly, in some rural areas the village blacksmith operates as a sole trader. However, the person concerned can be sued for his personal income and wealth if he falls into debt, and his business can expand only because his own personal income is put into new projects. In towns, the small retailer is usually in competition with many others, since housewives usually have good information on competitive prices. Therefore a situation approximating to perfect competition can exist and it is not difficult for new entrants to establish shops. However, some sole traders might be classified as monopolistic competitors in that they establish a special reputation for the particular special service provided by their shop, e.g., a hairdressing salon, which provides a unique personal service.

The Partnership The partnership form of industrial ownership is generally found amongst professional people such as solicitors, accountants, estate agents, etc. The partnership increases the flow of income into the organization, and deepens the financial reserves, differing in this way from the sole trader. Each of the three or four solicitors in such a partnership can also specialize in a particular area such as litigation, house purchase/sales etc., and thereby bring a greater range of expertise to the partnership. However, a major disadvantage is that the wealth and income of all partners can be called in if the partnership becomes involved in severe debt. It could be argued that partnerships of estate agents exist in a market that approximates to perfect competition. In a large town there are many such firms, information on property prices is widely circulated, and entry to the market is easy for newcomers. However, many partnerships are characterized by monopolistic competition. Solicitors, for example, provide a highly personal service to a client and so retain his custom by virtue of their unique knowledge of the client's affairs.

The Private Company A major form of ownership for small businesses is the private limited liability company. This type of company enables the owners to put into it only as much money as they wish, and its existence as a legal organization is separate from that of the owners. An example of this is a plant hiring contractor who rents bulldozing and other equipment to customers for developing building sites. As his business expands he establishes a private company to control the business. He may decide that his wife will become Managing Director; he will be the only other shareholder, and both shareholders will put, let us say, £20 000 into this company. Subsequently, if the firm is in severe debt, the owners can be sued only for the funds they have put into the company, since the company is a separate legal organization from them as persons. In this type of company only the limited number of shareholders can supply funds, but there are examples of large companies which survive with substantial funds and have a small number of shareholders confined to one family, e.g. Brinton's Carpets Limited, a major international textile company based in Britain.

Some private companies, such as many plant hire contractors, work in conditions approximating to perfectly competitive markets. Others are closer to monopolistic competition, such as product differentiating lock-and-key manufacturers, and even to oligopoly, as in the case of the carpet manufacturers mentioned earlier.

The Public Company The majority of large private businesses are public companies which not only have the advantages of limited liability but also can raise funds on the stock market by issuing shares to the public. There are therefore many owners (or shareholders) in such companies, and in most British companies institutional shareholders (i.e. insurance companies and pension funds) hold a substantial amount of the shares. At the annual general meeting of, for example, Imperial Chemical Industries the shareholders elect the company's main board of directors to run the day-to-day business of the firm. However, as long as the company is not in difficulties few shareholders usually turn up at the meetings, and the directors will be re-elected and their major policy recommendations accepted. This is true of most public companies. Such companies are nevertheless dependent upon performing successfully to be sure of raising funds, and such funds will not be easy to obtain from new issues of shares during a recession. In such circumstances the privately-owned family company can obtain more money more easily from committed family members. Monopolistic competition is in evidence amongst the public companies of the woollen textile industry, where there are many companies but differentiated products. Public companies also compete in oligopoly markets, such as the car industry with its four United Kingdom based companies. A few public companies are monopolies with huge market power such as Imperial Tobacco Company, discussed later in this chapter.

Summary There are four major forms of ownership in British private industry: sole trader, partnership, private company and public company. Monopolistic competition is followed by some organizations in all four types, perfect competition by some in the first three, oligopoly only in the last two, and monopoly only amongst public companies.

11.7 BRITISH MONOPOLIES AND OLIGOPOLIES: THE MONOPOLIES AND MERGERS COMMISSION

The domination of production in an industry by one firm (monopoly) or a few large firms (oligopoly) can lead to higher prices and lower production levels than the market system of allocating resources under perfect competition would. As we have seen in Section 11.2, if a firm has large power in the market it can fix prices above the level at which marginal revenue and marginal cost are equalized, and can further establish this high price by restricting production and availability of goods. The claims to efficiency of the free market economy are under serious scrutiny when such economies contain monopoly power. It is for this reason that in a mixed economy, one role of government as the economy's manager is to regulate monopoly and oligopoly.

Natural Monopolies Certain industries, of course, lend themselves to being natural monopolies, because the sheer capital costs of establishing a firm in the industry on a national network basis are huge. Postal and telecommunications services, and electricity and gas supply are examples. All natural monopolies, except water supply (which is controlled by local municipal and private monopolies) are nationalized in Britain and subject to parliamentary accountability (see Chapter 14, Section 7).

Monopolies Commission 1948–65 Other industries, however, have firms with dominant market power (e.g. in industrial gases, tobacco, and some sectors of chemicals) and the 1944 government White Paper on Employment Policy contended that the removal of the pricing and production restrictions of monopolies would expand trade and employment.

Therefore in 1948 the government set up a Monopolies Commission to investigate, whenever government requested, industries in which at least one-third of all the goods produced in the United Kingdom were supplied by one firm. The Commission could therefore probe all monopolies and most oligopolies, and government could take limited remedial action as a consequence. The size of the Commission was increased in 1953, and decreased in 1956, when documented restrictive practices agreements were referred to a newly established Restrictive Practices Court. As a consequence of making these written agreements between firms illegal and of the rapid increase in international firms' competition in British markets in the 1960s (due to lowering of tariffs), a spate of mergers between firms took place.

Monopolies and Mergers Commission since 1965 In 1965, the re-named Monopolies and Mergers Commission was strengthened in size and scope, by allowing it to investigate mergers leading to a one-third share of the market by a firm, and monopolies in service industries. More effective, however, was the strengthening of government powers to include price regulation and prevention of mergers, when the Commission recommended this type of action. Further powers of recommendation and inquiry were given to the Commission by the Fair Trading Act 1973, which required investigations of market dominance to include suggested actions to promote competition in the industry, and which allowed the Commission to look into price leadership in industries. Moreover, nationalized and local monopolies can be investigated, and any industry in which one firm produces one-quarter of all goods made in the United Kingdom can be probed. However, most situations of monopoly and oligopoly are not referred to the Commission, but stronger government action on its recommendations in the 1960s and 1970s, e.g. price regulation and merger prevention, and the power to investigate price leadership, helps promote competition in industries.

Monopoly in the Cigarette and Tobacco Industry Two examples of the Commission's work and of government's reluctance to intervene can be seen in the Supply of Cigarettes and Tobacco and of Cigarette and Tobacco Machinery Report (1960–61) and the Merger of British Motor Corporation Limited and Pressed Steel Company Limited Report (1965–6). The Tobacco investigation was a classic monopoly inquiry into an industry in which Imperial Tobacco Company held 75.4 per cent of the United Kingdom market (1954). The report showed historically the business tactics of non-interference in home markets used to limit United States firms' competition, and the devices utilized to prevent the success and ensure the takeover of a new United Kingdom Company which marketed a larger cigarette at the prevailing retail price. The company was combated by Imperial which, encouraged by other tobacco manufacturers, produced a similar cigarette, eroded the new company's profits and then took over the company. The situation in 1960 was that the industry contained 24 firms, marketing 400 tobacco brands. Imperial argued that each firm within its organization (e.g. Wills and Player) was a separate trading entity whose freedom was restricted only in the fields of capital, new products, pricing and advertisements. Apart from these implied historical criticisms of Imperial, the fundamental criticism of the Commission in its report was that the limited internal competition allowed to Imperial's constituent firms was not an effective substitution for real competition. The report believed, however, that the profits earned were not against the public interest, and that Gallaher's recently increased share of the market was a promising sign of increased competition.

BMC/Pressed Steel Merger Government took no action against Imperial's monopoly, but in the second example it delayed the proposed BMC/ Pressed Steel merger until the Commission reported. The case against the merger was that BMC was the largest car producer (45 per cent of the market) and Pressed Steel produced 40 per cent of the bodies for cars. The Commission concluded that the merger would integrate both firms' production in such a way as to create more efficiency, that indications were that BMC or Rootes would set up its own large body plant soon in any case, and that Pressed Steel's other main customers, Rootes and Standard Triumph, did not oppose the merger. Government approved the merger in the light of this report.

Action against oligopolies' market power has been even less than that taken against monopolies. Galbraith argues that modern capital-intensive industry usually results in two to four firms accounting for almost all the market, and that in this situation practices of price leadership and rigidity of company share of that market result. The tea supply industry in the United Kingdom is dominated by four such firms which account for 85 per cent of the market, and its price leadership practice was examined in 1970 by the short-lived National Board for Prices and Incomes. In April 1970 the largest firm, Brooke Bond (43 per cent of market), raised its price by 2d per $\frac{1}{4}$ lb, and shortly afterwards the other three firms did the same. The latter's main stated reason for being 'price-followers', said the Report, 'was that their competitive tea would have looked 'cheap' and therefore not as good as other leading brands'. The Report recommended that the tea companies should be more competitive in their marketing to retailers, but no action was taken by government. Nevertheless, their prices were not raised for another four years.

The Monopolies Commission makes few investigations of price leadership, however, but it does collect much information, and in the 1960s and 1970s government made greater use of its recommendations (e.g. price cut imposed on Kodak in 1966, and 20 per cent price cut imposed on household detergent manufacturers' new lines).

Summary By investigation, the government discovers the extent of monopoly and oligopoly in industries, but although at times it imposes price cuts and stops mergers, its efforts to promote competition through the Commission have generally been limited. Therefore one must assume that monopolies are charging prices above levels found at equilibrium of supply and demand in the perfect competition model, and oligopoly firms, guided by price-leaders, are behaving similarly.

11.8 GOVERNMENT ANTI-CARTEL POLICY: THE RESTRICTIVE TRADE PRACTICES COURT

Restrictive Trade Practices Court The government has developed a much stronger policy to deter price fixing (i.e. cartels) by firms in industries where there are many competitors, i.e. firms in a monopolistic competition market (rather than a monopoly or oligopoly dominated market). The main agent for this control is the Restrictive Trade Practices Court, which was set up in 1956 with the object of drastically limiting price determination by firms' collective agreements. All such agreements must be registered, and the onus is on the manufacturers to prove that the agreement is in the public interest. They have seven criteria for proving their case (called 'gateways') through the Court: (1) protection of public against injury; (2) making available 'specific and substantial' benefits; (3) counteracting restrictive practices of non-signatories of agreement; (4) dealing from strength with powerful purchasers; (5) avoiding serious unemployment; (6) aiding exports; (7) maintaining a restriction that is justifiable on merit. (This legislation was slightly amended in 1968.) The first four cases were lost by the manufacturers: e.g. the Cotton Yarn Spinners (1959) tried the unemployment 'gateway', but their excess capacity and their agreement's general effects were considered inefficient. Some agreements were upheld by the Court, such as that of the Water Tube Boilers (1959) which stimulated exports.

Glass Bottle Manufacturers' Price Agreement The Glass Bottle manufacturers in 1961 defended their agreement under the wide-ranging second gateway, 'specific and substantial' benefits to the public. The benefits in this case were argued to be those of very low stable prices and improvement in the quality of the product. These general claims were not supported by the Court, which felt that the manufacturers' use of weighted average profit figures could conceal inefficiencies and some very high profits, and that no price war (injurious to product quality) would result from the termination of the agreement.

It is interesting that the manufacturers then turned to informal methods of price agreement, such as 'information agreements' and price leadership. The Glass Container Information Bureau was short-lived, however, since many firms sold below the Bureau's reported prices, and the consequent attempt at price leadership through United Glass Co. soon failed due to price wars in the food-bottling industry. This example is taken from the three-quarters of the agreements which were not proved to the Court, and the result of the Court's decisions was that the overwhelming majority of registered agreements were voluntarily ended or drastically amended. Competition in pricing and allocation of resources were established in many industries therefore by this form of government intervention. The Fair Trading Act (1973) extended the Court's powers to include firms engaged in commercial services and the types of agreement requiring reorganization and investigation were extended.

Resale Price Maintenance The 1956 legislation, which set up the Court, paradoxically enforced one important feature of non-competition in retail markets: resale price maintenance (RPM). This situation enabled manufacturers legally to enforce a sales price on all their retailers, but in 1964 RPM was also made subject to the authority of the Restrictive Practices Court, in which manufacturers had to prove that their RPM arrangements were in the public interest. As with the other price agreement legislation there are criteria concerning the definition of the public interest which manufacturers must prove. This time there are five criteria (i.e. five 'gateways' through the Court): (1) quality and variety of goods would be reduced; (2) substantial reduction in retail outlets; (3) prices in the long term would rise; (4) goods would be sold unhygienically; (5) after-sales service would be substantially reduced. Groups of agreements were brought before the Court, and the vast majority of cases went against the manufacturer. The Court's decision, at its first hearing in 1967, to ban RPM in the confectionery industry was a major setback to firms, and by 1970 very few RPM practices existed.

Reductions in prices by supermarkets and discount stores varied from 20 per cent in paints, 5 per cent in furniture, 10 per cent in some cigarette brands, and 16 per cent in household appliances and electrical goods, in spite of the manufacturers' practice of recommending retail prices. The consequence of anti-RPM legislation was therefore a substantial move towards the competitive pricing system of allocation of resources.

The protection of the consumer as such was answered in the 1973 Act which has led the Director General to review firms' activities which he believes are against the consumer's interest. He has made voluntary codes of conduct with such service industries as motor repair, tourism and laundries to ensure independent arbitration for consumer complaints.

Summary Price competition amongst manufacturers, and price competition amongst retailers have been substantially encouraged by the government legislation which made restrictive agreements subject to criteria for a vigorously anti-cartel Court.

11.9 CONCLUDING REMARKS

Apart from Cournot's early contribution, the theory of imperfect competition was worked out in 1933 by Chamberlain and Joan Robinson, who pointed out that perfect competition was becoming an abstraction, and the real market forms were monopoly, monopolistic competition and oligopoly.

The main point for us is that the weakening of competition leads to the concentration of economic power and to a rather one-sided fixing of prices by the firms. Prices lose the flexibility they had under perfect competition and become more rigid. This means that changes in the circumstances of production no longer find a direct expression in prices. While a rise in raw-material prices is incorporated in the sales price, a fall in them is regarded as a source of extra profit instead of leading to a drop in the sales price. Moreover, even the most inefficient company can continue production under the protection of a cartel.

The allocation of resources to production units by the market under perfect competition is changed by monopolies, oligopolies and cartels. The British government, as manager of a mixed economy, has used legislation to attempt to remove some major features of these practices, and to ensure an allocation of resources less dependent on the monopoly and oligopoly power of firms. The cartels in industries which have many firms have been broken by the Restrictive Trade Practices Court, but oligopoly pricing and market sharing is only occasionally investigated by the Monopolies and Mergers Commission, which has concentrated its attention mainly upon monopolies. Only in the last 12 years has government made any real efforts to enforce some of the Commission's recommendations against monopolies, high prices and mergers. (The government's own monopolies, some nationalized firms, are dealt with in Chapter 14.)

QUESTIONS

1 Why is it impossible to derive a supply function in the case of monopoly?

2 To what extent is British Rail a monopoly?

3 What is resale price maintenance? How could a firm prove to the Restrictive Trade Practices Court that its RPM agreement was in the public interest?

4 What reports did the Monopolies and Mergers Commission produce in the last year? Has government taken any action against monopolies and oligopolies as a consequence?

5 Why is it difficult to recognize a position of economic power?

6 What is OPEC?

7 Describe the advertising policy of a manufacturer in one of the well-known oligopolistic markets.

8 List a few recent mergers. What reasons were given for them?

9 Name a multinational company that was in the news last week. Examine to what extent it has an oligopolistic position in Britain with respect to one or more products.

10 How can the power of a multinational company be manifested?

EXERCISES

1 What are the differences and similarities between consumer behaviour theory and producer behaviour theory?

2 What are the differences and similarities between the theory of perfect competition and that of monopoly?

3 Give some practical examples of oligopolies?

4 Compare the British Restrictive Trade Practices Court with the prohibition of cartels in the USA and Federal Germany.

5 Examine the advertisements of some detergent manufacturers in the papers in the next few months, and note any special offers and price changes.

6 How can the actions of the Monopolies and Mergers Commission lead to a lowering of the rate of inflation?

7 Name some oligopoly firms which are British owned.

8 Discuss the advantages and disadvantages of profit maximization. Can a final decision be derived from economic theory?

9 Discuss the question whether companies are responsible for environmental pollution, and if so, to what extent.

10 What is the significance of OPEC for the developing countries?

11 Why is the demand curve in monopoly and monopolistic competition an unbroken one, whereas in some cases the demand curve in oligopoly is kinked?

Chapter Twelve

The Price of Labour and Capital

The determination of the price of labour and capital often involves a fierce battle between unions and employers for a larger share of the national income, or 'national cake'. The share of the British national income accruing to wages of labour in recent years has increased to over two-thirds, whereas interest, rent and profit total about 30 per cent, and this situation is reflected in the falling profits of companies in the 1970s.

Marx and his followers depict a 'class struggle' between workers and owners of firms (or *capitalists*, as they are termed in Marxist literature), and they have analysed economic, political and social phenomena from this standpoint. According to Marx the capitalist, from employing workers and selling goods, obtains more revenue than he pays out in wages and the difference between the two amounts is broadly called 'surplus value'. This is siphoned off by the capitalist and used for capital accumulation and personal welfare. In this way the worker is 'exploited' by the capitalist. Furthermore, Marx argued that the introduction of labour-saving machinery and techniques leads to redundancies, an 'army of unemployed' and wages reduced to subsistence level (see Chapter 16).

Two points should be noted in this context. Firstly, although the position of the worker in the production process is often a dependent one the workers, by making a united stand in trade unions, can wield considerable power against the employer. Secondly, wages are now well above subsistence level in Western Europe and North America. Moreover, some workers identify themselves with what they produce in both capitalist and state socialist systems. In twentieth-century Britain, bargaining about wages and working conditions has generally been done by the various trade unions, representing the workpeople, and by employers' organizations, representing the employers. We shall now analyse the theory of the price of capital and labour in order to understand how incomes are determined in our society. We have seen how the prices of consumer goods are determined and how the producer operates in the market where he sells his goods. The producer must, before selling goods, however, first make the products, and for this he needs to buy the factors of production – land, labour, and capital – at certain prices.

It must be made clear that the demand for factors of production is a derived demand, and is based upon the market for consumer goods. The prices of the production factors are therefore related to consumer demand for goods. These prices of land, labour and capital are termed respectively rent, wages and interest, and are earned through the production of goods. We shall now examine the determination of each of these factor payments in turn.

12.1 THE MARGINAL PRODUCTIVITY THEORY OF LABOUR

Supply, Demand and Wages For a long time, economists tried to explain wages as follows, using a model in which perfect competition is assumed. The equilibrium price of labour emerges under the influence of the forces of supply and demand, and the lower the factor price, the more an entrepreneur wants to buy of it. This is how, for example, the individual demand curve of an employer for labour comes about. Employing more labour is not always an attractive proposition for the entrepreneur, since he may have to pay out more money in wages than the revenue he obtains from the sales of extra output.

It is assumed that a market supply curve for labour can be drawn showing that the higher the wage, the greater the total amount of labour offered. In this situation we are assuming perfect competition between many buyers and sellers of labour, and that all workers will be equally qualified to do the job. We also assume that the employer is not changing his use of other production factors such as capital and land. We thus

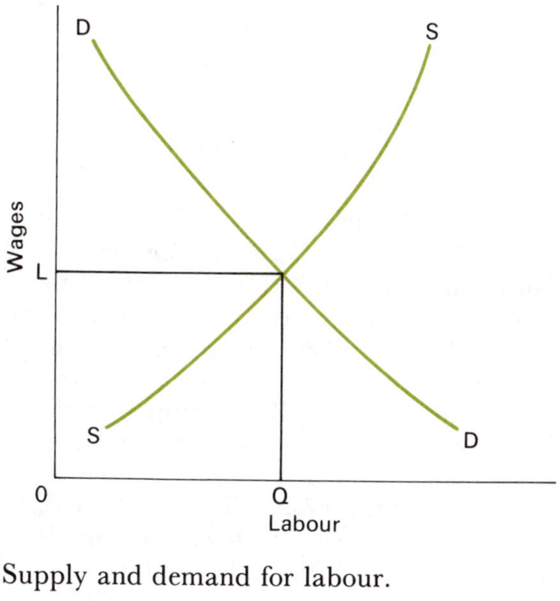

Figure 12.1 Supply and demand for labour.

obtain the real wage, together with the declining demand curve, and Figure 12.1 shows how the equilibrium wage L is assumed here to come about.

Marginal Productivity The demand for labour and the price paid to labour are explained more fully in terms of marginal productivity. The equilibrium wage, however, is still fixed by the free market, since we are still assuming that the firm is operating in a perfect competition situation. The demand for labour is governed by the money value of the marginal product of labour. The marginal product, we know, is the extra unit added to the production of a good. The marginal revenue product is the revenue the firm obtains from the extra unit of production. What we are most concerned with in this theory, however, is the last addition to revenue from the sales of goods due to the employment of an extra worker. We are therefore examining the relationship between the marginal revenue product and the employment of the last labourer.

In Table 12.1 below we see how the wage is related to the marginal product, and how employers demand certain amounts of labour for work. They will demand more and more labour as long as the extra units of output produced by the extra labour produce goods, which gain revenue when sold that is greater than the wage paid to the workers. However, when the employer reaches the point at which the revenue gained from the output of the last man equals his wage, he will employ no more workers. In other words, when the firm's marginal revenue product (i.e. the addition to revenue gained from the units produced by the last man) equals the wage, the maximum total of the firm's labour force, consistent with the maximization of profit to the firm, has been reached.

Table 12.1 Marginal revenue product.

Men	*Output (units)*	*Total revenue (£)*	*Marginal product*	*Marginal revenue product (£)*
21	1540	3080	–	–
22	1580	3160	40	80
23	1636	3232	36	72
24	1647	3294	31	62

In the table the revenue from each unit produced is £2. If the wage given in the market is £72 a week the employer will demand more workers even when he has 21 or 22 men in his factory. This is because the extra revenue he gains from employing the 22nd man (i.e. marginal revenue product (MRP)) is £80, which is greater than the wage. However, when he employs the 23rd man his marginal revenue product is only £72, the same as the wage. He will therefore demand no more workers; if he did this his MRP with 24 men would be £62, and he would pay out more to this last worker than he gained in revenue from employing him. The employer can only employ this last man if he lowers wages, and in the perfect competition situation the wage is determined by the combined forces of supply and demand, which the individual employer cannot change.

Criticisms of the Marginal Productivity Theory Keynes criticized the Marginal Productivity Theory on the grounds that if the wage was reduced in a recession it did not automatically mean that more workers would be employed, because a lower wage also implies a reduction in purchasing power. The theory is more generally attacked on the basis that it will apply only in perfect competition industries and in Britain these are few in number, as we saw in Chapter 10.

However, some economists would argue that the theory can be useful, in general terms, outside perfectly competitive markets. They suggest that if a trade union, through use of its economic power (e.g. strike action) forced the employer to pay a wage above the marginal productivity level, the company would be forced to take action to raise revenue or to lower costs. It could raise revenue by increasing prices, and if it were an oligopolist this could easily be done by a 'price leader' company (see Chapter 11). Motor car companies are sometimes cited as examples of this policy. On the other hand the company might cut costs by making some workers redundant. The steel industry is on occasions given as an example of this policy. However, a union strong enough to force wages above marginal productivity level is unlikely to allow large-scale redundancy.

It is suggested that British trade unions have resisted the development of new technology and preserved 'over-manned' situations in plants. The chemical industry labour force in British plants is a third larger than that for similar plants in Western Europe and North America (conclusion of study groups of employers and trade unionists in the Chemical Economics Development Committee). However, productivity deals in chemicals, oil processing, steel, railways and newspaper production have led to substantial reductions in the labour force in return for substantial rises in earnings and in the capital/labour ratio. Nevertheless, in most British firms there is still relative over-manning.

Non-monetary Rewards Advocates of the marginal productivity theory would argue that in the long run there will be a tendency towards equality of earnings for all workers, except for differences in pay due to particular conditions of work (i.e. due to net advantages). Lower wages may be compensated by non-monetary rewards, such as prestige in the job, which satisfies the worker (e.g. clerks in offices, who may be paid less than skilled craftsmen). Higher wages may compensate for non-monetary disadvantages, such as unsocial hours of work (e.g. public transport?), dangerous work (e.g. civil engineers?), dirty work (e.g. coalminers?). Opponents of the marginal productivity theory in this context argue that the dirty, dangerous, unsocial hours conditions in jobs are not compensated by higher pay. Wootton, the British social scientist, in her massive study 'The Social Foundations of Wage Policy' makes a major point that, 'most professional workers can expect to leave the average industrial worker behind well before they reach the top of their [pay] scales.'

Training and Wages The American economist Becker would contend that professional workers' salaries are higher in order to balance their loss of earnings and payments whilst training. The differential between a skilled and an unskilled worker is not simply the sum of the costs of training of the skilled worker, but also an additional amount necessary to equalize the rate of return on the skilled workers' investment in training with the rate of return on unit trusts or some other well used investment. The debate on the real determinants of the wage level is endless, but the argument that supply and demand (including marginal productivity) determine wages (allowing for non-monetary rewards and training costs) is tenable as long as we assume a perfectly competitive market for labour. However, it is necessary to examine monopoly factors in wage determination, such as unions, companies and employers' organizations, before reaching a definite conclusion in this matter.

Summary The determination of wages under perfect competition is an application of supply and demand analysis, in which marginal productivity is a key element. Under perfect competition the competitive pressures are such that wages in society tend towards equality, after allowance has been made for non-monetary rewards and training.

12.2 COLLECTIVE BARGAINING AND EMPLOYERS' ORGANIZATION AT NATIONAL AND PLANT LEVELS

The demand for and supply of labour meet in the labour market. This market is very diverse, since different types of labour are both required and offered. Labour and wage are therefore generalizations and in practice we have a whole set of wages based on skills and industries – a wage structure. The labour market is generally far from competitive, since over half of British workers belong to trade unions and the majority of employers belong to employers' organizations. Because of these constraints on competition the wage cannot be determined solely by supply and demand curves. There is in many cases a monopolistic situation on both sides of the labour market, so that the wage level and wage structure are the outcome of negotiations between unions and employers' organizations.

Collective Bargaining These negotiations are called collective bargaining, and in most British industries each side recognizes that the other has a right to bargain about minimum wages, hours, working conditions, holidays and shift payments. In Britain this bargaining has traditionally been at two levels; at a national level between unions and employers' organizations (at which the above mentioned are decided), and at plant level, at which supplements to the wage, such as piece-rates, bonuses and measured daywork are negotiated between the unions and the employer (see Figure 12.2). The earnings of the worker therefore are added to at plant level – a process known as *wage drift*. To give an example: between 1962 and 1967, in the chemical industry average weekly wages rose by 24.8 per cent, but average weekly earnings (including plant level supplements) rose by 38.1 per cent, the plant level payments alone increasing by as much as 13.3 per cent (see Table 12.2). An alternative two-tier structure of collective bargaining has been set up in some industries during the

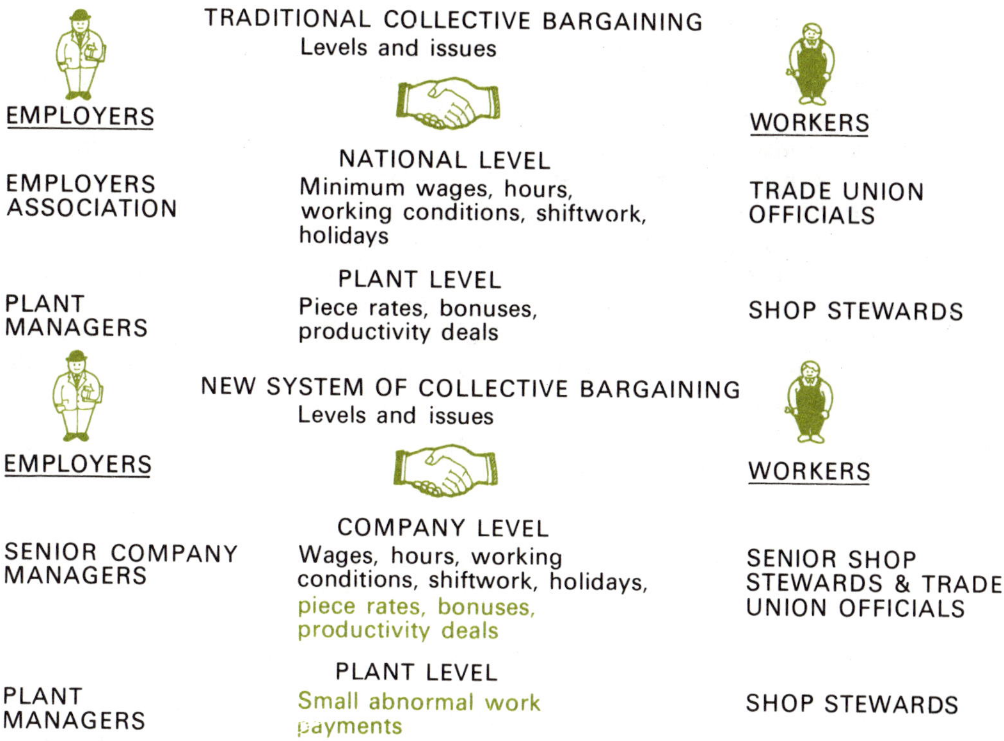

Figure 12.2 Collective bargaining.

last 20 years, consisting of company level negotiations and plant level negotiations. In this alternative system almost all earnings and conditions issues are discussed at company level, and only abnormal work payments are bargained at plant level. Nationalized industries and many multinational companies have adopted this alternative structure.

Table 12.2 Wage drift: chemical industry.

	Average weekly wages	*Average weekly earnings*	*Wage drift*
1962–7 (Income rises)	24.8%	38.1%	13.3%

Source: Royal Commission on Trade Unions and Employers' Associations: Report, 1968. Reproduced with the kind permission of the Controller of HMSO.

Traditional Collective Bargaining System How do these two structures of collective bargaining help determine the wage, and what economic reasons are there for determining wages through these structures? The traditional structure of national negotiations between employers' organizations and unions (represented by full-time officials) and plant negotiations between unions (represented by part-time Shop Stewards) and the employer developed out of late nineteenth-century employers' joint offensives against successful trade union demands for higher wages and recognition. The

Engineering Employers' Federation, for example, was founded in the 1890s to confront trade unionists, who had been successful in negotiations with individual firms. Soon employers realized that joint national bargaining about wages in multi-company monopolistic competition industries, such as engineering and textiles, helped ensure 'fairer' competition amongst firms, since all had to pay the same labour costs – there could be no undercutting. Since 1945 plant level bargaining has developed alongside national negotiations, largely as a result of labour shortages and the need for employers to increase piece-rates and bonuses at the plant to attract labour. National bargaining gave employers power to enforce wage cuts jointly in the inter-war depression years of labour surplus, but post-war plant bargaining has enabled union shop-stewards to influence strongly increases in earnings at a time of labour shortage.

New System of Collective Bargaining The alternative structure of collective bargaining – at company and plant levels – has grown up in newer oligopolistic industries such as chemicals, cars, oil and in nationalized industries. Recent research in the USA and Britain shows that large companies in oligopolistic industries with limited labour costs prefer to bargain their own employees' wages, since they can then adjust wages to give them some market advantage over other firms. The multinational company in particular aims to transfer emphasis from employers' organization negotiations to company based bargaining. An early pioneer of the company agreement was the giant chemical company I.C.I. whose Weekly Staff Agreement is negotiated entirely at company level with the exception of plant level payments for abnormal working conditions and other minor items. In some parts of the oil and gases industry British Oxygen Company controls so large a share of the labour market that it is virtually a one company monopsonist (i.e. the sole purchaser of labour in that industry). Some companies, however, do have a limited national agreement for the company, and measured day work (i.e. fixed payment based on work study) is negotiated at plant level. Nationalized firms concentrate bargaining for wages at company level and, as with I.C.I., little is bargained generally at the plant. The British Rail Board is a clear-cut example of a monopsonist, buying railwaymen's labour at national level, and paying only abnormal working hours and other minor items at local level. Such public and private monopsonists have real economic power in the labour market, but trade unions now organize at the same levels of bargaining to counter this strength. Research in the USA has shown that unionization of workers generally results in a 10 per cent increase in earnings compared with the non-unionized situation but in Britain little similar research has been done.

Summary In Britain wage levels and wage structures are determined largely by collective bargaining between employers' organizations and trade unions. Employers in monopolistic competitive industries tend to bargain in organizations at national level, but those in oligopolistic industries tend to negotiate at company level.

12.3 TRADE UNION ORGANIZATION AND COLLECTIVE BARGAINING ECONOMIC MODEL

Union Aims and Structure in Britain What are the aims of trade unions in the labour market? The Union of Post Office Workers' Rule Book gives as two major aims of the organization:

1. 'To obtain improved pay, hours, leave, superannuation and other general conditions . . .'
2. 'To encourage the amalgamation of organisations catering for Post Office workers into one industrial Union'.

Does this mean that the union aims to maximize the wage bill or to maximize membership? This latter is a powerful factor in increasing its bargaining strength, but British unions have usually concentrated on wage issues as their major aim.

The structure of British trade unionism is the result of a unique response to the historical conditions of the first industrial country, and does not have the industrial union structure of most countries. In Britain wages are bargained for by three major categories of unions: 'craft' (representing old-established skilled trades, e.g. Amalgamated Society of Woodworkers); 'industrial' (attempting to represent all workers in an industry, e.g. Amalgamated Union of Engineering Workers), and 'general' (able to represent workers in any industry, e.g. Transport and General Workers Union). In many industries groups of these diverse unions bargain with an employers' organization; for example 39 unions in the engineering industry negotiate with the Engineering Employers' Federation. Nevertheless six major unions account for over half of trade union members (see Table 12.3). In the traditional structure as we have seen, full-time professional officials representing the unions bargain with the employers' organizations, and their strength depends upon common agreement amongst the unions involved in a negotiating team. When this

Table 12.3 Trade union membership (1978).

1	Transport and General Workers Union	2 023 000
2	Amalgamated Union of Engineering Workers	1 423 000
3	General and Municipal Workers Union	945 000
4	National Association of Local Government Officers	709 000
5	National Union of Public Employees	693 000
6	Union of Shop, Distributive and Allied Workers	441 000
7	Association of Scientific, Technical and Managerial Staff	441 000
8	Electrical, Electronic, Plumbing and Telecommunications Union	420 000
9	Union of Construction and Technical Trades	301 000
10	National Union of Teachers	289 000

Source: TUC.

exists both unions and the employers' organization are in the strong positions of monopoly seller and monopoly buyer of labour respectively.

Employer Monopsony and Union Monopoly In the newer system of collective bargaining at company level, unions can also be monopolists, and this is discussed below. What is the position of the unions in plant level negotiations? When they involve substantial issues, such as piece-rates and measured day work, which deeply concern the worker, the shop stewards may have support for, and the ability to carry through, strike action in pursuit of a pay claim. Strike action affects the employers' short-term profits but, in the long run, the employer can draw on his company resources to rule out union efforts at plant level.

At the company level of bargaining unions also can (and do) put the full weight of their resources behind industrial action, and where both unions and employers are in monopoly and monopsony positions, as in the state coal industry and the private car company, Ford, massive clashes can result. The situation in the coal industry is such that there is one major union, the NUM, enforcing a closed shop of 100 per cent union membership, and one major employer, the NCB, and in the 1972 and 1974 national coal strikes there was just such a clash between monopolist and monopsonist.

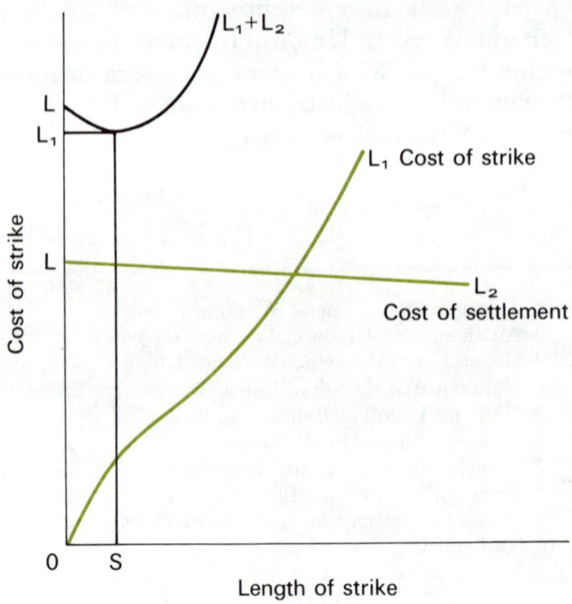

Figure 12.3 Strike: employers' calculation of costs.

Collective Bargaining Model The monopsony company is then faced by a trade union with monopoly power in selling wages. Each side is pushing for a different wage: the employer's aim is to negotiate a money wage increase lower than the union's first claim. The union's aim is a money wage increase higher than the employer's first offer. These money wage parameters set by both sides are the outer limits within which bargaining and struggle take place. Figure 12.3 shows the employers' calculation of strike costs and settlement costs.

An employer will only enter a strike over wage bargaining if he believes it will not last beyond S. If it does last beyond S, his calculated risk will have failed, and he will incur more costs than if he had settled before the strike. The miners' strikes of 1972 and 1974 showed the economic power of key workers who were able to resist longer than the NCB calculated, but in this example political power is involved too (e.g. power to close coal depots, to mount support in other unions, etc.).

Summary Trade unions, like employers, can be monopolists in collective bargaining if there is one major union per company or a group of united unions per industry.

12.4 INTERNAL LABOUR MARKETS AND WAGE DIFFERENTIALS

Internal Labour Markets We have analysed the major factors concerning why earnings of workers differ, such as non-monetary rewards and trade union and employer bargaining power. However, it would be wrong to omit internal labour markets from this analysis, since they are of increasing importance as industry and occupations rapidly become more specialized. The internal labour market is the labour market which exists within a particular occupation (e.g. electrician) or within a particular industry (e.g. chemicals). The skill involved in many occupations or industries is not readily acquired, and therefore the labour market for such skills is in the short run limited to those already trained.

This means that if there is a labour shortage in a particular occupational or industrial skill a firm will increase the wages of the workers concerned in order to retain them. For example, in the 1960s there was a serious shortage of trained graduate chemical engineers and workers in this occupation gained an additional rise in earnings in their internal labour market. Similarly, the shortage of skilled aircraft workers in the 1950s led to additional rises in earnings in the aircraft industry internal labour market. In both cases, however, the increase in specially trained workers in chemical engineering and in the aircraft industry during the following ten years moderated earnings increases.

Differentials and Inflation For the reasons we have studied so far in this chapter there exist differentials in pay between workers. *The earnings differential is the difference in earnings between two workers or groups of workers who are being compared*. Some differentials have existed for many years and have been accepted by all concerned, e.g. the differential between a railway engine-driver and a porter, the differential between a coalminer working at the coal face, and a coalminer working on the surface. Other differentials are of a more recent nature and owe their existence to the rapid pay changes of the highly inflationary 1970s or to incomes policy by government. An example of this is the substantial increase in miners' pay during the inflationary years 1972, 1974 and 1977, which altered the differential between miners and car workers in the miners' favour. A further interesting case of a similar type is the attempted rationalization of the British Leyland motor workers' pay structure in rapid inflation, which left the tool room workers at the Longbridge B.L. plants with a smaller differential in comparison with the car assembly line workers at Longbridge than they had previously.

Differentials and Incomes Policy Incomes policy during 1975–6 necessitated a flat-rate increase of £6 per worker, and the following year the policy was also mainly of a flat-rate nature. This resulted in lower paid workers obtaining as large a rise as higher paid workers, and the differential between them was therefore narrowed, because the lower paid were gaining a bigger percentage rise. This further reduced the differential between tool room men at B.L. Longbridge and car assembly workers on the same site. Such changes in differentials can lead to industrial disputes to restore the old differential, and the tool room men already mentioned were involved in such a dispute over a period of weeks in 1977–8, and nearly formed a new trade union because they had no official support from their union, the AUEW.

Differentials, Comparability and Industrial Disputes Changes in differentials are taking place between industries and occupations as regularly as changes in the tide. Workers are naturally worried not only about the actual money being paid, but also about the comparability of their pay with that of other workers. In Ireland the comparability issue is taken even more seriously than in Britain, and a classic example was a six-month coal strike by one company's mineworkers due to the differentials being altered in favour of coalface workers compared with lorry drivers. In Britain, disputes arise and are resolved by trade union power, employer power, economic circumstances, and intervention of conciliators such as the independent Advisory, Conciliation and Arbitration Service.

If wages were determined by one factor such as supply and demand pressure, then the labour market would be a simpler but perhaps a harsher place. However, the multiplicity of factors determining wages produce situations of changing differentials and conflict. Three solutions to this problem have been suggested. Clegg has argued for orderly wage bargaining units, based on plant or skills, within companies and industries. The 1965–70 government's incomes policy was designed to take account of differentials that change, in the approval of wage increases. The short-lived Pay Relativities Board set up by government in 1973–4 assessed differential changes and recommended policy prescriptions to government. Nevertheless, in a complex modern economy it is very difficult to control and plan earnings, since the number of skills is rapidly increasing with rapid technological change, and incentive schemes become more numerous and sophisticated in their operation. The worker, moreover, unlike insensitive natural resources and capital, has his own ideas on rewards, income distribution and means of attaining his financial goals.

Summary Wage differentials exist between groups of workers. They are subject to rapid change and give rise to industrial disputes over comparability of earnings.

12.5 INCOMES POLICIES AND GOVERNMENT

Government can intervene in wage determination through the operation of incomes policies, and it is sometimes suggested that this is necessary on the grounds that the monopoly power of some unions causes large scale cost inflation. To consider this question we need to examine the relationship between inflation and unemployment in the UK economy. A British economist, Phillips, argued in 1958 that there was a definite relationship between unemployment and money wages in the UK. This relationship showed that at lower levels of unemployment, the rate of increase in money wages tended to be higher (see Figure 12.4, where curve PP relates rate of change in wages to rates of unemployment). Incomes policy can be seen as a means to shift this curve to the left, that is to ensure that rates of change of money wage increases will be lower than otherwise at particular levels of unemployment (e.g. a shift from curve P to curve P_1).

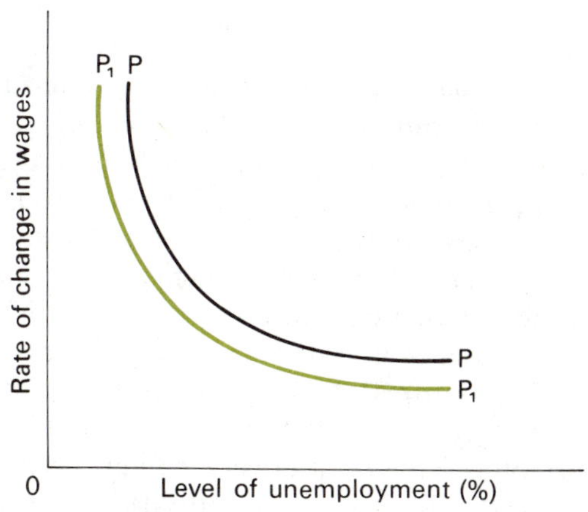

Figure 12.4 Phillips's curve.

Does incomes policy by government actually have this impact on wage determination? In Chapter 14 we examine a case study of incomes policy in the 1964–70 period in which the targets for incomes increases were related either to general economic growth or to increased productivity in a particular plant or company. Research shows that income growth was restrained only during the period of absolute freeze on incomes increases in late 1966 (when increases could be monitored easily), and during similar short wage freezes in 1961 and 1972. A major problem in assessing incomes policy is that we do not know what the situation would have been without it, and this point is not adequately examined by economists such as Parkin and Sumner whose investigations broadly conclude that the policy has no effect on incomes.

The Social Contract voluntary incomes policy of 1975–7 correlates with a period of declining wage rises, but is this attributable to the incomes policy implemented by government and unions or to the rapidly rising unemployment during these years? The demand for labour in general was declining during this period, but in coal mining it increased, yet the rise in the powerfully unionized miners' wages also declined.

Summary Incomes policy and its acceptance by unions with monopoly power can influence wage levels and the reduction of cost inflation in the mid 1970s owes something to this. However, the only incomes policy which has restrained wages at every attempt is the short 'wage freeze'.

12.6 THE RATE OF INTEREST AND THE CAPITAL MARKET

Classical Theory of the Rate of Interest The supply of money capital comes from saving, and the demand for it is sometimes called investment, i.e. the financing of the production of new capital goods. The higher the rate of interest, the less money capital is invested in financing production of new capital goods and the more saved in banks, etc., receiving a rate of interest payment. The point of intersection between the demand and the supply curve for money capital gives the equilibrium situation where as much money capital is invested as is saved. The corresponding rate of interest is shown in Figure 12.5. In the equilibrium situation an amount of money capital (OQ) is invested at OR rate of interest. This classical economist's theory of the rate of interest is called the Loanable Funds Theory, and it analyses the funds (money capital) in relation to the demand and supply for them. The rate of interest in this theory is therefore the price paid for loanable funds by borrowers.

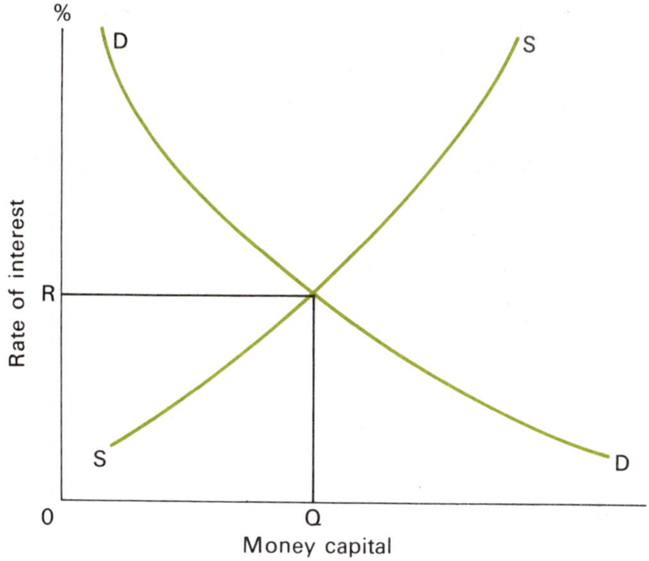

Figure 12.5 Supply and demand for money capital.

Although the lending of money by households to firms is presented above as a simple transaction, in actual fact there is a capital market in operation, involving supplies of, and a demand for, money capital.

Keynes's Criticisms of Classical Interest Theory According to classical theory, the supply of money capital comes from savings, while the demand for it stems from a desire to invest, and the higher the rate of interest, the less is invested by firms and the more saved by households. Keynes, however, regarded savings as more a function of the national income than of interest rates and said that the higher the income, the more is saved. Keynes also doubted the classical conclusion that the lower the rate of interest, the more is invested, and said that if firms want to invest, it is due to their expectations of profit rather than to one cost component – the interest rate. According to him, the interest brings about a balance between the supply of and the demand for money, and not between investment (I) and the saving (S). In other words, the interest rate affects the methods of saving and the methods of financing an investment which has already been made. Keynes thus emphasized the monetary aspect of the interest.

The Capital Market The capital market deals in money, short-term securities with a maturity of less than a year, and long-term securities with a maturity of more than a year (e.g. stocks and bonds).

The money supply comes mainly from banks wanting to put their temporary excess money to use in the short term, while the demand comes from firms and from banks needing liquid assets.

The London Stock Exchange is an important part of the capital market in Britain and it deals in securities of various kinds on a day-to-day basis. Thus, it deals in shares which make their holders co-owners of a firm, and, as such, risk bearers of it. The dividend they earn is not only compensation for abstaining from their money capital (i.e. not only the interest), but also a reward for bearing part of the risk. The shareholder therefore shares the debt or obligations of a firm. Firms needing long-term capital can raise it either on the Stock Exchange or from retained profits. The government, too, often turns to the capital market for long-term borrowing and issues government stock.

The supply in this capital market comes (a) from individual savers who want to invest their money via the banks, and (b) from institutional investors, such as pension funds and insurance companies, who have large assets which must generally be invested in a risk-free manner since the institutional investors must always be able to fulfil their obligations.

It can thus be seen that we cannot speak of *the* rate of interest any more than we can speak of *the* wage. In practice, there are several rates of interest, varying with the nature and term of the credit.

Summary The capital market deals with money and securities of different types. It is customary to speak of *the* interest, although in actual fact there are a number of different interest rates at any given time.

12.7 KEYNES'S THEORY OF INTEREST

The Demand for Active Money According to Keynes – as previously mentioned – the rate of interest brings about a balance, not between investment and saving, but between the supply and demand for money. The money supply is the total amount of money introduced into circulation by the institutions that create money. The demand comes from firms, government and private individuals who are demanding cash, i.e. primary liquidity. The required size of the former depends not so much on the rate of interest, but mainly on the nature and number of transactions between the households and the firms. In other words, a certain amount of money will be demanded for daily payments, irrespective of how high the rate of interest is, so that the demand curve for active money (L_1) is a vertical line (compare Figure 12.6).

The Demand for Inactive Money Inactive money, or investment funds, is held to buy stocks, shares, bonds and other securities for purposes of (a) precaution, and (b) speculation. In the former case the motive is to be secure against future risks, e.g. lengthy personal illness, and in the latter case the motive is to attempt to buy stocks and shares at low prices and sell them at higher prices. These investments, too, reflect the liquidity preference of the savers, i.e. their desire for cash. In Keynes's relatively

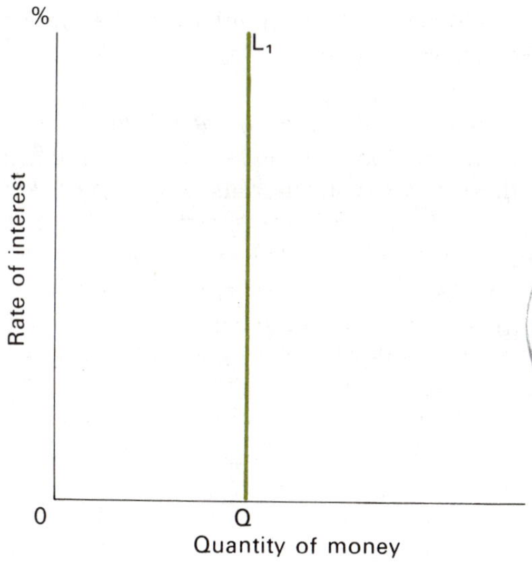

Figure 12.6 Demand curve for active money.

simple treatment, this liquidity preference is assumed to vary inversely with the interest. A high rate of interest is necessary, he argues, to persuade savers to part with their liquid funds, i.e. more money is held in the inactive form, which means that the demand curve for inactive money L_2 is a declining curve, as shown in Figure 12.7 (also called the liquidity preference curve). If the interest is low, people do not mind sacrificing it to bring their assets into the fully liquid form. Hoarding of assets is, in the Keynesian theory, encouraged by low interest rates, but high interest

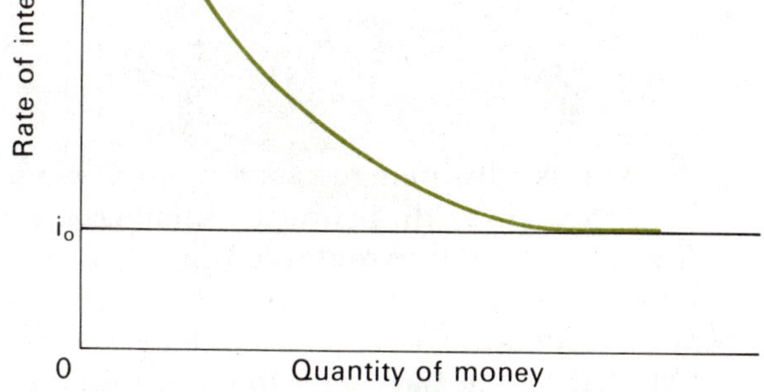

Figure 12.7 Demand curve for inactive money.

rates will be an enticement to individuals to abandon hoarding and to invest their money.

Determination of the Rate of Interest in Keynes's Theory In the case shown here, all the money is held in the inactive form when the interest rate is i_0. As the interest rate increases, however, keeping money in the inactive form involves a greater sacrifice through the loss of potential interest gains. We stress that the central issue in Keynes's interest theory is the demand for money – i.e. primary liquidity – on the part of the public, i.e. L_1 and L_2 are not money supply curves, but money demand curves, and the total demand for money is obtained by adding the two together graphically (see Figure 12.8).

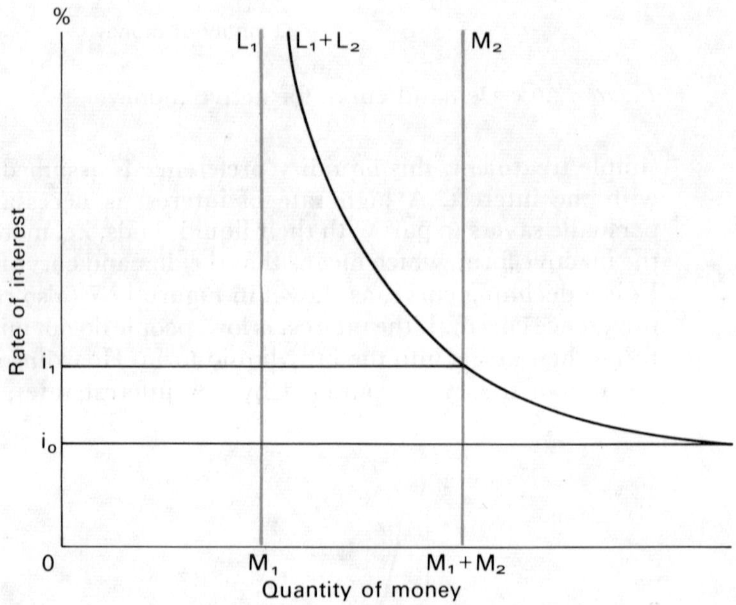

Figure 12.8 Equilibrium rate of interest: liquidity preference curve.

Against this demand for liquidity, we have the money supply M_2, which comes from the institutions that create money and is independent of the rate of interest, so that it too gives a vertical straight line. The point of intersection between this and the combined demand curve gives the equilibrium rate of interest i_1. At this point, the money supply is composed of M_1 and M_2, i.e. part of the money supply is in the active form and part in the inactive form. When the liquidity preference increases, so that the combined demand curve (L_1 and L_2) shifts to the right, a higher equilibrium increase arises, while an increase in the amount of money supplied is accompanied by a drop in the equilibrium interest rate.

Summary According to Keynes's liquidity-preference theory of interest, the equilibrium interest rate is determined by the demand for and the supply of money. Households and firms demand money for transactions, precautionary and speculative motives, while the supply is the total money supply brought into circulation. The interest rate is a payment to persuade households to part with their liquidity for a period of time.

12.8 RENT

The total supply of natural resources, including land, can be regarded as perfectly inelastic. The total supply is fixed regardless of price. The supply curve is therefore a straight line parallel to the vertical axis SS in Figure 12.9. Therefore, the actual rent is determined by demand forces, and in Figure 12.9 OP indicates the rent in a situation of normal demand.

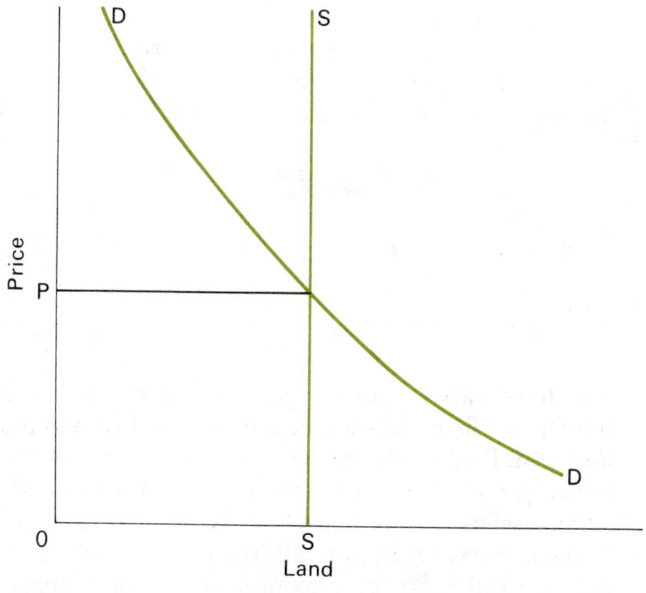

Figure 12.9 Supply and demand for land.

The amount of rent paid for farming land depends, however, less on inelastic supply factors than on the total supply of land. It is related to the acquisition of agricultural land for building purposes, and also to the reclamation of 'wild' land for agricultural use. The latter in eastern England in the early twentieth century has helped to modify rents, and the former has tended to increase land rents near to the major British conurbations in the post-1945 period. Rent income is proportionately less important than in the early twentieth century, since most housing nowadays is not rented from private owners but from local authorities (50 per cent of families own their own homes).

From the nineteenth-century writings on rent in economics, the term *economic rent* was developed to have a wider meaning than payments for lease of land or housing. Economic rent can be defined as *a surplus accruing to a factor of production over and above that which would keep the factor in its present employment.* Economic rent can therefore be applied to labour and called a *rent of ability.* For example, a pop singer who earns £100 000 per year might earn £5000 per year in his next best employment as a music teacher. He is earning an economic rent (rent of ability) of £100 000−£5000=£95 000 per year. That is, he is earning a surplus of £95 000 over and above the amount which would keep him in his present employment.

The supply of some forms of capital is inelastic in the short run, so economic rent on capital equipment can arise. An advanced computer system, for example, may be so well used by customers that its owners can increase the charge for use of it. This increase leads to earnings, which are a surplus accruing to the computer over and above that which pays for its upkeep and normal profit. This surplus is economic rent on capital, and is sometimes called *quasi-rent*.

Summary Rent, for land under perfect competition, is determined by demand only, since the total supply of land is fixed. Rent is however a declining proportion of factor incomes, since rent income from private housing has rapidly declined this century in Britain.

12.9 PROFIT

The fixed rate of interest paid to banks and to some preference shareholders by firms has been examined in a previous section, as have wages and rent. Profit is the element of income accruing to a firm after it has paid its wages to labour, its rent to any landlord, and interest to banks and some preference shareholders. Knight argues in his major book, *Risk, Uncertainty and Profit*, that 'all true profit is linked with uncertainty'. Profit, it is generally agreed by economists, is the financial return for a company taking 'non-insurable risks' (i.e. real uncertainty). A firm can insure against fire and flood, but it cannot take out an insurance policy to protect it if it is financially unsuccessful in building a new terylene plant or a new motor car works. The rate of return it obtains from sales of terylene or cars from the new plant may, it seems at first, be great enough to bring profit or small enough to incur losses.

Retained Profits and Investment In Britain profits finance over 50 per cent of investment. This means that over half the new buildings and machinery for firms are paid for from funds that the firm itself provides from successful previous sales of its products. Other sources of revenue to the firm are: (a) borrowing from banks and other savings institutions which of course incur interest charges; (b) a firm may issue more shares on the stock exchange, and thereby raise funds from savers although it must pay an annual dividend to them which is higher on average than they can expect from long-term government stock; and (c) the government or a government agency (e.g. Industrial Credit Finance Corporation) can be approached by a firm for a loan for a specific project, but this loan is repayable with interest and requires serious negotiation. The most secure source of finance for new expansion, and the least burdensome in the long run to companies, is profits, i.e. profits retained after payments to shareholders in the company. The large chemical companies (e.g. I.C.I., B.P.) often have to provide over half the cost of huge capital-intensive new plant through retained profits.

The causes and determination of profits have already been largely discussed in the last three chapters. In Chapter 11, Section 3 it can be seen that a monopoly firm can achieve abnormal profit from most projects it undertakes. Later, in Chapter 11, Section 4, it can be deduced that in the case of oligopoly a firm can achieve abnormal profits from, for example, the production of a new motor car. A firm operating under monopolistic competition (see Chapter 11, Section 2) is less sure of making abnormal profit from a new project, but may be able to achieve this through product differentiation. The perfect competition market permits abnormal profit by a firm only as long as the supply of the product is less than demand during a period of quantity adjustment in the market (see Chapter 10, Section 2). Indeed, the firm under perfect competition is involving itself in severe risk in undertaking expansion, since it has no privileged position in the market on which to rely if the project collapses.

Profit Sharing Schemes Should profits be shared more widely than to the company (as retained profit) and to the shareholders? This issue involves political and social value judgements, but there are also economic arguments for wider profit sharing. Since the 1920s I.C.I. has established a scheme of worker participation in receiving profits through the workers' acquiring, as of right, some shares in the company. It might be argued that, in so far as dividends to shareholders are based on profit and profits are based on maximizing output, worker share-ownership will bring about greater output per person. The link is debatable, but a small minority of British private firms operate this scheme. In Worker Cooperatives, such as Triumph Motors, at Meriden, Coventry (the largest in

Britain), the workpeople own the company, accept a flat-rate wage for everyone (£68 a week in 1978), and all are entitled to a share in any of the profits. The forms of ownership and profit sharing can be quite diverse.

The 1970s 'Profits Squeeze' Since the late 1960s in Britain there has been a fall in the proportion of firms' sales revenue accruing to profits. What has caused this, and could it have serious economic consequences? The rapid inflation of the 1970s has been paralleled by rapid wage increases to keep pace with prices, and to continue the post-war worker's expectation of a rising standard of living. Oligopoly and monopoly companies were able, until 1972, to pass on to the consumer such rising costs in the form of price increases. However, in 1972 some measure of statutory price control was introduced, which was strengthened in 1975 and again in 1978. Meanwhile, world raw material prices, especially oil, soared in 1973–5 and firms' profits were limited by rising wages, rising raw material costs, and problems resulting from price code restrictions on increasing their own prices. The world recession since 1975 has also hit sales severely and given a further blow to profits.

In 1978 the price code was eased, sales slowly began to rise, wages had been restricted for two years by a voluntary incomes policy, and raw material prices had stabilized. As a consequence the outlook for profits was much rosier in 1978, but their low levels, particularly in the mid 1970s, meant lower investment in buildings and machinery. Retained profits are so vital a part of capital financing in the modern economy that the profit squeeze was serious for the future economic development of Britain.

Summary Profit is a reward to a company for taking non-insurable risks. Profit gained will depend both on the success of the project, and the type of market in which the firm operates, e.g. perfect competition or oligopoly. Under monopoly and oligopoly firms will earn abnormal profits, which are not directly related to frequency and degree of risk-taking by companies.

12.10 INCOME DISTRIBUTION IN BRITAIN

As we discussed in Chapter 2 there has been a gradual trend in Britain towards a greater share in income by labour. Atkinson shows that percentage shares of gross national product to profits, rent and labour have changed from a ratio of 19:13:68 in 1930–38, to 21:6:73 in 1950–59, to 20:7:73 in 1960–69. This change is due to post-war labour shortages and in some cases trade union monopoly power (see Sections 2 and 3). Income distribution (on a percentage basis) shows, however, no redistribution in favour of the bottom 30 per cent of income earners. In 1949 the top 10 per cent gained 27.1, the middle 60 per cent 58.3, and the bottom 30 per cent

14.6. By 1967 the top 10 per cent had fallen to 24.3, the middle 60 per cent risen to 63.7, and the bottom 30 per cent had fallen to 12 per cent (see Figure 12.10).

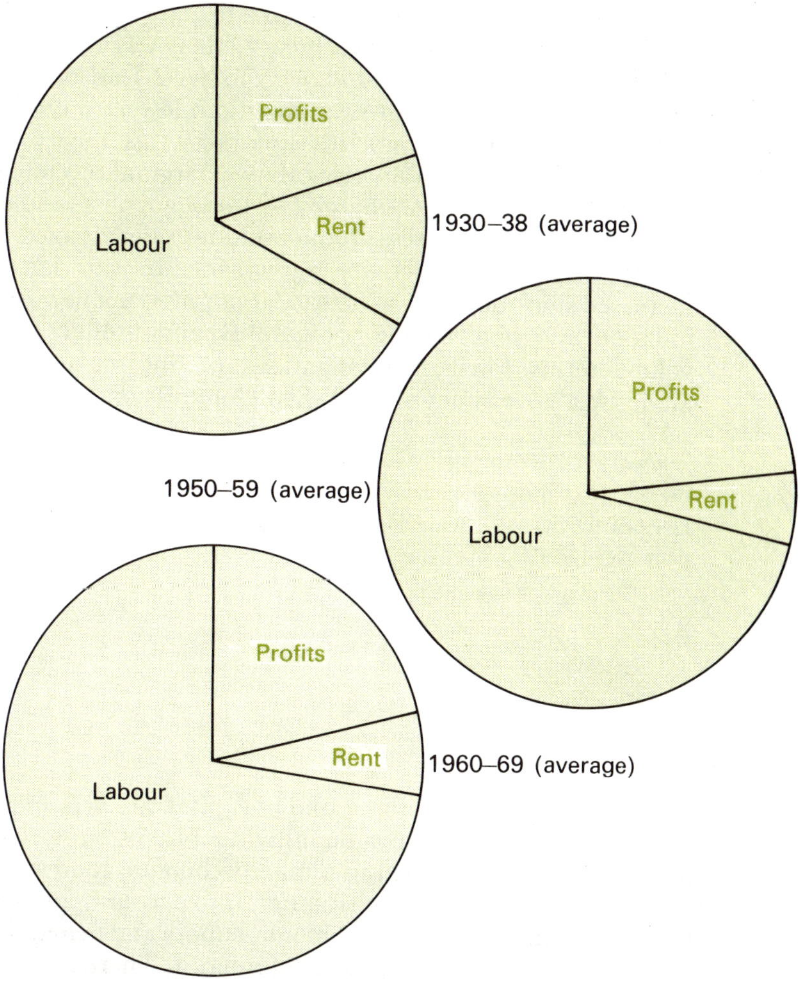

Figure 12.10 Income distribution in the UK. From B. Atkinson, *Economics of Inequality*, 1975, O.U.P. Reproduced with kind permission of the O.U.P.

Another British economist, R. M. Titmuss, in earlier research in the 1960s contended that if one took into account changes in the social and economic framework of life in Britain (e.g. trends in unemployment, social mobility, etc.) then a trend towards an increase in labour's share of national income was unlikely in the long run. Although there may be a gradual trend towards an increase in labour's share of income in Britain, there is a wide difference in distribution of wealth. Atkinson's researches show that in 1968 the top 1 per cent of the population owned 31 per cent of wealth and the top 5 per cent owned 56 per cent of wealth.

What can economic theory tell us about how changed income distribution might affect production and inflation levels? The marginal productivity theory predicts that production will be most efficient if returns to production factors are equal to marginal revenue product. If we apply the conclusions of this theory, then wage settlements by union monopolists and employers above this level lead to a less competitive product, and probably lower production, lower employment and lower profits. In perfectly competitive markets this theory is valid, but in oligopolistic markets, wage rises above marginal revenue product can be paid for by a higher price charged by the oligopolist (and consequent cost inflation) or by increased production and sales derived from a genuine union/company productivity agreement. In this latter situation an increased share of factor income to labour need not necessarily lead to cost inflation and may enable profitability and production to increase in volume terms. Further investigations into income and wealth are being made by a government-established Commission.

Summary Income and wealth distribution in Britain is unequal, but the post-war trend is towards an increased share of factor incomes to labour. Economic theory shows that this trend is compatible with greater production and profitability if wages are directly linked to production increases.

12.11 CONCLUDING REMARKS

The factor markets, of labour and of capital, are very important both for households and for firms on an individual basis, but wages, interest, and profit are better explained in a macroeconomic context. Incomes policy takes the general economic situation into account, and aggregate quantities like savings, investment, money supply and demand play an important role in determining the rate of interest. There has been in Britain a trend towards an increased share in income by labour, and this is due to post-war labour shortages, and to some trades union monopoly bargaining power. In oligopolistic industries an increase in incomes above marginal productivity can either be paid for by increased prices (which would lead to cost inflation) or by genuine productivity deals by which higher production and profits also emerge. But before going over to the macroeconomic domain, armed with the theory of factor pricing, it should perhaps be mentioned that, in the operation of the market mechanism, the level of income determines the amount of scarce resources that can be purchased. By virtue of the price system and the market, it is not people's wants that are expressed in the market, but their effective demand, which is backed up by purchasing power, and this is determined by their income and wealth.

QUESTIONS

1 How can a new wage level arise according to perfect competition theory?

2 Illustrate graphically the derivation of the labour demand curve described in Section 12.1.

3 What is wage drift?

4 What must happen before real capital is formed?

5 What does share price mean?

6 What is meant by collective bargaining, and which issues are bargained about?

7 What is factor-income distribution?

8 What is a monopsonist. Give examples of British monopsonists.

9 Describe Keynes's theory of interest.

10 What is meant by the equalization of income distribution?

EXERCISES

1 In what situation do wages tend to rise more steeply than productivity?

2 Follow the share prices of, e.g. I.C.I., in the newspapers for a few days and plot a graph showing the variations in them.

3 Explain why land prices have risen so steeply in Britain in the 1970s.

4 What is the effect of a decrease in liquidity preference on the rate of interest in Keynes's theory? Illustrate your answer with a graph.

5 Discuss the Social Contract Incomes Policy, 1974–7, and its success or failure.

6 Discuss the connection between trade union organization and cost inflation.

7 Discuss the criteria by which income differences may be considered acceptable.

8 Would the public disclosure of incomes contribute to bringing about a more equitable income distribution?

Chapter Thirteen

Technical Change and Variations in British National Income

In discussing the variations in the national income over time, we shall deal with the question why the British production level was higher in 1979 than, for example, in 1909. Keynesian theory tells us only what determines the national income at a given productive capacity for the economy, and if this limitation of his theory is not fully understood, it is likely that an incorrect answer will be given to the above question. The fact is that Keynes gave a short-term account in which he concentrated on effective demand; changes in the productive capacity of the economy were excluded from the analysis he made of the economy. Therefore the vital role of technical change on the long-term development of the economy is not part of Keynesian theory.

The obvious reason why the national income was higher in 1979 than in 1909 is that more could be produced in 1979. This is not only because society had more capital and population and exploitation of natural resources was greater, but also because technology was far more advanced and specialization of labour much greater. The factors of production, moreover, had not only increased in quantity but had also improved in quality: the capital goods available in 1979 were more advanced than those of 1909 since they embodied part of the technical development made over the past 70 years, and the quality of labour was better in 1979 due to more extensive education and training.

The answer to our question is therefore to be first sought on the supply side, in the supply of more and better means of production such as the factors we have just mentioned. We shall pay particular attention to the role of technical change in economic development and its consequences for the economy. However, the employment of all these improved and more numerous factors of production calls for sufficient expenditure in the economy, so that the Keynesian theory is examined again in the final answer to the question. We must also realize that economic growth is not a continuous development. On the supply side, the changes in technology and a lack of new capital development in firms and regions will lead to structural unemployment, whilst on the demand side there are recessions in trade which temporarily depress production and cause cyclical unemployment.

13.1 CHANGES IN THE NATIONAL INCOME: BRITISH ECONOMIC GROWTH

Economic growth means an expansion of production, and therefore of national income, during the course of time and it is usually measured in terms of the increase in real national income per person in a country during the course of time. We have so far dealt mainly with the level of national income within a given period, which is determined by the productive capacity or the effective demand.

The data shown in Table 13.1 for the British national income in the period 1948–77 indicate a sharp increase, but that during the 1970s was mostly due to price rises. If expressed in constant prices with 1974 as the base year, the national income for 1975 and 1976 is in fact lower than that for 1974. Therefore, the increase in the nominal national income here hides a drop, which is due to the recession, in the real national income. Prior to this, the growth of the national product was always about 3 per cent in Britain during the post-war period, but the recent figures indicate a 'negative growth'. However, in Britain a slow recovery of growth is expected for the coming years, particularly with the development of North Sea oil as a major new national natural resource.

When the expansion of the national income is charted over a period of years, we cannot say that the productive capacity is a fixed quantity, since the labour force increases with population growth, the stock of capital

Table 13.1 Changes in British national income.

Year	*National income (£m)*	*Year*	*National income (£m)*
1948	9479	1971	44574
1956	16465	1972	49679
1966	30380	1973	57915
1967	31983	1974	66574
1968	34146	1975	83060
1969	35937	1976	96676
1970	39487	1977	107990

Source: Annual Abstract of Statistics, 1977, Table 14.1, HMSO. Reproduced with the kind permission of the Controller of HMSO.

goods in particular industrial locations expands, more division of labour takes place and technology advances. These supply factors determine the production potential, while the demand factors determine the extent to which this potential is realized in practice.

The level of national income in the course of time thus depends on supply factors and demand factors, the first governing the development of the potential productive capacity, and the second governing the actual utilization of this capacity. The first are structural factors and are explained particularly by the theory of growth: the second are cyclical factors and are traditionally discussed in the theory of trade cycles.

If we examine the rate of growth in the British economy (or, put in other terms, the growth of British national income) in the post 1945 years, we can definitely conclude that it was a faster pace of economic development than that shown during the early part of the twentieth century, and also faster than that of the nineteenth century. However, the 3 per cent British average growth rate was well below that of her European neighbours, who averaged 4 to 6 per cent increases in production during the post-war years. There were two major reasons for the relatively slower growth: a smaller rise in the working population in Britain and, more importantly, a slower increase in output per man. This latter point was mainly due to the much lower rates of increase in quantity and quality of investment goods (i.e. new factories and machinery) in Britain than in her European competitors.

A further important facet of British economic growth in the last 30 years has been that it is not a consistent growth, but one of alternating booms and recessions. Each boom, however, has resulted in a higher growth of production than was present in the previous boom. Recessions took place in 1951–2, 1958–9, 1962–3, 1966–8, 1971–2, and since 1975. As discussed in Chapter 4, Section 10, in each of these recessions prior to the 1970s government intervention, by means of increasing investment goods production and a package of monetary and tax stimuli, led to an economic recovery well before unemployment became a serious problem. However, in 1971–2 the recession went deeper, and government did not take remedial action until unemployment had topped one million. During the recession of the mid to late 1970s government action of this type was still slower, not commencing until late 1977. A case study analysis of the British economy between 1964 and 1977 is included in Chapter 14. This most recent severe recession makes particularly relevant an examination in this chapter of the structural causes of unemployment, which are almost impossible to solve solely by government's increasing aggregate demand in the economy by new investment projects.

Summary The variations in the national income in the course of time are governed by supply factors and demand factors, the former determining the potential production capacity, the latter its utilization. In post 1945 Britain there has been an average increase in the national income of about 3 per cent per year, but this has been interrupted by six recessions, of which the mid to late 1970s recession was the most serious.

13.2 TECHNICAL CHANGE

This is perhaps the most spectacular influence upon economic growth and its impact now is greater than at any other time in the history of man. The term *technical change* covers a variety of changes including modifications to the way in which existing capital and labour are used (in order to increase the output per worker) and the creation of new products or new methods of producing existing products.

Invention and Innovation The creation of entirely new products or production methods depends critically on the rate of discovery, invention and innovation in society. In simple terms the rate of discovery will depend on the basic and applied research conducted in the country while the rate of invention will be dependent partly on the rate of discovery but also on the wants of society. Thus the invention of a hover-bicycle would not today follow from a basic discovery but rather from recognition of a consumer demand. Innovation, or the application of the invention to production (or having the invention produced as a product), may follow discovery or invention rapidly or slowly. The reasons for this are many and varied: for example, market research might have shown that wool and cotton would always be preferred to nylon and so delayed the introduction of nylon garments; or supersonic civil aircraft might not have been produced if most countries had legislated against such flights on hearing of the development.

Innovations will frequently stimulate invention and even discovery. For example, the early generations of computers, big and comparatively inefficient as they were, stimulated research and invention in the area of integrated circuits. Thus while inventions directly increase the body of technical knowledge, innovation can also achieve this indirectly.

It is difficult to establish a rigorous relationship between invention and innovation but certain generalizations can be made on the strength of the available empirical research. Thus the most important innovations follow inventions generally after an average time-lag of between 10 and 15 years. The shortest span between the two is in the petroleum industry, where it is only five years, and the longest is about 16 in a number of industries. This time-lag is shortest with mechanical innovations and longest with electronic ones; moreover, it is shorter for consumer goods than for capital goods. Inventions financed by the public sector are applied in practice after a shorter interval than those financed by the private sector. On the whole the average time-lag seems to be decreasing. However, the spread of an innovation to other firms in an industry is generally a slow process, often taking as long as 20 years. This spread of technical knowledge is an important part of the development of technology, and it mainly stems from the movement of creative technical people from one job to another. Publicly owned industries and rapid mobility of technical personnel are therefore spurs, it seems, to increased technical change.

Technical Change and Unemployment We must now examine the connection between technical development and the level of employment. According to Marx, technical development lowers the level of employment and leads to massive unemployment, because as human labour is replaced by capital, capital displaces some of the labour force from the production process, thus causing *technical unemployment*. This is completely different from cyclical unemployment, mentioned in connection with Keynes, where effective demand drops, and so neither labour nor capital is fully employed any more. Technological unemployment is due not to insufficient demand, but to a change in the factors of production on the supply side, and it is a special case of *structural unemployment* (see Figure 13.1) which quite generally results from changes in capital on the supply side, such as recent examples in the steel and car industries. The new steelworks at Teesside will produce 12m tons per year with fewer steelworkers than all those employed in north-east England at present. The new capital-intensive mini-car plant in Birmingham will employ fewer workers.

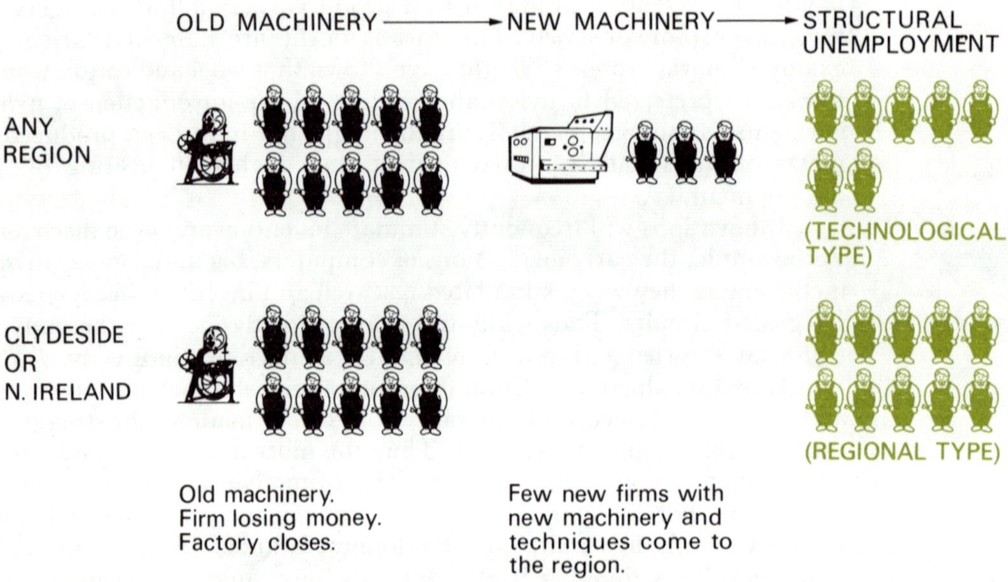

Figure 13.1 Structural unemployment.

Marx's prediction that technical development in capitalism would cause massive unemployment has not come true. This is partly because besides labour-saving technical development there is also capital-saving technical development, and partly because capital formation creates a demand for labour as well. In fact, there has so far been no great unemployment on a permanent basis.

Technical development therefore usually displaces workers on a relatively small scale, and these workers can find jobs elsewhere after some time. However, this involves considerable problems of re-training and adaptation to the new work environment. Persistent structural unemployment can also occur in certain regions called *depressed areas* where capital formation – e.g. in the form of new industrialization – is insufficient for keeping or creating new jobs for everyone. This structural shortage of capital is largely different from the shortage of effective demand, which causes cyclical unemployment. This distinction is particularly important from the point of view of economic policy, since the corrective measures to be taken differ according to the nature of unemployment. In general, anti-unemployment policy, as conditioned by technical development, requires a strongly microeconomic, long-term approach in which sufficient account is taken of the structural development of the economy, e.g. developments of new growth industries and new capital equipment. Such policies should therefore be applied to depressed regions, as should policies to increase effective demand for these products in those regions, as discussed in Section 5 below.

Technical Change and Unemployment in Oligopoly Industries Apart from unemployment caused by certain types of technical development, unemployment due to mergers and industrial concentration can also be regarded as structural unemployment, because it results from a change in the supply side, which is sometimes due to technical development. This is because concentration amounts to an increase in the scale of production, which in turn offers more scope for the application of new techniques, since it is then easier, and more readily justifiable, to make the large investments that are often necessary. The formation of the British Steel Corporation is an example of a merger leading to such consequences. Like the other forms of structural unemployment, this type is not part of Keynes's theory: none of them results from insufficient effective demand, and none of them can be remedied by increased spending. The firms involved in these mergers are very often oligopolies. What will be their reaction to technical development?

Oligopoly exhibits not only the different behaviour, reactions and expectations of oligopolists, but also different methods of updating technical knowledge. The power usually wielded by oligopolistic companies in the market does not mean that technical development within the firm can necessarily be channelled in the direction preferred by the management. Creativity by personnel can be organized within certain limits, but it does not take orders.

The likely future trend will be to base decisions about technical change not on simple criteria like financial yield, but on more basic, subjective preferences about the nature, direction and rate of technical development in the industry and its applications. This is already happening with the position of labour in some firms undergoing rapid and drastic technical change, e.g. British Leyland, Birmingham.

The more employees regard technical change as an inevitable fact, the more they will want to direct it and at least mould it to suit their own purposes. This will influence the rise of real incomes, as well as income distribution. A temporary opposition to the introduction of new techniques, for example to save some jobs, usually causes a drop in the firm's profits, so that often the income of others in the firm will also be affected. This in itself places high demands on the decision-making structure of the firm and these demands are increased by the international aspects of competition in the case of many firms. Technical change may also be deliberately hindered on the grounds that the external disadvantages of an increase in production (e.g. loss of jobs) outweigh the advantages of the application of new techniques (e.g. cheaper, more advanced products). In this way oligopoly firms can limit technological unemployment, and they can also limit it by reducing the working week substantially.

Summary **It is mainly technical development that urges us to take into account radical and rapid changes when attempting to explain economic growth. Technical change has important consequences such as mergers of companies, technical unemployment and structural unemployment in depressed areas. This section has dealt with structural unemployment, and therefore supplements the sections on causes of unemployment in Chapters 4 (Section 7) and 13 (Section 5).**

13.3 TECHNICAL CHANGE AND GOVERNMENT ECONOMIC POLICY

Technical change upsets equilibrium in economic situations, including full employment equilibrium, through the economies of scale it produces. In this respect it can be represented as a source of continuous uncertainty which leaves man at the mercy of uncontrolled forces. However, it is no longer justified, even if it ever was, to regard technical development as a process independent of the human will. Technical change embodies the core economic principle in that its development depends on the way in which scarce resources are allocated. When money and manpower are made available in a certain industrial area, such as the development of nuclear power for electricity, technical development is greatly promoted in that area. This technical change, however, has derived from an economic decision to allocate scarce resources to the development of nuclear power for electricity.

Control of Technical Change Control of technical change can be brought about by government as a coordinator and guide involved in the economic decisions of individual firms, but whether government should develop such a policy is a question concerning political, social and ethical value judgements.

The active guidance and control of technical development by the central government may perhaps be justified by the effects of technical change on employment and the environment. The need for participation of all employees in firms can be satisfied by designing suitable procedures for decision-making. Since decision-making without information and understanding is pointless, detailed policy models could be constructed with government advice in which various alternatives are given, as far as possible, in precise and quantitative form. It is possible that we may thus achieve agreement at the level of the firm between people with initially different viewpoints. Central government guidance of technical change will limit the problems caused by current technological unemployment, but the firms and their employees can none the less be the main decision-makers in this field.

Uncontrolled Technical Change and Energy Crisis Owing to the undirected nature of technical development by governments, the earth's energy sources are now being depleted relatively quickly. We are living off a finite stock of energy. Much energy is wasted in its own transport, use and conversion from one form to another, and production has become dependent on resources formed millions of years ago. Technical change can assist its conservation; so can pricing policies designed to limit fuel consumption.

In so far as nuclear energy is based on the splitting of uranium and plutonium, it also represents a finite source of energy. But this form of energy is an important temporary substitute for fossil fuels such as coal and oil, supplies of which are rapidly running out, particularly if use is made of fast breeder reactors which produce new fuel while producing energy. However, the use of this energy source raises difficult problems of thermal pollution and the disposal of radioactive waste. Atomic energy can also be obtained from nuclear fusion in which light nuclei are combined. This energy source is, in principle, inexhaustible, but the technology required for harnessing it is so complex that it will be some time before it contributes to the solution of the energy problem.

Nuclear fusion brings us to processes involved in the production of solar energy. The use of these forms of energy means that the conversion of various forms of energy into heat would be slowed down, which would make it possible to use the energy sensibly and profitably, and would accord with the natural cycles. As a result we would be living on interest rather than capital.

Technical development on a world scale should primarily be geared to these invariant natural energy systems, and attempts should be made to identify the most suitable type of energy conversion, find more efficient ways of using energy, and solve the problems of the transport, storage and location of heat released in bulk, together with the problem of thermal pollution. In the meantime it should be borne in mind that the most important current sources of energy, namely the irreplaceable fossil fuels, will run out, so that there is a theoretical upper limit to production. The gravity of the present situation mainly depends on how close we have already come to this limit.

It can be assumed that circumstances will force mankind to use solar energy and other invariant energy systems as sources of power for industrial and mechanical processes. However, technical constraints may make it necessary to develop nuclear energy – both fission and fusion – as an intermediate stage, though this has environmental pollution consequences. Although these considerations indicate that it should be possible to ensure the long-term energy supply of mankind, growth will still be limited by other factors, such as the finite size of the earth, the resources of raw materials and ecological principles. World technical development may require international economic policies under the aegis of the United Nations or similar bodies.

Summary Technical change in the late twentieth century is so rapid that it has enormous impact on employment and environment. The policies of firms, national government and international bodies are only slowly developing some economic control over this massive change.

13.4 INDUSTRIAL LOCATION AND ECONOMIC GROWTH

The location of industrial activity has a definite influence upon the rate of growth of the national income over time and is a consequence in part of the application of technical change in the form of new investment in capital goods. Industrial location itself depends upon the decisions of owners of firms, including those developing new technologies, and upon any controls by government over location of economic activity. Until the twentieth century, in Britain government influence on industrial location was very limited, and concerned such issues as location of royal dockyards, ordnance factories and communications development permission (e.g. for railways, canals and turnpike roads). Location of the manufacturing industrial basis of Britain during the period of its industrialization (1760–1820) was therefore almost completely determined by decisions of owners of firms at a time of massive technical change.

Laissez-faire Industrial Location in Theory and Practice Decisions were made in an atmosphere of laissez-faire and so location depended upon those geographical and cost factors which motivated entrepreneurs. This laissez-faire theory of industrial location simply predicts that firms will locate where profits can be maximized. Therefore they locate in places where costs of raw materials, natural resources and labour are low, and where geographical conditions (e.g. streams for water-power) are helpful. The iron industry of the early nineteenth century was primarily located in the West Midlands because iron ore, coal and lime were all available locally as raw materials and energy supplies, and a skilled craft labour force was also available locally as a nucleus of key workers. The cotton manufacturing industry of the same period in Lancashire was located there because initially water power, and later coal, were easily obtained as energy supplies, whilst non-guild workers provided a low-cost labour force, and Liverpool a port of access for raw cotton directly from the USA across the Atlantic.

During the twentieth century it is true that owners still make the final decision on where their factory is located, but since 1945 owners have required government permission to build a new factory or extend a factory substantially. In the development areas (see Figure 13.2) of northern England, Wales, Scotland, Devon and Cornwall, and in Northern Ireland, permission has normally been a mere formality. Location in those areas is therefore usually related to favourable geographical and cost conditions, in a way similar to that predicted by laissez-faire theory. Laissez-faire location of industry produced massive economic growth in

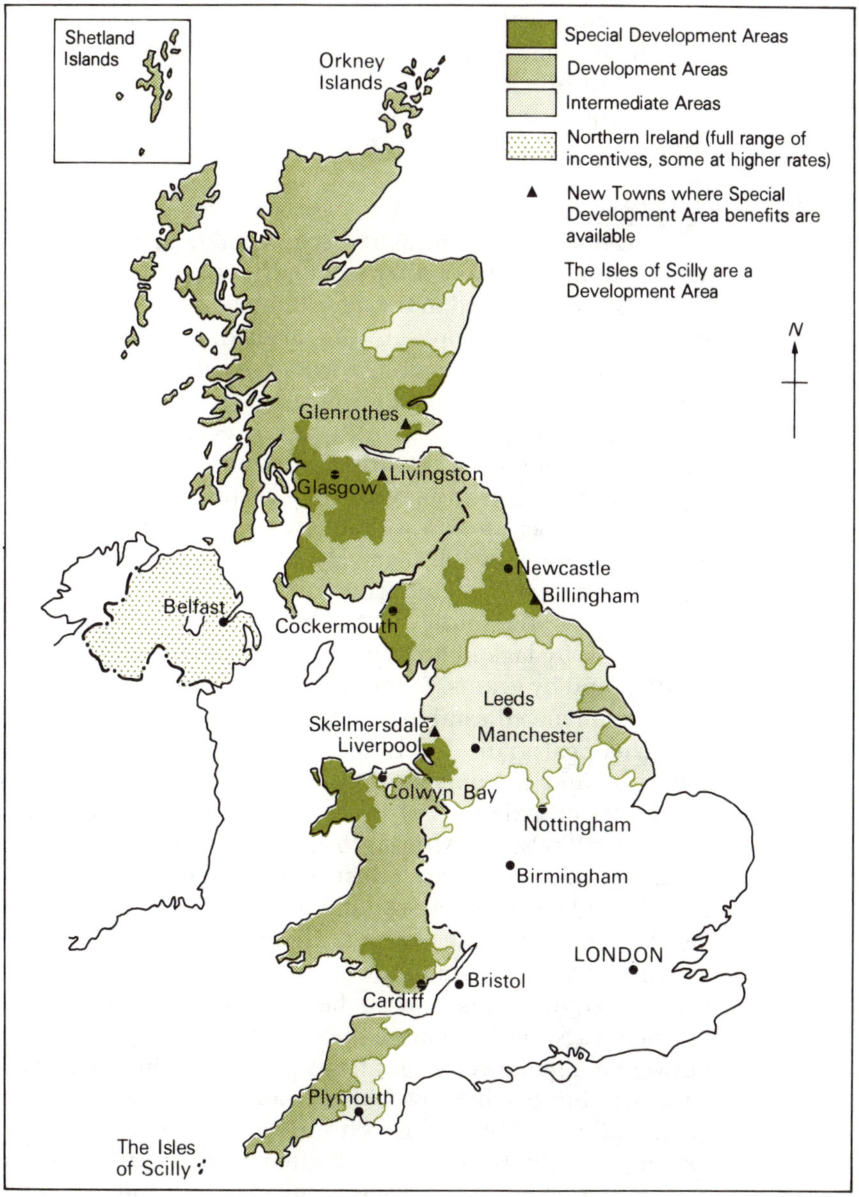

Figure 13.2 Development areas in the United Kingdom. Reproduced with the kind permission of the Department of Industry.

nineteenth-century Britain, but during the twentieth century labour as a factor of production became more immobile, and the capital stock of housing in a region of industrial decline also remained a nationally useful asset. The mass unemployment of workers in industry in the 1921–39 period in the present-day development areas was not accompanied by mass migrations of workers to the laissez-faire located growth industries of motors, chemicals, etc. in the Midlands and South-East. Economic growth in some regions was being held back by shortage of labour, whereas in other regions there was mass unemployment. Laissez-faire location of industry was to some extent failing to promote economic growth.

Government Industrial Location Policy: Advantages Since 1945 government-influenced location of industry became an overriding policy. Its economic justification was that growth industry short of workers in the south of Britain should expand in the development areas where labour was readily available. In this way, it was argued, economic growth would be promoted and mass unemployment of a structural nature largely avoided. The next section explains these measures as attempts to deal with regional structural unemployment. What, however, was the influence of this government-influenced location of industry policy on economic growth?

Over the 30-year period 1945–75 the British economy's growth rate of 3 per cent per annum was substantially higher than that achieved for most of the previous 100 years. However, as we saw in Chapter 2, it was far below the growth rate of economies of similar size in Western Europe. Large firms in the south and the Midlands which needed to expand were persuaded, by lack of government permission in their desired expansion location and by grants, to move to the development areas. Some moves of this type involved establishing a whole industry in a development area. The chemical giant I.C.I. set up a new factory in the late 1940s on Teesside, and so concentrated its development of chemicals there that economies of scale thus produced attracted new chemical firms to Teesside in the 1960s, e.g. Monsanto and Philips. Other development involved moving only a part of an industry, and the car assembly plants set up by B.M.C. and Chrysler in Scotland in the 1960s are examples of this limited development. No other parts of the industry followed, and no other car assembly plants. Costs of production of cars at these plants were higher because components had to be transported from the south, and the finished cars sent back to their main markets. Such increased costs outweighed the lower wages firms paid. Economic growth in such industries was limited by government policy, but where government could arrange for a whole industry to move economic growth was promoted. During the 1960s government attempted to attract more industry by developing social infrastructure in geographically favourable zones of development areas. The smaller scale type of industry, e.g. food industries and some science-based industry, was attracted substantially, provided employment and made goods with relatively small-sized components such that individual firms with low component costs added greatly to economic growth nationally.

Government Industrial Location Policy: Disadvantages The west Midlands region during the 30 years 1945–75 received 120 000 fewer jobs than it would have done if there had been no government control of location. It was the major manufacturing region not classified as a development area, and for most of this period it could not provide enough workers to produce its existing industrial goods. However, the location of industry policy has meant that new chemicals, steel, and engineering expansions went to other regions, and new industries themselves (e.g. computers and telecommunications – 'science-based' industry) by-passed the west Midlands. In 1972, for the first time in the twentieth century, the region's unemployment percentage was higher than the national average, and has remained above or near it ever since. Growing unemployment in the region has paralleled its narrowing (in modern industrial terms) industrial base, and its potential contribution to national economic growth has been seriously undermined. This regional experience does not necessarily condemn government location of industry policy in principle, but suggests that its aim should be one of balanced regional economies as well as balanced national ones.

Summary The decision factors in industrial location are the decisions of owners and the location policy of government. The impact of location decisions on economic growth is long term and fundamental to regional and national economies.

13.5 REGIONAL STRUCTURAL UNEMPLOYMENT

This section includes a further discussion on causes of unemployment which are also dealt with in Section 3 of this chapter and in Chapter 4, Section 7.

In addition to technological unemployment, the other major problem on the supply side is regionally based structural unemployment (e.g. in north-east England and in Scotland) which is due to insufficient new capital formation in existing industries and/or insufficient growth of new industry. Consequently employment declines. Unemployment rates in these regions are usually double the national average (e.g. United Kingdom 3.3 per cent, Scotland 6.1 per cent, Wales 5 per cent, northern England 5.7 per cent and Northern Ireland 7.1 per cent in December 1972) and are therefore a serious problem of mass unemployment at the regional level.

Regions of High Structural Unemployment One of the more intractable problem regions is Northern Ireland, whose industrial structure was largely dependent on the massively declining textile, shipbuilding and agricultural industries in which new capital formation was far less than depreciation. Similar regional structural unemployment existed in the following regions, due to the decline of the industries mentioned: Scotland (coal, shipbuilding, heavy steel, heavy engineering), north-east England (coal, shipbuilding, heavy steel, heavy engineering), South Wales (tinplate, coal) and north-west England (textiles, coal, heavy steel). The problem might have been solved if labour had been willing to move on a massive scale to the growth regions of the south and Midlands, but social pressures make most workers unwilling to change their work, home and regional environment.

Government Aid to Development Areas Government policy has been to intervene in the microeconomic market situation by attempting to increase growth of new economic resources in the regions of high unemployment and restricting such growth in the other regions, using the 'carrot' and 'stick' methods. The 'carrots' consisted of grants (sometimes tax allowances) to encourage firms to develop new plants in the regions of high unemployment, and partly on this incentive basis motor plants were established in the 1960s in Scotland and the north-west to modernize the regions' industrial structure. Within the regions, the government and regional planning councils designated *growth zones* (geographically advantageous areas) to which most new industry should be lured, and *special development areas* (where unemployment was severely high, e.g. Clydeside in Scotland) in which new firms would obtain extra grants. Local retrained labour was a further government incentive to new industry, brought about by training centres which enabled the unemployed to acquire the basic skills of the new growth industries and increase the supply of skilled labour.

The 'stick' in this policy has been the Industrial Development Certificate (IDC), which each firm requiring to expand its plant or offices by 1000 square feet or 15 000 square feet (the amount varied from time to time) needed to obtain from government. General policy was to refuse the IDC in the south and Midlands, and thereby force the firm to expand in a region of high unemployment or not expand at all, and this accounts for the other part of the reason why some motor plants expanded in Scotland and north-west England. In this way resources were re-allocated from regions of low unemployment to regions of high unemployment. The current IDCs (1978) apply to plants of 15 000 square feet, and the grants to firms to expand in regions of high unemployment (i.e. development areas) are 40 per cent of building and machinery costs.

Has this policy brought down the rates of regional unemployment? If we take a year of boom prior to the 1960s' regional policies, i.e. 1959, and a year of boom in the 1970s, i.e. 1974, it is clear that the problem persists in Scotland, Wales and northern England (see Table 13.2).

Table 13.2 Regional unemployment (%).

	Great Britain	*Northern England*	*Scotland*	*Wales*
1959	1.7	3.3	4.4	3.8
1974	2.6	4.7	4.1	3.8

Source: Annual Abstract of Statistics, 1977, HMSO. Reproduced with the kind permission of the Controller of HMSO.

The north-east of England provides a clear example of the attempt by government to overcome regional structural unemployment by the policies just outlined. During the 1940s and 1950s it was heavily dependent for employment on the old declining industries of coal, shipbuilding, heavy steel and heavy engineering, and one major new growth industry, chemicals. Undoubtedly government grants and IDC policy had pushed new factories into the region before the 1960s (including a major expansion of chemicals), but it was the regional planning policies of growth zones and special development areas in the 1960s which resulted in a large influx of new industry into the region. Three growth zones were designated in the government's Regional Plan (1963), Teesside, South Durham (i.e. Darlington/Aycliffe) and Tyneside, and a new social infrastructure of motorways, industrial estates, and housing and education facilities was established (including new towns at Aycliffe and Washington) to promote the natural geographical advantages of these flat zones. A wide range of light and electrical engineering firms, some telecommunication and computer firms, and further petro-chemical plants developed in the zones. Between 1959 and 1966 employment in new growth industries of engineering and electrical goods had risen from 90 000 to 135 000, in construction from 80 000 to 100 000, in professional services from 85 000 to 120 000, and in distribution services from 135 000 to 145 000 (Department of Employment and Productivity data, 1959 and 1966). Government policy was succeeding not only in attracting new manufacturing industry, but also in creating, to a limited extent by an internal regional economic expansion, new employment in consumer service industries due to the new higher incomes and spending of workers in manufacturing. Teesside, an area of rapid growth, became the major centre of the petro-chemical industry in Britain, and developed new industries ancillary to it such as construction of North Sea oilrigs.

The hilly country of West Durham was not suitable for large-scale new industry, and by the mid 1960s its towns began to register unemployment rates of over 10 per cent. It was made a special development area in 1967, and small to medium-sized firms moved into Consett (chemicals), Crook (man-made fibres) and Bishop Auckland, with the help of grants which paid more than 50 per cent of the firms' initial costs. This policy helped bring a substantial decline in unemployment to West Durham, but a major cause of this decline was the willingness of more and more West Durham workers to commute to jobs in the growth zones. By the early 1970s Teesside had so much recovered that its unemployment figures matched the national average in boom, but the regional economy generally had not yet been diversified enough. One particular difficulty was that capital-intensive firms as well as labour-intensive ones were attracted to the region and the former offered few jobs relative to the high government grants. The north-east is typical of the limited success and difficulty of eradicating regional structural unemployment by government policy.

Summary Government tries to increase growth of new economic resources in regions of high structural unemployment by incentives to new firms, and thereby to promote an internal regional economic expansion which raises local consumer demand for service industries. It therefore increases the supply of new productive capacity to a region in order to overcome that region's structural unemployment problem.

13.6 SPECIALIZATION

The application of technological change to actual production and the degree of specialization of the population in work tasks are the most crucial determinants of economic growth in most industrialized countries. The total population and working population are certainly important bases on which to build specialization, as was discussed in Chapter 2. The country with a large working population used to have more advantages over its rivals, because labour was a more important factor of production in the economy during the relatively labour-intensive development of the first industrial revolution. The rapid population growth of Britain in the nineteenth century was a positive stimulus to economic growth. Nowadays, however, the most important aspect of the production factor labour is not size of labour force but degree of specialization of labour in modern capital-intensive industry.

This highly specialized labour is sometimes spoken of by economists as *human capital*. In Chapter 12 (Section 1) we saw how the American economist Becker in his *human capital theory of wages* had argued that the differential between highly paid workers and others was the sum of the costs of training of the highly paid plus an additional amount necessary to equalize the rate of return on the highly paid workers' investment in training with the rate of return on unit trusts or some other well used financial investment. If this theory accurately predicts behaviour in the real world, a financial incentive is available to induce young people to train to be highly specialized workers. In Britain, do apprenticeships for skilled technicians, do degree courses, do post-degree applied science and business studies training courses lead to these pay differentials? The latter may do so, perhaps, but the differential between the skilled and semi-skilled in many British industries, e.g. motors and shipbuilding, is too small to act as a financial incentive for this type of specialization.

The degree of division of labour required in advanced industrial society demands education and training services capable of providing (1) a high level of general education, (2) an expert careers guidance service aware of national manpower planning and (3) a very high level of vocational training.

General Education In Britain recent reports by the Department of Education and Science bemoan the decline of general standards of literacy and numeracy in the schools. On the other hand, much larger numbers of students are attaining a high level of general education in the form of 5 'O' level GCE passes, 2 'A' level GCE passes and first degrees. The sixth-form education 'explosion' of the 1960s has been followed by the higher education 'explosion' of the 1970s, which provides the nation with students whose levels of intellectual development are capable of further intensive training for highly specialized employment. The government's Manpower Services Commission was set up in the early 1970s partly to inform government of labour shortages in highly specialized employment, e.g. aerospace, computer technology, and business services, and to provide high levels of planned training for initial entry and post-first career entry into them.

Manpower Planning The initial training pathway into these specialized jobs requires an expert careers guidance service for schools and a wider school curriculum to include engineering and business studies, since subject specialization begins so early in British schools. The Manpower Services Commission also recommends an expansion of post-degree vocational training in the applied sciences and business studies so that the desired greater number of students can in fact be placed in training. The Department of Education and Science's Green Paper *The Education Service* (July 1977) advocated a wider curriculum, more related to the need to train highly specialized workers in post-higher education, but places which offer training for them must also be expanded.

Vocational Training The national investment in education provided the means in the 1960s and 1970s for raising the general level of education to 'A' level school and to first degree standards. The occupational and task specialization which has made highly skilled jobs more and more skill-specific in the 1970s will require a further massive national investment in post-degree applied courses. The specialized worker now knows far more about a smaller area of knowledge but he is able, through his own specialized on-the-job research and by thought, to advance technical development further and thus to open up the possibilities of future economic growth.

Summary Intensive specialization of highly trained labour provides the means for firms and government to apply new technical developments and advance economic growth. Without such specialization, the application of new technical development and the achievement of faster economic growth are not possible.

13.7 ECONOMIC GROWTH AND DEMAND FOR OUTPUT

The excursions made above into the domains of specialization of labour, technical development and industrial location should not divert us from the other factors that determine changes in the national income during the course of time. Apart from the supply factors discussed, which determine what and how much can be produced, the demand factors are also important causes of economic growth.

The demands placed on the productive means of a country come from consumers, producers, government and foreign countries. The effective demand on the part of the first two has already been discussed in detail: the demand coming from the second two will be discussed – together with their other aspects – in the next two chapters.

Demand Less than Productive Capacity Demand may fall short of, exceed, or be equal to the productive capacity. In the first case, the actual level of national income is indeed determined by the demand, for the economy could produce more and there is some unemployed labour available, the only limiting factor being the demand. The recession in Britain in 1971–2 is an example of this situation in that effective demand was too low to create full employment. The national income ceases to grow under the influence of the demand factors, and we then speak of under-spending. In the second case (demand = productive capacity) the attainable output is in fact produced, and demand and supply keep abreast of each other. The labour market is at equilibrium, and there is no economic imbalance. The situation has been short-lived in Britain in the post-war years, but could be identified in 1953, 1959–60, 1963, 1969 and 1973. Finally, the third case is characterized by overspending, as explained below.

Demand in Excess of Productive Capacity: Trade Cycle When the four demand factors – consumers, producers, government and foreign countries – together call for a greater output than the available productive capacity permits, the real national income is determined by the productive capacity. Demand in this case, however, is ahead of the productive capacity – even though this is constantly increasing – and therefore prices must necessarily rise. Demands for labour, capital and natural resources are so high that their prices usually rise substantially. Economic life is then pervaded by a boom atmosphere: the labour market is over-extended, more of the labour force is wanted than is available, and persistent demand creates a favourable climate for investment. At first, money is forthcoming for firms from banks and the stock market, but eventually the demand is too great for the capital market as well: money becomes scarce, the banks grow reluctant to lend, interest rates rise, and some firms experience liquidity problems. Some entrepreneurs in investment goods industries find that they have over-reacted to the high demand and created an excess production capacity since the limited supply of labour and capital has now restricted the demand by consumer goods firms for these products. For example, a shipbuilding firm may have built more vessels than are needed to convey the now restricted demand of the consumer goods industries, e.g. cars, washing machines and television sets. If these symptoms are serious, the trade cycle has passed through the peak of the boom and some of the factors of production, such as shipyards and their workers, are not used. The Western economy was in a recession in the mid to late 1970s because of the slackening-off of world trade in 1974–5, worldwide inflation and the sharp rise in oil prices. All this has exacerbated the structural problems of the economy: on the demand side, exports and investment have dropped. Britain can now strengthen her trading position only with the aid of her North Sea oil and gas, the export price of which is increasing under the influence of rising world oil prices.

Britain and the Mid to Late 1970s Recession If viewed from the supply side, the cut in investment in a recession amounts to some unwillingness on the part of the entrepreneurs to expand their production capacity, their willingness having diminished together with their profit. Cost inflation, where manufacturers' prices are pushed up by a sharp rise in labour costs, has played a role in limiting such high cost production (e.g. motor industry). For this reason unemployment in Britain will not recede at the same rate at which the world economy recovers and demand for goods increases. Slowing down the wage rises is one of the main means of guaranteeing full employment again in the long run, although of course some unemployment may remain due to technical change. In any case, to understand the present situation we must take into account both the demand factors and the supply factors that govern our economic growth.

However, the current recession is not as serious as the Great Depression of the 1930s. This is partly due to the more important role in economic life of the government, which intervenes to smooth out fluctuations in total investment by programmes of increasing government investment (begun in the United Kingdom in 1977–8). Therefore the government stimulates economic life in periods when spending in the private sector falls off. Social security guarantees some purchasing power, and thus a basic livelihood, whenever a worker cannot work for some reason or other. Finally, the progressive income tax system is a built-in stabilizer, since it automatically takes less money from people in difficult times, e.g. when they are on lower earnings or on Social Security payments.

Summary The course the national income takes over a period of time must be explained by a combination of supply and demand factors. The demand factors are vitally important in ensuring that increased productive capacity is used, full employment is achieved, and economic growth is made a reality.

13.8 CONCLUDING REMARKS

While Chapter 4 dealt with national income within a given period of time, and a fixed productive capacity could be assumed, this chapter has explained variations in the national income during the course of time. We have here therefore taken into account changes in the productive capacity, and have particularly focused upon technical change and specialization.

Technical change can lead to the development of rapid economic growth through the innovation and swift application of new inventions and new work methods. However, the impact of technical change upon the economy can be so rapid that it produces consequences which may be economically as well as socially undesirable. Such features are structural unemployment and environmental pollution. Government policy is important here, since the state is in a position to influence the consequences of technical change and even the direction of technical change itself.

Structural unemployment is a major problem of the late 1970s, and it has been an important contributor to the large-scale unemployment experienced in Britain since 1975. Industries such as steel and car manufacturing shed labour even when they have made major developments in new plant, and regions dependent on still older industries in decline, such as textiles and shipbuilding, are particularly affected. Structural unemployment and environmental pollution can often coexist. Noise, oil pollution, smoke, fumes, and the destruction of natural beauty are the negative effects of economic growth and technical change.

Technical change and economic growth are dependent upon a highly specialized labour force, trained through specific vocational schemes, and possessing a high level of general education. The British education system has been adapted gradually to meet these demands, but the shortage of highly qualified labour has increased. It remains to be seen whether the creation of new jobs in this way will eventually lead to a reduction in general unemployment.

Technical change and specialization have therefore led to a large increase in British national income since 1945, and as technical change accelerates the production capacity increases still further. Until the mid 1970s, demand for goods and services outwardly kept pace with the increase in productive capacity, although overmanning of plant existed in many firms. We are faced in the late 1970s with a lack of effective demand and consequent slower rates of economic growth, but also still confronting us is the challenge of accelerating technical change and of potential productive capacity.

QUESTIONS

1 What are the causes of an increase in the productive capacity of a country?

2 When is the nominal increase in the national income equal to the real increase in it?

3 Who exerts a demand on a country's means of production?

4 What phenomena are observed during a boom?

5 Give some examples of technical development.

6 What is the effect of computers on the demand for (a) bookkeepers and (b) programmers?

7 Can mergers lead to unemployment?

8 What is the connection between industrial production and the pollution of rivers?

9 What forms of structural unemployment are there?

10 What is the role of the Manpower Services Commission?

EXERCISES

1 Design a clear graphical illustration of the figures given in Section 13.1. What would you deduce from the graph?

2 Discuss some aspects of technical development that affect life in the home.

3 Someone wants to build a factory near your home. Who should be involved in the discussion about it, and what welfare effects should be considered?

4 Discuss unemployment, including the following aspects:
(a) Is it the right to work or the right to an income that should be guaranteed?
(b) People's attitude to leisure time.
(c) Can the available work be shared out fairly?
(d) How can unemployment be reduced?

5 Name some positive and negative aspects of technical development, and discuss the role of government in guiding it.

6 Discuss the connection between booms and demand inflation, and compare this situation with that of cost inflation and structural unemployment.

7 In what ways does industrial location determine economic growth?

Chapter Fourteen

The Public Sector and British Government Economic Policy

The public sector normally comprises the central government, local authorities and nationalized industries, but we shall sometimes use the word *government* to mean the whole of the public sector. The economic role of the government has been mentioned in previous chapters, but this chapter is devoted to a systematic discussion of this subject.

This topic often leads to heated political arguments, for some people want to minimize the role of the government in economic affairs while others want to maximize it. In countries like the USSR, China, Cuba and the state socialist countries in Eastern Europe, central planning and the collective approach predominate in deciding what, where, how and how much should be produced, and for whom, leaving less room for individual initiative and personal preference. There is usually a Central Planning Commission whose role is to control economic life rather than forecast its trends. In such planned or command economies, the state provides for almost everything from the cradle to the grave. The lack of markets makes it difficult to adjust the production to the consumer's requirements, and the economic allocation of scarce resources may sometimes be secondary to the fulfilment of plans worked out for the state-owned firms.

By contrast, in other countries, like those in the rest of Europe, the USA and Japan, the free-enterprise or capitalist economy tends to predominate, with entrepreneurial production, free markets and decentralized decision-making. However, in most Western European countries, government has a large role in the economy through ownership of nationalized industries, being backed by a large civil service and having a policy of intervening in the large private sector in order to attempt to eliminate fluctuations in the economy. Certain aspects, such as the power of multinational companies, the exorbitant profits companies sometimes make, the authoritarian decisions made by firms, unequal income distribution, and environmental pollution, cause public disquiet. However, these political questions lie outside the scope of this book, and we shall simply mention that the major social issues of recent years such as unemployment, the energy crisis and environmental pollution are related to technical development, as is their solution.

Whatever position the public sector occupies in economic life, one of its fundamental problems concerns the use of scarce resources, since this is not decided in the public sector by market forces and the price mechanism but by collective decision-making processes. Through these processes the expenditure on education and defence will be determined. The questions involved here are how to organize the decision-making apparatus, what weight to attach to individual preferences, and what importance to attribute to pressure groups and to the interests of future generations. These questions encroach on the political field of parliamentary democracy, which illustrates once more how the boundaries of economics are expanding.

14.1 THE GOVERNMENT

The government is a producer unit, just like a factory making shoes. It produces goods and renders services of value to individuals and to society and thus contributes to welfare. Unlike the private sector, it is motivated mainly by the interests of the community as reflected in the national Parliament to which it is responsible. Its economic aspect is reflected in the demands it places on scarce resources which have alternative uses, for it, too, must constantly make a choice. Decisions about the allocation of the factors of production are largely left, in the private sector, to the market forces while in the public sector they are made mainly by means of the national budget. In a parliamentary democracy, the various and often conflicting interests of the people are, in principle, weighed up by Parliament, but Parliament is often subjected to the operation of pressure groups (e.g. trades union congress, I.C.I. and anti-nuclear power groups). The individual, as an individual, usually influences government expenditure only through his membership of such pressure groups.

Although the public sector also comprises the local authorities, government organizations and institutions (e.g. in the sphere of social security and health services), the education service and nationalized industries, the present discussion is largely restricted to the central government. The connection between the various parts of the public sector is quite close; for example, they all tend to pursue a common wage policy, such as government's 5 per cent norm for 1978–9. A speciality of the public sector is the supply of public goods, like justice, administration and defence, for the use of which an individual's payment is practically impossible. These goods cannot be split into smaller units that could be supplied to some and withheld from others – they are available to all and paid for by all. Moreover, as they are produced they are available, by definition, to everybody (see Figure 14.1). Some goods – called *quasi-public goods* – can or could also be purchased on an individual basis (e.g. roads and education), but these are mostly financed from public funds, since direct payment for them would be undesirable due to cumbersome administration. The government also supplies goods and services, such as railway services, which could equally be supplied by the private sector, but not without a serious risk of monopolies arising. The government also

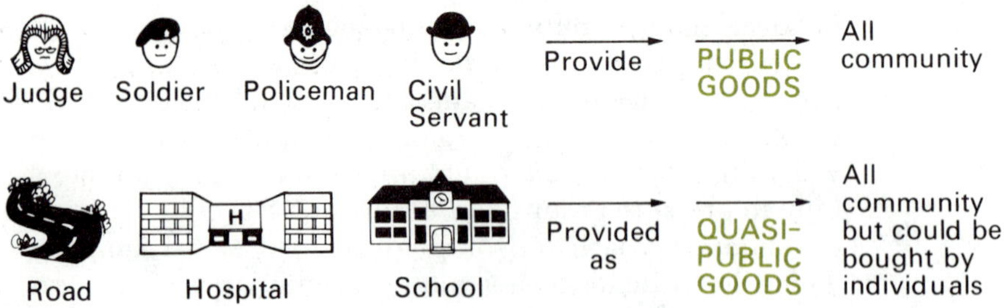

Figure 14.1 Public and quasi-public goods.

provides services for individuals, e.g. the postal services, electricity, gas and water supplies, and public transport. One of the advantages of this is that projects which benefit the public (e.g. rural railways) but which the private sector would not contemplate because of their unprofitability are accomplished, and the financial loss incurred in these ventures is of course covered by public funds. Some basic manufacturing industries providing individual commodities such as coal, steel and aerospace are also in public ownership.

Summary The public sector is motivated by the welfare of the community as a whole, reflected in the decisions of the national Parliament, and accomplishes its aims mainly by means of the national budget. However, like any other economic organization, it has to allocate scarce resources in government ownership to satisfy many wants.

14.2 THE ANNUAL NATIONAL BUDGET

The important role the government plays in economics is reflected in the annual national budget which the Chancellor of the Exchequer presents to the House of Commons in March or April every year. This comprises a summary of the various budget items and shows how the government budget fits into the overall economic and financial situation of the country. The government budget contains proposals for government expenditure and the means (i.e. government revenue) of financing it. Government expenditure applies to education, sciences, social security, defence, transportation and public works, while the main source of revenue derives from taxes, namely direct taxes (income tax and taxes on profit and capital) and indirect taxes, which act as price surcharges (such as value-added tax).

When revenue does not cover expenditure, the government raises government loans which can be either 'funded' or floating. The first consists of long-term loans with a fixed interest rate, while the latter consists of short-term loans (with a term of less than a year), such as treasury bills. The conversion of floating debt into funded debt is called 'funding'. These loans make up the public sector borrowing requirement.

Those who prepare the national budgets are restricted in many ways. For example, the national budget cannot vary drastically from year to year, since many projects, such as the nuclear submarine programme, take several years to complete, and once the government has committed itself to a long-term project it must continue to finance it year after year. Occasionally, however, some such projects are cancelled, usually with serious unemployment consequences (e.g. the TSR.2 aircraft in the 1960s). Furthermore, numerous items of government expenditure are complementary to those made in the private sector, that is they depend on the growth of the economy and the population, examples being investments in the infrastructure such as roads and housing. Besides, cutting back on government spending can harm the structural development of the economy (e.g. in re-training of skilled labour and education) so the Chancellor must be careful.

Finally, it is very time-consuming to implement a budgetary change in taxation. The changeover from purchase tax to value-added tax in 1973 involved enormous expenditure and time in re-training staff as well as printing new information. Even a change in the standard rate of income tax or the personal allowances on income tax involves much work on the part of the income tax staff.

According to classical economic liberalism, budget items should be minimized, and revenue should balance the expenditure. According to Keynes, on the other hand, the government must balance the trade-cycle trends in the private sector and therefore pursue a counter-cyclical budgetary policy. In this framework, when during a recession expenditure in the private sector drops, the government intervenes by raising public spending and cutting government revenue derived from taxes, so that a budget deficit arises. This is covered by a budget surplus that occurs when, in a boom period either before or after the recession, the expenditure in the private sector rises and the government can cut public spending and raise the revenue from taxes. In such periods, the government may still inject money into the capital market, but it does not do this to finance the private sector but to 'mop up' liquidity from the money and capital market, to make investments less attractive for the private sector. This is how the national budget aims to smooth the fluctuations in effective demand in the private sector. This counter-cyclical budgetary policy fits into the trade-cycle policy of the government, but goes far beyond any interventionist role the government plays in the structural development of the economy. An emergency budget, often called 'mini-budget', is introduced by government at times of serious inflation or unemployment, when government cannot wait until the annual budget to take stringent budgetary measures to control the problem.

A budgetary control geared more to the supply side is effected by government grants to areas of high structural unemployment to eliminate this type of unemployment in the long run. (This subject was discussed in Chapter 13.)

Summary The differing views on government's economic role are reflected in the various policies proposed for the national budget. One of the ways government attempts to eliminate fluctuations in economic activity is through the annual budget, as well as by using it to raise revenue to pay for government expenditure.

14.3 GOVERNMENT EXPENDITURE

Government expenditure comprises expenditure on public goods (such as defence) and on quasi-public goods (such as roads and education), mentioned before, and transfer payments (such as old-age pensions and unemployment benefits). In the case of transfer payments, the government acts as a redistributor of income. A fourth type of government expense is incurred in the provision of goods and services below cost price, as was the case with milk and some other essential foodstuffs in 1974–6. In such cases, it is not considered right to ask the users to pay more, so that the difference has to be made up from public funds. Some important items of central government expenses featuring in the British national budget for 1976–7 are shown in Table 14.1.

Table 14.1 British government expenditure, 1976–7 (£m).

Defence and external relations (UK)	
Defence	5 621
Overseas aid and other overseas services	1 062
Commerce and industry	
Agriculture	1 003
Industry and employment	3 074
Environmental services	
Roads and transport	2 716
Housing	4 680
Other environmental services	2 560
Law and order	1 848
Social services	
Education	7 519
Health and personal social services	6 533
Social security	11 168
Northern Ireland	1 627
Government lending to nationalized industries	800
Other public and common services	1 687
Total programmes	51 898
Interest on National Debt	1 800
Total	53 698

Source: Britain 1978: Official Handbook, Table 22, p. 332, HMSO. Reproduced with the kind permission of the Controller of HMSO.

Since the total for 1976–7 is over £50b, each of the first two items is seen to receive one-sixth of the total figure. The increase in government expenditure has been very substantial in the past few years, partly because of inflation. This has been accompanied by a desire to keep a tighter grip on government spending by comparing the expected utility of an item with the sacrifice involved in financing it, and by carefully deciding what to spend money on in order to maximize its utility. New methods, such as the planning–programming–budgeting system, have recently been developed in which the costs of government activities are compared with their benefits. For example, the third London airport proposal was subjected to vigorous cost–benefit analysis in order to find the 'best site' – before the whole project was abandoned.

The economic aspect is more obvious if the money spent by the government is classified as real government expenses on the one hand and transfer payments on the other. The former comprises the money with which the government buys its share of the productivity capacity, and it consists of wages and salaries for its employees, as well as outgoings on government consumption and investment. By contrast, transfer payments do not belong to the sphere of commodity exchange, and so they make no direct demand on the productive capacity. The government does not buy anything in these cases, but transfers money from wealthier to poorer people (who can of course buy goods with it for themselves). Capital transfers made to alleviate disasters are also counted with transfer payments.

A special class of income transfer payments, namely social security benefits, has recently received increased attention, mainly because of the mid/late 1970s recession. These payments include not only unemployment benefits, sickness benefits and benefits to people too incapacitated to work, but also family allowances, old-age pensions, widows' pensions and orphans' pensions. All social security payments are made to help people whose earnings have diminished for one reason or another. The social security system is so comprehensive in Britain that its financing in recession out of limited national resources is becoming increasingly difficult.

When the government discharges part of the national debt or gives loans to industry, we speak of business capital transactions.

Summary The high level of government expenditure illustrates the great importance of the government to our economy, and that government can change its expenditure to influence fluctuations in economic activity. Fifty per cent of public spending is on the social services.

14.4 GOVERNMENT REVENUE

The biggest source of revenue is taxation, and – as mentioned before – we distinguish between direct and indirect taxes. The former include income tax and corporation tax, bringing in an estimated revenue of £18 039m and £2587m, respectively, in 1976–7. Indirect taxes include value-added tax (£4240m), oil tax (£2400m), tobacco tax (£2150m) and alcoholic drink tax (£2050m) in 1976–7. The total figures for direct and indirect taxes were about £21 000m and £15 000m, respectively, in 1976–7. The most important non-tax revenues, 4 per cent of total revenue, are profits from government companies, interest, radio and TV licences, crown-land leases, fines, and penalties for discharging wastes. Table 14.2 shows the sources of British government revenue for 1976–7.

All the sums spent on education are channelled to local authorities and supplemented at local level by rates. They provide the finance for state schools, colleges and polytechnics.

Table 14.2 British government revenue (£m).

Taxation	*1976–7*	*1977–8 (forecast)*
Inland revenue		
Income tax	17 030	18 039
Surtax	63	30
Corporation tax	2 650	2 587
Petroleum revenue tax	–	5
Capital gains tax	300	330
Development land tax	1	5
Estate duty	124	70
Capital transfer tax	260	320
Stamp duties	272	320
Total	20 700	21 706
Customs and excise		
Value-added tax	3 750	4 240
Oil	2 060	2 400
Tobacco	1 885	2 150
Alcohol	1 355	2 050
Gaming	285	315
Car tax	295	250
Protective duties	725	690
Agricultural levies	60	135
Other revenue duties	10	10
Total	10 425	12 240
Motor vehicle duties	835	1 068
National Insurance surcharge	–	1 159
Total taxation	31 960	36 173
Miscellaneous receipts		
TV licences	237	275
Interest and dividends	140	225
Other	860	935
Total miscellaneous receipts	1 237	1 435
Total revenue	33 197	37 608

Source: Britain 1978: Official Handbook, Table 23, p. 337, HMSO. Reproduced with the kind permission of the Controller of HMSO.

When funds are insufficient for covering expenses, the government can ask for credit, usually in the form of either treasury bills (three-month) or medium- and long-term government stock. When there is a clear deficit at the end of the financial year it is usually funded by government stock. The deficit in 1976–7 was funded in these ways.

During the 1970s taxation on income has tended to increase relatively and that on expenditure to decrease relatively. In 1969–70 central government taxation was 39 per cent on both income and expenditure but by 1976–7 the taxation on income had risen to 44 per cent and that on expenditure had declined to 27 per cent.

The major tax on income is, of course, income tax, which has a basic rate of 33 per cent. However, the first £1535 (1978–9) earned is not subject to any taxation. It is often suggested that taxes on income are a deterrent to individual initiative in work. Studies by economists on this matter tend to suggest that the disincentive operates only at the higher levels of income tax, when individuals are being taxed at the rate of 75 per cent or more of their extra income. In line with other EEC countries, Britain's major expenditure tax has become value-added tax, levied at 8 per cent, with food exempt. Large revenue is derived from the tobacco and the alcoholic drink taxes which, taken together, almost pay for government health services! There is perhaps scope for further taxation on expenditure through increases in the relatively low gaming taxes. Taxes on expenditure, unlike those on income, relate very little to the individual's capacity to pay.

Summary The main source of government income is taxation. A proportion of the money thus raised is channelled to the local authorities to enable them to pay for local services, in particular for education. Taxation in Britain in the 1970s increased in proportion on incomes and decreased in proportion on expenditure.

14.5 A KEYNESIAN MODEL INCLUDING THE PUBLIC SECTOR

Now that we have introduced the public sector into the economy, we can add real government expenditure (G) and taxes (T) to the macroeconomic quantities discussed in Chapter 4. Real government expenditure does not comprise transfer payments such as social security benefits and taxes we rate in the net sense, subsidies being deducted. The national product is now composed not only of consumer goods and capital goods, but also of the production of the government: this gives us, as far as Britain is concerned, a much more real-world picture since government production equals about 37 per cent of production. We can therefore say that output in money terms is equal to the sum of the value of consumer goods produced, investment goods produced and government production:

$$O = C + I + G. \tag{1}$$

Similarly, the national income by the expenditure approach (Y) now consists not only of the money spent on consumption (C) and the money saved (S), but also of the taxes (T). In the mixed economy, taxes play an essential role in financing the public services, and we are now integrating them into macroeconomic theory. Therefore we can say that national income is equal to the sum of consumption, saving and taxes:

$$Y = C + S + T. \tag{2}$$

It follows from Eqs. (1) and (2) that the actual (*ex post*) values of saving and investment now need not be equal to each other. The identity now reads

$$I + G = S + T. \tag{3}$$

Only if real expenditure by the government is equal to the level of taxes is ex post investment equal to ex post saving.

The Keynesian method of determining the equilibrium level of the national income in a given period of time, during which a fixed productive capacity can be assumed, can now be worked out.

We have to make an assumption about the behaviour of consumers. Let us say that planned expenditure on consumer goods depends on the disposable income of the consumers, where disposable income is defined as the difference between national income (Y) and taxation (T). To be more specific, postulate a linear relationship between consumption (C) and disposable income (Y − T), so that the consumption function reads:

$$C = c(Y - T) + C_0 \qquad 0 < c < 1 \text{ and } C_0 > 0 \tag{4}$$

In Eq. (4), C_0 is autonomous consumption and c is the marginal propensity to consume.

With respect to T we make the rather simple assumption that the level of taxes is proportional to national income, so that it is a constant fraction t in relation to Y. We therefore have

$$T = tY \qquad 0 < t < 1 \tag{5}$$

Eq. (5) implies that the government receives more through taxation as national income (Y) rises.

Also to be added to the Keynesian analysis is the real expenditure of the government (G), which we assume to be autonomous and therefore not related to national income. If G_0 is the symbol for autonomous government expenditure, we arrive at

$$G = G_0 \tag{6}$$

Let us finally assume that private investment has again an autonomous character, so that it does not depend on national income. We then have

$$I = I_0 \tag{7}$$

In Eq. (7), I_0 is the symbol for autonomous investment.

In order to close our model, we need an equilibrium condition. To this end, we assume that for equilibrium in the economy total expenditure or effective demand should be equal to national income. This means that the sum of consumption, investment and government expenditure equals national income. The equilibrium condition therefore reads

$$Y = C + I + G. \tag{8}$$

If we substitute in Eq. (8) the expressions we have introduced for C, I and G, we easily see that

$$Y = c(Y - tY) + C_0 + I_0 + G_0. \tag{9}$$

From Eq. (9) we can derive the equilibrium value of national income:

$$\bar{Y} = \frac{C_0 + I_0 + G_0}{1 - c(1 - t)}. \tag{10}$$

The multiplier no longer equals $\frac{1}{1-c}$, but $\frac{1}{1-c(1-t)}$. The levying of taxes has made the multiplier smaller, since taxes mean that people have less of their income to spend.

Let us give a numerical example to conclude. If $c = \frac{3}{4}$, $t = \frac{1}{5}$, $C_0 = 10$, $I_0 = 40$ and $G_0 = 30$, the equilibrium value of national income ($\bar{Y}$) according to Eq. (10) equals 200.

Summary The public sector can be included in a Keynesian model of the determination of national income, by adding government expenditure and taxation to the macroeconomic variables already studied.

14.6 GOVERNMENT ECONOMIC POLICY

Before examining the government's spending policy, we shall deal with some general aspects of economic policy. Economic policy embraces all the measures by which the government aims to influence and control economic life, as well as the instruments used for this purpose. We are thinking here primarily of the behaviour of the central government, but the measures of local authorities can also be included in economic policy. The objectives of the central government's economic policy are of course more far-reaching than those of the economic policy of a district or metropolitan county council. For example, the state aims to influence trade cycles and thus eliminate fluctuations in economic activity by adjusting the level and composition of government spending, and this lies outside the scope of the Wyre Forest district council. The government can, of course, include other public bodies in the implementation of its trade-cycle policy. The economic policy of the central government also differs from that of local governments in its instruments. For example, the central government can announce a price freeze to curb inflation, but the local authorities cannot. The next few sections will deal predominantly with the objectives and instruments of the central government's economic policy in Britain.

It is important to realize that the contents of economic policy cannot be deduced only from economics. The choice of objectives and instruments is a political question, governed not by positive statements ('what there is') but by normative statements or value judgements ('what there ought to be'). These views often relate to desired changes in the economic system and to the ways of bringing these about. These judgements are based on political and ideological convictions and – as mentioned before – cannot be deduced from economics. Of course, economics can help in formulating, and particularly in quantifying, the objectives and instruments, since it offers a very efficient apparatus for elucidating the consequences of various policies. The debate on government economic policy among the Labour, Conservative and Liberal parties involves value judgements in specific arguments on economics issues.

We distinguish between trade-cycle policy and structural policy of government. The former deals with the demand side of economics, its aim being to influence the level and composition of expenditure in the public and the private sector. An increase in expenditure leads to more employment, of course, and helps overcome a recession trade-cycle situation. Examples of ways used by government to correct this trade-cycle situation in Britain are cuts in income tax, company tax, value-added tax, excise duty on beer and the tax on petrol. An example of increased government expenditure to strengthen structural policy would be grants to firms to set up plants in areas of high unemployment. In many cases, there may be a conflict between trade-cycle policy and structural policy. Thus, a reduction in public investment during a boom can slow down the improvement of the infrastructure (roads, railways, water supply, schools, etc.) upon which depressed regions rely to attract new industry and employment. A constant complaint in Scotland, Wales and north-east England is that government has reduced expenditure in those regions during booms in spite of high unemployment there.

Although the improvement of education may be desirable for structural development, the economic situation in a period of severe inflation may not be able to bear the extra investment. The fact that investment affects both spending and the productive capacity emerges clearly from economic policy: Keynes puts the stress on the spending effect, while growth theory puts it on the productive capacity effect. Basically the same distinction is encountered in the theory of public finance when one speaks of the government's influence on spending and on planning. The choice between trade-cycle considerations and structural considerations, when these are in conflict, is based on value judgements that do not follow from economic issues.

We also differentiate between short-term and long-term economic policies. The difference between these in time is arbitrary, one year being short-term and five years long-term. However, this interpretation is not entirely satisfactory. It is sometimes believed that trade-cycle policy is short term to eliminate the fluctuations in economic activity while structural policy is long term, to improve labour and capital quality, etc., but this concept is just as unsatisfactory as the previous one. The real difference lies mainly in the number of constants versus variables included in the formulation of economic policy: the greater the number of variables amenable to changes, the stronger the long-term character of the treatment. Let us take the labour market as an example. If the supply of labour is considered to be constant, so that the demand for labour is a key variable, then the labour market policy has a stronger short-term character than it has in the case when the volume and composition of labour supply are also regarded as variables that can be influenced.

Summary Although economic theory should not be confused with economic policy, a study of the latter reveals that scarcity imposes choices and decision on us. Government economic policy is related both to eliminating fluctuations in economic activity (i.e. trade-cycle policy) and to overcoming structural economic problems (e.g. improving quality of labour).

14.7 USE OF NATIONALIZED INDUSTRIES IN GOVERNMENT ECONOMIC POLICY

State-owned firms produce about 11 per cent of British gross national product and employ about 18 per cent of the working population. They are therefore not only a very important contributor to national economic resources, but also provide in themselves a powerful tool which government can use to modify fluctuations in the economy such as inflationary booms and slumps. The nationalized industries were taken into state ownership for three basic economic reasons. (1) Natural monopoly: some industries involve so much capital expenditure and geographical coverage of the country that they tend to be dominated by one firm (e.g. the Post Office, electricity and gas). (2) Basic industries: these supply all other major industries, but do not necessarily tend to be monopolies when in private ownership (e.g. coal, steel and transport). (3) New highly technological industries: some new industries involve so much capital and risk that a country of Britain's size finds few or no British firms able to cope with such projects, and the state becomes involved (e.g. aerospace).

How does government use its ownership of these industries to manage the economy? In this case it is important to realize that a government minister in charge of the industry is responsible for all general policy decisions (e.g. investment, pricing and wages), and the managerial board is responsible only for day to day management.

Therefore, in the nationalized firm, the government, through the minister, can carry into effect policies to help control national unemployment and inflation. During the recession of 1971–2 the government through the minister responsible for the British Steel Corporation (steel industry) initiated a £1200m investment programme, which provided new jobs in construction and allied work to help overcome unemployment (it was also, of course, a means of modernizing the industry). Similarly, in the 1975–9 recession, the Government made credits available to British Shipbuilders (state shipbuilding industry), so that ships for a Polish company should be made in regions of high unemployment (e.g. Clyde and Mersey).

Examples of the use of state firms by government in controlling inflation are the price restraint measures of British Rail and the Electricity Distribution Boards in 1977 and the implementation of a 10 per cent pay norm for 1977–8 in the state industries (e.g. electricity supply and coal). These policies may contribute to the easing of national macroeconomic problems, but they may also militate against the economic efficiency of the state firm itself, by under-pricing the product, by low wages which do not attract sufficient labour, and by unnecessary investment in some sectors of the firm.

Summary Nationalized industries are used by the British government to increase investment and jobs in recession and to control prices and wages in inflationary times.

14.8 OBJECTIVES AND INSTRUMENTS OF GOVERNMENT ECONOMIC POLICY

The government's economic policy in Britain has the following objectives: (1) full employment; (2) stable prices; (3) equilibrium in balance of payments; (4) economic growth. Some of these objectives conflict (e.g. the pursuit of full employment can easily clash with prevention of inflation). This illustrates the need to view the objectives as a single interrelated complex. Let us examine the objectives in more detail.

Full Employment This means prevention of both unemployment and over-full employment. Situations of disequilibrium in the labour market include both unemployment and a large influx of imported labour.

Stable Prices The problem of inflation has come to occupy a central position in government economic policy. Since the British economy is an open economy, it is also subject to the effects of inflation abroad, particularly on imported raw materials and foodstuffs. Prices in the 1970s were pulled up by the great demand on world markets ('demand pull' mechanism of inflation), and at the same time pushed up by the great increase in labour costs at home ('cost push' mechanism of inflation). Depending on their market power, home producers also raised their prices in this situation. In view of all these pressures, government finds it difficult to achieve an inflation rate below 10 per cent.

Equilibrium in Balance of Payments To achieve a balance of payments that shows an equilibrium requires equilibrium conditions to be created between Britain and foreign countries in the transactions in goods, services and capital. This aspect is discussed in more detail in Chapter 15, which is devoted to international trade.

Economic Growth This objective requires the increase and improvement of the productive capacity. Attempts to raise production per head, come what may, can have some external disadvantages such as pollution, and we are more and more often faced with the choice between a pleasant environment on the one hand and a high level of growth on the other. A pleasant environment is just as much part of economic welfare as are more goods, and some might suggest it is taken as a fifth objective of economic policy. Some British governments have made income-redistribution an additional objective of economic policy (e.g. Labour governments, particularly in 1945–51 and 1974–).

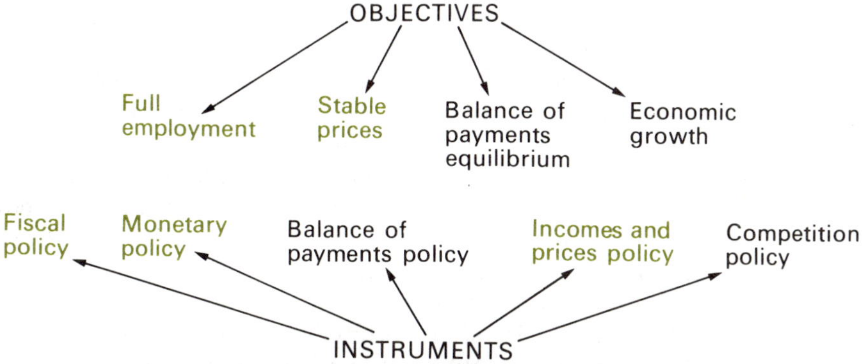

Figure 14.2 Objectives and instruments of British government economic policy.

To achieve the above objectives, government utilizes economic policy instruments (see Figure 14.2), of which the most important in Britain are: (1) fiscal policy; (2) monetary policy; (3) incomes and prices policy; (4) balance of payments policy; (5) competition policy. The last-named involves control of monopolies, oligopolies and mergers (as discussed in Chapter 11) in order to limit price rises and promote expansion of industries. Balance of payments policy involves principally exchange rate and capital movement control in order to bring into equilibrium outflows and inflows of goods services and capital. The mechanisms of control have been discussed in Chapter 7, and will be analysed further in Chapter 15. The other three policy instruments will be examined through short case studies of their use in dealing with economic policy objectives: in the case of incomes and prices policy, the 1964–71 Labour government; in the case of monetary policy, the 1970–74 Conservative government; and with fiscal policy, the Labour government since 1974.

Summary **Economic policy is based on weighing up the possible effects of different objectives and instruments, and in making choices between them. The ever-changing pattern of interplay between the objectives and instruments of economic policy can be disentangled by closely following the latest developments.**

14.9 CASE STUDY: INCOMES AND PRICES POLICY; 1964–70 LABOUR GOVERNMENT

The basic macroeconomic setting in which the Labour government was implementing incomes and prices policy was one of a 4 to 5 per cent inflation rate, relatively high by the 1950s and 1960s experience, and a large balance of payments deficit. To counter the inflation and attain its major objective of price stability, government at first relied mainly on fiscal and monetary policy but in 1966 turned to incomes and prices policy, not only as one means of easing the problem but as the major method of doing so. The first general report of the newly formed National Board for Prices and Incomes (NBPI) in 1966 put the case for emphasising this: '... the country has a choice: to pitch demand so much below the limits of capacity that the uncertainties attendant on its fine regulation are diminished and the power of managements and unions to contribute to inflationary pressure is reduced; or to secure appropriate behaviour by managements and unions with regard to prices and incomes so that demand can be pitched nearer the limits of capacity and a higher rate of growth achieved'. In other words effective counter-inflationary monetary and fiscal policies would have to be so strong that they would lead to a substantial fall in consumer demand, production and employment. Therefore incomes and prices policy should be given a chance to work.

The machinery for implementing incomes and prices policy established in 1965 was quite elaborate. The NBPI had the task of vetting price and income increases submitted to it by government, according to criteria propounded by government. Any increase not supported by the NBPI could be statutorily withheld by a Government Order for a very limited period (varying between three and 12 months). In July 1966 government emphasis on this policy was made much firmer when the statutory limit was extended to 12 months, the 'norm' for general wage increases reduced to 0 per cent, and no exceptions to this 'norm' permitted for six months (nor any price increases). During the next six-month period the policy was slightly relaxed to permit exceptions to the percentage norm on grounds of increased productivity, and to allow price increases if import costs or taxation went up.

This severe policy was relaxed in mid 1967, when a general pay norm of 3½ per cent was permitted, and increases above that could be justified on the pre-1966 criteria of increased productivity, low pay, shortage of labour or comparability with other occupations. Similarly, price increases could also be allowed on the pre-1966 criteria of unavoidable cost increases.

A further main objective of government policy at this time was the elimination of the large balance of payments deficit, which it was believed would be removed if incomes restraint led to fewer imports being needed and prices restraint led to more exports being won.

What were the effects on inflation of the incomes and prices policy? Studies show that the period of 'freeze' and 'severe restraint' in 1966–7 was successful, but that the periods before this and later in 1968–9 were little influenced by the policy. Weekly earnings rose from (1959 = 100) 140.4 (1965) to 149.4 (1966) to 154.4 (1967) to 166.8 (1968) to 179.6 (1969). Retail prices also rose sharply between 1965 and 1966 from 120.1 to 124.9, much less sharply from 1966 to 1967 (128.0) and again rapidly increased to 134.0 (1968) and 141.1 (1969). Even in 1966–7 the policy was not fully successful in halting earnings and price rises, but that year's strong policy did have a clear impact by substantially reducing the rise in earnings and prices. The less severe policies earlier and later in the 1960s appear to have had little practical impact, but we do not know, of course, what the rate of inflation would have been without them. Moreover, in 1968–70 the government became increasingly subjected to trade union pressure to relax policy, and fewer cases were referred by government to the NBPI in 1969–70. The policy had little or no impact on the balance of payments, which worsened in 1967, and to counter this the currency was devalued that year. Table 14.3 shows incomes and prices under these policies.

Table 14.3 Prices and earnings under incomes and prices policy.

	Weekly earnings (1959 = 100)	*Retail prices (1959 = 100)*
1965	140.4	120.1
1966	149.4	124.9
1967	154.4	128.0
1968	166.8	134.4
1969	179.6	141.1

Summary **The incomes and prices policy instrument works successfully in short periods of severe wage and price restraint, but appears to have very limited influence in achieving the policy objectives of stable prices and balance of payments equilibrium over a longer period.**

14.10 CASE STUDY: MONETARY POLICY; CONSERVATIVE GOVERNMENT 1970–74

The general economic background to the monetary policy pursued by the Conservative government was initially one of rising unemployment (to over one million in 1971: 4.1 per cent of the working population) followed by a persistence of inflation and renewed balance of payments deficit. During 1970–71 inflation was still 8 to 10 per cent per annum and interest rates were kept high to restrict demand. After 1971 the prime objective of the monetary policy instrument was to bring down the high rate of unemployment, and to this end fiscal policies were also utilized. Interest rates were reduced (to 5 per cent), and Bank Rate and hire purchase rates were reduced, but much of the expansion in the supply of credit to firms from banks for investment purposes, and therefore to raise employment, was due to the new policy of competition and credit control introduced in 1971 (see Chapter 7). The liquidity ratio of 30 per cent was replaced by an eligible reserve assets ratio of 12½ per cent, and this enabled banks to lend more in long-term advances to firms although not at the increased rate implied above since reserve assets ratio is related to a more limited section of deposits. The strict 8 per cent cash ratio was abandoned, cash reserves fell to 5 to 6 per cent, and credit expanded further. Government also expanded the cash basis of the money supply very rapidly and therefore enabled more credit to be created and lent by banks to firms for investment/employment purposes. In 1972–3 £5000m was the increase in credit. (It should be pointed out that some of these funds went into property speculation rather than into physical investment.)

Unemployment fell from 4.1 per cent (January 1971) to 2.2 per cent (November 1973), and this was due not only to the monetary expansion (which tends to be gradual in its impact because of its indirect nature) but also to large injections of government spending and increased consumer demand as a consequence of fiscal policy measures. The impact of both these policy instruments also raised business confidence and enhanced the willingness of private firms to bear risks in increasing production, investment and employment.

A consequence of the massive monetary expansion was a rise in consumer demand to the point of accelerating inflation as well as production, and a worsening balance of payments. The objective of monetary policy in 1973 changed to control of inflation, and a 'squeeze on credit' was introduced in which minimum lending rate (MLR) was raised to a (then) record 12 per cent, special deposits called in and directives given to banks to limit personal loans. Allied to this, funding and open market operations were used to tighten the squeeze. It was assumed that the objective of rectifying the adverse balance of payments would be achieved by the automatic devaluation during inflation of the (since 1972) floating pound. The monetary measures used to combat unemployment had been successful, but when the Conservative government left office in early 1974 it was too early to assess the impact on inflation of the restrictive monetary, fiscal, and incomes and prices policies which had been imposed.

Summary Monetary policy instrument works slowly because it affects industry indirectly, and its cumulative effectiveness can be seen only over an 18- to 24-month period. The massive money supply expansion of 1971–2 was still stoking the fires of inflation in 1973.

14.11 SHORT CASE STUDY: FISCAL POLICY; LABOUR GOVERNMENT AFTER 1974

The economic setting for this Labour government in 1974–5 was an increasing rate of inflation, a rising rate of unemployment (from 600 000 to over one million), and a worsening balance of payments. In this complex situation government initial moves were to maintain the monetary squeeze, relax the incomes policy, strengthen the prices policy, and to use fiscal policy at times to counter rising inflation (March 1974 budget) and at times to counter rising unemployment (July and November 1974 budgets). By spring 1975 government chose to make the reduction of inflation its main objective, and fiscal policy its major instrument. Public expenditure was cut by £1100m and taxation was increased by £1251m, and in 1976 there were two further large reductions in public spending, of £1000m in both July and December. The impact of these measures on inflation was directly to reduce consumer demand by taxation increases, and directly to lower the public sector's demand by the cuts in its expenditure. Inflation was reduced to single figures by mid 1978.

Allied to the fiscal policy's direct impact, there were reductions in the increase in money supply in 1976 and 1977, and a strong prices policy and a stronger voluntary incomes policy in 1975–7, implemented with union support. It is difficult to assess the relative importance of the fiscal policy instrument in reducing the rate of inflation, but it was the most direct instrument in its impact, and also the most flexible one in the government's armoury. This last point was particularly illustrated in late 1977, when government changed the emphasis from counter-inflation to counter-unemployment, and did so by cutting taxes (£1049m) and raising public spending (£1000m). This policy was confirmed by further substantial tax cuts and spending increases in April 1978. It is true that a more relaxed incomes policy had been adopted in late 1977 and that interest rates had been allowed to fall from the 15 per cent record MLR in 1976 to 5 per cent, but these measures had not been accompanied by any increase in the money supply.

The balance of payments situation improved in 1975–7, partly due to home-produced North Sea oil, and to reduced demand for imports during the recession. The new Cambridge school of economists have emphasized the importance of fiscal policy in restoring equilibrium to the balance of payments by reducing the public sector's demand for imported goods.

Summary The direct and fairly immediate effects of the fiscal policy instrument mean that it is a more flexible, and in the short run more effective, instrument than the others in dealing with inflation, except for the very short-term incomes and prices freeze. Monetary policy may be more effective in the long term, but even in that time fiscal policy is far more powerful than incomes and prices policy, according to research studies so far produced. (None are available yet on the 1975–7 government/TUC joint incomes policy which may reveal a strength in the long term of government/TUC incomes policies.)

14.12 CONCLUDING REMARKS

The economic function of the government is reflected in the goods it produces and the budgetary policy it pursues. The former include public goods which are placed at the disposal of the community as a whole, but they also include individual goods whose use the government wants to promote or restrict, or in the case of which it wants to prevent any exploitation of the consumers. Government expenditure normally increases from year to year, since the provision of the various goods and services requires more and more investment, which either keeps pace with or increases more steeply than the national income. The local authorities spend much of the money involved because numerous responsibilities are delegated to them by the central government. The government revenue comes from various sources, but mostly from taxes. Any gap between revenue and expenditure is filled by loans and credits. In Britain the nationalized industries, together with the rest of the public sector, are also used to moderate unemployment and to counter inflation, as agents of government economic policies.

As we have just seen, the government plays various important roles in economic life and these are basically determined by the prevailing economic system. In Britain's mixed economy, the objectives of economic policy determine its instruments, but are themselves determined by policies. In this sense, both the objectives (and their order of priority) and the use of the instruments depend on value judgements that lie outside the scope of economics. The instruments can be used separately but it is better to apply them in conjunction with one another, if only to prevent serious conflicts arising between policy on a trade cycle and that on the structural aspects of the economy. We have analysed the impact of three major policy instruments through short case studies of the last decade or so. It is clear that in the short run the fiscal policy instrument enables government to change its policy objectives and their impact more effectively, due to its direct influence. In the longer term, monetary policy has a powerful influence, but incomes and prices policy is strongest in the very short-run 'freezes'.

QUESTIONS

1 What are the objectives of economic policy? Give a brief description of each.

2 Name the instruments of economic policy and describe them briefly.

3 What are public goods?

4 Give an example of transfer payments.

5 What are the main items of government expenditure in Britain?

6 What are the sources of government revenue in Britain?

7 What is the difference between direct and indirect taxes?

8 What is the difference between government expenses and transfer expenses?

9 What are the main nationalized industries in Britain?

10 Give examples of fiscal, monetary, and incomes policy in post-war Britain.

EXERCISES

1 What is the explanation of the fact that for some years now the share of the government in the production of the national income has been increasing considerably?

2 Discuss the economic consequences of an increase in the indirect taxes.

3 Imagine a closed economy in which the connection between saving (S), disposable income (Y) and taxes (T) is $S = 0.2(Y-T) - 20$, the autonomous investment is 30, the autonomous government expenditure is 20, and the taxes (T) are proportional to the national income at a rate of $T = 0.1Y$. Assume that at equilibrium the planned investment and government expenditure are together equal to the sum of planned taxation and saving.
(a) Calculate the equilibrium value of Y.
(b) Calculate the multiplier.
(c) How will Y change if the tax rate is increased to 0.2?

4 Should the major aim of a national budget be to balance revenue and expenditure, and thereby maintain strong anti-inflationary conditions in the government's sector of the economy?

5 How has the British government used its nationalized industries to eliminate fluctuations in economic activity?

6 Compose your own short case study of a recent use of (a) monetary, or (b) fiscal, or (c) prices and incomes policies by the British or the Irish government.

Chapter Fifteen

International Trade, the European Economic Community and Britain

Britain has numerous economic ties with other countries: world trade has been in its blood for centuries. In the late nineteenth century Britain established an empire which included one-quarter of the world's population and operated as a free trade area for British goods.

The growth of tourism in this century has allowed large numbers of individuals to visit and experience other countries. While our grandparents hardly ever crossed the Channel we are European travellers and our children will see other continents as well. However, we cannot rely on the links thus created to exclude all conflicts.

We are now in the European Community, the aim of which is to unite the member countries into a single economy, which might eventually extend to cover all other aspects of the economy. We still have far to go, and national differences may hinder progress in these developments, but practical results can already be seen by all of us: it is easier to travel in the EEC countries, there is not the same delay at frontiers, and changing pounds into foreign currencies is easier.

By extending our field of vision beyond our frontiers in this chapter, we come face to face with a problem that will long cast a shadow over our world – poverty and human suffering in the developing countries of Asia, Africa and Latin America, where per capita production is so low that many people die of hunger. Here Malthusianism reigns, wages are depressed to subsistence level, and food production cannot keep pace with the high birthrate.

The difference between the national income of rich countries and that of poor ones is even greater than the inequality of the income distribution within one country. Previous colonial policy provides an added reason why the West cannot turn a blind eye to the enormous differences in welfare between itself and the developing countries. Aiding these countries means supplying money, goods and knowledge in the framework of a worldwide policy, but we can also open our frontiers to products coming from them. Whether we want to do this or not is a political question. Tinbergen, the great Dutch economist who has specialized in the study of the developing countries in the past 20 or so years, has warned that a world catastrophe is inevitable unless the gap is narrowed between the standard of living in the rich and that in the poor countries.

15.1 THEORY OF COMPARATIVE ADVANTAGE AND FREE TRADE

Specialization or division of labour exists not only within a country but also between countries: one country may specialize in the production of butter, while the other concentrates on the manufacture of aircraft. This specialization results from natural conditions and the relative immobility of labour across frontiers. Each country concentrates on the production of those goods which it can make the cheapest, or comparatively cheaper. The word 'comparative' is important, because in absolute terms – i.e. in comparison with another country – its production of all goods may be cheaper, but this cheapness does not exclude trade with other countries. Absolute advantage is illustrated in Table 15.1 in the case of two countries, A and B, and two products, butter and cars, the figures referring to the number of units of work (u.w.) needed to make these goods in the two countries: in other words, they represent the production costs.

Country A thus makes butter cheaper than country B, while the latter makes cars cheaper than country A. Here country A has an absolute advantage in the production of butter and country B in that of cars, and it is obvious that they will concentrate on making these and exchange their goods with those of the other country. For example, butter can be produced cheaper in Ireland than in Britain, and motor cars can be made less expensively in Britain than in Ireland. So each country specializes in its cheaper product and the two countries exchange them to mutual advantage.

Table 15.1 Absolute advantage.

	Country A	*Country B*
Butter	3 units of work	6 units of work
Car	30 units of work	10 units of work

Table 15.2 Comparative advantage.

	Country C	*Country D*
Coal	3 units of work	9 units of work
Wheat	30 units of work	40 units of work

However, trade is still possible between them if one country – say country C – can make *both* products cheaper than country D. Imagine that the situation is as depicted in Table 15.2.

At first sight, country C will make both products and it is not worth its while buying either one from country D. However, the important point is not this absolute advantage but the comparative advantage, calculated on the basis of the ratios between the costs. Country C has a greater relative advantage in the production of coal (where the cost ratio between the two countries is 3:9, i.e. $\frac{1}{3}$) than in the production of wheat (where the cost ratio is only 30:40, i.e. $\frac{3}{4}$). Country C is therefore better off by concentrating its factors of production on the manufacture of coal and buying wheat from country D. The reason for this is that country C is clearly better at producing coal than it is at producing wheat. It therefore gains more in terms of coal produced and overall national income than it loses in terms of wheat when it transfers its resources from the production of the latter to that of the former. It can concentrate its resources on coal production, and produce far more at lower cost than if it were to devote some of its resources to producing wheat. Conversely, country D is better off producing wheat, selling some of it to country C and buying from the latter coal, in the production of which it has a comparative disadvantage. Country C thereby produces far more wheat and at a lower cost for two countries than it would for itself alone. In short, both countries have a higher national income if they trade with each other than they would otherwise (i.e. they produce more at lower cost per unit). As a result of international trade and the underlying factors (namely a better allocation of the factors of production and the more efficient use of the available labour), production, national income and real wages for both countries will be higher. For example, Britain can produce both wheat and coal cheaper than France. Both countries benefit, however, if France specializes in producing the less expensive good wheat, and Britain specializes in producing the good in which it has greatest relative advantage.

The transfer and application of technical knowledge is a major factor influencing changes in the comparative advantage of countries. Technical knowledge, when rigorously applied to industrial development, leads to more advanced and greater volume methods of production, and this enables a country to produce cheaper good-quality articles. Japan benefited in the immediate post-war period from the transfer of American 'know-how' in many industrial fields (e.g. electronics and shipbuilding). She then applied this technical knowledge and also researched it further. The result was a massive application of advanced technology to such industries as electronics and shipbuilding, which enabled her to make cheaper high-quality ships and radios, etc. Japan thereby gained a comparative advantage in international trade in these products over such countries as West Germany and Britain.

A further advantage of national specialization referred to above is an increase in the scale of production with a fall in relative costs. This is called *economies of scale*, and can be listed with comparative cost advantages in justifying national specializations and international trade. The national specialization by Britain in North Sea oil leads to economies of scale in production not only of the oil itself but of oilrigs and other equipment needed to develop the product. Another reason for international trade lies in national consumer preferences. Thus, if the Irish like potatoes more than the British do, and if the British like fish more than the Irish do, the exchange of British potatoes for Irish fish enhances the satisfaction of wants in both countries. In this theory we have assumed equal transport costs, perfect mobility of production factors, constant returns and full employment.

These advantages are reduced or destroyed if trade is restricted by the introduction of import duties or quotas by a country for any reason. This may be done to protect the home industry from foreign competition and thus to safeguard against unemployment. This policy is pursued if more is thought to be gained by protection than lost by deviating from the model of optimum allocation of the factors of production under terms of international free trade.

As mentioned above, free foreign trade may be curbed to safeguard jobs at home: for example, unrestricted entry of textiles from the developing countries would soon annihilate the textile industry in Western Europe. Another reason for controlling imports is to protect infant industries at home, which – once they are vigorous enough – are expected to hold their own without any protection in the face of foreign competition. Australia has tariffs on imported manufactured goods, so that the manufacturing section of her economy can develop to an economically workable size. In such cases, the optimum allocation of the means of production comes second to economic growth in the country concerned.

Free international trade may also be hindered by the sluggish adjustment of prices and wages to the requirements set by specialization and by imperfect mobility of labour. Thus, if wages in areas of potentially high unemployment do not fall fast enough to make moving elsewhere attractive to workers, the re-employment of the workers elsewhere is difficult, so that a combination of inflation and unemployment may occur, with an undesirable effect on the balance of payments.

Summary International trade is based on specialization and the principle of comparative advantage, and leads to greater efficiency and higher national income. However, it is not given full scope when the protection of jobs and infant industries at home is considered more important. The sluggishness of market forces and the price mechanism also hinders free international trade.

15.2 THE BRITISH BALANCE OF PAYMENTS

The balance of payments is a record of the transactions in goods, services and money between Britain and other countries during a year. The current account balance is a part of the balance of payments: it shows the transactions in goods and services, but not in money (see Table 15.3).

Visible Trade This consists of exports and imports of physical goods, e.g. British aircraft to the USA, British cars to Germany, Italian refrigerators

Table 15.3 British Balance of Payments 1977 (£m).

Visible trade	
Exports	32 176
Imports	33 788
Visible balance	− 1612
Invisible Trade	
	15 801
	14 024
	+ 1777
Current account balance:	+ 165
Current account balance	+ 165
Investment and other capital transactions	+ 4357
Balancing item	+ 2839
Balancing for official financing	+ 7361
'Balance of payments'	–

Official financing	
Net transactions with IMF	+ 1013
Foreign currency borrowing by government and public sector	+ 1014
Additions to official reserves	− 9588
Total official financing	− 7361

Source: CSO Monthly Digest of Statistics, October 1978, Tables 15.1 and 15.3, HMSO. Reproduced with the kind permission of the Controller of HMSO.

to Britain and Bulgarian jam to Britain. It was in deficit by £1612m in 1977.

Invisible Trade This consists of services exported and imported and such items are 'invisible' (i.e. they cannot be seen), unlike the 'visible' goods such as cars and jam mentioned above. 'Invisible' exports include insurance and banking services to foreigners by companies based in Britain (e.g. Barclays Bank D.C.O. and Royal Insurance Company), and shipping and air services to foreigners by British merchants ships and aircraft. 'Invisible' imports include similar items such as banking services provided in Britain by foreign-based companies (e.g. First National City Bank [US], Mitsui Bank [Japan]). Tourism is also in this category, and has rapidly expanded as a source of 'invisible' export to Britain in the 1970s. Interest, profits and dividends earned by British companies abroad are part of invisible exports (e.g. I.C.I. profits in Australia, BP profits in the USA). Similarly, interest profits and dividends earned by foreign companies in Britain are part of invisible imports (e.g. the American-owned Esso petro-chemical company's profits in Britain and the Dutch-owned Philips electrical company's profits in Britain). Another invisible import service is the use of foreign military bases by British armed forces (e.g. in Germany and Belgium), and an invisible export is the use of British bases by US armed forces. In virtually every year there is a surplus on invisible trade in the British current account balance, but this is often more than counterbalanced by a deficit on visible trade. During the 1970s the balance in visibles weakened until North Sea oil was developed, and the balance for invisibles strengthened. In 1977, for the first time since the early 1970s, the current balance overall moved into surplus (£165m).

Balance of Payments This is the current account balance plus accounts of money flows between the United Kingdom and other countries. It includes the total currency flow between the UK and other states.

Investment and Other Capital Transactions This is the major item in money transactions between the UK and other countries. It involves overseas investment of money in the UK. This amounted to £4357m in 1977 and represented foreign firms' investment in British industry (e.g. new petro-chemicals work by Philips Petroleum USA). At the same time, of course, British money is invested overseas by British firms. This amounted to £2100m in 1976 and included, for example, BP petro-chemicals work in the United States. Two other important items in the money capital transactions are exchange reserves in pounds and import–export credit. Since the pound is a major international currency, some foreigners hold their savings in pounds (e.g. in UK companies' shares). In 1976 there was an outflow of £1407m worth of exchange reserves in pounds from the UK, which reflected a change made by foreigners from holding their savings in pounds to holding them in other currencies. Export credit (i.e. credit extended by UK banks and UK businesses to overseas firms) was so extensive in 1976 that it amounted to £1178m. Import credit (i.e. credit facilities extended by foreign banks and businesses to UK firms) was relatively small at £169m. Due mainly to high export credit and an outflow of exchange reserves in sterling, the money flow accounts were in deficit in 1976 by £2814m. Due to a balancing item (representing the net total of errors and omissions in other items in the capital account) of £591m, the actual deficit in money flow accounts was £2223m. By contrast, in 1977 reverse movements of foreign exchange helped to create a surplus in money flow accounts of £4357m. If we add the £7196m surplus in money flow accounts to the £165m surplus on balance of trade, we reach a *balance of payments* surplus of £7361m. Balance of payments is also known as a *balance for official financing*, to clarify purposes of action.

Official Financing of Balance of Payments Surplus The UK uses this 1977 surplus by adding to reserves of gold and scarce currencies (£9588m), but also carries out foreign currency borrowing by its public corporations and local authorities (£1014m) and has a loan from the International Monetary Fund (IMF) (£1113m).

Summary **The balance of payments gives a systematic survey of all Britain's economic transactions with other countries. The balance of payments or 'balance for official financing' consists of two parts and must end with the same figure on both sides for accounting purposes.**

15.3 THE EFFECTIVE BALANCE AND BASIC BALANCE

The effective balance is the sum of the current account and the capital account. It may be imagined for the sake of simplicity that there is a zero effective balance when no overall change is needed for formal balancing purposes, in the currency position, which embraces foreign currencies, gold, and special drawing rights (SDR) (concerning a new type of international money) with the IMF (see Section 6). This can happen spontaneously in practice only if the balance on current account and that on capital account fully offset each other, i.e. if the surplus in one is equal to the deficit in the other. However, not even the effective balance tells us enough of the country's real foreign trade position, since equilibrium seems at first sight to prevail when, for example, a large deficit on the current account is offset by temporary trade credit or loan from abroad. If this credit or loan suddenly comes to an end, equilibrium can be maintained only by dipping into the currency reserve.

The concept of 'basic balance' has been introduced to make the equilibrium less dependent on such temporary and fortuitous factors. For this reason, the capital account is split into regular, or structural, transactions and occasional ones, and the latter are ignored. The basic balance is thus the sum of the current account and that part of the capital account which features only the regular items which, owing to their recurrent nature, have a more or less permanent place in the balance of payments. The basic balance concept is gaining ground internationally.

However, the distinction between regular and occasional capital transactions between countries is somewhat arbitrary. The second type is admittedly uncertain and depends on the monetary situation and the economic climate, but exactly where the dividing line lies is left to the monetary authorities to decide. It is perhaps more to the point that these items are no less real for being occasional. In fact, a basic balance showing an equilibrium may hide a flow of gold and currencies abroad because of the occasional capital transactions.

Summary To find out whether a balance of payments shows an equilibrium, one must examine the credit/debit difference under the various headings. The totality of transactions with foreign countries can be viewed against the background of regular transactions year by year.

15.4 CAUSES OF DISEQUILIBRIUM IN THE BALANCE OF PAYMENTS

We have seen that the effective balance may show a disequilibrium, but have not yet discussed how a surplus or deficit can arise. This will now be done in an example of two countries, Britain and Germany, and will be related to the current account.

Owing to Britain's open economy, imports and exports account for as much as 28 per cent of the British national income, so that both the latter and the British balance of payments depend on the economic situation in other countries. Let us assume, for example, that there is a wage increase in Britain which is not supported by an increase in the productivity of labour. The purchasing power of the British worker thus increases, so that he buys more goods, and therefore also more German goods, thereby increasing the volume of German exports to Britain (the volume of British exports to Germany may change at the same time). The wage increases may urge the British firms to raise their prices, particularly if productive capacity is used to the full, and this will raise prices in Britain. Owing to the higher prices and wages, British industry is now less competitive both in Britain and abroad. On the home market, the British consumer buys more and more of the relatively cheaper foreign goods, and the German consumer buys less and less of the more expensive British goods. The British balance of payments may then show a deficit and the German one a surplus.

How bad this is for Britain depends on how much of her national income comes from foreign trade. As it happens, this is as high as 28 per cent so that the fall in British exports and the rise in German imports will have serious consequences for the extent to which productive capacity is utilized in Britain. However, the situation for Germany is different: the increased exports to Britain tie down a greater proportion of the German productive capacity, and the strain on this is further aggravated by the fact that the home industry must also satisfy the demand that British goods satisfied before their prices went up.

In monetary matters, the situation is that, on balance, Britain owes Germany money, and the payment of this debt means that foreign currency flows into the German commercial banks. The Bank of England cannot prevent the increase in German money supply caused by people changing this foreign currency into Deutschmarks. This increase in the money supply and the concomitant increase in spending in turn push German wages and prices up, particularly if the productive capacity is in full use. Thus, Germany has, as it were, imported the British price rises with the surplus in her balance of payments, resulting originally from the British wage rises. Conversely, a decrease in effective demand in Britain, caused by a decline in economic activity here, may lead to a deficit in the German balance of payments. Both these causes are of a cyclical nature, that is they are connected with fluctuations in spending.

A disequilibrium in the balance of payments may also come from structural causes, in which case the surplus or deficit is due to a change on the supply side. Technical development changes the supply relationships between countries, with countries moving ahead and others falling behind; this can of course change the pattern of world trade and the international division of labour. For example, the advanced Western countries are no longer the best place for making unsophisticated cotton articles. The production of these can be left to South Korea, Hong Kong and the other developing countries. By contrast, Western exports will include technically more advanced finished products such as computer systems, aircraft and telecommunications equipment.

Besides cyclical and structural factors, foreign trade may also be adversely affected by accidental events such as disasters, poor harvests, revolutions and wars. For example, Britain has lost a large market in Iran because of the drastic change in the political situation there. Furthermore, the formation of an economic block like the European Community can introduce a sharp division between its member countries and others, and while trade within the bloc increases that with countries outside it may decrease.

Summary A disequilibrium in the balance of payments may be caused by cyclical, structural and accidental factors. Technical development in Third World countries is changing the structure of world trade, such that Western countries must now specialize in advanced industrial products to maintain equilibrium in balance of payments.

15.5 FLOATING AND FIXED EXCHANGE RATES

The rate of exchange is the ratio between the values of two currencies and gives the price of one currency in terms of another.

With a floating or flexible exchange rate, this price is determined by the free interplay between supply and demand for currencies. For example, French francs may be in demand in Britain to pay for cars bought from France, while the supply may come from French tourists visiting Britain. If the demand for francs exceeds the supply, the price of the franc goes up or, in other words, the price of British currency, expressed in francs, decreases. French cars then become more expensive for us, and holidays in our country become cheaper for French tourists. As a result, fewer French cars are imported (so that the demand for francs will be much less), and more French tourists will visit Britain (so that the supply of francs increases). The change in the rate of exchange has thus re-established the equilibrium in our balance of payments with respect to France, which was disturbed by paying out more for French cars than Britain was getting from French holidaymakers.

Fixed Exchange Rates 1944–71 However, the use of the floating rate in the 1970s has brought mixed blessings, and the international payments situation was particularly unstable between the two World Wars. The fluctuations in exchange rates discouraged international trade, and the uncertainty involved in the calculation of the value of imports and exports in particular reduced the volume of world trade, even though it was already possible, to some extent, to cover the risk of exchange on the forward speculative market for currencies. Speculative capital movements (i.e. money movements out of one country and into another) further enhanced the fluctuations of exchange rates, so that the equilibrium in the international payments situation could not be re-established. As a result, the leading trading nations returned to fixed exchange rates after the Second World War. This ensured more security in the field of international payments in general, and in particular abolished the risk of losing on deferred payments and many capital supplies through a change in the exchange rate in the intervening time.

The rates were fixed at the Bretton Woods Conference in 1944, where the International Monetary Fund (IMF) and the International Bank for Reconstruction and Development (IBRD) were also founded. The IMF was established to put the post-war monetary system of the member countries on the solid foundation of relating all currencies to the (then) strongest, the US dollar, which in turn was related to gold at a fixed price. The IMF can use the money deposited with it by the member countries to help countries out of their balance-of-payments difficulties. The IBRD was established for the provision of long-term loans to developing countries. The IMF has been joined by nearly all the non-communist countries. The Bretton Woods Conference established a free payment system in the case of current account items, and fixed exchange rates with respect to the dollar and gold.

Fixed exchange rates did not exclude fluctuations; in fact they allowed fluctuations within certain agreed narrow limits. But when these limits were reached, the central bank in the country in question was obliged to correct the exchange rate by buying or selling currencies. However, the central bank generally did not wait until one of these limits was reached and instead tried to correct at an early stage any rise or fall in the exchange rates.

Devaluation of Currency Fixed exchange rates imposed some monetary discipline on the trading partners, since a country with higher inflation would have falling exports, rising imports and deficit in its balance of payments. Furthermore, to pay for this deficit, gold and currencies flowed out of the country and eventually confidence in the country's currency severely deteriorated; speculators sold this currency and moved their assets into stronger currencies. These pressures generally forced the government to devalue the currency, particularly when the IMF found that the situation reflected a fundamental disequilibrium in the country's balance of payments (in fact, the approval of the IMF was needed for any devaluation exceeding 10 per cent). This means that the official value of the currency with respect to the dollar was reduced. In 1967 the pound was devalued from $2.8 to £1.00 to $2.4 to £1.00. Since the price of gold in dollars is fixed, devaluation means an increase in the value of the gold reserves at the country's central bank, as expressed in terms of the home currency (i.e. pounds). Besides, devaluation curbs imports and stimulates exports to an extent that depends on the price elasticity of imports and exports. After the 1967 devaluation £100 worth of British goods sold in the USA for $240 instead of $280, whereas £100 worth of American goods sold in Britain for £116 rather than the £100.

The greater this elasticity, the more effective the devaluation will be. Furthermore, devaluation can be effective only if the country's spending abroad is curbed, by considerably reducing imports from overseas. This makes sense since devaluation became necessary in the first place mainly because this spending exceeded the home productive capacity. In fact, devaluation without cutting spending abroad has hardly any effect.

Revaluation of Currency On the other hand, it may happen that the country's currency is undervalued, e.g. when the country manages to combine steady growth with stable prices. This leads to a constant surplus in its balance of payments, since its low-priced exports are large and imports are relatively small in number and the gold and currency reserves increase to pay its surplus on balance of payments (unless capital is exported at the same time). Prices and wages will eventually be affected, since the steady demand for home products makes the demand for labour excessive. Admittedly, the rising productivity of labour helps, but in the long run it is neutralized by the upward trend of prices and wages. To avoid a rise in these, the country will have to revalue its currency, so that exports are curbed and imports stimulated. During the 1960s Germany experienced this situation and revalued the currency several times. A 5 per cent revaluation of the Deutschmark would mean that German exports were 5 per cent dearer, and imports into Germany from abroad 5 per cent cheaper. Confidence in fixed exchange rates in the early 1970s was shaken by the large deficit in the US balance of payments, which has had a worldwide effect, since the dollar is not only the home currency of the USA, but also an international means of payment. As we have seen, from 1944–71 the dollar had a fixed direct gold equivalent. This means that when the US introduced too large an amount of dollars into international trade by importing more than exporting, and paying out in dollars, the central banks in the countries into which the dollar was flowing built up larger and larger claims against American gold reserves. When these short-term dollar liabilities of the US greatly exceeded her official gold reserves, her trading partners could no longer rely on the convertibility of the dollar into gold. In fact, this convertibility had to be abandoned in 1971, and it was not reinstated by the International Monetary Agreement (the so-called Smithsonian Agreement) in Washington in December 1971.

Floating Exchange Rates 1971–8 The fixed, dollar-based exchange rates and the fixed price of gold have together greatly contributed to the problems about the position of gold in the international monetary system. The fact is that accelerating inflation and serious economic troubles worldwide do not provide a suitable climate for fixed exchange rates, because these put too great a strain on the central banks' supporting action when the dollar is a weak currency, as explained above. The re-adoption of floating exchange rates was therefore understandable, and since 1972 the pound has floated, on balance, downwards (see Table 15.4 for 1978 exchange rates). A mixed system was actually in operation from 1971 to 1978 among some Western countries (i.e. The Netherlands, Belgium, Germany, Denmark and Luxembourg) as a result of an agreement whereby the exchange rates are allowed to fluctuate between an upper and a lower limit, like a 'snake in the tunnel'. The central banks step in to support currencies only when the 'snake' threatens to get above or below these limits. In 1979 all the European Community countries except Britain adopted a developed version of the 'snake' called the *European Monetary System*. Exchange rates fluctuate between upper and lower limits but can be supported when under pressure by a massive central fund of currencies.

Table 15.4 Foreign exchange rates and the pound (21 September 1978).

£1 equals the rates below			
Australian dollar	1.71	Japanese yen	371.00
Austrian schilling	27.95	Dutch guilder	4.20
Belgian franc	60.90	Portuguese escudo	89.30
Canadian dollar	2.31	Spanish peseta	144.70
French franc	8.65	Swedish krone	8.72
German mark	3.86	Swiss franc	3.00
Italian lira	1632.00	American dollar	1.98

In Britain, floating exchange rates developed in the early 1970s. In 1971 the pound was declared by the British government to have no fixed parity to gold or the dollar. At first the pound strengthened, but high rates of inflation in Britain relative to other major trading nations led to the pound's automatically losing value. From $2.4 in 1971, it fell to $1.60 in 1976, and strengthened to $2 by 1978. This massive fall was accompanied by large bulk selling of pounds, Bank of England intervention to prevent a more drastic fall in value, and the relative rise of the Deutschmark, Swiss franc, Dutch guilder, French franc and Japanese yen in value and in use as reserve currencies. Since 1976 the Bank of England has intervened more often to control rapid fluctuations in the pound's value, and the government has had to modify its interest-rate policy to maintain a relatively high rate of interest in order to attract overseas funds. By these means of government-managed 'floating', the pound became a more stable currency in 1978, and the falling rate of inflation in Britain also played a part in this. None the less, the inflation rate in Britain was still sufficiently high to prevent her joining the European Monetary System in 1979.

Summary Confidence in a system of international payments is undermined when the trading partners establish large surpluses or large deficits on their balance of payments, and do not revalue or devalue the currency. Floating exchange rates allow almost automatic appreciation and depreciation and were necessary to cope with rapid price rises in many countries in the 1970s.

15.6 INTERNATIONAL LIQUIDITIES

There is a fear that there will not be sufficient funds to finance a growing world economy in the future. The increase in the value of world trade is a fairly good indication of how much money will be needed to balance deficits in the balance of payments, and gold production is undoubtedly insufficient to meet the growing demand for money; besides, gold is increasingly withheld from the monetary authorities by speculative hoarding by individuals.

Special Drawing Rights It has been customary since the Bretton Woods agreement of 1944 to use the dollar as international money on a large scale, in addition to the pound sterling which originally qualified in this capacity before the war. These two are major reserve currencies in the sense that European countries keep a large part of their reserves in them (as well as in gold). They also have some credit facilities, as a result of agreements with the IMF, known as *special drawing rights*. The Group of Ten (industrial countries) also has special credit arrangements. At present, the monetary authorities in Western European countries keep their reserves in these three means of payment in readiness to correct any balance-of-payments deficit.

In the case of credit facilities, whether and to what extent these special drawing rights count as international liquidity depends on the conditions agreed: long-term credits with a strict repayment scheme are difficult to regard as such.

The drawing rights with the IMF, on the other hand, do represent international liquidity: they are credit facilities available to the member countries of the IMF in the event of payment difficulties. The IMF decided in 1967 to create special drawing rights (SDRs) as a new type of international money, and the resolution was ratified two years later. These special drawing rights were originally expressed in gold, but in July 1974 gold was replaced by a combination of 16 currencies. In fact, the role of gold is being increasingly taken over by SDRs, and the function of gold as an international monetary system was drastically curtailed by the 'Gold Agreement' in Washington in 1975, which came into force in 1977, when the articles on gold in the statutes of the IMF were deleted. Gold will disappear as a method of international payment if international confidence grows in a currency or set of currencies issued by an authority which is supra-national.

Decline of Pound Sterling as Reserve Currency The pound sterling and the US dollar have been steadily declining in importance as international currencies, since the war in the case of the former and during the 1960s and 1970s in the case of the latter. Why is this so? During the 1939–45 war the Commonwealth countries provided Britain with goods and forwent payment. Instead, they were issued with *sterling liabilities*, IOUs expressed in pounds sterling. By 1945 these sterling liabilities exceeded Britain's gold and scarce currency reserves. Such a situation inspired little confidence in foreigners, who might otherwise have wished to hold their reserves in pounds. Those who did hold reserves in pounds were often tempted to sell them, fearing a devaluation of the pound. The Bank of England regularly had to intervene to buy pounds on the international foreign exchange markets in order to maintain the fixed value of the currency. In 1949 it was devalued, but for the next 18 years, during a period of rapid world economic expansion and some substantial growth in the British economy, the pound strengthened, although there were important financial crises in 1951, 1957, 1961 and 1964, when the Bank had to buy pounds on a large scale to maintain the currency's value. The further devaluation of 1967, and depreciation of the currency under floating exchange rates since 1971 have reduced international confidence in, and therefore international use of the pound sterling as a reserve currency even more.

Decline of American Dollar as Reserve Currency The US dollar lost international confidence as a reserve currency in the 1960s because the country incurred massive balance-of-payments deficits. These deficits led to an outflow of dollars and gold from the USA during the 1960s and 1970s on a scale which gives rise to concern about the country's ability to perform over a long future period the role of provider of international reserve currency. The US dollar therefore lost value during the period of floating exchange rates in the 1970s, as worried holders of the currency sold it and bought instead appreciating currencies such as Deutschmarks, Swiss francs, Dutch guilders, Japanese yen and sometimes French francs. Current lack of confidence in the US dollar and pound sterling as reserve currencies has hastened the development of SDRs as a form of international money which may eventually replace those currencies and gold as international reserve currency.

Summary Examination of international liquidity shows that eventually gold will cease to be an instrument of payment in international trade. It is gradually being replaced by international paper money, i.e. the special drawing rights and leading world currencies (dollars, marks, pounds, guilders, francs and yen), although both $US and pound sterling roles in this capacity are declining.

15.7 THE DEVELOPING COUNTRIES AND THEIR GROWTH THROUGH WORLD TRADE

World trade is at present deeply affected by the problems of the developing countries, stemming from their low per capita income. Savings are very low in those countries so that investments must be financed with capital from abroad. Apart from the low per capita income, which is a common feature of them all, the developing countries show more differences than similarities. Their income per head may be increasing, decreasing or constant; their population growth may be very high, as in India, or less high, as in Africa; they may be rich in natural resources, or not; and they may have only agriculture or also some industry. Malthus's pessimistic view on the future of economic systems, while it may not hold for the Western countries, certainly holds more than a grain of truth with regard to a number of developing countries where the per capita income is low, the population growth is high and the economic structure is predominantly agrarian. The internal features of these countries' economic growth were discussed in Chapter 2, Section 4.

Owing to their unfavourable ratio between imports and exports, many developing countries are struggling with balance-of-payments problems. Their exports generally lack diversity (e.g. primary products, minerals) and run the risk of being made unnecessary by technical development in the West. Furthermore, the prices of their exports often tend to fall.

The developing countries can be helped only by a worldwide aid programme, which means that the rich countries will have to give up part of their wealth in the same way as the government transfers income from rich to poor people within a country. But what form should this international income redistribution take? First of all, it should not be a transfer of money, since this would probably feather the nest of the ruling elites. It should take a form that results in a rise in the home production and thus in the standard of living of these countries.

Britain and most other Western countries use about 1 per cent of their national income for such aid every year. This money can be used either in the field of consumer goods (e.g. to devise a scheme of nutrition) or in the area of development projects (so that capital formation is promoted on the spot). But should the aid come from the rich countries' national income or consist of the encouragement of international division of labour in such a way that the developing countries benefit via international trade? The answer is probably both, but the stress seems to be more on aid than trade,

According to Tinbergen, we need a completely new international economic system, in which the Western countries concentrate on advanced production processes needing highly trained labour, while the developing countries concentrate on less sophisticated methods of production, with the rich countries thus becoming, as it were, the instrument-makers of the world. In other words, the poorer countries would become richer through reorganized international trade.

The 1973 oil crisis and the subsequent steep price rises reshuffled wealth to some extent, but the Third World, except for its oil producers, has not benefited much from it; in fact, the higher energy prices made its balance-of-payments position even more difficult. It is true, however, that the oil-producing countries are beginning to use some of their suddenly new-found wealth for helping the poor countries. The oil crisis also further accelerated the already appalling inflation in some South American developing countries, and the IMF decided in January 1976 to set up a special fund to aid developing countries.

The technical knowledge of the industrialized countries is one of the important resources largely still waiting to be tapped by the developing countries. Japan is a good example of what can be achieved here, having herself changed from an underdeveloped to a leading industrial country in a few decades, originally by copying and applying Western technology with the aid of dynamic and inventive managers and entrepreneurs. It is doubtful, however, whether Japan can serve as a model for all the developing countries, and the cultural and social conditions in some countries may favour a more tightly controlled development, based on central planning.

Summary When aid to developing countries is being organized, it is important to take into account the economic and other characteristics of each of these countries separately. Aid may not be enough to solve their problems, and a reorganization of international trade may be essential.

15.8 INTERNATIONAL ECONOMIC ORGANIZATIONS TO PROMOTE TRADE SINCE 1945

The following international organizations will be discussed here:

GATT	(General Agreement on Tariffs and Trade)
OEEC	(Organization for European Economic Cooperation)
EPU	(European Payments Union)
EMA	(European Monetary Agreement)
OECD	(Organization for Economic Cooperation and Development)
Benelux	(Customs union between Belgium, Netherlands and Luxembourg)
EC	(European Community)
EFTA	(European Free Trade Association)
CMEA or COMECON	(Council for Mutual Economic Assistance)

(OEEC and EPU did not exist in 1978).

The aim of the GATT, which dates back to 1947, is to eliminate or reduce the restrictions on international trade, such as customs duties, non-tariff barriers and quotas (i.e. quantitative limits on imports). By virtue of the Most Favoured Nation clause, if a member country grants tariff advantages to another these must be extended to all the other signatories. The latter participated in the Kennedy Round (of Trade Negotiations), organized at President Kennedy's suggestion with a view to stimulating trade between Europe and the USA by considerably reducing import duties. When Japan and numerous developing countries joined, these negotiations acquired a worldwide importance. As a result of an agreement in May 1967, the import duties on 80 per cent of the world trade were reduced by an average of 35 per cent in five years. In addition, the rich countries donated 4.5 million tons of grain to the developing countries every year, and special arrangements were made to help these countries by facilitating their exports (including manufactured goods). Such trends for reductions in tariffs were further developed by the Tokyo Round Agreements of 1978–9.

The OEEC was founded in 1947 to administer the Marshall Aid from the United States to Europe, and was joined by 17 countries. Over a period of years, the OEEC concentrated on reducing trade restrictions and facilitating multilateral payments. For this second purpose, the EPU was set up as a clearing system of credits and debits among the member countries, as well as to extend credit to them. When the post-war recovery in Europe was completed in 1958 and the convertibility of these European currencies was re-established, the EPU was replaced by the EMA. This agreement set up a European Fund, which plays more or less the same role in Europe as the IMF does in the world.

In 1961, the OEEC was renamed OECD (Organization for Economic Cooperation and Development) and was joined also by Spain, the US and Canada; while Japan joined it in 1963. In comparison with the OEEC, the stress has shifted to aid for underdeveloped areas and coordination of economic policy.

For the European economic groups to be discussed here and in following sections, see Table 15.5.

Table 15.5 European economic groupings.

EEC	*EFTA*	*Comecon*
United Kingdom	Norway	USSR
West Germany	Sweden	Poland
France	Iceland	East Germany
Italy	Austria	Czechoslovakia
The Netherlands	Switzerland	Hungary
Belgium	Portugal	Romania
Denmark		Bulgaria
Ireland		
Luxembourg		
Applicants		*Non-European members*
Greece		Cuba
Portugal		Mongolia
Spain		Vietnam

Comecon was founded in 1949 to promote economic cooperation among state socialist countries. It includes, outside Europe, Mongolia, Cuba and Vietnam, but the majority of its members are European countries (Bulgaria, Czechoslovakia, East Germany, Hungary, Poland, Romania and the USSR). The organization does not attempt to coordinate the national economic central plans of each country, but to encourage, to a limited extent, specialization of production in particular countries.

Summary The post-1945 world saw a deliberate attempt to extend free trade by the establishment for this purpose of international economic organizations. They were particularly successful in the 1950s and 1960s, but have been faced with a big trade recession in the mid 1970s.

15.9 EUROPEAN ECONOMIC ORGANIZATIONS

Benelux The Benelux was a customs union set up by Belgium, The Netherlands and Luxembourg in 1948, following a decision to do so in

1944. It abolished customs duties and other mutual trade restrictions and established a free trade area, with a common external tariff towards other countries. In 1960, it became an economic union – a further step towards full economic integration, characterized by:

1. free movement of goods, services, people and capital;
2. common trade policy towards other countries;
3. joint institutions;
4. coordination of economic policy (monetary, fiscal, social, agricultural, etc.).

Agricultural cooperation is as yet incomplete: Belgium is worried about cheap imported dairy products and horticultural produce. Nevertheless, the Benelux has accumulated a great deal of useful experience for further European integration. It is in this wider EC context that Benelux is of real interest to Britain, since it demonstrates methods of economic integration which might be used by the EC.

European Coal and Steel Community The European Coal and Steel Community (ECSC) was set up in 1952. Attempts, dating back to just after the war, to prevent a new conflict between France and Germany led to the Schuman Plan in 1950 for bringing French and German coal and steel production under one organization, to be joined by others as well. This community comprises France, Germany, Italy and the Benelux countries – the first members of the EEC – and (since 1973) Britain, Ireland and Denmark. The aims of the ECSC are twofold: to set up a common market with free trade in coal and steel, and to pursue a common policy, particularly on competition, prices, production and investment. While the organizations discussed so far are inter-governmental, where the authority lies with the various national governments, the ECSC is supra-national, i.e. it is above national governments. The ECSC has brought about a more intense competition and thus more efficient production: for example, when unprofitable coalmines have been closed down the social problems involved have been taken into account. Other major sources of energy such as oil and gas are not similarly controlled, so that there is no European energy policy in spite of the ECSC. Since 1967, ECSC has been part of the European Community, which includes the EEC and Euratom.

Aims of EEC The EEC Treaty and the Euratom Treaty were signed in Rome in 1957, and came into force on 1 January 1958 under the name of the Treaty of Rome, by France, Germany, Italy and the Benelux countries as the original member countries. Associated countries are Greece and Turkey in Europe, and, outside Europe, some countries in what were formerly French, Dutch, Belgian, British and Italian colonies in Africa, the Caribbean and the Pacific. Figure 15.1 illustrates the present membership of the European Community. Every European country can apply for membership, but France vetoed Britain's applications in 1963 and 1967. At the beginning of 1972, however, Britain's application was accepted, together with that of Norway, Denmark and the Irish Republic, and these countries duly joined the EEC in 1973 except for Norway, where

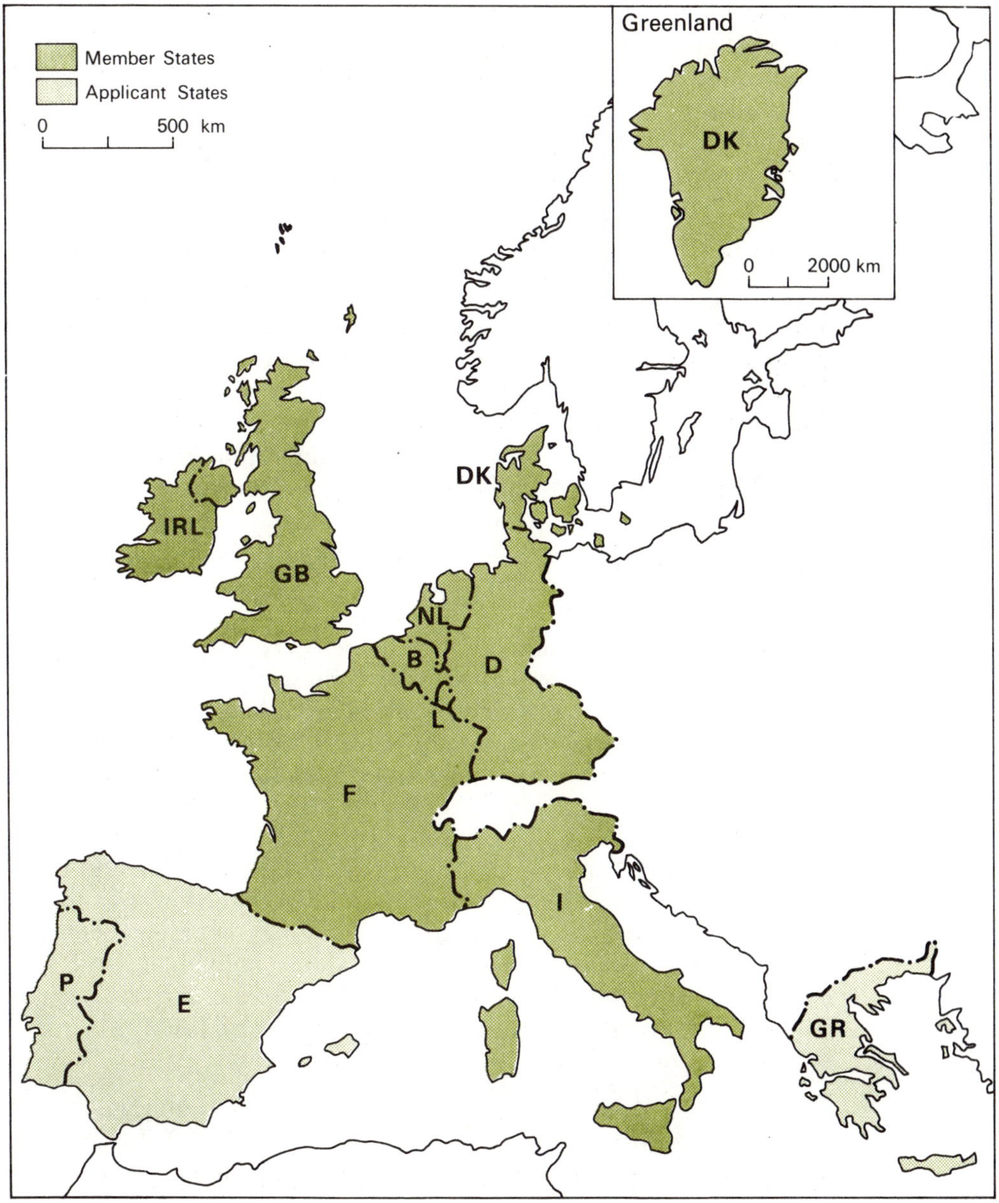

Figure 15.1 Member states of the European Community.

the people voted against it in a referendum. In 1977 Greece made a formal application for membership, and this is being studied by the EEC members, together with 'informal applications' from Spain and Portugal. One of the two main aims of the EEC is to ensure free movement of goods, services, people and capital. In the case of goods this was done by the abolition of customs duties (1 July 1968). There is now a common external tariff towards other countries. The privileges the EEC countries grant to one another appear to conflict with the Most Favoured Nation clause of

GATT, but the latter has made an exception of customs unions and economic unions. As regards the free movement of capital and labour, the aim is to use these factors of production where they can make the greatest contribution to welfare. For this purpose, the member countries accept one another's social security systems, requirements for the establishment of businesses, etc.

The other main aim of the EEC is to pursue a common economic policy comprising, first of all, the coordination of macroeconomic policy, especially on agriculture, transport, industry, competition and trade. This is a very difficult task, partly because the national governments of the member countries must give up some of their sovereignty in the process, and the national laws on agricultural, social, fiscal, transport and other matters must be harmonized (e.g. the policy of growth, money, budgets and payments).

The previous executive bodies – the High Authority of the ECSC and the Commissions – were combined in 1967 to form a single Commission for EEC, Euratom and ECSC which now has 13 members. This must be seen as the first step in the unification of the three founding instruments for the EEC, ECSC and Euratom.

The abolition of internal tariffs has led to a great increase in trade between the member countries, by 700 per cent between 1958 and 1972. However, a great deal remains to be done in policy coordination, and agreement on a common agricultural policy has been particularly difficult to reach and maintain. The specific sections which follow deal with EEC economic policy, decision-making and the impact of EEC on the British economy.

The European Free Trade Association (EFTA) was set up in 1959 by Britain, Sweden, Norway, Denmark, Switzerland, Austria and Portugal (Iceland joined later) as a reaction to the EEC. The aim was to abolish import duties on industrial products among the member countries (attained on 1 January 1968) while retaining individual tariffs toward other countries; that is, there is no common external tariff here. On joining the EEC, Britain and Denmark left the EFTA.

Summary The Western European countries have established a customs union with full free trade and a common external tariff. In terms of the theory of comparative advantage they are one economic unit.

15.10 DECISION-MAKING BY THE EEC'S INSTITUTIONS

The EEC's aim is formally to unite the economies of the nine member states, but so far its scope has been limited to the formation of a customs union with a common external tariff, the operation of a common agricultural policy, and the development of other common economic policies mainly in the regional, social and industrial structure fields. How does it reach its decisions in these fields and what is the influence of British representatives on these decisions? The answers to these questions entail consideration of the Council of Ministers, the Commission, the Parliament, the Court of Justice and the Economic and Social Committee.

The Council of Ministers No major decision can be made without the approval of the Council of Ministers, on which are one minister from each member state and a representative of the Commission. The Council meets several times a year as a Council of Foreign Ministers (i.e. all foreign ministers of the nine countries), three times a year as a Council of Heads of Government (i.e. all prime ministers/presidents), and as many times as necessary as a Council of Agricultural Ministers, of Social Affairs Ministers, of Industry Ministers, etc., depending upon which issues are discussed. In 1975 the large increase in the Regional Fund for the poorer regions of the EEC required Council's approval, and in any major issue such as this unanimous approval is required. Put at its most nationalistic, the British or Irish or any other government can prevent any major economic decision by its veto.

The Commission The initiation of economic policies comes from the civil service, called the Commission, of the EEC. It employs about 7000 workers, headed by 13 Commissioners who are appointed for four years by the member states but swear an oath to the European Community. Each Commissioner except the President has a department (or Directorate-General) to run (e.g. Overseas Trade, Regional Affairs). A Commissioner is appointed by each country (two from the four larger countries, Germany, Britain, France and Italy). The Commission also has power to implement the decision of Council. It is the Commission which intervenes in the agricultural markets to buy products whose prices are falling below the level at which a reasonable minimum for farmers' economic wellbeing can be maintained. The Commission is therefore a very important organization in the operation of EEC economic policy and for initiating a policy proposal, but no proposal can be put into practice without the approval of national ministers on the Council of Ministers (see Figure 15.2).

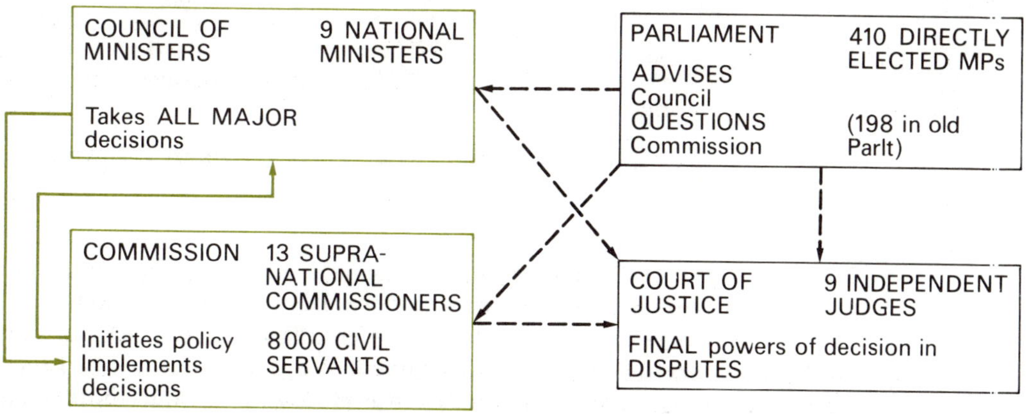

Figure 15.2 EEC institutions and decision-making parties.

The Parliament The other Community institutions are at present largely advisory bodies. In the old system, the European Parliament consisted of 198 MPs, nominated by their national parliaments (36 from Germany, Britain, France and Italy, 14 from Belgium and the Netherlands, 10 from Denmark and Ireland and six from Luxembourg). In the new system instituted in 1979 it is directly elected by the European voters for the first time, and such a democratic mandate may lead to an increase in its powers. At present it can force the Commission to resign, but cannot appoint a new Commission. Its main power lies in consultation by the Council over the Commission's budget, and in this way, although the Council has the final word, the Parliament can exercise some influence over how much is allotted to the Regional Fund, the Social Fund, the common agricultural policy (CAP), etc. In the old Parliament, the 36 British MPs had influence on this through the political parties to which they belonged in Parliament. Therefore Labour MPs influenced the largest Parliamentary party, the Socialists (63 seats), Liberal MPs were in the Liberal and Democratic Parliamentary Party (27 seats), and Conservative MPs in the European Conservative Parliamentary Party (17 seats), and the Scottish Nationalist MP sat as an Independent. Similarly, the Irish MPs had influence through the Parliamentary parties to which they belonged: Labour in the Socialist Party, Fianna Fail in the European Progressive Democrat Party (17 seats) and Fine Gael in the second largest party, the Christian Democrats (52 seats) (see Figure 15.3).

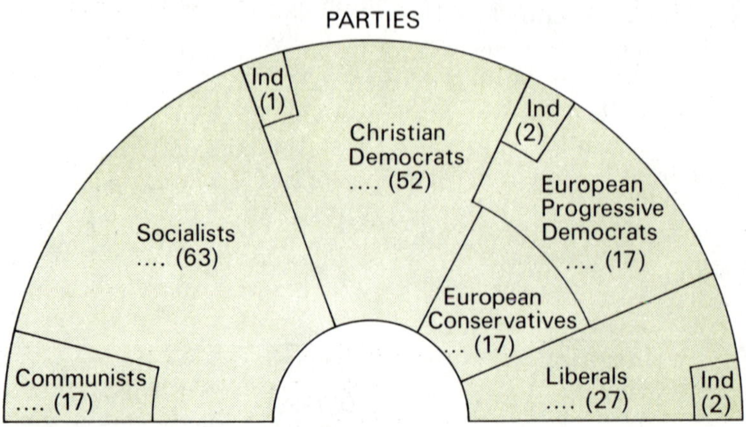

( ) indicates numbers in old parliament

SEATS BY COUNTRY

	NEW	OLD
France	81	(36)
Germany	81	(36)
Italy	81	(36)
U K	81	(36)
Netherlands	25	(14)
Belgium	24	(14)
Denmark	16	(10)
Ireland	15	(10)
Luxembourg	6	(6)
	410	198

Figure 15.3 European parliament – parties and seats by country.

The Court of Justice The European Court of Justice deals with breaches of the law in applying and interpreting the EEC treaties. French duties imposed on Italian wine imports were referred by Italy to the Court, and the Court ordered the French government to end the duties. The French agreed, as every state has done when served with a Court judgement. Finally, the Economic and Social Committee must be consulted by the

Council and Commission on free movement of workers, firms and services. It can also act on its own initiative to follow up matters with Council, Commission and Parliament. The Committee represents trades unions, employers and other major interest groups in social and economic activity. It has 144 members (24 from Germany, Britain, France and Italy, 12 from Belgium and the Netherlands, nine from Denmark and Ireland, and six from Luxembourg).

Summary **There are now some large areas of British economic life administered by the Commission, e.g. agriculture, external trade, and some aspects of regional, social and industrial policy. Changes in the policies themselves, however, can be made by the Council, which can also extend Community administration to the whole economic life of the nine countries. In making these vital economic decisions the national governments have maintained their influence by insisting on the power of veto.**

15.11 COMMON AGRICULTURAL POLICY

The largest of all the EEC's internal economic activities is the agricultural policy, and it is also the most costly and controversial, especially in countries with low numbers of workers employed in agriculture, e.g. Britain and Germany. The Common Agricultural Policy has five major objectives: (1) to stabilize markets; (2) to ensure availability of supplies; (3) to ensure supplies to consumers at reasonable prices; (4) to promote a higher standard of living for farmers; (5) to increase agricultural productivity by promoting technical progress and rationalizing production.

What has been the impact of CAP in achieving these objectives generally within the EEC, and especially with regard to Britain?

Stabilization of Markets and Prices The stabilization of markets and prices is an attempt to combat the very variable prices of agricultural commodities on the world market. Small increases in demand lead to large changes upwards in price, and vice versa. For example, the variations in the monthly price of wheat on world markets between 1968 and 1974 was as much as 11 per cent. Within the EEC countries the monthly variation for the same product over the same period was 3 per cent under the CAP. It is fair to conclude that price variations in Britain and the EEC countries are now less than on world markets, but this does not mean that EEC prices are necessarily lower than world prices.

Self-sufficiency of Food Supplies The availability of food supplies to all the EEC is something which CAP can almost achieve, since EEC is 90 per cent self-sufficient in agricultural products. Britain is only 46 per cent self-sufficient in agricultural products, and it is argued that in a world of food shortages Britain's population is much more secure for food now that she is an EEC member. This was a particularly strong argument during the world wheat shortages of the early 1970s, and its validity does depend upon growth of world population (which is certainly very rapid) in relation to growth in world agricultural productivity.

Levy on Agricultural Imports The consumer obtains his food under the CAP largely from within the EEC, and this is achieved by establishing a common external tariff on world supplies to the EEC. This tariff means that a levy is placed on most imported food since EEC products are usually higher in price. The levy is equivalent to the difference between the EEC 'threshold price' and the (usually) lower world price. This threshold price is fixed as the minimum price necessary to maintain farmers' standards of living plus the transport cost of the product.

When prices fall drastically within the EEC this does not fully accrue to the consumer's benefit, because as soon as the falling price of, for example, butter drops below the minimum necessary to maintain reasonable farmers' living standards the EEC Commission intervenes to buy up butter and maintain a price which is not too low for this purpose.

Raising the Level of Farmers' Incomes We have seen that although the consumer generally pays a higher price for food in normal years within the EEC and does not benefit when the bottom falls out of the market for a product, the farmer on the whole does achieve a reasonable standard of living. In the 1950s agricultural incomes in all nine countries were well below urban incomes. The rapid industrial growth of the six original EEC members in the 1960s led to further substantial rises in urban incomes. So that in spite of the CAP, farmers' incomes rose more slowly than that of urban workers, but nevertheless they rose substantially. In the first year of EEC membership Irish farmers' incomes rose by 36 per cent. In Britain, farm incomes have benefited but to a lesser degree, since Britain had its own system of subsidy to farmers prior to joining the EEC.

Increasing Agricultural Productivity The CAP uses the funds obtained from levies on imports to provide aid to farmers to improve output. The consequence of this has been that between 1961 and 1971 the labour productivity index for agriculture rose from 100 to 188, compared with from 100 to only 166 in industry. Output per man increased also, after better equipment had been introduced and 5.5 million agricultural workers had moved to other employment. British farmers had already become the most capital-intensive in the EEC when Britain joined, but output per head in Britain is continuing to develop under the CAP.

Summary The CAP is the largest of the community's policy ventures and in net terms is financially disadvantageous to Britain. However, it ensures the supply of sufficient food at stable prices.

15.12 COMMON ECONOMIC AND SOCIAL POLICY

The EEC has as a basic aim the unification of all aspects of the economies of its member countries, and the nine countries have formally agreed to an economic and monetary union by 1980. However, the most effective developments so far have been towards common policies for (1) regions; (2) social affairs and (3) industrial structure.

Regional Policy The basic objective of this policy is to reduce differences in income between the richest and poorest regions of the EEC. The highest per capita incomes are in Germany and the Benelux countries, and the lowest are in southern Italy, Ireland, Scotland and some parts of northern England.

In order to improve industrial development and living standards mainly in the poorer areas the European Regional Development Fund has been established. Italy receives 40 per cent of the Fund, Britain 28 per cent, France 15 per cent and Ireland 6 per cent. By contrast, only 1.5 per cent goes to Belgium, 1.7 per cent to The Netherlands and 6.4 per cent to Germany. The fund has been specifically used in Britain and Ireland to attract firms to poorer regions, and to develop roads and other social infrastructure to attract firms. It is an important supplement to the national governments' own policies to encourage new growth industries in north-east England, Clydeside, and the west and south-west of Ireland (see Figure 15.4).

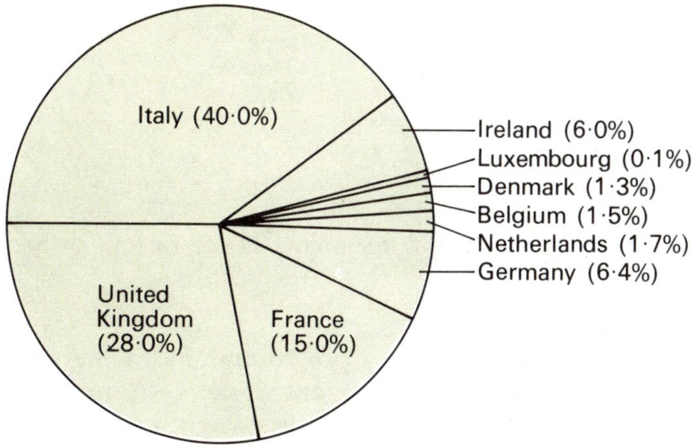

Figure 15.4 Recipients of European regional fund (1975–7).

In addition to the Regional Fund, the European Investment Bank approves loans in accordance with banking criteria for commercial projects in less-developed regions. Again, Ireland and Britain have made substantial use of this facility. Britain, in economic terms, probably gains most from its EEC membership through the availability of funds under regional policy.

Social Policy In 1974 the EEC adopted a wide-ranging social action programme, the goals of which are full employment, improvement in living and working conditions, and participation of both sides of industry in economic and social decision-making. The social action programme's main tool for this task is the European Social Fund, established in 1971. The Social Fund is designed to combat unemployment by enabling funds to be made available for training workers in new skills. In this way the fund helps counter the regional imbalance within the EEC caused by decline of or lack of industry in the poorer regions. The main countries to benefit by the fund have been Britain (28 per cent), Italy (27 per cent), France (19 per cent) and Ireland (7 per cent). However, the Fund is not large enough yet to make a substantial contribution to the problem of large-scale unemployment in the nine countries in the mid-1970s recession (see Figure 15.5).

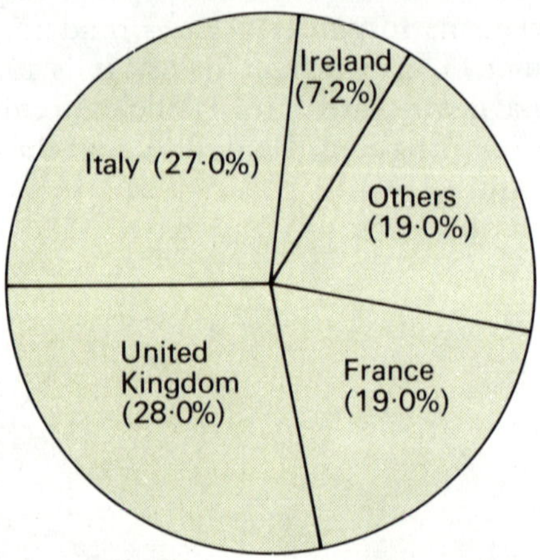

Figure 15.5 Major recipients of the European Social Fund (1975).

The social policy programme has achieved coordination of social security benefits for migrant workers within the EEC, so that a British worker with a job in Germany is entitled to his home country's social security payments. About two million workers a year benefit from this. The social action programme includes directives on safeguards against mass dismissals of workers, a 40-hour week in all nine countries and four weeks' annual holiday (by 31 December 1978), and migrant workers to have trade-union rights which are equal to those enjoyed by indigenous workers. A European Foundation for research into the improvement of living and working conditions has been established in Ireland.

Industrial Structure Policy The EEC industrial structure policy envisages five main action areas:

1. Abolition of technical barriers to trade. This aspect of policy involves standardization of weights, measures and product descriptions, so that non-tariff barriers to trade between member countries are removed. This aim derives from the basic feature of the EEC, i.e. free trade within the Customs Union for all products. The policy reduces product differentiation by manufacturers in monopolistic competition and oligopoly, but it does not remove it, as the EEC-wide advertisement policies of Philips electrical goods and Rolls-Royce aero engines clearly demonstrate.
2. Liberalization of public and semi-public contracts. This section means that national governments and state firms in the member countries should put out contracts so that any company in the nine countries may make a quotation. In this way oligopoly and monopoly tendencies within the nations are meant to be reduced by competitive tendering by many EEC companies.
3. Promotion of competitive European-scale firms. The process here is to support the amalgamation of medium-sized companies on a national level into larger firms to supply the product to a European-scale market. This means elimination of tax laws, which at present make European mergers difficult. The industrial policy is therefore concerned with achieving a European-scale market in commodities where the present markets are national. In this way, it is argued, costs of production can be reduced and, theoretically, so can prices.
4. Promotion of advanced technology industries and industrial sectors in difficulties. It is recognized in the industrial policy that the EEC countries' international specialization lies in advanced technology industries, e.g. aerospace and computers. The Commission's task is to investigate the development of an efficient and competitive industrial structure in these areas, and to encourage research and speedy research dissemination. As we saw in Chapter 13, the results of technological change require rapid implementation, and in the EEC context this means that firms must be made large enough to pay for new equipment and competitive enough in EEC markets not to create an EEC monopoly firm. It is a difficult balance to achieve.
5. Establishment of a business cooperative centre. This centre encourages mergers and cooperation between firms in the different member states, by discussion, intervention with national governments and advice on concluding mergers.

As a world leader in advanced technology industries, Britain has gained new markets for her products in the other eight countries, but costs of technical development are also encouraging British firms to seek mergers and cooperation agreements on products with other EEC firms. Firms in such industries in Britain are usually monopolies or oligopolies. In an EEC context national monopolies should become European oligopolies or be involved in a monopolistic competition market.

Summary Some development towards common policies can be seen in the fields of transport and energy, but the main areas for common economic and social policies are regional, social and industrial structure. Britain and Ireland have benefited in net terms from the regional and social funds of the EEC.

15.13 THE IMPACT OF EEC MEMBERSHIP IN THE BRITISH ECONOMY

In January 1973 Britain, together with Ireland and Denmark, joined the EEC, and in 1978 they became fully integrated members of the community. What has been the effect of this on the British economy and on British economic policies?

Customs Union Prior to entry into the EEC, British trade was expanding rapidly with the 'Six' (i.e. the first six member countries) – in 1965–72 exports to the EEC rose by 140 per cent and imports by 170 per cent – so that the EEC in 1972 was the United Kingdom's largest market. Since membership in 1973 this trend has continued strongly, but imports from the EEC remain greater than exports. In 1973–6, United Kingdom imports from the EEC rose from £5205 million to £11 384 million, whereas United Kingdom exports to the EEC increased only from £4034 million to £9160 million. Has the Customs Union created both more trade and more jobs in Britain than would have happened if the United Kingdom had been outside the Customs Union? It is absolutely certain that more EEC/United Kingdom trade has developed as a result of EEC membership, but the difficult economic question is whether more employment in the United Kingdom has been created by this trade than would have been created if the United Kingdom had imposed import controls on EEC goods to provide more jobs at home. The theory of comparative costs would argue in favour of the Customs Union approach, even in a recession such as that of the mid 1970s, but the question nevertheless needs thorough empirical research. The trade deficit between the United Kingdom and the EEC is not, however, simply due to a high propensity to import manufactures from the EEC; it is also due to the increased value of imports as the pound depreciated strongly in 1972–6, and to increased food imports from the EEC rather than from outside.

Common External Tariff Before 1973 not only was United Kingdom trade with the EEC increasing, but trade with the USA and the Commonwealth was declining proportionately. In 1970–72, imports from the Commonwealth declined from 23.9 per cent of total imports to 19.3 per cent and exports to the Commonwealth fell from 21.0 per cent of total exports to 18.9 per cent. In the same period, imports from the USA declined from 13.0 to 10.5 per cent, and exports to the USA slightly increased from 11.6 to 12.4 per cent. When Britain began the transition in 1974 to implementation of the Common External Tariff this meant that the number of agricultural products and textiles requiring import duties was reduced, and the agreement between the EEC and developing associated states was extended to Commonwealth countries in Africa, the Caribbean and the Pacific. The Asian and developed Commonwealth countries were excluded from the Association Agreement and consequent free entry of their products into EEC markets (including the United Kingdom), but this controlled imports of their manufactures to Britain, and imposed the kind of tariffs on these countries which they had imposed on Britain in the 1950s and 1960s. Britain retained her industrial free trade area links with her former partners in the European Free Trade Association, due to an EEC/EFTA agreement gradually to abolish tariffs on industrial products.

As a consequence of these external trade arrangements, United Kingdom exports to EFTA countries in 1973–6 increased at roughly the same percentage rate as exports to the EEC, but the percentage rise in imports from EFTA was less than from EEC countries. As a consequence, the United Kingdom's balance of trade with EFTA improved. The percentage increase in trade with the Commonwealth (except for oil-rich Nigeria) and the USA was considerably less than with the EEC during 1973–6. The United Kingdom acceptance of the Common External Tariff simply extended the trend towards a decline in the United Kingdom's proportion of trade with the Commonwealth and the USA, and an increase in trade with Western Europe, both the EEC and EFTA (see Table 15.6).

Table 15.6 UK external trade pre- and post-EEC entry.

	Exports			*Imports*		
	1969	*1973*	*1976*	*1969*	*1973*	*1976*
EEC	2070	4030	9170	2150	5210	11 380
Sweden[a]	300	510	1050	330	740	1190
Norway[a]	145	240	470	180	330	620
USA	900	1510	2450	1130	1610	3040
Canada[b]	310	410	630	510	740	1160
Australia[b]	320	400	690	240	340	390
Nigeria[b]	80	170	770	100	210	320
India[b]	70	130	210	110	150	360
Hong Kong[b]	90	130	200	130	260	440

Source: Annual Abstract of Statistics, 1977, HMSO.
[a]EFTA members; [b]Commonwealth members.

Balance of Payments and Economic Growth What were the effects of trade liberalization and changing trade patterns on the balance of payments? Between 1969 and 1972, balance of trade deficit on visibles (i.e. goods) between the United Kingdom and the 'Six' worsened from −£79m to −£495m, whereas the deficit with the rest of the world improved from −£1006m to −£897m. The deficit in the balance of trade on visibles with the rest of the world worsened only slightly in 1973–6 from −£1181m to −£1347m, whereas the deficit with the EEC sharply worsened from

−£1172m to −£2224m. Clearly the lowering of trade barriers between United Kingdom and EEC had helped worsen the balance of trade on visibles, but there were other major factors at work such as higher rates of inflation in the United Kingdom than in the EEC generally, and massive rises in raw material and food prices on world markets. The high inflation reduced the competitiveness of British exports to the EEC, in spite of the depreciating pound, and the commodity price rises fuelled the fires of inflation in a country in which 80 per cent of raw materials in 1978 was imported.

When the balance of trade on invisibles is examined (e.g. services such as banking, insurance and shipping), a marked improvement in 1973–6 from a surplus of £1431m to one of £2166m can be seen. It can be surmised that London, as the major European centre for commercial services, gained substantially from United Kingdom entry into the Customs Union, and since 1974 it has also developed a key role as the financial services centre linking the oil-rich Middle East with the EEC. The Customs Union has brought to the United Kingdom a larger market than the United Kingdom brought to the Customs Union, of course, but the main advantages so far to Britain have been in the services sector.

What has been the impact of trade liberalization on United Kingdom economic growth? Between 1969 and 1972 output rose by about 4 per cent, but in the first year of EEC membership it soared by nearly 10 per cent. However, the 1973–4 European and world boom was short-lived, and in 1974–5 output fell back to 1972 levels in the European and world recession.

Agriculture It was forecast by the British government that food prices would rise by 16 per cent as a result of Britain's being part of the Common Agricultural Policy. The price rise due to the CAP was in fact lower (12 per cent), but Britain, like the rest of the EEC from 1972 onwards, was hit by a massive rise in world food prices. However, this rise in world food prices was less severe in Britain because in 1973–5 the CAP provided food at a lower price than the high world prices. Since 1975 world prices have fallen below the CAP price levels, so that the British consumer is paying more for food. On the other hand, CAP food is a secure supply at a time of rapid world population increase.

Regional Social Policy The world recession of the mid 1970s has made particularly acute the problem of unemployment in Britain, especially in the northern and western regions. The big increases in EEC Regional and Social Funds in 1974–5 available to Britain might have made a substantial contribution to solving regional unemployment before the recession. During the recession, however, they have been large crumbs of comfort in a situation which requires much more massive-scale solutions.

Fiscal Policy British agricultural policy has been changed substantially as a result of EEC membership, but monetary policy has been little affected since Britain refused to tie its currency to other EEC countries. In fiscal policy, however, the value-added tax was introduced to harmonize with EEC countries' taxes, but its wider range, compared with that of the old purchase tax, has made government reluctant to use it as a means of increasing taxes whilst pursuing anti-inflationary policies. Industrial structure policy at EEC level has had only a very limited effect so far on Britain, but its encouragement of advanced technological industry could be of great potential value to British firms.

Summary The mid 1970s recession makes it difficult to analyse the true impact of EEC membership on the British economy. The CAP has been less severe in its impact than anticipated, and regional and social funds have contributed positively to the UK economy, but Britain's loss of freedom to control imports in a recession has meant that solutions to the unemployment problem have to be made at EEC level – a task as yet hardly begun.

15.14 MACROECONOMIC THEORY AND INTERNATIONAL TRADE

We know that in a closed economy, i.e. one without any movement of goods, services and factors across frontiers, the national product is the sum of consumer goods (C), investment goods (I), and government production of goods and services (G), i.e.

$$O = C + I + G.$$

The corresponding equation for the national income (Y) is national income (Y) = consumer spending (C) plus saving (S), plus taxes (T), i.e. $Y = C + S + T$, where taxes are again to be understood in the net sense, subsidies being deducted. If we now want to consider an open economy, we have to introduce two further macroeconomic quantities, namely the stream of exported goods and services (X) and the stream of imported goods and services (M). We must therefore include exports in the national product since the goods exported were also produced in the country, but we have to subtract the imports, since the goods imported do not belong to the national product of the country. Therefore national product (O) will now equal consumer goods (C) plus investment goods (I), plus government production of goods (G), plus exports (X), minus imports (M), i.e.

$$O = C + I + G + X - M. \qquad (1)$$

We know that the national income (Y) equals consumer spending (C) plus saving (S), plus taxes (T), i.e.

$$Y = C + S + T. \qquad (2)$$

It follows from Eqs. (1) and (2) that the actual (export) values of saving and investment are no longer equal to each other. The identity now reads:

$$I + G + (X - M) = S + T.$$

The identity between saving and investment now holds in this situation only if (1) taxes exactly balance government spending and (2) exports are equal to imports in value. If G = T the difference between S and I is equal to the difference between X and M.

The Keynesian method of determining the equilibrium value of the national income in a given period of time, in an economy open to international trade, can now be worked out. We assume, as in a closed economy, that productive capacity is fixed, and that the national income is determined by effective demand.

We now again bring into this explanation material already examined in Chapter 14 Section 5. We assume that investment (I) and government spending (G) are autonomous, i.e. their levels are independent of the national income. Therefore investment (I) equals autonomous investment (I_0),

$$I = I_0, \tag{3}$$

and government spending (G) equals autonomous government spending (G_0).

$$G = G_0. \tag{4}$$

We also assume that taxation (T) is a constant fraction (t) of the national income (Y). This means that taxation increases or decreases in proportion to the national income. We therefore have

$$T = tY. \tag{5}$$

Total planned consumption again equals the autonomous consumption plus the part which is proportionally related to disposable income.

$$C = c(Y - T) + C_0 \quad o<c<1,\ C_0>o \tag{6}$$

We now introduce into the explanation the open character of the economy. We assume that exports (X) are autonomous, i.e. independent of changes in the national income. Therefore, exports of goods and services (X) equal autonomous exports:

$$X = X_0. \tag{7}$$

We also assume that imports (M) are a constant fraction (m) of national income (Y). This means that imports increase or decrease in proportion to national income:

$$M = mY \quad O<M<1. \tag{8}$$

In order to establish the equilibrium value of national income, we need an equilibrium condition. It is that effective demand is equal to national income:

$$Y = C + I + G + (X - M). \tag{9}$$

If we substitute in Eq. (9) the expression for C, I, G, X and M, we arrive at:

$$Y = c(Y - tY) + C_0 + I_0 + G_0 + X_0 - mY. \tag{10}$$

We therefore obtain the following expression for the equilibrium value of national income:

$$\bar{Y} = \frac{C_0 + I_0 + G_0 + X_0}{1 - c\,(1 - t) + m}$$

The multiplier is not now $\frac{1}{1 - c(1 - t)}$ as in Chapter 14, Section 5, but is $\frac{1}{1 - c(1 - t) + m}$, because the introduction of international trade, by which people can purchase imported goods, has made the multiplier smaller.

We now therefore have the following expressions for the multiplier k.

Case 1. A closed economy without government (as in Chapter 4) $k = \frac{1}{1 - c}$

Case 2. A closed economy with government (as in Chapter 14, Section 5) $k = \frac{1}{1 - c(1 - t)}$

Case 3. An open economy with international trade and government $k = \frac{1}{1 - c(1 - t) + m}$

The multiplier therefore decreases as we change from a closed economy without government to one with government, and then to the real-world situation of an open economy with government.

Summary The Keynesian model for explaining the level of national income now includes both government spending and revenue and trade with foreign countries. The multiplier effect of increased domestic investment has less impact on an economy open to foreign trade than in a closed economy.

15.15 CONCLUDING REMARKS

In this chapter, in which foreign trade has been brought into the picture, we have discussed the balance of payments, exchange rate, revaluation, devaluation, special drawing rights, international liquidities and international organizations, in particular the EEC.

The aim of a country in this connection is twofold: to control spending (which depends on the economic climate and trade cycle) and to stimulate production (which depends on economic structure and growth). With steady technical development, growth means the rate at which present consumption is replaced by future consumption, and it varies from one geographic area to another. For Britain, for example, it is particularly the growth of exports that is important. The rapid growth of population in Ireland calls for a constant growth of production, unless people are prepared to accept a drop in the per capita income. However, since they seem not prepared to accept this, exports must be increased all the time. On the other hand, we must not forget the less material requirements connected with the environment, even though the unemployment problem will now have to be given a higher priority.

Though social conditions are constantly changing, the economic problems remain essentially the same: they always boil down to a choice from the available scarce resources to achieve the best possible balance between many wants and satisfaction, supply and demand, and spending and production, both at the microeconomic and at the macroeconomic levels.

QUESTIONS

1 What are comparative cost advantages?

2 Why is the balance of payments always at equilibrium in the official accounts?

3 What does devaluation mean when imports are considered?

4 Why is the multiplier smaller in an open economy than in a closed one?

5 What are the differences between a customs union, an economic union and a free trade area?

6 What is the gist of the Most Favoured Nation clause?

7 What is a supra-national organization?

8 Which countries may be eligible for EEC membership?

9 How can developing countries be helped?

10 What factors upset the effective balance in the balance of payments?

EXERCISES

1 What items are affected in the balance of payments in the following cases?
(a) an American tourist spends some money while on holiday in Britain;
(b) dividends are paid out to foreign shareholders;
(c) credits granted to a foreign country are repaid.

2 How does a wage increase affect the equilibrium in the balance of payments of the same country?

3 The following values are given in this exercise for an economy open to international trade:
$C = \frac{2}{3}(Y - T) + £40m$; $I = £50m$; $G = £30m$; $D = \frac{1}{10}Y$; $T = \frac{1}{10}Y$; and $E = £20m$.
(a) calculate Y;
(b) find the value of the multiplier;
(c) if the government spending (G) increases to £40m, how is the national income (Y) affected, assuming repetition of this in each period?
The equilibrium in this model is given by the equality between the sum of the national income and imports on the one hand and the sum of expenses on the other.

4 What advantages would a further enlargement of the EEC have for consumers?

5 What effect does the abolition of import duties have for the establishment of industries in EEC countries?

6 Discuss how competition in the European market can just as easily increase as decrease.

7 Is it right from a macroeconomic point of view to raise wages in the case of overspending and a static productivity of labour? Who will press for such an increase? Does it make any difference to the argument when international trade is brought into the problem?

8 Describe the role of gold and special drawing rights as international currencies.

9 What possibilities exist for the transfer of technology from rich to poor countries?

10 Assume that Britain decides to use 2 per cent of her national income for aiding developing countries; what would the consequences be?

11 In your estimate would it be possible to create an international currency, and if such a currency system were introduced would it have any practical advantages?

Chapter Sixteen

Centrally Planned Economies

Scarce resources to satisfy many wants can be allocated by the state at national level, rather than by firms and households at market level. Such centrally planned economies are often called *command economies* because the central authorities give orders which usually must be obeyed by industries and firms. Most economies of this type derive from Marxism the theory which influences their policy, and therefore in this chapter we shall first examine Marxist economic theory as developed by Karl Marx and modified by Lenin and Mao Tse-Tung. We shall then study the mechanism of allocation of scarce resources through central planning and apply the ideas and techniques discussed to the USSR, the largest advanced industrial economy of that type. The practice of central planning varies so widely that it is necessary to go on to study planned economies with many market features, e.g. Yugoslavia, those with a huge agricultural sector, e.g. China, and, indeed the use of aspects of central planning in mixed/market economies such as Britain and France.

16.1 MARX AND CAPITALISM

In order to grasp fully the relevance of Marx's ideas on the command economy in a socialist state, it is necessary to examine briefly his critique of the capitalist market economy. Marx places capitalism as the third in a series of inevitable stages of socio-economic development for nations: (1) slavery; (2) feudalism; (3) capitalism; (4) socialism; (5) communism. Society passes from one stage to another because the economic interests of different social classes are opposed and from their clash come changes. Capitalism, for example, succeeds feudalism following a clash between feudal landlords (earning rent income) and the emerging middle-class merchants and factory owners (earning profits) whom Marx calls the capitalists. Under capitalism a new working class of factory workers (earning wages), selling their labour to the capitalist class, emerges.

Marx maintains that the source of all value of a product (e.g. a locomotive) is the socially necessary labour put into producing that product, and this forms the basis of his labour theory of value. However, from empirical studies of mid-nineteenth-century British industry Marx could conclude that the worker did not obtain the full value of the product, but normally just a subsistence wage. At least half the value, what Marx called *surplus value* went to the capitalist as profit. In a 12-hour working day the labourer might make in only six hours enough of the product to pay for his wage. This is called *necessary labour time* (= v). The remaining six hours of labour is surplus labour (= s), whose production revenue accrues to the capitalist as profit. Marx called this surplus value the 'exploitation' of the worker by the capitalist (see Figure 16.1).

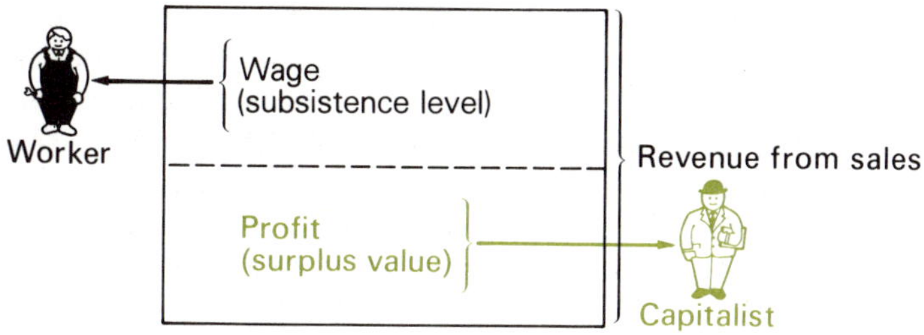

Figure 16.1 Surplus value.

However, as capitalism develops further, Marx argues, the lot of the working class becomes still worse. Technical change takes place in the form of mechanization of production, such that craft labour diminishes and workers simply man the new equipment. Competition between firms to produce more per man leads to increased mechanization, the elimination of weaker firms, and concentration of ownership of firms into fewer hands. Parallel to these developments are the increased output per man and a lowering of prices and of profits in the intensity of competition. The culmination of this process for many workers, however, is unemployment, caused basically by the replacement of labour by mechanization, and this in spite of some selective increase of demand for 'luxury articles' and servants by the wealthy class. Demand for labour under capital accumulation in this situation is not sufficient to compensate for labour-saving technical change which renders workers redundant.

Employers confronted by competition on this scale, and in a strong position in relation to the mass unemployment of workers, attempt to lower wages to absolute subsistence levels and to extend hours of work. Moreover, each depression in the trade cycle, argues Marx, becomes worse in these later stages of capitalist development, so that all workers are haunted by the spectre of unemployment. In this situation of inevitable class struggle and increasing poverty there is the overriding motive for wage-earning workers and the unemployed to organize revolutionary action to take control of the firms and the state. The opportunity to do this also exists, since hundreds of thousands of workers are living in huge industrial cities in which they can easily organize together the required action.

Summary Marx argues that in the later stages of capitalism, not only does the worker obtain half the revenue from sales of his output (the remainder – surplus value – goes to the employer) but his wages fall, hours of work lengthen and unemployment increases. In this situation organized workers will overthrow capitalist ownership of firms.

16.2 THE COMMAND ECONOMY AND MARXIST THEORY

Marx's Theory Marx himself wrote only very sketchily about the organization of production in a socialist society. One of his main themes was that the common production of goods should be regulated by society for social use. He did not clearly work out the actual nature of organization for fulfilment of this goal, but thought that the state would be required for two major purposes: (1) to employ labour; (2) to allocate social consumption. It is therefore implied in the former that the state has an important role in organizing production, since it ensures the employment of the labour force. It is clearly stated in the latter that the state has control over allocation of resources for consumption, which Marx specified as schools, health services, sickness and industrial injury benefits, etc. provided free by the state. The costs of social consumption would be deducted prior to incomes paid out to workers, and there would be other prior deductions for replacement of capital equipment and the state's administrative costs. Payment to labour would depend on the labour time put into the production of goods and services by the worker. Payment would also vary, however, in relation to the needs of society for particular types of work. As Marx puts it: 'Its [labour time] apportionment in accordance with a definite social plan maintains the proper proportion between the different kinds of work to be done and the various wants of the community.' The social plan would also ensure that market prices of goods would be equal to their value, and goods would therefore be sold in relation to the labour employed in their production. Marx saw this framework as a temporary one for the socialist stage of production, but when abundance of material goods had been created in this new system of society, and human nature transformed, the final stage of communism would evolve. At this point workers would be paid according to their social need rather than their output, or as Marx put it, 'From each according to his ability: to each according to his need.'

Lenin's Policy It was left to Lenin, as leader of the first country to implement Marx's theory of the centrally planned economy, to develop these ideas in practice. He had already extended Marxist economic theory by the thesis that imperialism was the highest stage of capitalism, i.e. that the competitive struggle by firms for markets led to the development of economically integrated colonial empires. Lenin's action plan after the 1917 Russian Revolution was that all citizens should be employed by the state, and that industrial output should be planned by the state and firms owned by the state. The state's decision-making would be placed under the control of Soviets (Councils) of workers in factories and towns, and principally at national level. The Communist Party would have an organization at all levels parallel to the Soviets to maintain the working-class ideological purity of the decision-makers. In this way it developed in the USSR a major control of national decision-making. Stalin, Lenin's principal successor, extended state ownership to agriculture and intensified industrial planning. In China, the Russian planning experience was applied to industry after 1949 by the communists under the leadership of Mao Tse-Tung, but in agriculture the land was now owned by rural communes of farmers, and more emphasis is placed in Maoist theory than in Leninist theory on practical consent by the governed.

Summary Marx outlined the organization of a socialist economy, and placed the state during the socialist stage of development in the central role of employing labour and allocating social resources.

16.3 RESOURCE ALLOCATION UNDER CENTRAL PLANNING

The main characteristic of modern central planning in the state socialist countries of Eastern Europe is the central management of the economy in accordance with detailed plans for allocation of resources, e.g. production, distribution, investment and consumption, including targets and methods for implementation of plans. The State Planning Commission whose chairman is normally a government senior minister develops the central plan (for usually a five-year period), which includes the economic targets to be attained by the nation and firms, and the coordination of

Table 16.1 Countries with command economies.

Europe	*Asia*
Albania	Cambodia
Bulgaria	China
Czechoslovakia	Laos
East Germany	Mongolia
Hungary	North Korea
Poland	South Yemen
Romania	Vietnam
USSR	
	North America
	Cuba
Africa	
Angola	Ethiopia
Congo	Mozambique

these targets to make sure they are mutually possible, e.g. coal production has to be consistent with steel production targets. The Commission is also responsible for developing methods of monitoring and ensuring the plan's success, and for justifying its targets for the economy in the light of the real-world economic conditions of the nation. Nowadays, the Commission normally revises the plan each year to account for changing economic conditions. (See Table 16.1 for list of countries with command economies.)

Inter-branch Balances A major feature of the plan is the coordination of targets between the different branches of the economy, and this is done by a scheme of 'inter-branch balances'. Flows of production from one industry to another form one essential element of coordination, but the following are also balanced with production targets: (1) incomes to the branches, i.e. industries; (2) consumer and investment spending; and (3) state spending and private spending (see Figure 16.2). The Commission attempts some optimalization of plans through detailed calculations of the feasibility and benefit of more than one plan. Its recommended plan is then sent for comment to economics ministries, firms and local authorities, returned to the Commission for final revision, and sent to Parliament for discussion and implementation into law.

What are the major advantages and disadvantages of this type of planning? Economists in state socialist countries argue that experience in Eastern Europe indicates that slumps and unemployment are generally avoided, growth rates are higher, and income distribution is more equitable than in market economies. On the other hand, Western economists argue that these countries have problems in the microeconomic allocation of resources to consumer preferences, lower per capita consumption, prices not related carefully to costs, and instances of decisions by ill-informed senior politicians, clumsily carried out by a central bureaucracy. (These criticisms and commendations are discussed more fully in Sections

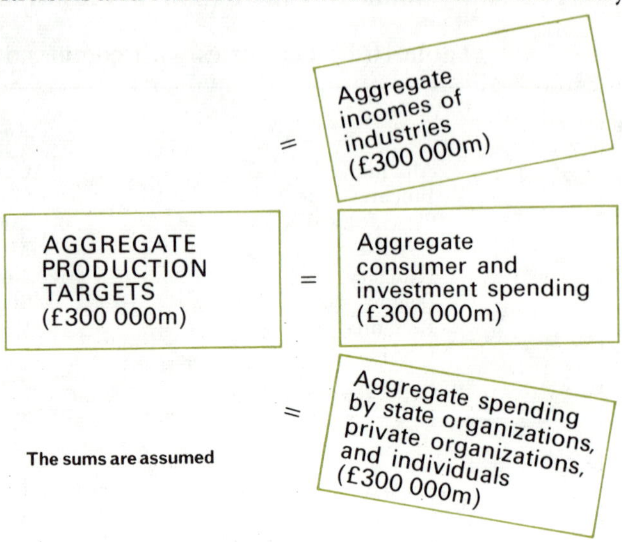

Figure 16.2 Major inter-branch balances.

4 and 5 of this chapter in relation to the USSR.) The economic reforms of the 1960s have attempted to overcome some disadvantages by involving market forces and consumer preferences much more in microeconomic allocation. Some state socialist economists, however, would argue that modern mathematical models, using computers, can make better microeconomic decisions than the market in terms of reconciling social goals and consumer preference.

Investment, Consumption and Pricing What are the main features of the modern centrally planned economy? The levels of investment and of consumption are determined by the plan and resources allocated centrally, and the former is generally higher than in decentralized market economies. New fixed capital and working capital usually make up about 75 per cent of investment, and consumer durable goods and social capital the remainder; a decision on quantities made centrally in advance of actual production. However, the recent growth of finance for investment from firms' profits has helped them develop small investment projects, and the use of bank credits gives some freedom to firms as long as investment decisions accord with the framework of the plan. Consumption decisions are planned centrally in terms of quantities of social and private consumption. Pricing decisions for raw materials and consumer goods are made centrally, but prices of other goods are determined at lower levels, although the state can adjust prices to deal with scarcity. Nevertheless, prices are not normally used to allocate resources, that function being mainly left to physical planning from the centre.

Profits and Wages Profits are used in state socialist central planning as a measure of efficiency of the firm, but the firm has to fulfil other more important goals, which are of course the production and investment targets in the plan. The state takes the lion's share of profits in the form of taxes (between 60 and 80 per cent), but the remainder goes to small investment projects in the firm, the firm's cultural and housing funds, and an incentives fund for workers and managers. In Eastern Europe the incentives fund receives between 6 and 20 per cent of the workers' income, and is usually proportional to basic earnings. Some small allocation of resources for investment is achieved through profit, but wages are a more powerful mechanism for allocation of the major resource, labour. Actual wage funds for firms are determined by the central plan in such a way as to give incentive to workers to go to regions of new economic development, and to jobs where the skills are in short supply. These central planning decisions are made, after consultation with lower levels, by the Council of Ministers, Parliament and the State Planning Commission, and carried out by the economics ministries, by the industries and local authorities themselves, and finally by the firms.

Summary Central planning therefore involves major resource allocation by physical controls from the centre on investment, production, consumption and distribution (including wages). Some price decisions and profit decisions are decentralized, but these allocate resources only to a limited extent.

16.4 CENTRAL PLANNING AND RESOURCE ALLOCATION IN THE USSR

In the USSR, unlike Yugoslavia and China, which we discuss later, the detailed central economics plan still dominates the economy. This plan is drawn up by the State Planning Commission (called Gosplan) and then referred to economics ministries, the 17 constituent Republics, industries and firms for comments. These modifications are then passed upwards to Gosplan which coordinates the final draft (containing 200 to 300 commodities of national importance) and sends it to the Council of Ministers and Supreme Soviet (Parliament) for discussion, approval and legislation. Alongside the national plan each economics ministry, Republic, industry and firm has its plan for the same period of time. (See Table 16.2 for examples of realized production figures.)

Table 16.2 USSR production figures.

	1968	*1971*
Coal	416m tons	441m tons
Crude oil	309m tons	377m tons
Steel	167m tons	181m tons
Vehicles	282 000	529 000

Source: UN Statistical Yearbook, 1975, Tables 52, 54, 124 and 135. Reproduced with the kind permission of the UNO.

Balances between sectors of the economy are an essential part of the national plan and in the USSR this means the following important items: (1) a balance between output and employment of the whole working population; (2) a balance between physical output and financing of this output; (3) a balance between output of final products and the raw materials, components, etc., required for making them; (4) a balance between output of the national economy and output of individual firms. Due to current rapid economic change the plans are revised annually. In this process Gosplan proposes a revision, the firms and other lower echelons add their development to the plan so far, and Gosplan uses this to produce the revised plan. Investment, production, consumption and distribution, unlike those in Yugoslavia, are largely determined by physical allocation of resources through the national plan, as described in Section 3 of this chapter. To supplement physical controls, exhortation through media campaigns is important, such as the advice campaign to farmers and fishermen during the 1972 drought.

Pricing in Soviet central planning is used as a measure of value, but not normally as a method for allocating resources. Retail prices tend to remain stable over several years, unless substantial shortages are reflected in agricultural products, for which collective farm prices are determined by supply and demand. The Soviet price system does not of itself respond to changing consumer preferences, and firms in making business decisions cannot use the price system effectively to reflect the opportunity cost of these decisions.

Since the 1960s, profits have been more fully introduced to give a measure of plant and firm efficiency, whilst the number of physical plan targets for firms has been reduced from between 20 and 30 to eight. The state receives 70 per cent of profits as taxation, and 24 per cent goes to firms' social funds and 6 per cent to the workers' and managers' incentives fund.

Therefore, approximately 10 per cent of workers' earnings, on average, comes from firms' profit distribution. Firms' profits allocate resources only to a very limited extent, but the state plan, by determining wage funds, attempts with more powerful tools to allocate labour to job-shortage and regional labour-shortage areas.

The major sector of the Soviet economy, lacking spectacular growth, has been agriculture, in which relatively low rural incomes and relatively high prices of consumer goods are a disincentive to collective farmers' work motivation. The 1970s are witnessing an increase in investment in agriculture, however, according to national and industrial plans.

Summary In the Soviet economy, the national central plan allocates resources for production, investment, consumption and distribution by physical controls, although some limited resource allocation function is performed by firms' profits and by pricing.

16.5 MACROECONOMIC POLICY IN THE USSR

Do problems of fluctuation in levels of economic activity exist in a centrally planned economy such as the USSR? During the 1920s and 1930s the Soviet Union deliberately reduced foreign trade to a minimum both for military strategic reasons and to protect herself from the effects of world slumps on the production levels of the country. The establishment in 1949 of Comecon (Council for Mutual Economic Assistance) among the state socialist countries of Eastern Europe (excluding Yugoslavia and Albania), Mongolia, Cuba and Vietnam has led to an expansion of Soviet foreign trade with these states. All such countries have centrally planned economies, however, and they are free from substantial trade recessions. The concentration in the USSR on planning through physical controls has also left little room for monetary factors to cause disturbances to intended production levels. However, in an economy which sets an absolute priority on full employment, from time to time situations occur in which goods are overproduced in relation to realized demands of customers. The goal of full employment is easier to attain in the USSR, which provides larger-scale employment in space research, defence and central planning administration, than in Yugoslavia and Western Europe.

The other major fluctuation in economic activity, the production boom and associated shortages of products, occurs fairly frequently in the Soviet Union, and shows itself in the form of bottlenecks in manufacturing industry, non-availability of some consumer goods, and in selective price rises at times of severe inflation. This quite frequent disequilibrium between production and spending was not originally believed possible by Soviet economists since the central planners controlled both. From the early 1960s even the retail price index, which is rigidly controlled, has shown yearly price increases of 1 to 2 per cent. The aim of the authorities is to keep retail prices as stable as possible for as long as is feasible. A tendency develops, therefore, to avoid major changes in such prices, and spending eventually exceeds production. The disequilibrium situation becomes worse, and the authorities normally respond to this by raising prices substantially. This measure restricts demand for goods internally and brings about a situation in which production and spending balance each other better. (In Poland, the authorities have allowed inflationary disequilibria to develop much more seriously and an example of this is given in Chapter 17, Section 4.) The recent world shortages of commodities such as grain and oil have been reflected in higher prices of limited amounts of Soviet imports, which has had a minor effect on price levels.

A further macroeconomic problem, that of maintaining a fast rate of economic growth, has become a matter of concern to Soviet planners because the growth rate appears to fall in percentage terms whilst the economy becomes more industrially advanced. The high growth rates of the 1950–68 period, averaging 8 per cent per annum, exceeded those reached in Western Europe and North America. However, during the 1970s the combination of an increase in consumers' expenditure, a rise in agricultural investment and high military expenditure on research and development resulted in a lower rate of economic growth, particularly in the earlier show-piece sector, heavy industry.

Summary Central planning removes the macroeconomic problem of high unemployment, but it does not remove inflation, and it still remains to be seen whether high rates of growth can be produced in an advanced industrial society under a command economy.

16.6 CENTRAL PLANNING IN STATE SOCIALIST COUNTRIES: YUGOSLAVIA AND CHINA

Yugoslavia Yugoslavia and China are state socialist countries which have developed central planning in a different way from that of the other

Eastern European countries, including the USSR. Since the 1950s Yugoslavia has introduced many market features into an economy that was once tightly controlled from the centre. Production, price, wage and consumption controls were dismantled in the 1950s, and in 1963 government central planning of investment was relinquished in favour of bank finance for investment. A further source of investment for firms is self-generated profit, most of which accrues permanently to the firm and can be used to increase earnings of workers as well as investment. The firms are still owned by society in the form of the firms' workers, however, but central planning now consists only of medium-term indicative plans, i.e. of future estimated trends, to give guidelines to firms.

Yugoslav economists argue that strict central planning, with emphasis on heavy industry, helped rapid economic growth during the late 1940s, but that as living standards rose consumer choices multiplied and 'market socialism' was adopted to solve more effectively the microeconomic as well as the macroeconomic allocation of resources. Market socialism enabled highly profitable firms to expand investment and raise wages, however, especially in the north and in Serbia, whereas less profitable firms have indulged in less investment and raised wages much less, particularly in the south of the country. Consumer choice and living standards have improved with market socialism, but unemployment has reached 10 per cent of the workforce, and it is arguable that Yugoslavia is no longer a centrally planned economy, although firms are still communally owned.

China China, like Yugoslavia, followed the Russian model of central planning until the late 1950s, when production and investment decisions were decentralized to the provinces and counties because of the hugeness of the country, the different levels of technology in different provinces and counties, and the very large agricultural sector. The production and investment, now centrally planned, is confined to a few large firms. Regional plans in the 1970s have led to a massive development of small firms, with a regional market, in the machinery, cement, steel, chemicals and coal industries. National plans for large firms have particularly concentrated in the 1960s and 1970s on 'military' industries, including nuclear, aerospace and telecommunications sectors, and on the chemicals industry, including fertilizers.

Several attempts have been made to collectivize agriculture, the livelihood of the majority of the population. During the 1960s farmers in most provinces were organized into communes of 4000 to 5000 families, and these were later subdivided into *production teams* of 40 to 60 families. It is in fact the 'production team' which is the agricultural accounting unit, and profit accrues to it, thereby providing a financial work incentive. At times in the 1970s the national planners have raised commodity prices to increase output via increased profits from production teams (e.g. sugar in 1972). However, the main incentive to agricultural production is seen by national planners to be exhortation (e.g. 'Learn from Takai' – films and eulogies of a successful commune) and the self-reliance of production teams. Agriculture provides an economic surplus for industrial development (through taxes) and the urban food supply, whilst the development in regional plans of small-scale commune industries places less demand on urban industrial capacity. In China, central planning has been adapted to the differing stages of economic development of provinces, and to a nation the majority of whose workers are rurally based. The Chinese economy is in some ways similar to the situation in developing Third World countries.

Summary The state socialist countries contain a variety of experience of planned economies, including Yugoslav market socialism, which has social ownership but not much central planning, and the Chinese attempt to plan for a huge agricultural sector as well as advanced industrial development.

16.7 ELEMENTS OF CENTRAL PLANNING IN MIXED/MARKET ECONOMIES: FRANCE AND BRITAIN

France Mixed/market economies can include elements of central planning, and the most highly developed elements in a Western country are practised in France. Pierre Massé, former Commissaire Général of the French General Planning Commission, defined planning as '... a development in thought paving the way for a development in practice ... It [the French plan] does not attempt to dictate to business firms what they ought to do, but it does make clear to them the overall objectives of economic development, and the specific objective of their branch' (industry). These specific objectives of each industry are drawn up first by committees, representatives of firms and unions in the industry, and the objectives include production targets for the industry. Next the General Planning Commission, utilizing the industry plans, produces a four-year national plan indicating national targets for production, consumption, investment and incomes. These targets are indicators to firms of national trends and industry trends, which do not require firms' obedience but aim to give security and confidence to firms' planning decisions. Since unions and firms participate in drafting the plan, they are prejudiced towards its success.

The French government helps the plan, as far as changing macroeconomic circumstances permit, by liaising its fiscal and monetary policies to the objectives of the plan, and by using its 50 per cent control of investment similarly. Senior French civil servants in the 1960s and 1970s have worked with the General Planning Commission experts in the execution of the plan to such an extent that their decisions, too, are now taken in the context of the plan. The continuous, rapid post-war growth of the French economy, French planners argue, has been due not simply to the concept of indicative central planning, but to its active acceptance and implementation by firms, unions and government.

Britain Unlike France, Britain has not developed indicative central planning over any length of time, but has made several attempts at doing so. In 1962–4 the National Economic Development Office produced a four-year plan, and in 1965–6 the short-lived Department of Economic Affairs published a five-year National Plan, very similar in development and features to the French plans. Throughout the post-war period the Treasury has produced short- and medium-term forecasts of production, consumption, investment and incomes, but this has involved no active central planning of the economy, although it has been of use to industries and firms. See Table 16.3 for a comparison of economic growth.

Table 16.3 Comparisons of economic growth.

	Industrial Production (1963 = 100)			
	1948	*1958*	*1968*	*1971*
Yugoslavia	25	58	139	186
France	40	77	127	160
Britain	62	84	120	125

Source: UN Statistical Yearbook, 1975, Table 50. Reproduced with the kind permission of the UNO.

Since 1975, the government has again attempted some indicative central planning called the *industrial strategy*, which is designed in particular to develop production and investment. Working through the National Economic Development Office (NEDO), government has set up over 30 industry-based committees to analyse obstacles to investment and production growth. For example, in diesel engines and steel these obstacles have been identified, and mergers and government assistance recommended. The latter is carried out by a specialist organization, the National Enterprise Board, which has authority to provide funds to rationalize production and investment organization in firms, and thereby links national planning to industrial reorganization. A further intended development of the industrial strategy is voluntary planning agreements between the large firms and government. This form of indicative planning, however, does not include incomes and consumption targets.

Summary An element of central planning, called indicative (or 'outline') planning, is used in some mixed/market economies, such as France and Britain, and provides national and industrial economic guidelines and targets for firms, which they may use in making business decisions.

16.8 CENTRAL PLANNING AND THE POLITICAL SYSTEM

Central planning is normally associated with one-party states. In the USSR a one-party administrative elite controls the central planning decision-making at the top, and there is no regular way, in practice, of conferring and withdrawing supreme authority from this elite. A substantial amount of economic decentralization in planned economies tends to induce the emergence of some political opposition, such as Yugoslavia's internal region-based opposition or an opposition based on cultural factors such as occurred briefly in Czechoslovakia in 1968. However, in theory, one could have a multi-party state with central planning of the economy, as the British Labour Party envisaged in the 1930s and 1940s for the UK.

The mixed/market economy is normally associated with multi-party states, but for over 40 years in this century Spain and Portugal were one-party states, yet ran a decentralized economy. Yugoslavia and Hungary have been involved in a programme of substantial decentralization of economic decision-making, and although this process has gone much further in Yugoslavia than in Hungary, considerable control of investment and production has been given to firms in the latter without this leading, so far, to the development of a political opposition.

Summary Central planning and one-party states normally go together, but it is possible to have detailed central planning in multi-party states and a market economy in a one-party state.

16.9 CONCLUDING REMARKS

Central planning in the allocation of scarce resources has generally led to a more rapid rate of growth during a country's industrialization phase, in which economic choices are few. In an advanced industrial society, however, planning from the centre is normally insensitive to microeconomic consumer choice, and, particularly in Hungary and Poland (as well as of course Yugoslavia), market forces are being introduced to supplement by use of the free price mechanism the central physical allocation of resources. Meantime, in Western Europe, elements of central planning are being used to supplement market forces in business decision-making, and the European nations' economies therefore show a limited trend towards convergence. The current macroeconomic problems in Western Europe cause us to examine particularly central planning and Marxist economic theory as vehicles for solutions. It can be argued, however, that like rival economic policies and theories they provide only recommendations which, when acted upon, may lead to a lessening of the seriousness of certain specific economic problems at a historical moment.

QUESTIONS

1 What is the Labour theory of value?

2 What is the economic role of the state in a socialist society, according to Marx?

3 What are the main functions of the State Planning Commission in a state socialist country?

4 Explain the meaning of 'inter-branch balances'.

5 List the state socialist (communist) countries in the world.

6 What are the main features of French indicative central planning?

7 Define the UK's industrial strategy of the mid 1970s.

8 List the main authorities which are consulted in the drawing up of Soviet central plans.

EXERCISES

1 To what extent does Marx's advocacy of a socialist economy remove the major weaknesses he attributes to the capitalist economy?

2 Discuss the advantages and disadvantages of allocation of resources at a practical level in a centrally planned economy.

3 Why have Yugoslavia and the USSR made changes in their systems of central planning? And discuss the main differences in central planning in the two countries.

4 Discuss the importance of the role of profit in the allocation of economic resources under central planning.

5 Has the Chinese form of central planning followed directly from the economic theories of Mao Tse-Tung, or does it owe more to the economic theories of Marx and Lenin?

6 Do the Chinese, Yugoslav and Soviet forms of central planning have more in common with each other than with central planning in France or Britain?

7 Which economic problems does central planning deal with less successfully than the mixed/market economy?

8 Does the form of economic central planning depend upon the political system in a country?

Chapter Seventeen

Comparative Review of Economic Theory

The study of Marxist economic theory and of centrally planned economies leads us finally to compare that theory with economic theories of the mixed/market economies, such as Britain and the other EEC countries, which we have studied earlier in the book. The aim of this chapter is therefore to compare the advantages of different major economic systems from the standpoint of concrete specifications of economic welfare, such as efficient allocation of resources and income distribution. In earlier chapters we examined four major explanations, i.e. theories, of the economy, and how they might operate: classical, Keynesian, monetarist and Marxist. In the last chapter we compared the advantages and disadvantages, at a practical level, of the operation of centrally planned economies, largely derived from Marxist theory, with the operation of mixed/market economies, mainly derived from the other three theories. As we saw, in communist countries the pure centralist command economy of Marxist economic thought in practice involves some market decentralized elements. The pure decentralized market economy, envisaged by classical theory, also has some important elements of central government decision-making (see Chapter 14).

A very important feature in comparing the theories is what they have to say about the levels at which economic decisions might be made. Who has the power to take the decisions? In classical theory, and very largely in monetarist theory, the consumer in the market is the sovereign, whereas in Marxist theory it is the state through the government and central planners. Keynesian theory proposes a combination of consumer and state decision-taking, in which the influence of the former is normally greater. These points, of course, over-simplify what the theorists actually wrote. For example, Marx envisaged some market elements in the state socialist economy, especially in its early stages, and Adam Smith saw no role for the consumer in economic decision-making concerning defence, police and the judicial system. However, in essence there is a substantial difference between levels of decision-making proposed in Marxist, monetarist/classical and Keynesian theories.

The theories and the levels of decision-taking advocated in them have had an enormous impact upon the views of businessmen and politicians concerning the levels and the persons who make the decisions. The view of

Marxist and social democrat politicians in Western Europe that the state has an important central planning role in the economy has had a significant impact on the gradual development of planning and state ownership of industry in most of these countries. The view of many businessmen and conservative politicians in North America and Western Europe that most economic transactions should be determined in the free market has helped substantially to make permanent, as it were, the basic predominance of market economics in these countries. Keynes's remarks about businessmen being the disciples of some defunct economist have come true about him personally, now that many of them, since 1945, have advocated ideas, based on his own, of the mixed/market economy in post-1945 Western countries.

We must not only study economic theory but must also assess its manifestations in various economic systems in a comparative way. From this analysis we can establish which theories might be most applicable to the British and EEC economies. This comparative review of theory and economic systems is presented as a concluding section and summary of the economic discussion contained in the book.

17.1 THE CLASSICAL SCHOOL AND THE MARKET ECONOMY

The pioneers of the classical school, especially Adam Smith, were the first to attempt to explain the workings of an economy, and they argued that free competition between firms and production factors ensure optimal economic efficiency and allocation of economic resources. The public goods of justice, police and armed forces were all they exempted from the 'economic law', that pursuit by everyone of economic self-interest, led to maximization of profit and high output. Perfect competition was the market form that these late-eighteenth/early-nineteenth-century economists believed generally to exist in reality, and where it did not exist governments, they argued, should permit it to develop. As we saw in Chapter 10, perfect competition leads to equilibrium of prices for a product throughout the market, and also of equalization of average costs. In economic decision-making the consumer is king, since allocation of resources is based on individual consumer preferences. For example, if consumer demand for a product rises the price goes up, which is a signal to the profit-maximizing manufacturer to increase the output of the product. When he boosts production, more of the goods become available in the shops, and this increase in supply leads to a fall in price, ensuring satisfaction for the consumer.

This free market economy, it is argued, would also ensure for the most part full employment, since the available quantities of production factors (e.g. capital and labour) determine what output can be produced. When any unemployment occurs wages fall until they reach a level at which employers are prepared to take on unemployed workers. The classical theory, refined by the late-nineteenth-century economists Marshall and Pareto, postulated that consumer welfare and efficient allocation of resources in an economy were optimized through marginal quantity changes. The proposition that perfect competition fulfils the optimum conditions and gives rise to efficient allocation of resources is called the *theorem of Pareto-optimality*. Naturally, the classical school believed that if free competition was extended to international trade the optimum conditions and efficient allocation of resources would be achieved on a worldwide scale, and, in the nineteenth century, governments with free-trade ideals, such as the British government, pressed other governments to establish a world economic order based on classical economics.

These preferences expressed by consumers through the market are of course individual and not collective ones, and we are not considering in this theory an efficient allocation of resources for situations where pressure groups play an active role. The power of the consumer to influence allocation of resources depends upon his income and wealth, so that the free market economy provides efficient allocation of resources within a given income distribution for the population. The role of government is minimized to that of providing essential public goods, and it is argued that this can most efficiently be done by balancing government revenue and expenditure. Such a government would see no value in price and wage policies since these would interfere with the free market forces which were already bringing optimal allocation of goods and labour. That perfect competition brings about efficient allocation of economic resources is a positive statement of one school of economic thought. The implementation of policies based on this type of economic theory requires political and social value judgements about the kind of society and income distribution people wish to develop.

Summary The classical theory postulates that perfect competition leads to optimum efficiency in allocation of economic resources because firms and consumers make decentralized economic choices in their own interests. This allocation of resources is particular to a given income distribution.

17.2 MARKET FAILURE AND ECONOMIC INSTABILITY

Critics of classical economics would refer to the real world of economics in order to attack the theory, and we also need to refer to it in order to account for the development of Keynesian and Marxist theories. The non-operation of perfect competition in many parts of the real world is sometimes referred to as *market-failure* and examples of such situations can be easily cited in the twentieth century. External economies of companies in geographically favourable locations will lead to abnormal profit, and therefore an allocation of resources to production factors different from that postulated by perfect competition theory. However, one of the sharpest divergencies from the free-market model is the development of firms with oligopoly and monopoly power. As we discussed in Chapter 11, such firms in Britain obtain abnormal profits, and can restrict output in order to maintain shortages and high prices. Even under monopolistic competition there is some element of abnormal profit to firms, and thereby an interference with optimum resource allocation as envisaged in completely free markets.

Wage determination in some real-world conditions of monopsony buyers (monopoly companies) and monopoly sellers (100 per cent organized trade union workforces) is an outcome of a collective bargaining economic power struggle rather than a result of equating the wage of the marginal worker with that of the marginal revenue product (see Chapter 12). The recent trend in British industry has been towards oligopolistic, powerful companies and unions with closed shop membership in plants. In such cases employers can obtain abnormal profit and workers gain wages above marginal productivity levels, all of which results in pricing and allocation of resources quite different from those obtaining under free competition. During this century we have of course witnessed throughout most of the industrialized world both substantial cyclical and substantial structural unemployment, which again differs in actual results from the predictions of classical theory. Large-scale cyclical unemployment persisted in Britain during the period 1921–39, although it could be argued that substantial wage reductions might have eliminated it. Throughout this century structural unemployment has persisted in many northern and western regions, although classical theorists would argue that labour was too immobile. Moreover, government increased its role above that prescribed by the classical school, and took over natural monopolies such as electricity supply as well as postal services.

Summary In the twentieth century real-world persistent unemployment and the development of oligopoly and monopoly resulted in divergencies from the free-market model of efficient resource allocation.

17.3 KEYNESIANISM AND THE MIXED ECONOMY

Government intervention in the market economy is the catalyst, which in Keynes' theory, developed in the inter-war period of persistent unemployment, enables full employment to be reached and maintained. As we discussed in Chapter 4, the government, in the Keynesian model, increases its spending on investment goods, which, through the multiplier effect, raises consumer goods production much more substantially. Meanwhile, government's example and low interest rates encourage private firms to boost their production and employment. Nationalized industries are also used by the state, as owner, to expand production (e.g.

steel, coal and aerospace), and also in some cases to provide services the market would not ensure (e.g. subsidies to rural buses). Therefore, through fiscal monetary incomes policies, aided by some indicative planning (e.g. NEDO, industrial strategy), government attempts to manage effective demand for goods and services such that full employment is maintained (as discussed in Chapter 16, Section 7).

Other government roles in tackling market failure are to restrict the power of oligopolies and monopolies by methods of intervention which we discussed in Chapter 11, and to cushion the structural unemployment's effects of technical change by the methods discussed in Chapter 13. Government commissions and courts to curb oligopoly power, and regional policies to induce firms to go to areas of high regional structural unemployment are two major features of the British mixed/market economy. Government also influences income distribution by its incomes and social security policies. Social security payments, which are bare subsistence level, to pensioners and unemployed, and flat-rate incomes policies increase consumer demand and to some limited extent re-distribute income. Through restrictions on environmental pollution by firms, and on sites for development of new industries, government intervenes to allocate resources between competing needs of manufacturing industry and other social needs. In Britain, government is now responsible for over 50 per cent of research and development in industry and therefore has substantial indirect control in the development of technical change in state and private firms. This indirect influence is another feature of the growth of government involvement in the modern mixed economy.

The basic structure of the economy in the Keynesian theory is a market form, but with the addition of government intervention to ensure a more efficient allocation of resources through such devices as maintaining full employment, curbing oligopoly and re-distributing income. The decision-making structure in the economy is a mixture of decentralized choices by consumers and small firms, 'and centralized choices by government and oligopoly firms.

Summary The mixed/market economy has developed in Britain in the post-1945 period and is partly a consequence of the acceptance of Keynes' ideas of government intervention to help ensure what is argued to be a more efficient allocation of fully employed resources than the market alone would achieve.

17.4 A REVIEW OF MARXISM

Marxism, the details of which were studied in the last chapter, was a response in the nineteenth century to the market theories of classical economics, but Marxism and a modified form of classical economics called *monetarism* can be seen in the 1970s and 1980s as a response to the real-world problems of mixed/market economies and the associated apparent failure of some Keynesian policies. The high and persistent unemployment in mixed/market economies, including Britain and the EEC countries, in the mid and late 1970s, accompanied by high rates of inflation undermined some confidence in the Keynesian policy prescriptions for governmental management of effective demand in the economy. However, Keynesians would argue that proper application of his actual policies (as prescribed in his writings) required, in full employment conditions, the moderation of earnings rises by organized labour, and price increases by employers, but it is also the case that his theories did not deal with the serious structural unemployment problem.

Marxist economic theory and its agent the centralized command economy attempt to ensure full employment and price control by the state planning apparatus (as discussed in Chapter 16, Section 3). In this way it is recommended that the problems of concurrent high unemployment and rapid inflation can be overcome, and central planning ensure efficient allocation of resources. Moreover, Marxist theory would reduce income and wealth distribution differences more substantially, and eliminate private oligopolies as well as the market mechanism. Marx argued that unemployment would be overcome by state employment of the labour force, and by implication through state organization of all production. Lenin developed the theory further to argue categorically that the state should own and plan all production. This technique of central planning to ensure full employment has been a success in state socialist countries, and one can argue that in this way an important contributor to economic inefficiency is overcome. Unemployment due to massive new mechanization would be avoided in Marxist theory by central planning of labour, re-training, new jobs and changed hours of work.

Marx wrote little, directly, on inflation as a major macroeconomic problem, but his view that prices should be fixed relative to the labour value of the product would be an important defence against price inflation. In fact, prices change less in communist countries due to subsidies to protect the price of basic necessities and the use of waiting lists for some major non-essentials. Sometimes the long-run stability of prices of necessities in these countries causes such a divorce between price reality and price actuality that a massive (e.g. 25 per cent) change is announced. Riots by Polish workers forced their government to modify such a price-change measure, and firms find that prices with unknown degrees of subsidy pose difficulties concerning opportunity cost decisions. Marxist economic theory involves a more equitable income distribution than the market achieves, and its central planning, it is argued, allocates resources in an optimal efficient way. However, central planning theory is insensitive to the many microeconomic choices which consumers could make, and has some minor problems of over-production to maintain full employment and some major ones related to inflation.

Summary Marxism contends that efficient allocation of resources and a more equitable distribution of income can be achieved by central economic planning.

17.5 MONETARISM

Monetarist economic theory, in contrast with Marxist and Keynesian theories, would limit government's role in a market economy to that of provider of essential public goods, controller of the money supply and watchdog on oligopoly development. The American economist Milton Friedman has led this renaissance of quasi-classical economics in the last two decades, and in the book *A Monetary History of the United States* (Friedman and Schwartz) he defends the stability of market economies and the successful use of monetary policy. His ideas, applied to the highly inflationary British economy of the 1970s, would mean that government would reduce the money supply so firmly that general price rises would gradually be eliminated. A consequence of this, it is argued, would be so much less cash flow for private companies and state firms to pay wage increases, and thereby less unemployment created. More stable competitive prices would lead to an increase in firms' exports, and the increased production and limitations of wage rises would raise profitability of companies, stimulate investment and enable a more efficient allocation of economic resources nearer to the market model idea.

Monetarists, like Friedman, would accept the unequal income distribution consequences of an economy operating nearer to the market model, but would maintain that the increased economic growth so promoted would provide increased incomes generally. Other key aspects of monetarism would involve the dismantling of state ownership of industry, apart from provision of essential public goods, and substantial reduction in the use of fiscal policy to manage effective demand in favour of a balanced budget. The decision-making structure of the economy would become much more decentralized but, unlike the classical economists, monetarists would maintain government intervention over money supply and to limit oligopoly. Indeed, control of the money supply is argued to be the essential tool of economic management, and use of fiscal policy largely unnecessary since stimulation of money supply can increase employment and its reduction eliminate inflation.

The development of monetarist economic theory has undoubtedly made its mark on Western governments in dealing with the massive inflation of the mid 1970s. The British government very substantially cut the original increases in money supply proposed for 1976 and 1977, and, as monetarists would predict, the inflation rates in 1977 and 1978 dropped sharply. Some other EEC countries, especially Federal Germany, and also the USA and Japan made earlier and more drastic reductions in money supply, and in Germany this brought about an 'old-time' inflation rate of less than 2 per cent by 1978. The British government used fiscal policy more extensively and this, due to its flexibility, also had the advantage of stimulating the economy in 1977–8 when unemployment reached its peak.

In the regular meetings of the seven leading industrial nations (the USA, Japan, Federal Germany, France, the UK, Italy and Canada) there has been a manifest caution over reflating their economies in order to stimulate reflation of the world economy during the late 1970s. Monetarist theory has given them such a sure tool of controlling internal inflation through control of money supply that they are afraid that monetarist theory's predictions will be realized, i.e. increases in money supply will fuel not only rapid inflation but also unemployment. Such fears and inaction by the 'Big 7' worsen the cyclical unemployment and consequent resource allocation problem, particularly since the spread of unemployment is an international phenomenon.

Keynesians and Marxists would contend that monetarist economic policy does not provide government with a wide enough range of policy instruments to manage demand and thereby allocate resources efficiently in a complex advanced modern economy. A criticism of all four strands of economic thought is that they concentrate too much upon the national rather than the international economy, and therefore deal inadequately with the impact of extra-national economic changes upon the nation's economy and upon the need for growth of underdeveloped nations' economies.

Summary Monetarism proposes a return to the market economy, but with government intervention to manage the money supply, control oligopoly and provide essential public goods, and thereby ensure efficient allocation of resources.

17.6 CONCLUDING REMARKS

The development of Keynesianism and the mixed economy was a limited convergence between the classical market economy and the Marxist command economy. Recent developments in economic theory make greater divergence, in the form of a movement towards Marxist economic ideas and towards quasi-classical monetarist ideas. The British and other EEC economies are still mixed/market ones, and the reader is now able to consider whether monetarist or Marxist theories' policy prescriptions might be of help in dealing with British economic problems in the late 1970s and early 1980s. We come back, in fact, to those economic problems referred to in the first section of Chapter 1, i.e. inflation, unemployment, balance of payments, environmental issues and economic growth. Now, however, we are armed with economic theories, concepts and knowledge which enable us to understand the probable consequences of proposed solutions to these problems.

QUESTIONS

1 Define classical, Marxist, Keynesian and monetarist theories of the economy.

2 What is the theorem of Pareto-optimality?

3 What did classical economists advocate concerning international trade?

4 What is 'market failure'?

5 Which aspects of the market economy did Keynes recommend that government control?

6 What was Marx's solution to the problem of mass unemployment?

7 What is Friedman's solution to the problem of rapid inflation?

8 Which aspects of the market economy do monetarists recommend that government controls?

EXERCISES

1 In what respects do Keynesians and monetarists differ concerning the methods of practical organization of an economy?

2 How does the role of the state differ in terms of economic management in the Marxist and Keynesian theories?

3 Is monetarism simply classical economics re-stated for modern times?

4 Compare and contrast in a country the levels of economic decision-making recommended by the Marxist and monetarist theories.

5 To what extent might Marxist economic theory prescriptions help solve current major British economic problems?

6 Compare the 'market failure' of the classical model in the early twentieth century with the 'failures' of Keynesian theory in the 1970s. To what extent are they failures inherent in the theory or due to a lack of full implementation of the theory?

7 To what extent might monetarist economic theory prescriptions help solve the current major British economic problems?

8 Which economic theory most effectively argues its prescriptions for optimal efficient allocation of economic resources?

Glossary

Active Money Quantity of money which is held by households and firms to meet regular purchases of goods and services.

Advances Short-term lending to individuals, and short- and medium-term lending to nationalized and private firms by the banks.

Assets This refers to the methods by which the banks use deposits in the economic system.

Autonomous Investment Investment which does not depend upon the level of the national income.

Average Propensity to Consume The ration of consumption (C) to national income (Y).

Balance of Payments A record of all economic transactions in goods, services and money between a country and all other countries during a given period of time.

Balance of Trade A record of all economic transactions in goods and services between a country and all other countries during a given period of time.

Bank Money This consists of credit created by the commercial banks.

Capital A stock of physical assets in being at a given point in time. These are termed, more simply, 'capital goods'.

Capital Deepening Growth of the stock of capital goods more than proportional to the growth of the labour force.

Capital Market The facility through which the supply of and demand for capital are related to each other.

Capital Widening Growth of the stock of capital goods proportional to the growth of the labour force.

Cartel An agreement by the producers in an industry to restrict competition among themselves (e.g. an agreement to sell their goods at the same price).

Ceteris Paribus (Latin: other things being equal) The scientific method of keeping other factors constant in order to isolate one or some factors which the economist wishes to analyse.

Circular Flow of Income This consists of four flows: (a) flow of goods and services produced by firms for households; (b) flow of money from households to firms as payment for these goods and services; (c) flow of the production factors, labour, capital and land, from the households to the firms; and (d) the flow of money payments from firms to households in the form of wages, rent, interest and profit.

Collective Bargaining The negotiations between trade unions and either employers' associations or companies to decide jointly upon employment conditions in an industry, firm or nation.

Command Economy An economic system of central planning in which even minor details of economic life are subject to a national economic plan.

Commercial Banks The multi-purpose banks which have power to create credit (e.g. Lloyds, Midland).

Common Market A type of international economic integration, which includes a customs union and free movement of the factors of production (labour, capital) in the member countries.

Consumption The process of using goods and services to satisfy wants. It can therefore refer, legitimately, to the purchase by an individual or family of goods and services supplied by firms.

Consumption Function Behavioural equation expressing the relationship between C (consumption) and Y (income).

Customs Union A type of international economic integration characterized by reciprocal abolition on the part of the countries concerned of tariffs and other barriers to free trade. There is free trade in goods, within the customs union, and a common external tariff towards countries outside.

Deductive Method A method of logical reasoning, in which conclusions are reached from one or several hypotheses.

Deflation A state of disequilibrium characterized by an excess of the sum of money being destroyed and dishoarded over the sum of money being created and hoarded, during a period of time.

Demand The willingness and ability to pay for a particular good or service.

Depreciation The wearing away of fixed capital goods during a given period of time (e.g. one year).

Devaluation An official reduction in the value of a national currency in terms of gold and other currencies.

Dishoarding A movement of money from inactive cash to active cash.

Economics The study of the relationship between many wants and scarce resources which have alternative uses.

Economic Growth An increase in national income due to the development of the productive capacity of the country.

Economic Union A type of international economic integration, which includes a common market and the harmonization and coordination of economic policies of the member countries.

Effective Demand The total demand for consumer goods (C), and the total demand for investment goods (I).

Elasticity The responsiveness of one variable to changes in another, expressed in relative terms.

Engel Curve The Engel curve shows the relationship of the demand for a good and the income of the consumer.

Entrepreneur The person or group of people (e.g. Board of Directors) who both combine land, labour and capital in the production process, and take non-insurable risks through production. (The entrepreneur, it can be argued, has a specialized type of labour.)

Exchange An action between two economic units (e.g. family, firm), in which one offers a product for another product, and the other accepts and offers the latter product for the former.

Exchange Equalization Account An account held and managed by the Bank of England, and used to prevent undesirable fluctuations in British currency. Utilizing funds from this account the central bank buys pounds whenever there is large-scale international selling of pounds. In this way the central bank attempts to maintain the exchange rate of the pound. Conversely, the central bank sells pounds whenever the currency is gaining in value too rapidly.

Expansion Investment An increase in the stock of fixed capital goods by a firm, in order to attain a higher production level.

Expenditure Comprises purchase of goods and services by households for consumption and purchase of goods and services for investment.

Expenditure Equilibrium A state in which, during a period of time, effective demand is such that full employment prevails.

Factors of Production Resources used to produce other goods and services. These resources are land, labour and capital. The first two are the primary factors of production, whereas capital is a derived factor of production.

Fixed Capital Capital goods which can be used repeatedly in the production process (e.g. tools, machines).

Financial Market A section of the capital market dealing with long-term transactions of two years or more to maturity (e.g. long-term government stock).

Fixed Exchange Rates A system of exchange rates in which currencies are exchanged at standard rates, which have been previously agreed.

Floating Exchange Rates A system of exchange rates in which the price of one currency against another is fixed by the interaction of supply and demand for the currencies in the market.

Full Employment The level of full employment is reached in an economy when all offering themselves for work are in jobs, with the exception of those unemployed due to switching from one job to another (i.e. frictional unemployment).

Funding The conversion of short-term holdings of government stock into long-term holdings of the same by the inducement of attractive rates of interest.

Geographical Market Fragmentation The division of the market for a product into geographical areas or regions in which some producers have strong geographical location advantages over other producers.

Good Anything which satisfies a want (e.g. consumer good, service).

Gross Added Value The difference between the market value of the product and the original value of new materials and components. This is also called *Gross National Product*.

Hoarding A movement of money from active cash to inactive cash.

Homogeneous Goods Goods which are completely identical to each consumer and to each producer. The consumer therefore cannot distinguish the good produced by one firm from that produced by another.

Inactive Money Quantity of money which is held by households and firms for emergencies (e.g. ill-health) or for buying securities, such as shares in firms or government stock.

Income The money accruing to an individual, firm, financial institution or government during a given period of time.

Indicative Planning The establishment by government of general targets for the major sectors of the economy, to serve as recommendations and inducements to firms' decentralized economic decision-taking.

Indifference Curve A curve which depicts all those combinations of quantities of products, which give the consumer the same level of satisfaction (i.e. of utility).

Individual Demand Function A function which accounts for the demand for a good by an individual in terms of the prices of all other goods and of his income.

Individual Goods Goods which by their nature could be made available for purchase by individuals, and which are paid for by individuals.

Individual Sales Function A function which shows the quantities of a product that is offered for sale by the individual producer (i.e. firm) at different prices.

Inductive Method A method of logical reasoning, in which one reaches conclusions from empirical observation of numerous economic facts.

Inflation A state of disequilibrium characterized by an excess of the sum of money being created and hoarded over the sum of money being destroyed and dishoarded, during a period of time.

Institutional Investors Collective savings institutions, a leading aim of which is to place their funds with the most secure firms, private and state financial institutions. Examples of institutional investors are insurance companies and pension funds. This type of investor plays a vital role nowadays in the financial market.

Inter-branch Balances The coordination of targets in the major sectors (e.g. industries, consumption) of a centrally planned economy.

International Liquidities Internationally acceptable funds which are used by countries to pay for temporary deficits on their balance of payments.

Investment An increase in a stock of physical assets over a given period of time (e.g. one year). Investment, on other words, is new capital goods.

Labour Human resources which offer themselves for work and constitute a factor of production.

Labour Theory of Value The source of all value of a product is the socially necessary labour time put into producing that good.

Land A production factor the supply of which is fixed in the short run (i.e. one to two years), and is limited in the long run by the total available. (It includes all natural resources.)

Law of Diminishing Marginal Rate of Substitution A consumer is less willing to give up one good for another as his consumption of the latter increases in relation to the former.

Law of Increasing and Diminishing Returns When more and more units of a factor of production are added to another factor of production that is held constant, the total product rises at first more than in proportion to the variable factor, and then less than in proportion to it.

Liabilities The deposits made with banks by individuals and firms.

Liquidity The property of being acquired and disposed of quickly and easily without loss in nominal value.

Liquidity Preference The desire by individuals and firms to keep their funds in the form of inactive money so that it is available to assist with their own precautionary and speculative motives.

Macroeconomics The study of the totals of economic activity in a nation (e.g. national income, investment).

Margin The last increase or decrease of a small quantity in the total amount of an economic variable (e.g. production, consumption, cost).

Marginal Cost The cost incurred in the production of an extra unit of a good.

Marginal Product The last small increase in the total quantity of a good produced, due to an increase of a factor of production.

Marginal Productivity The marginal productivity of labour is the change in production due to increasing the labour force by an extra employee.

Marginal Propensity to Consume The ratio between the extra consumption and the extra income that makes the extra consumption possible.

Marginal Revenue The revenue which accrues to a firm from the production and selling of an extra unit of a good.

Marginal Utility of a Good The increase in total utility derived from the last small increase in consumption of a good.

Market The facility through which demand and supply for a good are related to each other.

Market Demand Function A function which accounts for the demand for a good by all consumers in terms of the prices of all goods and the income of all consumers.

Market Economy An economic system in which the economic decisions are freely taken at a decentralized level by firms and consumers.

Market Sales Function A function which shows the quantities of a product that are offered for sale by all producers of the product at different prices.

Market Socialism An economic system in which the means of production, distribution and exchange are socially owned, but economic decision-making is performed mainly at the decentralized level of firms and households (e.g. Yugoslavia).

Microeconomics The study of the behaviour of individual economic units (e.g. household, firm).

Minimum Lending Rate The key rate of interest in the London money market which is usually set by the Bank of England acting on government instructions. If the government does not intervene this rate is determined in the market as a rate ½ per cent above treasury bill rate.

Model A simplified representation of reality in which the simplification is achieved mainly by the introduction of certain assumptions.

Monetary Equilibrium A state in which, for a period of time, the sum of money being created and being hoarded is equal to the sum of money being destroyed and being dishoarded.

Money at Call Very short-term (one to 14 days) lending by banks to the discount houses in the London money market.

Money Market A section of the capital market dealing with short-term transactions of up to one year to maturity (i.e. money at call, treasury bills, other government securities of up to one year maturity).

Monopolistic Competition A market form characterized by a substantial number of buyers and sellers whose products are similar but not perfect substitutes for each other due to product differentiation and/or geographical fragmentation of the market.

Monopoly A market form characterized by one seller, in which he determines his prices for himself.

Multiplier Numerical coefficient which relates a change in a component of aggregate demand (e.g. investment) to a consequent change in national income.

National Income The value of the flow of goods and services becoming available to a nation during a given period of time (e.g. one year).

National Income by the Expenditure Approach The total expenditure on consumer goods and on investment goods during a year.

National Income by the Income Approach The total of all incomes derived from working in the production of goods and services during a year. It is composed of wages, rent, interest and profit.

National Income by the Product Approach The total added value of all goods and services produced during a year.

Net Added Value The difference between gross added value and depreciation. This is also called *Net National Product.*

Net Investment The difference between total investment and depreciation of fixed capital.

Oligopoly An industry in which production is controlled by only a few firms (e.g. motor car and tyre manufacturers).

Opportunity Cost The forgoing of the next best alternative good or service in favour of the good or service actually used.

Overspending A state in which, during a period of time, effective demand is greater than the productive capacity of the economy.

Perfect Competition A market form in which there are very many producers and consumers operating in a perfect market.

Perfect Market A market in which there is (a) full transparency of information, (b) goods sold are homogeneous, and (c) free entry and exit for producers.

Price Elasticity of Demand A coefficient which expresses the responsiveness of demand for a good to variations in price of the good in relative terms (prices of other goods and consumer income being constant).

Price Elasticity of Supply A coefficient which expresses the responsiveness of supply of a good to variations in the price of the good in relative terms (prices of other goods and consumer income being constant).

Product Differentiation A method by which goods are given real or imagined differences by their producers. Such devices as branding, packaging, advertising, etc. are used to differentiate between such goods (e.g. branding, packaging and advertising of instant coffee products).

Production The provision of goods and services through combining the factors of production (i.e. land, labour and capital).

Productive Capacity The total amount of goods and services that a nation is capable of producing if all the factors of production are used maximally.

Profit The financial reward to a firm for taking non-insurable risks. It is the residual item left over after wages, interest, rent, raw material and component payments have been made by a firm.

Public Goods Goods which because of their nature cannot be subdivided for sale to individuals. They are therefore provided for all the nation by the state (e.g. defence services, administration of justice).

Quasi-public Goods Goods which by their nature could be made available for purchase by individuals, but which the state finds administratively more convenient to provide for all the nation (e.g. education, roads).

Rate of Interest The price paid to an individual or firm or financial institution for the use of their money during a period of time by another individual, firm, financial institution or by the government. For example, a rate of interest is paid by a firm to a shareholder in the firm.

Rent The payment made for use of land and durable goods during a given period of time.

Replacement Investment The production or acquisition of new fixed capital goods to make up for the wear and tear on old fixed capital goods.

Reserve Assets Ratio Total eligible bank liabilities (i.e. all deposits except foreign currency deposits) must be matched by the bank's having 12½ per cent of its assets in the form of short-term bills, money at call and other short-term loans to government.

Reserve Currencies National currencies in which the monetary authorities of other countries hold a large proportion of their international currency savings. The US dollar and pound sterling were the main reserve currencies until their decline in the 1950s and 1960s. The Deutschmark, Swiss Franc, and some other West European national currencies have become to a limited extent reserve currencies in the 1970s.

Resources The physical supplies of land, labour and capital, i.e. the factors of production in quantitative and qualitative terms.

Revaluation An official reduction in the value of a national currency in terms of gold and other currencies.

Saving That part of income not spent on consumption.

Scarcity The eternal tension between wants and the possibility of satisfying wants.

Solvency The capability by banks to finance from their own resources any losses.

Special Deposits A transfer of a specified percentage of a bank's assets from the bank to the Bank of England, at the latter's request.

Specialization (or division of labour) A situation in which each worker concentrates upon one particular aspect of the production process.

State Money This consists of notes and coin.

Supply The quantity of a particular good or service which sellers are prepared to offer.

Surplus Value The difference between the revenue gained by the employer from a worker's production of goods sold, and the wage paid to that worker.

Tax The transfer of funds by sanction of law from individuals, firms and financial institutions to the government.

Technical Change The installation of new capital (e.g. machinery) in a firm or the public sector or the application of new methods of work. The development of new technical methods and products is also taken into account.

Trade Cycle Well-defined and repetitive oscillations in economic activity over a period of years, caused by fluctuation in demand.

Transparent Market The market in which all producers and consumers have full information on all prices asked for and offered in the market.

Treasury Bill A short-term (up to three months) borrowing by the government.

Underspending A state in which, during a period of time, effective demand is lower than the productive capacity of the economy.

Utility The capacity of a good to give satisfaction of wants to the consumer.

Value The utility given by a particular good.

Wants The desires of the population for goods, services and intangible resources such as leisure time.

Wealth A stock of physical assets, financial assets and non-tangible assets which can be exchanged for money.

Welfare The level of satisfaction of the wants of an individual or a community in so far as it is based on the allocation of scarce resources which have alternative uses.

Working Capital Capital goods which will be transformed into other goods during the production process (e.g. oil transformed into plastics).

Bibliography

CHAPTER ONE
Donaldson, P. *Economics of the Real World*, Penguin, 1976.
Harbury, C. D. *Introduction to Economic Behaviour*, Fontana, 1971.
Stewart, M. *Keynes and After*, Penguin, 1975.

CHAPTER TWO
Bailey, R. *Problems of the World Economy*, Penguin, 1973.
Donaldson, P. *The Great Divide*, Penguin, 1977.
Khan, M. A. *Economic Development of Bangladesh*, 1971.
Parkinson, J. *Bangladesh: Test Case for Development*, 1977.

CHAPTER THREE
Hays, S. *National Income and Expenditure in Britain and the OECD*, Heinemann, 1971.
HMSO. *Annual Abstract of Statistics*, HMSO.
United Nations Department of Social and Economic Affairs. *Yearbook of National Accounts Statistics*, UN Publications, 1979.

CHAPTER FOUR
Lewis, W. A. *Economic Survey 1919–39*, Longman, 1970.
Stewart, M. *Keynes and After*, Penguin, 1975.

CHAPTER FIVE
Anthony, V. S. *Banks and Markets*, 2nd ed., Heinemann, 1974.
Bank Education Service, Leaflet 4. *The Clearing System*, B.E.S.
Bank Education Service, Leaflet 10. *How a Banker Looks at a Balance Sheet*, B.E.S.

CHAPTER SIX
Herbert, G. *The Management of the Economy*, Ginn, 1978.
Jones, A. *The New Inflation*, Penguin, 1973.
Trevithick, J. *Inflation*, Penguin, 1977.

CHAPTER SEVEN
HMSO. *Competition and Credit Control*, HMSO, 1971.
Revell, J. *British Financial System*, Macmillan, 1973.
Williams, R. M. *Sample Studies of Financial Institutions*, Ginn, 1979.

CHAPTER EIGHT
Farquhar, J. D. and Heidensohn, K. *The Market Economy*, Philip Allan, 1975.
Harbury, C. D. *Introduction to Economic Behaviour*, Fontana, 1971.

CHAPTER NINE
Farquhar, J. D. and Heidensohn, K. *The Market Economy*, Philip Allan, 1975.
Harbury, C. D. *Introduction to Economic Behaviour*, Fontana, 1971.

CHAPTER TEN
Farquhar, J. D. and Heidensohn, K. *The Market Economy*, Philip Allan, 1975.
Leftwich, R. K. *The Price System and Resource Allocation*, Dryden, 1976.

CHAPTER ELEVEN
Galbraith, J. K. *The New Industrial State*, Penguin, 1976.
Yamey, B. S. (Ed.) *Economics of Industrial Structure*, Penguin, 1973.

CHAPTER TWELVE
Atkinson, A. B. *The Economics of Inequality*, O.U.P., 1975.
Burton, J. *Wage Inflation*, Macmillan, 1972.
Clegg, H. A. *System of Industrial Relations in Great Britain*, Blackwell, 1978.
Ingham, G. K. *Strikes and Industrial Conflict*, Macmillan, 1974.
Parkin, M. and Sumner, M. T. (Ed.) *Incomes Policy and Inflation*, M.U.P., 1972.

CHAPTER THIRTEEN
Brown, A. J. *Framework of Regional Economics in the UK*, C.U.P., 1972.
Freeman, C. *Economics of Industrial Innovation*, Penguin, 1974.
Heertje, A. *Economics and Technical Change*, Weidenfeld and Nicolson, 1977.

CHAPTER FOURTEEN
Herbert, G. *The Management of the Economy*, Ginn, 1978.
Prest, A. R. *Public Finance*, Weidenfeld and Nicolson, 1974.
Prest, A. R. and Coppock, D. J. (Ed.) *The U.K. Economy: A Manual of Economics*, Weidenfeld and Nicolson, 1978.
Tivey, L. *Nationalised Industries Since 1960*, Longman, 1973.

CHAPTER FIFTEEN
Swann, D. *Economics of the Common Market*, Penguin, 1978.
Tew, B. *The Evolution of the International Monetary System*, Hutchinson, 1977.
Young, D. *International Economics*, Intertext, 1972.

CHAPTER SIXTEEN
Carew Hunt, R. N. *Theory and Practice of Communism*, Penguin, 1974.
Friedman, R. (Ed.) *Marx on Economics*, Penguin, 1973.
Leeman, W. A. *Centralised and Decentralised Economic Systems*, Rand McNally, 1977.

CHAPTER SEVENTEEN
Le Kuchman, R. *The Keynesian Revolution*, Penguin, 1970.
Robinson, J. *Economic Philosophy*, Penguin, 1970.
Roll, E. *Development of Economic Thought*, Longman, 1972.

Index

Numbers in italics refer to Figures and Tables